S.L. SUTHERLAND is associate professor in the School of Public Administration at Carleton University.

Devoted to the study of political attitudes and behaviour, this analysis attempts to improve the predictability of the activity from attitudes. Through an analysis of data relating to the attitudes and behaviour of students at the University of Alberta toward the social phenomenon of 'student power' in the late 1960s, Professor Sutherland addresses three main questions: what proportion of students form internally consistent and coherent viewpoints about student participation in the affairs of the university? what are the characteristics of the attitude 'clusters' which facilitate activity? and what social attributes encourage an activist posture, either for or against student power?

This analysis reflects the conviction that any one attitude will be only weakly related to a specific behaviour because the meaning of that attitude, and thus its implications for action, will vary depending on other attitudes held by the individual and on the social context in which the attitude is learned and held. Thus, before behavioural implications are drawn, a whole complex of viewpoints must be identified and the meanings of actions must be viewed in their context of manifestation.

This study makes a significant contribution to the field of attitude-behaviour research and studies of political radicalism and will be of particular interest to sociologists and social and political psychologists.

S.L. SUTHERLAND

Patterns of Belief
and Action:
Measurement of Student
Political Activism

UNIVERSITY OF TORONTO PRESS
Toronto Buffalo London

© University of Toronto Press 1981
Toronto Buffalo London
Printed in Canada

ISBN 0-8020-5534-6

Canadian Cataloguing in Publication Data

Sutherland, S.L. (Sharon Lynn), 1940-
Patterns of belief and action

Bibliography: p.
Includes index.
ISBN 0-8020-5534-6

1. Students – Political activity. 2. Student
movements. I. Title.
LB3610.S97   371.8'1   C81-094371-9

The book is dedicated to
Thomas and Constance Sutherland,
my parents.

Acknowledgments

I have incurred many debts of gratitude during the preparation of this manuscript. My good friends and colleagues Eric Tanenbaum and Jerry Ezekiel must be mentioned first: some of the mistakes may even be theirs. Both share most of my theoretical preoccupations, but we have worked together through many nights in computing centres as well. Jerry Ezekiel and I jointly developed the university-specific attitude scales which are at the centre of this book, and Eric Tanenbaum and I together refined all the other attitude measures and indices. Ken Macdonald and David Braybrooke were central to the book's development as well. Jennifer Ehly, Ian Budge, Richard Merelman, John Reed, and R.I.K. Davidson were generous with time, helpful comments, and criticism. Lorraine Ourom, senior manuscript editor for the University of Toronto Press, made the last stages of production a pleasure. My profound thanks also go to Gail Stanton, who typed the final manuscript. Finally, I must thank W.H. Maidens, who was more energetic and helpful than any of that crew of much-thanked academic wives, although also perhaps more headstrong and temperamental.

The project from which data are drawn was funded by the Canada Council to the name of Dr Christian Bay. Drs Susan Hunter-Harvey and Ted Genet Harvey directed instrumentation, fielding, and preparation of the machine-readable data. They kindly allowed me to add the measures developed earlier by Jerry Ezekiel and me to the data collection schedule for the Canada Council funded study. Jerry Wilson and Grace Skogstad were also involved in the project's day-to-day operations. I am grateful to the project personnel for the steady quality of their work, for there were very few 'gremlins' in the raw data. Once these raw data were compiled, we have worked independently of one another.

The Canada Council has since funded my study at the University of Essex. The book has been published with the help of a grant from the Social Science Federation of Canada, using funds provided by the Social Sciences and Humanities Research Council of Canada, and a grant from the Andrew W. Mellon Foundation to the University of Toronto Press.

Contents

PATTERNS OF BELIEF AND ACTION:
MEASUREMENT OF STUDENT POLITICAL ACTIVISM

Introduction

They do things in groups, he explained.
Alone they would say, 'Yes, sir' and 'No, sir.'[1]

From the early 1960s, an outburst of collective dissidence generally called the youth movement challenged most western democracies for ten or twelve years. A part of this general opposition to the status quo was focused upon substantive politics, and a part was dedicated to the politicization of major institutions of society. Students demanded participation in the running of educational institutions, and that their elders respect ethics and morality in 'real world' politics. In effect, students were demanding justice for everyone, as well as the right for themselves to make policy that would affect the whole society. Students said they wanted, among other things, self-government of the universities, which meant to many people that students intended to take over the administration of higher education; free university education for everyone (including training in the professions); the waiving of university admission requirements for some minorities; an end to the conduct of applied military research; and an end to the American war in Vietnam and the 'complicity' of national governments in that war. Most observers did not think that these were legitimate student demands. Even among those who were sympathetic, many regarded the movement as one of children, on a misconceived children's crusade. Authorities panicked as often as not and there were deaths as demonstrations got out of hand. Strangely, with almost the same co-ordination across campuses and societies with which it had arrived, the movement was judged to be over. Yet still, across the whole of North America, student representatives take their seats at senate meetings and meetings of departmental committees. New generations of student representatives are sometimes even coaxed and recruited into their seats by faculty. The melody, or malady, lingers on. One small aspect of 'student power' has rooted, however tentatively.

The student power movement was of wide interest, because at first it appeared to be a rebellion within the upper middle class of youth against age. Was society transforming itself, observers asked themselves. University students drew perhaps more than their share of attention and concern, because they were so conveniently observed by academic commentators. Student power was really only one of many crusades then current, most arising out of the youth movement, being taken up by it, or affiliating with it in some way. Indeed, in so far as there was a common theme, it can be thought of as the 'participation decade.' All kinds of participation were demanded, and studied. People demanded 'power,' be it community power, black power, red power, power for women, or student power. But people wanted not only or primarily the last word but *roles.* They wanted to be empowered to do things for themselves, not to be consulted and obeyed by an administrative class in the manner of a binding plebiscite. At a minimum, the movement asked that people take part in whatever decision-taking machinery was operative, that they be contended with in every serious sense.

Social shifts like the student power movement promise much to social psychologists. They suggest provocative questions. How many people, and which ones, will be reached by the message of the movement? Of those exposed to the message who will attend and therefore learn the message? Who will be convinced? Of sympathizers, who will be recruited to take an active part in the movement? Indeed, is action undertaken from conviction about the ideas? Or do all but the movement's elite move lemming-like in a welter of fashionable ideas? How many participants are 'action freaks,' available to any movement? How *do* the movement's ideas establish a place on the agenda of social concern and gain a broad base? Why and how do social movements move out of the limelight of public attention, sometimes dying virtually overnight, and at other times fading slowly away? All of these questions are interesting; and all are important. The present study chooses one basic issue to examine, in the hope that the effort will help to structure the general area.

STUDENT POWER AS RESEARCH OPPORTUNITY

Substantive aims
The basic question of this book concerns the proportion of a public that might be mobilized to a cause. Unfortunately, even this one question is too general to be directly illuminated. We must learn more about particular pub-

lics and particular 'causes' before we can speak of people in general. The present study is therefore an examination of one public, and one cause: the public for the cause of 'student power' at one North American university.

Still, the study reflects on some broader issues. That student power was so much 'in the air' created a good research opportunity. Most people are not very much interested in public events and, of those who are interested, only a small minority are ever moved to action. American and Canadian scholars are pretty generally agreed that only 3 or 4 per cent of voters can be classed as 'ideologues' in the sense that they hold several logically consistent opinions about politics. The proportion of activists in the mass population is often guessed at about 1 per cent.[2] American research conducted during the last half of the 1960s with known groups of radicals indicated that about 2 per cent of all students at any one university were 'principled leftists' (Peterson, 1968, 1970). But here was an intelligent, educated population which was daily being exhorted to activity. And unlike standard systemic politics, where opportunities for action are formal and infrequent – voting, etc. – the student movement provided an opportunity for formal opinion-relevant activity almost daily. It even virtually legitimized informal, 'anomic' political activity. In short, here was an opportunity to discover what proportion of an almost-ideal population would form a set of consistent ideas about a problem which was of direct relevance to them. Survey data collected from university students at the height of the movement could therefore answer broader questions not only about proportions of principled leftists, but also about principled conservatives (vis-à-vis student politics) and about the proportion of principled individuals who carry on to become active.

The 'student power' movement began in the early 1960s with two broad kinds of demands. One was for 'participation.' The other called for changes in substantive policy being made for the whole society. Both were illuminated by the conviction that the juggernaut of the anonymous, non-accountable corporate-government alliance was self-motivated and self-programmed. Growth was 'the system's' only goal. It cared nothing for 'people.' The student movement held that social values – hard cash, social respect, and roles in governance – should be redistributed to accomplish absolute equality. Perhaps the best-known summary statement is Mario Savio's rallying cry: 'The time has come to put our bodies on the machine and stop it!' Savio was one of the most prominent figures of the Free Speech Movement which had begun in Berkeley in 1964.

The general demand for participation did not deal with policy content. It was acceptable to a larger, less ideologically radical group of students. So far as it had any detail, it was a demand for citizen roles in governing – of the university, of the community, of the whole society. Perhaps the best-known statement of this ideal is the 'Port Huron Statement' issued by the Students for a Democratic Society, and attributed to Tom Hayden: 'As a social system we seek the establishment of a democracy of individual participation, governed by two central aims: that the individual share in those social decisions determining the quality and direction of his life; that society be organized to encourage independence in men and provide the media for their common participation' (Jacobs and Landau, 1966: 160). With remarkable optimism students began where they were. They attempted to 'democratize' one of the most elitist, expertise-based, paternalistic, and subtle of all social institutions – the university. This attempt to achieve 'significant and meaningful participation in the processes of decision making' (Sampson, 1967: 21) is not accepted by scholars of the movement as the one common long-range goal of student power advocates, more general even than the other unifying theme, opposition to American foreign policy.

It is pleasant to sit in one's chair some time later and state that the student demand for participation for its intrinsic good – 'for the sake of it' – was clearly distinguished from the policy demands for radical change. But in the mid-sixties, things were not so straightforward. In part, the rhetoric of the movement was continually being worked out. There was also a confusion in the public media between the generally non-political hippies and the militant new student radicals: an apprehension that there was about to be a revolution followed by compulsory free love and raggedness. This confusion affected the university milieu to some extent as well.

Nor did the academic 'fire house' research conducted during the early years of the movement clarify matters. Social scientists composed questionnaires virtually upon hearing of a sit-in or demonstration. They administered their 'instruments' to whoever remained at the scene. They seldom paid much attention to defining the event around which the activity centred. Thus early studies 'discovered' what now seems comically obvious: for example, that those who were taking part in demonstrations tended to be politically left. A great deal of effort went into distinguishing student activists from hippies. Otherwise, characteristics were attributed out of any useful context. Radical students were often described without a comparison group. Or radicals were compared to the general student body rather than to students who were politically active but not left. Radical activists, it was found, were intelligent, humanistic, idealistic, dedicated, well reared, and rich. But these were also the characteristics of all political activists. Lester Milbrath's *Political Participation* (1965), a contemporary summary of empirical research which stated that political activity, interest, and skill increase with increasing income, education, and social status, was not noticed by those who re-searched student politics. Early results therefore hardened into a portrait of 'the activist' which was like a gem-stone without a setting: lovely, but it couldn't be hung anywhere.

This lack of context for findings about student activists was bothersome. Therefore when my friend Jerry Ezekiel and I thought it might be interesting to study 'student power,' we wanted to know, first, what students thought it was and, second, where the student 'radical' fitted in the context of the whole student body. How we went about discovering what 'student power' meant to our subjects is the basis of the second chapter of this book. But the second idea of establishing a comparative context for findings about student radicals deserves some additional discussion at this point.

Methodological goals

The problem of establishing a social context inspired the method of study pursued in the whole project. To many readers, the methodology of the study will be equally as interesting as the findings of substance about student activists. The methodological focus of the work concerns, in effect, the possibility of performing in representative populations meaningful study of 'attitudes' and reported behaviours through the method of once-only ques-tionnaires. In short, is the method of survey research of any real utility in the study of individual differences and political preferences and activity of indi-viduals? Is the survey researcher limited to discovery of the obvious? The case study in which the usefulness of the method is determined is the study of the incidence and correlates among university students of coherent opin-ion or 'belief system' concerning student power. The characteristics of known groups of activists has been described by a multitude of other studies. Although some findings are in contention, there was a clear core portrait. Could one select analytical aggregates from a random survey sample – groups which one stipulated by sets of opinions and behaviours – of which *one* silhouette of 'the activist,' the others forming the context against which the activists' portrait should be judged? Attitudes per se – ones which could be shown to identify something like known groups – would be searched for at the same time as one searched for the activists. Indeed, success in finding the types would indicate that one had the method right.

Scholars of verbal measures of 'attitudes' and their connection – or lack of connection – to reported behaviours will see the interest in this problem. Other readers may think of self-reported attitudes as being guiding motives of a sort and therefore in exact correspondence with an individual's activi-ties. They will therefore be interested to know that even with the most pertinent and reliable of measures of individual 'personality' differences (whether called opinions, attitudes, values, traits, or beliefs), researchers seldom predict more than 10 per cent of the variability in the non-verbal behaviour of interest (Wicker, 1969). Such relationships mean that, at best, 90 per cent of the variance in behaviour remains as a puzzle for explanation by recourse to factors other than the attitude or trait.

This lack of success has been regretted for some time. As long ago as 1940, C. Wright Mills identified the 'disparities between talk and action' as 'the central methodological problem for the social sciences' (Deutscher, 1966, 238). In the same year, Merton pointed to the centrality of the problem, regretting that no systematic research had been conducted on whether 'the amount and direction of spread between opinion and action [is] relatively constant for members of different groups' (1940: 21–2). The first chapter of this book argues that the situation is not much improved some forty years later. Therefore, as social psychology is often defined as the study of attitudes, it seemed worthwhile to concentrate upon the observed connection between words and deeds, and to try to show how 'attitude' might figure in larger schemes which attempt to relate aspects of social structure to behaviour. This study attempts both these goals, perhaps sometimes in an experimental and imperfect way, and emerges with some improvements and insights which other researchers may well find useful.

Chapter 3 shows that it is possible to improve the amount of variance explained in behaviour by attitude measures beyond the usual threshold. The 'theory' or guiding notion behind these manipulations can be quite simply stated. It can be routinely applied in survey research. It can be modified for secondary analyses of much existing data. The idea is that any one attitude will be only weakly related to a specific behaviour because the meaning of that attitude (and therefore its implication for action) shifts depending on what other attitudes are held by the subject, or depending on the 'psychic consequences' to the subject of his or her own social attributes. Irwin Deutscher put one basic problem very clearly when he wrote: 'A question put to me by an interviewer concerning how I feel about Armenian women forces me to respond to the words and to the interviewer; standing face-to-face with a real flesh and blood Armenian woman, I find myself constrained to act toward a very different set of symbols' (1966: 248). Without claiming any firm base in symbolic interactionism, this view extends nicely to student activism. It is easy to imagine that a student might favour an increased student role in university decision-making and yet not participate in student activity because he or she feels ill at ease with the radical student group which is dominant and would therefore gain power from student participation. The student here might feel ill at ease for a variety of reasons, ranging from disagreement with other aspects of the radical platform to a sense of social discomfort because of a different cultural background or social class of origin. Thus a whole complex of attitudes may need review before behavioural implications can be drawn with any safety. By the same token, actions may have different meanings (be connected with different attitudes) and a different value for future predictions as to continued activity depending on their specific manifestations in a particular context.[3] Obviously, 'participation' in student political activity will have different attitudinal correlates depending on whether one is speaking of participation in a radical action group or in a traditional student council.

The reader will now understand why the word *theory* was caged in modest quotation marks at the beginning of this account. This is not a theory of human behaviour in the same sense as is, say, Milton Rokeach's view that behaviour is predicted by an interaction of the attitude toward the social object of action with the attitude toward the situation in which action is to take place (Rokeach, 1968). One may wish to make love to one's spouse, for example, but not in a rowboat. In a much less neat way, the 'theory' deals with improving predictive capacity. It says that, in order to develop attitudinal measures which effectively predict behaviour one can do the following: (1) identify samples of the target behaviour(s); (2) review the context(s) in which the behaviour takes place; (3) identify the obvious social object which is accepted as 'the inspiration' for the activity and develop measures of attitude toward it by questioning the actors; (4) ask oneself whether the context of activity is shared, even incidentally, among more than one social object, and develop measures of the others as well; and then (5) develop predictive complexes or syndromes of attitudes which fit the logic of the actual historical context. This procedure may seem messy and tedious, but four decades of incisive scientific research have shown that there is no easy way.

To the extent that the current attempt is successful, it is, as noted, of considerable interest to the secondary analyst: the scholar who examines survey data for purposes different from those the research was designed to serve. Secondary analysis is both the duty and the almost-certain fate of the survey analyst during the next decade. It is a duty because survey data are always expensive and almost always under-analysed, merely tasted and abandoned. At a minimum, existing data stored in university archives form a cheap resource for the pre-testing of hypotheses. Scholars will necessarily turn to these data as funds for large surveys become more scarce.

The study on which this work is based is of student political activity in Edmonton, Alberta, at the height of the student power movement. It analyses student political activity and political preferences with reference to demands upon the university setting for participation and to preferences about the larger society's politics.

It can be noted that the study design does not require the reader to generalize as a matter of faith from the substantive findings to any broader population of 'students in general.' In terms of substantive findings, the work can be treated as a case study to the point where the profiles of Alberta students are compared with profiles for activists elsewhere. The latter profiles are developed from available empirical evidence to provide a plausible baseline for judgment of findings about the Alberta activists. Student activists at the University of Alberta were found to resemble activists from a great variety of other locations. The empirical matching exercise is conducted precisely to check their representativeness. However, a loose claim as to what proportion of a population has the propensity to become politically active is implied by the present analysis. That is, it is suggested that the University of Alberta, and indeed Alberta in general, can be said to be as 'typical' as any other North American locale in regard to the proportion of the population that could be recruited to a social movement.

According to the conventional wisdom of eastern Canadians the whole of Alberta, let alone Edmonton and its major university, is an out-of-the-way oil patch with conservative, indeed biblical, propensities. This is not the place to lay that particular complacency to rest, but it can be noted that the view was of limited relevance even in 1969–70. The city of Edmonton was then, as now, an economic growth area and was experiencing a population boom. The discovery of Canada's largest petroleum fields near Edmonton had occurred in 1947, and during the 1950s the city doubled in size. The growth rate continued through the 1960s, the Edmonton Chamber of Commerce then claiming that the city was Canada's fastest-growing metropolis (Kasahara, 1968).

The increase in population to 1969–70 could be largely attributed to migration from rural Alberta and from the other western provinces. Data collected in a large random sample survey of the Edmonton electorate in 1970 illustrated the trend. Eric Tanenbaum (1980: 5) reports: 'Less than 5% of the city's residents were born in Edmonton, whereas 19% had moved to the city within a five-year period before the survey. Overall, less than 35% of the population had resided in the city for more than twenty years. Nevertheless, the majority of the population (56%) had spent the first fifteen years of their lives in Alberta. Just over one-fifth lived outside Canada during this period of their lives. Some ... evidence of the rural movement to urban areas is provided by the 41% of the population who come from farm backgrounds.'

The city is perhaps more truly a mosaic of ethnic groups than most other Canadian locations. The same survey reported upon by Tanenbaum found British Canadians to be the largest group, accounting for almost 40 per cent of the city's residents, with notable representation from other groups as follows: Ukrainian Canadians, 9 per cent; Polish Canadians, 7.6 per cent; German Canadians, 7 per cent; and Scandinavian Canadians, 5.7 per cent; French Canadians, 3 per cent.

Ethnic origin in the city had then, as it likely does still, some fairly profound associations with status. Ethnic origin was associated with the distribution of occupation-types, and with the level of education attained by the individual. Tanenbaum found that British Canadians contributed a disproportionate share of Edmonton's professionally employed people and executives. Eastern Europeans were over-represented among manual labourers and among persons with only a primary-school education. The distribution of income across groups was, of course, parallel.

The median yearly family income in the city at the time of the study was $7,000, slightly above that for the nation as a whole. The industrial base of the city was heavily dependent upon the petroleum industry. This situation made for somewhat more economic stability than for other cities of comparable size, because of the steady demand for the products.

Alberta's provincial politics have been the subject of considerable interest (see Irving, 1969; Macpherson, 1968; Smith, 1967; and Young, 1969). At the time of the study, at least 40 per cent of the population of the city as a whole had never known anything but a Social Credit government provincially (Tanenbaum, 1980). The Social Credit League, which had been elected in 1935, held power until August 1971. For most of this period, the league was virtually without an opposition in the Legislative Assembly. Government was by a strong cabinet, and was low-profile, small-'c' conservative. The premier for much of that period, Mr E.C. Manning, continued in a minor way the Bible broadcasts of the radio evangelist who had brought the movement to power, Mr William Aberhart. The continued success of the league, however, was probably due less to religion than to the continuous prosperity of the region as it diversified from agriculture to a shared dependence on the oil industry. Albertans never voted heavily for a federal Social Credit party.

The University of Alberta at Edmonton was and is the major institution of higher education in the province. It had a tradition of intellectual opposition to the provincial government from within faculty ranks, although the university administration itself was always fairly conservative. Just as the city grew during the 1960s, so did the university. By 1969 the university was an enormous educational plant, serving more than 18,000 full-time students. Without wishing to activate the 'Americanization' debate of the time, I might mention that the rapidly expanding social science departments were being generously studded with both young American lecturers and draft-dodging graduate students[4] (see the Symons Report, 1975; and Matthews and Steele, 1969). In so far as intellectual political debate and the radicalization of the campus depended upon outside sources, then, it seems fair to say that the movement on campus depended directly on the south and not on eastern Canadian sources.

By the late 1960s, demands for participation by students in the running of the university were reaching a peak. The Edmonton campus had an active and visible contingent of radical prosyletizers in three main groups, each of which emphasized the issue of university 'self-government' – perhaps as an issue for education of the study body. These groups were the Students' Union for Peace Action (SUPA), which had been active since 1965, the Student Christian Movement (SCM), an older body, and the Students for a Democratic University (SDU), active since the early spring of 1968. The SDU was formed on the model of the American SDS, the more modest title being a Canadian phenomenon. Richard Price has written a detailed historical review of these groups and early episodes in the founding of the 'new left' in Alberta (see Price [1970]; Harding [1968] and Reid and Reid [1969] also provide useful background). The radical groups engaged in the full program of teach-ins, educational films, and 'celebrity' guest appearances that characterized campuses across North America. One notable visitor was Karl Deitrich Wolff of the German SDS. Another was yippie Abbie Hoffman, whose politics were to be outrageous. He came to address several thousand students and was beaten at his own game by a dissenting group of 'mooners' in his audience. Harold Cardinal[5] of the Indian Association, with American Indian Movement brothers, introduced those of us who were familiar with black power and student power to red power.

Alberta radicals capitalized effectively on a series of incidents such as the university's denial of tenure to popular left-wing professors in the anthropology and sociology departments, and a tactless refusal, at a teach-in, by the dean of arts to waive the university's academic admission requirements for Alberta Indian students. The university administration responded to student activity with fairly dramatic increases in the numbers of campus security forces, and also brought city police onto campus to contain a number of apprehended insurrections (which never materialized). The radicals were first rate at orchestrating activity for maximum media impact. They had two principal purposes. First, they felt a need to 'probe the system' to find out where power lay in the university, in order to frame sophisticated demands for roles in governing the institution. Second, full coverage of events meant that other students would be educated and recruited to the movement.

At least one teach-in, on the topic of control of tenure decisions by faculty and administration and the general issue of the 'authoritarian' university, drew close to a thousand students. But the event which marked the high point of support for the movement was a bread-and-butter march on the provincial legislative buildings in the late winter of 1968. More than a thousand students marched across the bridge spanning the river, in fierce Alberta cold, protesting an increase in fees. In addition, there was basic, day-to-day 'organizing' activity within all social sciences and humanities departments. Sociology and political science were perhaps most active. Graduate students first, then undergraduates, negotiated for roles on departmental committees. During this time, representation on the university senate was granted and a very liberal slate was elected to the student council (see Price, 1970). In short, a large number of local events occurred in front of a background of both routine activity and well-publicized world-wide student protest. In 1969 attention was focused on the issue of student power.

In summary, here was an intelligent, educated population which was the target of daily proselytizing on campus and the natural clientele for the intense general-media coverage. Hence, there was every reason to hope that this would be an 'economical' population within which to insist that opinions be consistent and 'strong' before testing their relationship to actual behaviour. (As it happened, only about 20 per cent of sample students satisfied the rather loose criteria for grasp of the 'ideology' described later. Only a subset of these were highly active.) A university sample would also be a sample which was implicitly controlled for effects arising from differences in social class. The habit of tracking media for politically relevant information is related to considerations of social status, most notably education. In more representative populations, 'attitude' variables explain only the most minimal amount of variability in behaviour in comparison with even the most gross of status indicators. In short, an opinion-engaged university sample offered a good opportunity to test the potential of 'attitudinal' indicators for prediction of behaviour. Limitations would be those endemic to survey research: since a cross-sectional survey offers no means of controlling for time, results would indicate only that factors were related and say nothing of direction of causation.

There are many related issues that this book does not examine. One noteworthy untouched problem demands special mention. Interesting although the topic is, this book does not attempt to explain student power as a movement, that is, it does not consider when and how and why the movement developed, and why it dissipated. Instead, it attempts to identify the people who took up the ideas of the student movement and made 'student power' visible in their own university setting. Social movements, of course, do not depend alone on the personal characteristics of individuals, but 'are a combination of social conditions and the availability of people able and ready to view them as problems and to take the actions necessary to solve these problems' (Tallman, 1976: 140).[6] A study of the social conditions – the whole *context* of society which provided a moment in time for the gladiators – is analysis at another level, and is ably treated by a great many other writers.

Some early commentators on the movement almost ignored the role of social conditions, imputing causation for the whole phenomenon of student protest to individual personality factors. They held that permissive child-raising practices had created a generation of self-confident and rebellious young people whose individual personality tendencies aggregated to a 'critical mass' at the best universities and eventually summed to the movement. Other writers have allowed that the social context was important, and that it intersected with personality variables in so far as available kinds of activity presented a solution to the individual's personal problems and personality needs. Still others have held that the student movement was only one aspect of a general movement of political restlessness challenging the 'establishments' of western democracies. In this view, the student movement was blown out of all proportion to its true (relative) importance within the general phenomenon of challenge for several reasons. One was the skill of the students in manipulation of the mass media. Another was the facile tendency of the establishment media to concentrate upon the then-current upheaval as a cultural-cum-generational ruckus rather than as a truly political challenge. Students (long-haired, shabby, and sexually promiscuous, but still middle-class children) lent themselves to this interpretation. In a word, it was in the interest of the establishment to let the student movement hog the spotlight while the system covertly defended itself against 'real challenges.'[7] While the present work cannot shed light on the prior causes of the facilitating social conditions, its findings can inform an examination of the mechanism which linked the movement to the participants. My findings would support the view that 'student power' did not draw upon either pathological personality needs or superior psychological strength, but that the aims of the students concerned rational preferences for real-world politics. Chapter 4, for example, shows that views of student power were a part of a much broader set of political viewpoints of the whole society.

The data for this study are drawn from a large study sponsored by the Canada Council, 'Determinants of Citizenship Orientation,' conducted by the University of Alberta during the period 1968–70. The study was funded to Dr Christian Bay, and directed by Drs Susan Hunter-Harvey and Teddy Genet Harvey. Nine hundred and fifty-nine interview schedules were completed and usable from a target of 1,200. This sample was random within strata: the first through fourth years of undergraduate enrolment, graduate studies, and postgraduate professional studies. There is a good fit for basic parameters (sex, age, place of residence, and grade average where applicable) as derived from the registrar's records and sample estimates within strata. Details of administration and the questionnaire are given in chapter 2. 'Student power' measures were adapted from independent surveys conducted a year earlier by me and Jerry Ezekiel.

CONTENTS OF BOOK

In chapter 1 I give an account of 'attitudes' as defined and studied by social psychologists over the last forty years. I discuss the failure of 'attitude' to predict other non-verbal behaviour, and the sterility of the study of attitude (henceforth 'verbal reports') when it is shorn of other overt behavioural implications. It is said that the problem of measuring the empirical relationship between verbal reports and other behaviour is a pseudo-problem, because they should never have been separated. In the chapter I argue that verbal reports and other non-verbal behaviour should be regarded as being in a relation of mutual on-going causation, instead of the more standard view of 'attitude' as the necessarily temporally prior motivational aspect of goal-directed action. The argument is that this theoretical alteration (plus a number of minor adjustments to current ways of regarding verbal reports) could form an improved guide to research practice. The way that these adjustments could translate into broad research procedures which are appropriate to cross-sectional questionnaire-based survey studies is outlined. In brief, it is suggested that it is the total stance of an individual toward a social object that is important. Coherent opinionion should be combined with an action component in the definition of 'stance.' Those individuals who do not have consistent belief systems toward social objects should be put in a separate group. The belief system can then be investigated for its relation to independent variables (and the 'non-existent stance' can be investigated for its social correlates, as when an individual holds no views and performs no activity toward, say, protecting the civil liberties of a threatened group). It is intended that the empirical study to be reported can be used as a case to show that adoption of these recommended views and practices will have a pay-off in generating more powerful and interpretable results.

Chapter 2 is addressed to defining what 'student power' meant to students at the University of Alberta. A multi-staged research program was devised and carried out during the period 1968–70, in which students themselves could provide the definition of student power. This practice is consistent with an earlier recommendation about ensuring relevance to subjects of stipulated social topics. The definition, however, had to be assessed in the context of a 'dictionary' of other agreed terms. Hence it was thought necessary to administer a wide-ranging final questionnaire to a random sample of students. This instrument included many so-called standard scales as well as the autochthonous student power measures.

These final questionnaire measures are divided into three groups for discussion and refinement: (1) student viewpoints about student power and the university experience in general, (2) orientations to the society, and (3) orientations toward the self. The last two categories contain many scales of interest to the practising social scientist. Orientations to the society include versions of the California F-Scale (Authoritarianism), Rokeach's Dogmatism, Budner's Tolerance-Intolerance of Ambiguity, Rosenberg's Faith in People, and Srole's Anomy. Among self-orientations are strong versions of the Institute for Personality Assessment and Testing's Anxiety measure, the General Mental Health Index, and Rosenberg's Self-esteem and Sensitivity to Criticism. The theory behind the 'standard' scales is discussed before refinement procedures are outlined and defended.

Refined scales are reported in full in the text or appendixes. In a final section the concurrent or 'context' validity of central verbal measures is assessed. Throughout, measurement assumptions are strong.

In chapter 3 I take up the measurement of opinions toward student power. I ask how three central verbal report scales might be combined into a test for a tight criterion ideology dealing with student participation in the running of the university. Subjects at consistent extremes of the measures Student Power, Rejection of Radicals and Radicalism, and University Militancy are said to possess a syndrome of opinions either favouring or against 'student power.' The utility of creating a syndrome or belief system is established by showing that the syndrome is more effective in predicting university political activities than is any one of the component scales on its own. Four criterion 'types' (for stances vis-à-vis student power) are then stipulated, on the basis of an ideology dichotomy (radical-conservative) and an action dichotomy (active-passive). This split will allow the later assessment of the likeness of the types' other viewpoints and social origins to members of known groups investigated in other research, such as student radicals, alienated students, and Smith, Block, and Haan's 'constructivists.' Those students who do not qualify for entry to a 'type' because their opinions do not conform to the criterion syndrome, or because their beliefs are not matched by an appropriate activity component, are used throughout as a comparison group. 'Types' whose social viewpoints and backgrounds are investigated in later chapters are: (1) active radicals; (2) passive radicals, that is, students of coherent pro-student-power opinion, but who do not act; (3) active conservatives, who are consistently against the student power movement but *are* active in university political affairs; and (4) passive conservatives.

In chapter 4 I take these four university political types and add the flesh of opinion and activity in the wider environment to the bare bones of preferences about university politics. I show that the belief systems tapped by preferences about university politics show characteristics of high constraint and wide range. One can successfully predict from the criterion student power beliefs to further compatible political and social opinions and actions (or lack thereof), and to statements of a broader personal world-view which illustrate the moral aspects of the belief system. It can be claimed, therefore, that this is a successful attempt to specify operationally 'political ideologies' as defined by Converse (1964b: 207): belief systems which are characterized by high constraint, wide range, and a centrality of political items. In Merelman's image, these rudimentary ideologies of the university do reveal that the actor has an 'intellectual handle' on the world (1969: 751). Views of the self, more usually called 'mental health and psychological functioning,' are here treated as part of the total world-view. Claims are sometimes made that the student radical acted from a superior psychological make-up. Findings here help to rehabilitate the active conservative, and show that the active radical moved outward from intellectual conviction rather than from any markedly superior psychological strength.

Chapter 5 is a systematic review of findings of the research on activism, presented in summary tables. Until now, the primary question of interest has been: 'How clearly can one predict other behaviour from verbal self-reports of affect for an object?' Certain improvements have been demonstrated. But the improvements lack a validating context: that is, how can we know that the analytical aggregates isolated by the ideology-defining techniques of this research are the 'real' groups of individuals with whom other research on student power has been concerned? Here, therefore, the question shifts to: 'What are the characteristics of those individuals who have been seen to favour student power?' The way to establish the characteristics is through a review of the descriptions of active individuals provided in the literature. Therefore, research findings for a wide range of variables are reported under the headings used for this study's results in chapters 6, 7, and 8.

Chapter 6 investigates the parental characteristics of the four types of this research. The aim is to discover whether the groups differ systematically from one another, and to see if there is a match in characteristics of radical activists here and those outlined in chapter 5 for the known groups of radicals. 'The literature' indicated that a highly educated, high-occupational-status mother had some special importance in the families of radical activists, and that Jewish or secular backgrounds were associated with left activism. The working hypothesis for this research is somewhat more complicated, however. It is suggested that both active types (radicals and conservatives alike) will share a characteristic of having been reared in a well-structured environment, unlike their passive ideology-mates. Acting conservatives will have been reared in the most traditional families, and radicals in the most modern households. The underlying idea is that politics is peripheral to most people; hence an environment in which there would be the highest number of *congruent* sources for transmitting a criterion ideology would be the household most likely to rear activists. Findings support the 'coherent learning' hypothesis of this work and are in keeping with the major consensus of the literature. In a sense, 'stereotypical' environments do best at transmitting political messages.

Interest then shifts to the problems of establishing whether, if one separated types into ideology groups, different parental factors will affect activity differently for the radical and conservative groups. The working hypothesis is supported. Radical activity is associated with having a highly educated father and a high-status mother. But a working mother constitutes a damper on conservative activity. Secular backgrounds are associated with increased radical activity but decreased conservative activity. Gender is really important only in social-helping (non-political) activities, which is a particularly feminine sphere of action even among the young. When the analysis is repeated without controls of consistency of opinion, or direction of ideology, substantive effects are cloaked. It also then takes more variables to account for less variance in intensity of activity.

Chapter 7 follows the same analysis procedure, but deals with the socialization or upbringing characteristics reported by the four university types.

The working hypothesis is the same as for the previous chapter: backgrounds of those who are most active will show most evidence of 'structure,' and different factors will be important (in terms of amount of variance accounted for in prediction of activity intensity) depending on whether the university ideology is radical or conservative. Socialization factors which were isolated in the literature as being characteristics of left-wing student activists are also shown to be characteristics of the radicals of this research. These are primarily being first-born and reared in disciplined and highly interactive families. This match supports the procedure of selecting 'types' on the basis of strong opinion-activity stances. Again findings are confounded in substance and weakened in strength by removing the ideology constraints (direction and consistency).

Chapter 8 again follows the outlined procedure, in analysis of the students' own characteristics. The consensus of the literature was that left activists were located in humanities and social science faculties, and that activists were oriented toward social service and intellectual occupations and were non-religious. In this research, it is found that active radicals are 'planless, single and secular, and have fairly clear academic orientations.' They are over-represented in arts faculties and under-represented in science and education studies. The students' own 'career' characteristics are of greatest importance in explaining variation in activity intensity among the group of radical-ideology students. The single most important factor is whether or not the student has formed the desire to acquire more than one academic degree. For radicals, activity in the university increases markedly with commitment to a long academic career. Next most important is the number of years already spent at university. These characteristics of the student appear to be far more powerful in explaining intensity of opinion-congruent activity than any other factors – be they parental or upbringing characteristics. Interestingly, it appears that the student power message did reach and activate almost the upper limit of its potential clientele. That is, the *passive* radicals do not appear to have formed a potential recruitment pool. They are located in fringe disciplines and are quite markedly non-academic in orientation.

In chapter 9 I compare the results of this work with those from research on activism. I evaluate the quality of results generated here using dual criteria of convincingness and explanatory power. I discuss the importance of the findings for democratic theory and enlarge upon the 'coherent learning' mechanism.

Some readers will be interested in both threads of this work: (1) the theoretical and methodological worries about how to improve prediction from attitudes to behaviour, and (2) the substance of student power and how to explain most effectively the emergence of developed political personalities by reference to their backgrounds. Those who are concerned with student activism only can concentrate on chapters 3, 4, 5, and the conclusion. Others should follow the procedure through each of the chapters.

The bibliography is of necessity very long as it covers the literatures of the student power movement, the attitude-behaviour consistency controversy, general attitude theory, and general political psychology. Particularly for the first two areas, many references are included which are not explicitly discussed in the text; other readers may find them useful, and they have certainly informed my thinking.

1

Attitudes in theory and research

It is difficult to conduct a discussion of the usefulness of 'attitudes' to the survey researcher without becoming entangled in a morass of philosophical, psychological, and psychometric problems. What is an attitude? Is it a property of a person, in the sense of being a motive or a drive, that might describe the 'reason' a person undertook an action? What is the status of such properties? Or is 'attitude' a summary description of a person's characteristic mode of behaviour, inferred by an observer from the person's words and deeds, perhaps revealing more about the observer than the subject?

And how should we conceptualize the process by which attitudes – and, indeed, opinions and personality traits, and values – are acquired? Much of the literature simply treats all such characteristics which vary from individual to individual as initial posits, but they must stem from somewhere. If they are learned, by what social agencies are they transmitted? What weight should we put on the analytic distinctions we can draw between opinions, attitudes, values, personality traits? What inferences should we make about the relationship between dispositions once their boundaries have been imposed? How much correspondence should one expect to find between measures of attitude based on verbal behaviour and other reported behaviour – what *is* the relation between words and deeds?

Psychometric considerations involve a superhuman alertness to sources of technical bias and invalidity. One must choose one's scaling method, balance one's statements, achieve unidimensionality of measure (one thing at a time), and do this with sufficient reliability that another researcher's replication would yield substantially the same results. One must triumph technically *after* the philosophical-theoretical questions above have been satisfactorily answered or avoided; otherwise, one measures fog to three decimal places. And if one concentrates upon validity to the neglect of measurement problems, one is a cabinet builder with a perhaps wonderfully pure conception, but coarse and quixotic tools.

But the purpose of this chapter is not to address these ongoing difficulties in the measurement and validation of attitudes. Rather, it is to suggest a means by which many of these problems can be avoided. In brief, it is suggested that we should avoid working with attitudes conceived of as distinct motivational states (and stages) to the occurrence of other kinds of overt behaviour. Instead, we should return to a still-earlier conception in which attitude and behaviour – words and deeds – are thought to develop together in a relation of mutual causation. An individual's stance toward a social object – as measured by both traditional attitudinal measures and indicators of other overt behaviour – can then be validated by reference to other independent variables. Initially, I discuss here conceptualizations of attitude as they have been developed over the past forty years. I conclude with a discussion of problems peculiar to the method of survey research, and suggest a number of procedures which would build on the strengths of cross-sectional survey studies.

SEPARATION OF VERBAL AND OTHER BEHAVIOUR

The reigning conception of attitude in social psychology remains that stated by Gordon Allport in the 1930s and restated in the 1950s in what is often said to be the best short history of the concept. Allport was not stipulating an original definition, but was providing a succinct 'official' definition of the concept: 'An attitude is a mental and neural state of readiness, organized through experience, exerting a directive or dynamic influence upon the individual's response to all objects and situations with which it is related.' The objects towards which an attitude 'readies' response are values. Values are objects which society has agreed upon, 'objects of common regard on the part of civilized men' (Allport, 1954). Allport continued to say that measurement can only work for attitudes that are common, and that there will be few attitudes common enough to be profitably scaled.

It seemed a reasonable expectation that an individual's 'state of readiness,' organized as it was by experience of the social object, would be an enduring state. It would operate in individuals across situations, making future behaviour predictable from a knowledge of the attitude. The effect of the specific situation upon behaviour could be covered under the caveat 'all other things being equal.' While a behaviourist might be made unhappy by the suggestion that an attitude was a real state of the organism, there is nothing transparently flawed in this reigning conception. Indeed, the behaviourist would be able to cover the notion of 'state' by thinking of an individual's history of reinforcement as having affected his or her propensities for action.

But, crucially, the official conception was not and is not the working conception. The measurement techniques developed by Thurstone, Likert, and Guttman tapped only the individual's reaction of liking or disliking the object of the attitude. By the mid-1940s, nearly all researchers had accepted that they could adequately measure Allport's predictive state of readiness by that which was captured by the new techniques – the pro-con evaluative, or 'affective' character. Further, attitudes as they are gathered in research are individuals' *own* verbal reports of affinities for and aversions to some part of the environment. Other broad classes of evidence might include the researcher's observations of both verbal and other overt behaviour; the subject's responses to incompletely structured stimuli, that is, projective techniques; physiological reactions; and the subject's responses in engineered situations in which an underlying disposition is thought to be important. But, as Daryl Bem points out, even the most grand theoretical conceptions virtually always boil down to operationalizations depending on self-reported verbal affect (Bem, 1968a: 197).[1]

This acceptance that 'attitude' was adequately captured through verbal self-reports of direction of affect was disastrous for social psychology. It is easy to understand how it came about.

William I. Thomas and Florian Znaniecki in *The Polish Peasant in Europe and America* (1918) showed how important attitudes were for individuals. 'Attitudes' described the imprint of culture on the individual, and the motility of attitudes explained the success or failure that an individual would have in achieving growth in the new American soil. It is the Thomas and Znaniecki conception of attitude which is behind Allport's official definition. In Thomas and Znaniecki's work, attitude was a favourable or unfavourable disposition toward anything in the value realm: a process of consciousness which determined real or possible activity. Attitude bore with it a motivation for activity. Motivation could be the link in the organism that led from environmental stimuli through to a response shaped by the organism itself (Fleming, 1967: 326). Attitude is philosophical stance. The individual can only go forward from the basis of what he had learned from his past.

Unfortunately, just when social psychologists were recognizing the interest of 'attitudes' as a way of talking about the retention of culture by the individual, Thurstone's method swept the field by allowing researchers to readily collect 'objective' descriptions of individuals' attitudes as statements of pro or con feeling. Further, these attitudes could be compared with one another for degree of favourableness or unfavourableness. Later, Likert's method made the task easier still.[2] The sheer ease with which vast quantities of 'empirical' data on so-called attitudes could be collected generally led to their collection in an interpretive vacuum. Other kinds of behaviour in the life context were not assessed. The attendant or antecedent structural and cultural conditions were not independently observed and recorded.

The crucial problem created for social psychology was that Humpty-Dumpty has to be put back together again. In comparison with overt physical activity, verbal behaviour is so very free, so easily generated and recorded. Acceptance of this methodological course separated verbal behaviour from other overt behaviour, and created quite gratuitously the task of specifying the empirical relationship between the two. Once they are separated, the relationship must be specified, because social psychologists are primarily concerned with willed action. This verbal dimension of affect had become the stand-in for will, for motivation.

The problem was compounded by the fact that a great many social psychologists did not seem to notice that Humpty-Dumpty had been broken in two. The breakage was perhaps cloaked by the connotations of the word *attitude*: Darwin had used it to describe an overt physical posture, 'frequently an exaggerated whole body posture' (Fleming, 1967: 294). This very strong sense of the union of intentional and physical readiness by the individual was effectively retained by the official definition's phrase 'mental and neural state of readiness.' This meant that researchers could and did make inferential leaps from individuals' statements of affect to activity. 'Readiness' to act was virtually the deed itself.

In short, with acceptance of verbally reported affect as an adequate indicator of attitude, the stage was set for more than thirty years of disappointment with the attitude concept. This thirty-years' waste can be reviewed by touching on a few scholarly landmarks.

Social psychologists had been warned early. LaPiere anticipated the bitter consensus of the 1960s by thirty years, with his study of innkeepers' attitudes toward Chinese persons. He showed that what people said they would do and what they did were different; that verbal statements of intent to exclude Chinese and equable overt acceptance of Chinese as customers were *both* norms. The 1960s saw many theoretical-polemical retrospectives of where attitude had led us. Allan Liska has provided excellent reviews of these contributions. Notable are Donald Tarter's assessment of his seven years as a scholar of attitudes, 'Attitude: The Mental Myth' (1970), and Irwin Deutscher's 'Looking Backward: Case Studies on the Progress of Methodology in Sociological Research' (1969). In his article, Deutscher analyses three studies of prejudice which had been conducted over a thirty-year period, and shows the steady refinement in design and conceptualizations. Unfortunately, Deutscher runs the film backwards so that it is the 1934 LaPiere study which is shown to be the most advanced. Although Deutscher's goading produced a series of very strong replies, the most useful of these, by Ajzen et al., concludes that while research does not support Deutscher's contention of an actual regressive trend 'there is no indication of a significant advance either' (1970: 271).

Less polemical and dramatic but more deeply disturbing contributions were made during the same period by scholars who did concerted searches of research reports and notes, looking for signs of empirical robustness of the attitude conception. Tittle and Hill in 1967 and Wicker in 1969 and 1971 provided powerful summaries of existing work. Overall, the studies suggested that, with the mainstream conception of attitude as verbal effect toward the object, using standard scales or single statements, attitudes were only slightly related to overt kinds of behaviour. Correlations were often near zero, and rarely exceeded 0.30. 'Only rarely can as much as 10 per cent of the variance in overt behavioural measures be accounted for by attitudinal data' (Wicker, 1969: 161). Walter Mischel's impressive *Personality and Assessment* (1968) attacks the entire range of theoretical personality contents, attitude among them. Mischel reviews psychoanalytic and trait personality theories based on the supposition that individual personality characteristics should exhibit stability over time and across situations. He examines hundreds of empirical reports, and concludes that 0.30 is about the natural limit for the ability of an index to predict behaviour across situations. He concludes that behavioural continuity is a function of similarity in situations. Bem's defence of Mischel's work against a critique by Alker (1972) suggests that there may be two kinds of people, 'those with traits and those without' (1972: 23). Bem's work since 1972 expands upon and qualifies his position, but in no case does he suggest a return to the traditional tactics (see Bem and Funder, 1978: Kenrick and Stringfield, 1980).

It had thus taken more than thirty years for mainstream scholarship to grapple with the empirical results: attitude did not predict behaviour. Even so, many scholars continue research on attitude which makes no mention whatever of behaviour other than verbal test behaviour. Robert Salisbury notes that what was hailed as the 'behavioural revolution' generated remarkably little analysis of actual behaviour as an irony peculiar to political science (1975: 323). But behaviour-free studies of social viewpoints other than political exist in abundance. In a kind of orgy of respectful attentiveness to the aggregated elicited agreements of mass populations, researchers assumed that it was useful to study all individuals' reactions to every social value (and everything was a social value). The way in which these reactions related to one another was assumed to be of intrinsic interest.

Survey research generated perhaps the worst abuses. Controlled experimental manipulation was of necessity abandoned for large-scale investigations and with it was abandoned the right to impute non-obvious 'causes' of viewpoints. But the habit of making such imputations was not abandoned. Nor was the logic of significance testing, which asked only whether the finding was one that could have occurred by chance. With large sample surveys, virtually every 'finding' was significant. In a study of 1,500 people, if it is found that height predicts one-half of one per cent of the variability of intelligence, that finding will almost certainly reflect population parameters. With ill-defined attitudes, virtually every attitude was just slightly, but significantly, related to every other attitude. The substantive contents were often in logical contradiction. (For critical review of this research, see Sutherland and Tanenbaum [1977, 1980].)

There was one clear trend in the welter of operationalizations and vague relationships: attitudinal contradiction and confusion, and disvalued personality characteristics and social attitudes, were attributed to mass publics in contrast with elites, and to lower socio-economic groups in contrast with the middle and upper classes. The corpus of work would hardly be worth criticizing were it not for this 'finding,' which has given comfort to the functional apathy theories within modern democratic theory. That is, functional apathy theories connect these attitude findings with the empirical discovery that members of lower strata are less active politically. These theories find the coincidence lucky for liberal democracy.[3] Notable theoretical challenges to this corpus are Bachrach (1967) and Pateman (1970). Richard Hamilton (1972) and Mischel (1968) present the most comprehensive critiques on empirical grounds.

In summary, first the limelight and then the recrimination belonged to the conception of 'attitude' which had been shorn of any physiological or non-verbal behavioural implications. Behaviourists (in distinction from the political scientist behaviouralists), interested in the responses of individuals to environmental contingencies, were not so much beaten from the field as defined out of it. They ignored mental contents per se in favour of the more overt behavioural signs by which one would have to, in any event, infer the mental contents. (Of course there has always been interest in attitudes as dependent variables, that is, as *learned* predispositions. Hilgard [1980] notes an increasing interest in cognition by experimental psychologists.)

Probability versus latent process debate

In any event, DeFleur and Westie had been able, in 1963, to identify a coherent but very minor conceptualization of 'attitude.' This alternative to the Allport formulation given above is the 'probability conception.' 'Attitude' is inferred from the historical record of all an individual's responses toward an attitude object, including both verbal and other overt behaviour: 'a series of responses toward a given stimulus is likely to show some degree of organization, structure, or predictability. Responses of a specified type, say verbal rejection behaviour, may be more likely to occur than, say, acceptance or indifferent responses for a given individual when he is confronted repeatedly with a defined attitude stimulus. If this is the case, such a response organization can be termed a negative attitude. The attitude, then, is an inferred property of the responses, namely their consistency' (DeFleur and Westie, 1963: 21).

To say that someone has a negative attitude toward French Canadians, then, means that in the presence of stimuli relevant to French Canadians all possible expressions of negative responses are more probable than are positive responses. Overt behaviour was being bootlegged back in.[4] The advantage of the probability conception, DeFleur and Westie said, was that it linked the attitude concept firmly to observable events.

The attitude concept had been attracting unfavourable notice from philosophers of science because it was often not linked to observable events. A personality theory, May Brodbeck says, remains in the realm of fantasy when there is no possibility of falsifying claims (1968: 4). The scientific method entails that if one claims that an individual has a property, it must be possible to state the observable conditions under which a sentence containing the claim is true or false. Verbal behaviour is still admissible evidence under this stricture. But observance would curb the licence to infer a trait from *any* overt manifestation. An example of such abuse is when both obedience to parents and rebellion against them can be seen as overcompensation for the dependence. The psychologist Robert Sears had earlier objected to the growing interest in disembodied 'attitude' from a stronger stand: 'the basic events to which behavior theory has reference are actions ... There is no virtue in a descriptive statement that a person or a class of persons possesses such and such a trait or need unless that statement is part of a larger one that concludes with a specification of a kind of action to be performed' (1951: 477).

DeFleur and Westie addressed this issue by side-stepping. One disadvantage of the probability conception, they said somewhat disingenuously, was that according to their conception 'attitude' could *not* be used to explain behaviour. A consistency of response could not be used to explain itself. Explanatory formulations bearing on identified response consistencies would necessarily rely on propositions relating them to truly independent variables. These would be variables which were not part of the network of evidence from which one inferred the attitude in the first place. Again there is analytic support for the position. It is argued (for example, Winch, 1958, and Davis, 1968) that causal statements connecting attitudes with actions are at best redundant because actions are only distinguishable as such (as willed activity rather than as 'accidental' or entailed behaviour) by reference to the motives which we impute to describe them. MacIntyre (1967) argues, similarly, that the relation of belief to action is not external and contingent, but internal and conceptual.

The alternative conception of attitude DeFleur and Westie referred to as the 'latent process' conception. This is another name for the Thurstone-Thomas conception. Latent process conceptions begin with the same observed response consistency, but explain that consistency (and predict from it for the future) by postulating a mediating inner process. Attitude becomes a hidden mechanism which is *real*, is inside the individual, and compels his responses to the stimulus object. This latent something, DeFleur and Westie said, echoing Skinner, is 'simply unnecessary.'

Skinner held that the question of existence of real inner states, available only to the individual, was better bypassed than directly confronted, because direct confrontation led only to philosophical paradox and to epiphenomenal 'empirical' psychology. Certainly the definition of attitude as pure affect, stored inside the person like little barrels of emotion which a homunculus can inventory and put on tap in response to appropriate social values, had run out of usefulness. And certainly a conception of man's behaviour as elicited solely by contemporary environmental presses had never been tenable. The realms of private psychic experience and publicly observable overt behaviour needed to be opened to one another, if only as translation between two bodies of theory. What was needed was a new conception of attitude. This would state that individual tendency systems were established by the individual's experience, attempt to incorporate the modes of establishment and predictive power of such systems into knowledge about learning processes, and treat these tendency systems/behavioural repertoires as open processes whose durability was an empirical matter rather than an assumption. That is, if one thought of attitude as being a probability of getting a favourable or unfavourable response toward an object, it would be natural to assume that as behaviours continued to be performed, future probabilities moved toward more, or less, certainty.

Contributions from cognitive theory

In fact, such formulations were available and in use in experimental social psychology from the mid-1950s. They did not, however, affect atemporal cross-sectional survey research because most of the new formulations involved some specification of process. Thomas Ostrom, in 'The Emergence of Attitude Theory: 1930–1950' (1968), did a major service by ignoring his own title and providing a succinct evaluation of major contributions to theoretical formulations of attitude developed *since* 1950. His two major categories are learning-behaviour theory and cognitive integration theory. The first 'draws upon principles resulting from the study of human and animal learning, while the latter is based on analyses of the individual's phenomenal representation of his world' (Ostrom, 1968: 2). Both theories do man the honour of thinking of him as being adaptable and teachable, and as shaping his behaviour to environmental contingencies after some deliberation. Attitude is alternatively a dependent or independent variable, sometimes thought of as a motive and sometimes not.

Ostrom makes no mention of attribution theory as such in his review, but he does note the contributions of Daryl Bem to attitude theory under the heading 'eclectic.' Attribution theory, as applied by its main proponents (Edward Jones and Keith Davis, Bem, Richard Nisbett and Stuart Valins, and Harold Kelley),[5] addresses itself to the description of processes by which an individual comes to form understandings of the causal structure of his environment. To quote Conrad Morrow, 'the individual will attempt to analyse and understand the events in his life based upon the information he has about himself, his life, and his world. With this information, he will attempt to explain the cause of events in terms of internal causes (causes relating to the self) and/or external causes (causes relating to the non-self)' (1971: 3).

Typically, the individual is said to pursue a causal chain from the effects of a deed to the intentions of the actor (taking into account the extent to which the actor appeared to be autonomous of situational constraints), thence to imputation of more stable characteristics or dispositions of the actor (see Jones and Davis, 1965). The individual could reflect on his own experiences in a similar manner, imputing dispositions to the self.

The particular importance of Daryl Bem is that, in 'Attitudes as Self Descriptions' (1968a: 198), he suggests 'specific mechanisms through which attitudes can function as both independent and dependent variables in the attitude-behavior link.' Bem's argument traces out the implications of Skinner's 'radical behaviourism' for attitude-as-statement-of-affect. Latent process conceptions imply that 'attitude' is a *clear* internal stimulus which is accessible only to its possessor. Bem argues that the individual *learns* to make discriminations between different kinds of internal stimuli (including the pro and con feeling of attitude). This learning, like all learning, takes place through the socializing community: for example, a child learns names for various aches and pains by echoing the words his mother utters as she watches his physical signs. Discriminations between inner stimuli are few, and gross. Skinner makes the elementary physiological point that there is very little inner sensory equipment with which to make discriminations. Further, the subject's own discriminations are easily overridden: Valins (1966), Schachter and Singer (1962), Schachter and Wheeler (1962), and Laird (1974) have all demonstrated that manipulation of an individual's expressive behaviour mediates the quality of his emotional experience as he reports it. Earlier, Arnold Tannenbaum (1957) had demonstrated that personality changes can be brought about by persisting change in environmental conditions. Hence 'inner states' may be neither clear, well-bounded, nor 'private' except in the sense that the individual alone experiences the 'state.'

Bem argues, in effect, that one of the individual's best sources of information about his own attitudes is the behaviour that would be seen by an outside observer. The individual takes his self-descriptions, in part, from internal affective cues (which he will be able to name to the extent that, in the past, he has been reinforced by others for the 'correctness' of the name). The individual does have access to certain collateral products of his own genetic and environmental history (Skinner, 1976: 19). The point is that his own behaviour is a good source of information for the individual. The individual knows he likes brown bread because he recalls eating it. It is, of course, not strictly necessary that an individual be able to recall perfectly the events and evidence on which attitudes are based.

And how might attitudes function as directives for behaviour? Bem suggests that they might work as internalized directive speech, a form of self-instruction (1968a: 207). In one of Bem's brown bread experiments, he found that where subjects were repeatedly *told* that they liked brown bread, their consumption increased.

Now it is worth noting, if only briefly, that the Bemian account of how individuals come to take their stands about who and what they are, and what they do, very closely parallels the account given by Gilbert Ryle in *The Concept of Mind* (1969: 154–95). Here Ryle is anxious to dispose of the 'ghost in the machine.' Ryle denies that the individual has privileged access to 'real' mental states, as does Skinner. We do not 'introspect' and come out with full and fresh information about our inner selves. Instead, Ryle says, we *retrospect* from time to time on the activity we have just performed, and perhaps plan more activity. To claim to introspect implies puzzles of divided consciousness: we watch ourselves watch ourselves as we consciously perform tasks. Hence, if retrospective knowledge (in which the individual explains to himself the import of what he was doing, or simply rehearses a sequence of events) is the only knowledge available to an individual, the person has exactly the kind of information about himself that he can have of anyone. More recently, Richard Nisbett and Timothy Wilson (1977) have provided a review of existing empirical work which suggests that individuals have little or no direct introspective access to higher-order cognitive processes. Smith and Miller (1978) follow up on the problem.

Behaviour, therefore, in both the Bem and Ryle formulations, is a prime source of information for the individual about his or her own attitudes. If we accept this idea, the problem of the causal relationship between attitudes and behaviours dissolves as a pseudo-problem. To thus consider attitude and behaviour as inseparably existing in a feedback relationship to one another is the philosophical solution. It is also being pointed to as the practical or applied solution by such doyens of attitude research as Herbert Kelman (1974).

Kelman identifies only one major potential problem with the attribution theory conception that an individual's attitude is gleaned from the same sorts of evidence that are available to another observer. The objection is that attitudes might be construed as being merely epiphenomenal to action. That is, 'attitude' loses the sense of actually shaping future activity, whether as 'real' mediating inner process *or* as behaviour rewarded in the past in similar eliciting circumstances. Kelman argues on two grounds that attitudes are not epiphenomenal, that is, that there is a link from attitude to action. He notes that cognitive dissonance and cognitive attribution theorists have devised a number of experiments in which a person's beliefs were ascertained, then his behaviour was manipulated in some fashion and consequently shown to have some consequences for his beliefs. The different processes inferred by the two groups of theorists need not concern us here. Of interest is the fact that both made the point that the individual's behaviour could and did form his interpretation of his own motives. Kelman says that there *must* be a connection between attitudes and action, otherwise people could not be made sufficiently uncomfortable with attitudes as self-descriptions that they would feel obliged to relabel their attitudes.[6] Kelman's other major point is that all major reviews of research to date show that there is some persistent attitude-action connection: people have emphasized the disappointing magnitude of the connection, but the connection is equally sensibly pointed to as being always there.

Kelman's recommendation for a working definition of attitude therefore brings us back to the Darwinian synthesis: 'Attitude ... is not an index of action, but a determinant, component and consequent of it. Furthermore, it is not an entity that can be separated – functionally or temporally – from the flow of action, but is an integral part of action. Attitude and action are linked in a continuing reciprocal process, each generating the other in an endless chain. *Action is the ground on which attitudes are formed, tested, modified, abandoned*' (Kelman, 1974: 316; emphasis added).

Definition to be employed
The time is now ripe to state the definition of attitude that will be employed in this research, and to forecast the happy consequences. First, attitudes will be accepted as being dispositional; summary descriptions of the probability that an individual will (continue to) respond in a certain way to certain social objects. Second, it is held that the individual infers his or her dispositions as the result of self-perceptions of his/her own behaviour and also from such information about inner states as may be available. Behaviour feeds back into attitude.

The consequences of accepting such a definition are obvious. First, acceptance means that the connection between attitude and action per se is no longer a matter of great intrinsic interest. The two cannot be thought of separately. Therefore one cannot learn anything new by predicting one from the other, a thing from itself. We should think of verbal reports of affect for an object, and activity toward that object, as being collateral indicators of an individual's stance toward a social object. We can sensibly work to improve the relationship between scores on verbal scales of affect and reports of other overt behaviour if we conceive of the task as a technical exercise to improve internal validity. We may also use these two things to describe 'attitude' as response probability. But to 'explain' attitude we must relate it to independent sets of variables. That is, because we take both verbal scale scores and other overt behaviour as the evidence from which we infer a pattern of approval or disapproval of an object (in which we may find no pattern) we shall not speak of affect as causing the act. Possible candidates for causes and effects will be sought outside the object-related verbal and overt behaviour.

SURVEY RESEARCH: THE PROBLEM OF
ESTABLISHING COMMON VALUES

Up to this point, although the use of attitude in survey research has been the implicit focus, the discussion has also been relevant to uses of attitude in experimental research. The following remarks, in contrast, are restricted in application to cross-sectional surveys.

Obviously, for the study of individuals' preferences to have generated so little return over thirty to forty years of endeavour, there had to be more wrong with it than the fact that the working definition of the master concept had precipitously omitted one major source of evidence – behaviour. It seemed, in fact, that findings about 'attitudes' were not sufficiently precise so that anomalies could be generated. Results were so unstructured that the world of facts could find no avenue through which to strike back and force adjustments in definition and theory. To adapt Dennett's analogy (1978: xiv) not only were researchers unable to 'carve nature at the joints,' it seemed that nature had no joints to suggest lines for carving. Even with attitude re-conceptualized, it still remains interesting that a person's verbal reports of affect for an object were being measured so badly that they scarcely correlated with other overt behaviour, which one could think of as being criteria for validity.

There are at least two very different discussions which tempt one at this point. It would be logical to launch next onto topics of technical improvements; or further to suggest that as behaviour prediction is a multivariate problem, we must include attitudes toward the situation, social constraints, role considerations, information, intelligence, and developmental considerations. These concerns will be taken up in chapter 3, which attempts to incorporate such suggestions for improving the 'attitude-behaviour' relationship. But it is my opinion that a much more basic corrective must precede even these improvements. We now turn to a basic characteristic of survey measures.

Let us accept that an individual can give us an adequate verbal description of his or her affect for some social object. Let us also accept that this description is at least part of what we need to talk about attitude, and that it ought to indicate the probability for other behaviour toward the attitude object. Now, how adequate is a cross-sectional survey's objective measure of verbally reported affect as a description of an individual's verbal behaviour toward an attitude object? Can one capture each individual's attitude, even if the definition is restricted to such a simple dimension as a pro-con response to verbal stimuli? The answer, of course, must be 'no.' At the most, one can secure an individual's agreement or disagreement to a small set of statements. These statements are stipulated by the researcher, who has some reason to believe that they are relevant to the object in question.

Indeed, the statements may well be relevant to the object in question. In political studies, there is every reason to want to measure the incidence and chart correlates in mass publics of interesting political opinions. The prior

Figure 1.1 Relationship of response choices to behaviour

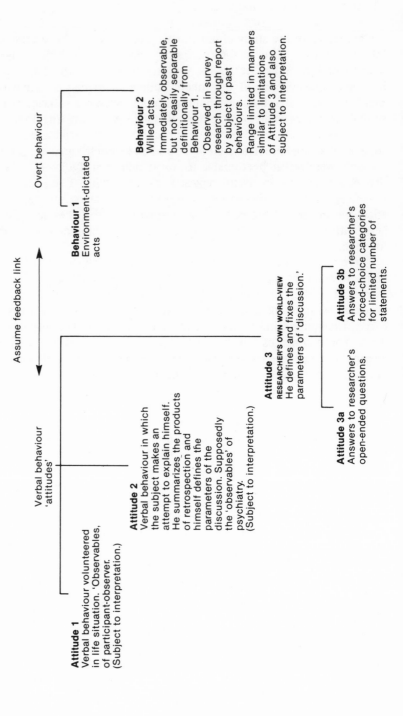

Assume feedback link

Verbal behaviour 'attitudes'

Overt behaviour

Attitude 1
Verbal behaviour volunteered
in life situation. 'Observables',
of participant-observer.
(Subject to interpretation.)

Attitude 2
Verbal behaviour in which
the subject makes an
attempt to explain himself.
He summarizes, the products
of retrospection and
himself defines the
parameters of the
discussion. Supposedly
the 'observables' of
psychiatry.
(Subject to interpretation.)

Attitude 3
RESEARCHER'S OWN WORLD-VIEW
He defines and fixes the
parameters of 'discussion.'

Attitude 3a
Answers to researcher's
open-ended questions.

Attitude 3b
Answers to researcher's
forced-choice categories
for limited number of
statements.

Behaviour 1
Environment-dictated
acts

Behaviour 2
Willed acts.
Immediately observable,
but not easily separable
definitionally from
Behaviour 1.
'Observed' in survey
research through report
by subject of past
behaviours.
Range limited in manners
similar to limitations
of Attitude 3 and also
subject to interpretation.

problem is, rather, that the statement might not be relevant to the person in question.

In development of the best scales, statements to which subjects will respond are developed through a process of consultation with the milieu. The attitude statements are developed from people's observations about the social phenomenon to be studied. At the worst, scholars solemnly record reactions to statements which were written decades ago by other scholars for other purposes. These are stilted and outdated, but rather perversely interesting because response rates are available for other samples. But, regardless, the researcher *does not have* a record of the individual subject's unguarded verbal expressions of liking or disliking for a social value. Rather, the researcher has placed his or her subjects in a response situation in which they are constrained (to an unknown extent) by the lack of variety of choices. There is therefore little reason to expect high correspondence between the individual's scale score and his spontaneous in-situation evaluations of any social object. The problem here may be elucidated by reference to figure 1.1. This is an attempt to show that survey research may well not come very close to capturing anything but measures of how many people can be coaxed to endorse or reject the researcher's statements. It is drawn in an attempt to show a major source of attenuation in the verbal/other overt behaviour relationship. The general assumption in survey research, one expects, is that the record of *constrained* choices is in fact an adequate evaluation of what unguarded (or unguided) verbal behaviour would reveal, and that therefore, when other overt behaviour has been observed not to fit, the verbal/overt behaviour relationship (or attitude-behaviour link in the latent process model) has been adequately tested and found wanting. I suspect that in most research there is no reason to think that this test has been performed. There is the additional problem, of course, that 'opinions,' whether researcher-stipulated or subject-volunteered, tend to be cast in general, situation-free terms. An act, in contrast, is always situation-bound and specific as to purpose.

The different cue value of statements for different individuals, unconscious response biases, and conscious impression management are other sources of attenuation. Still another major and less often mentioned difficulty is the 'instant salience' effect which often occurs when one presents a co-operative subject with a universe of statements which may or may not have formerly been a part of his opinion repertoire. In this situation, the subject may respond in a random fashion. Or the subject may reflect and form views on the spot, perhaps inferring them from past reactions. The researcher is thus measuring an 'instant attitude,' which may or may not remain a part of the individual's repertoire of conclusions (opinions) about the world. It therefore makes some sense to regard each attitude statement as an attempt to influence the subject to endorsement. In cases where the subject endorses contradictory statements, he is yielding to persuasion and is in an ongoing 'opinion change' process. Evidence of ongoing self-contradiction in the course of completing the series of questions would indicate lack of salience of the attitude object, as well as persuasability.

Philip Converse discusses the same problem area in his article 'Attitudes and Non-attitudes: Continuation of a Dialogue' (1970). Converse, in the reported longitudinal study on attitude evolution, had urged people not to respond to a statement unless that statement was salient to them. In co-operation, 35 per cent of his sample admitted they had no genuine opinion on an item, and did not answer at all. Still Converse found enough 'attitude inconsistencies' that he concluded that a good deal of 'noise' in the test relationships was caused by the endorsement and rejection by subjects of 'non-attitudes.' It is worth emphasizing that Converse was eager to cope with the problem of great amounts of missing data. In contrast, most proponents of questionnaire studies tend to equate success in gathering 'good' data with success in getting people to succumb to forced-choice categories.[7] The category 'neither agree nor disagree,' instead of being treated as missing data, is traditionally treated as a mid-point on an ordinal scale of negative to positive affect for an attitude object.

The probability notion of attitudes as conceived by DeFleur and Westie, however, makes attitude measurement as sensible a task as is possible under the circumstances:

The probability conception of attitude makes measurement a rather straightforward task. This is particularly true when the definable set of behaviors is called *verbal* behavior. With the aid of various scaling techniques, the individual can be confronted with graded sets of statements which are representative selections from the universe of possible (verbal) responses to the attitude stimulus. If the individual clearly endorses only statements of a very complimentary nature regarding the attitude object, his probability of favorable verbal responses outside the measurement situation (or in a later repetition of the measurement situation) is thought to be high and he is characterized as having a favorable attitude. If one starts an investigation of attitude variables with the probability definition in mind, the measurement task can logically be conceived of as a determination of response probabilities. (1963: 23)

But how do we specify the constructs that we are interested in assessing? That is, what makes any particular statement a 'representative selection' from the universe of possible responses to a particular attitude stimulus? The question is a return to one aspect of the earlier concern about establishing relevance-to-subject of the 'attitude' statements presented for his or her affective reaction. Also, the idea that there is a 'universe' or a 'population' of statements which might be made about a social value sheds some commonsense constructive light on the problem.

But the social scientist might be interested in *two* varieties of attitudinal universe rather than in just one. First, there is the task in which the researcher wishes to discover the incidence of support for some intrinsically interesting criterion ideology. The writers of *The Authoritarian Personality* wished to learn about the potential for fascism in the American public. Fascism was defined and cast in operational form by the researchers. In this kind of task, 'relevance' to subject should mean only that the statements are cast in easily understood straightforward contemporary prose, *and* that the subject is given every opportunity to show that the ideas are of no concern to him. The second variety of attitudinal universe would be one where the important question is how the subjects themselves think of the social object. There may be no known criterion ideology. Or it may be necessary to draw the set of views out of the population before its incidence (popularity) can be investigated. In this case, the researcher can interview people about all aspects of the value, and emerge with a 'representative sampling' of the universe of reactions to the social value.

Dating or, rather, outdating of statements is a problem in both measurement tasks. In the first case of measuring amount of agreement with a criterion ideology, the problem is more easily spotted. Elite analyses are always highly visible and hotly debated, and make clear claims to clarity and temporal relevance. For example, the scholar studying socialism in Saskatchewan would necessarily be alert to the need for the theory to accommodate approval of the family farm. In the second task, where the population specifies its own definition, it is less easily remembered that the 'universe' itself will date quickly. Prejudice, for example, is a phenomenon that exists over time and across societies. But to manifest prejudice, the individual must do some thing, or say some thing. Each temporal and spatial context carries its own variety of deeds and means by which individual persons can harm and exclude one another. Each population will have a universe of capsule descriptions of, and sentiments about, the social value. The researcher must be able to translate accurately between the language of the social scientist in which prejudice is a universal social phenomenon and the language of life-in-context. In daily life, prejudice is manifested in the deeds and statements which are systematically hurtful to actual persons, say, Ukrainians on the

Canadian prairies. Cronbach has argued eloquently that 'the special task of the social scientist in each generation is to pin down the contemporary facts' (1975: 116).

Attitude researchers have often denied that such adjustment to real social time and locations is necessary, or desirable. Social scientists are said to be more than opinion pollsters, and are not to be so hustled by time. One can answer that where measures of attitude are inappropriate to the people and the times, we are pollsters of yesterday's opinions. Validity, like relevance, must be built up stage by stage, every link specified in the chain of abstraction from what is observed to the desired broad social 'law.' If such a procedure 'discovers' only islands of narrow-range laws, of 'limited range of relevance, beyond which it makes no sense to affirm or deny' (George Kelly, 1973: 202), so be it. It will be more useful to have specific propositions which may well be irrelevant to most contexts, than to have general propositions which are irrelevant to all contexts. To quote Cronbach again: 'To know man as he is is no mean aspiration.'

THE PROBLEM OF OWNING UP TO A-TEMPORALITY

In his useful interpretation and review 'Behaviour Theory as Personality Theory' (1968), D.E. Berlyne describes what a stimulus-organism-response law might look like in such a theory. At least four terms referring to the organism would intervene between stimulus and response:

$$S,_oTransient, {}_oDevelopmental, {}_oLearned, {}_oCongenital^R.$$

Each of these capacities or states of the organism will have some effect on what is to emerge as response, once the stimulus has been given. By 'transient' is meant factors such as mood and fatigue and the effects of the measurement situation. This term can be seen as an error term. 'Developmental' refers, of course, to the age of the organism. In a way it is concerned with an implicit comparison of that organism relative to 'normal' development in the species. Piaget's work would be of great interest here; that is, has the individual reached an age at which he can manipulate certain concepts like volume, and so forth? Under 'learned' is all learning that the individual has undergone to date – every possible individual variation that is acquired, such as habits, attitudes, opinions, beliefs, and self-view. Most of what we think of as character and personality would fall under this term. It represents the residues of the interaction of the capacities of the organism with the environment, over the organism's entire history. 'Congenital' refers to constitutional and inborn predispositions: the limitations of that particular individual. This may not be a trivial term even for the survey researcher. Recent thinking in psychophysiology suggests that the ability to *have* affect ('emotion,' or visceral involvement), as well as the amount of affect displayed, is physiologically controlled. It appears that there is great variability even within the 'normal' range (see, for example, Lykken, 1968: 423). Further, the health of an individual, his intelligence, and usual energy level will have an impact upon the amount of energy the individual will have left after looking to immediate needs.

But, when we collect data from an individual in a cross-sectional survey, we are working virtually completely within the 'learned' term, relating the contents through the use of correlation. More often than not we simply accept conventional ideas about direction of causation and perpetuate them in our interpretations and 'results.' We think of people as not voting because of 'alienation,' for example. What one 'knows' is that non-voting and reports of estrangement vary together. In a sense, one is continually assessing responses, knowing nothing about whether or when a stimulus might have been presented to an individual. Therefore, in survey research, we should suggest only response-response probability laws. We should not impute contemporaneously reported 'stimuli' as 'causes' of 'responses.'

Another aspect of owning up to a-temporality in cross-sectional survey research concerns the attribution and interpretation of broad 'commonsense' dispositions. 'Authoritarianism' is such a disposition. As proposed by the California researchers, it is a high-level abstraction arrived at through consideration of many subtly varied kinds of behaviour over time and across situations: the 'gist' of a behaviour history toward *many* social objects. In principle, one could pursue the delineation of the various aspects of the syndrome by developing one scale for each aspect. These scales could then be correlated to see if the syndrome is, in fact, a phenomenon. Do its aspects as stipulated vary together empirically? But having described a manifestation of a set of views does not mean that we have discovered its genesis, nor does it mean that one can attribute a dynamic psychic function to the syndrome.[8]

In short, when we work solely with cross-sectional survey data, we do not know *why* individuals believe what they do. In particular, psychoanalytic dynamic interpretations of a-temporal survey research findings constitute a barrier to serious scholarship. Imputation by the researcher of an indirect dynamic can 'explain' any association between any set of variables. One simply invents some 'underlying organizational principle that can account for the phenotypic behavioural differences in terms of a genotypic description of that person's psychic structure' (Wachtel, 1973: 324).

The third way of owning up to a-temporality is to refrain from making distinctions on the basis of the presumed durability of mental contents. These distinctions simply re-emerge in interpretation of findings as unjustified causal inferences. First, it is generally assumed that the individual characteristics which we describe through survey studies are enduring orientations. Some may be, some may not. We need panel studies to address the problem. Similarly, it is generally assumed that some aspects of personality are more durable than others. The accepted hierarchy, increasing in generality and durability, runs through judgments, opinions, attitudes, values, and self-image (Yinger, 1963: 589). Thurstone embarked on this course when he first held that verbalized opinions were the evidence from which one inferred attitude (1928, 1931). The hierarchy exists in many refinements, but the assumption is that general dispositions are deeper and more stable, and stand in causal or mediating relations to the more specific, particular dispositions.[9] But this is purely a presumptive hierarchy (Elder, 1973: 792). Unless it is involved as either axiom or theorem, its invocation as window dressing in survey research would seem to cause only confusion.

WHAT IS TO BE DONE?

There are a number of proposals to extract from the discussion of attitudes in use over the past forty years. The proposals can be briefly restated for emphasis, since the next chapters will attempt to explore them.

First, as it makes theoretical sense, and as it bows to the fact that in cross-sectional survey research we do not know whether attitude precedes behaviour or vice-versa, we can think of 'attitude' as the combined probability of the occurrence of favourable or unfavourable behaviour *and* of other overt behaviour toward a social value.

Second, let us measure one thing at a time, responses toward one clear social value in one measure. This is more in the nature of a goal to aim at than a goal to be realized. William Scott makes the point that a group of test items can be 'only relatively unidimensional, and that the number of additional dimensions required to encompass them will depend on the larger set of items that are included with them in a common factor analysis' (1968b: 1001). While it makes more sense to ask whether one attitude can and should be distinguished from another, the technical term in use is 'uni-dimensionality' of measure; hence we shall follow this use.

Third, the 'attitude' that is being measured must be one that is relevant to the population being studied. Consultation of the milieu to be studied, when appropriate, must obviously take place before the one-off survey. When the data are in, wholesale discard of statements which do not scale with their intended measures is a second safeguard against the promulgation of nonsense. In the case in which the incidence of a population's adherence to some criterion attitude or 'ideology' is at issue, a third tactic is possible. (The term is used in the sense of a broad belief system.) This tactic is of great importance for establishing incidence and correlates of student power ideology, the task of this study. The idea is simple: before the subject is said to have the ideology, he or she must show consistency across all of the discernible unidimensional (or merely separable) aspects. Working with as many one-topic measures as is appropriate, the researcher cross-examines his subjects. The tactic allows subjects who might have formed 'instant attitudes' to each of the facets of the ideology a chance to indicate that their instant opinions are not relevant to the social object being studied. They do this by being in contradiction in terms of the criterion syndrome. In a way, the tactic extends the validity rationale that favours long unidimensional scales whose statements are carefully graduated for extremity, to *batteries* of unidimensional scales. But there is a major difference in interpretation. The subject who agrees with only some of the component scales is not said to possess the ideology in small amount. Inconsistent subjects are excluded as not manifesting the ideology.

Parenthetically, this third 'consistency' tactic entails a change in the way non-experimental social scientists think of handling their total sample. The tactic is explored empirically in chapter 3. Briefly, the researcher no longer talks about the target attitude in the whole sample, but only in the portion of the sample to which the attitude is relevant. The residual group, rather than being 'waste,' becomes an explicit comparison-cum-control group. How are the 'attitude-holders' different in their other characteristics or views from this residual group? If there are no differences, the researcher faces the fact that the attitude, while possible to isolate, does not resonate to the hypothesized independent variables.

Fourth, indicators of behaviour, other than verbal, toward the attitude object should be selected with as much care as are the verbal indicators. One can work back and forth between the verbal scales and other behavioural indicators to establish reciprocal predictability. If action is the ground upon which attitude is formed, and vice-versa, then the exercise is sensibly conceived as ensuring concurrent validity of the two types of indicators of the 'probability of response-syndrome' toward the social object. Where it is important that the viewpoint be 'actionable,' then the tactic is a method for testing.

The fifth proposal is the logical extension of proposals three and four: validate with reference to completely independent criteria. What should these criteria be? The enterprise of social science presumes that human behaviour is lawful, that it is determined. Thus, where there is consistency across a variety of expressions of verbal affect and reports of other activity, this consistency must have arisen because responses have been routed toward stable patterns by patterns of reinforcement. The pattern that exists, then, exists first in the environment. This is not to say that all learning is systematic, nor that all learning has come about through conditioning (see Skinner [1976: 148] on superstitious learning and Bandura and Walters [1963] and Bandura [1971] on other modes of learning). The question is the degree and kind of relatedness between patterned attitude and activity and characteristics of the social structure. Elder's recommendation is to establish 'links' between aspects of the environment and the characteristics of individuals – their capacities, dispositions, and concepts of self and others (1973: 790). It will also be a matter of interest to elucidate the criterion ideology by showing the extent to which it exists in other systems of social viewpoints. Ideas are more interesting as they impinge upon society than as neural and mental states: 'Systems of ideas as they are actually held by people and social groups, or, as Mannheim would say, ideas existentially considered, are facts. As such, we know they are potent causes. But what is a cause is also of necessity an effect. In other words, rationales are themselves causally determined; accordingly, it is the business of social science to discover their causes as well as their effects' (Bergman, 1968: 130).

The final cautions deal with the interpretation of cross-sectional survey research findings. A cross-sectional survey which is not an integral part of a larger multi-method study of one population is a study of correlations of phenomena. This means that attribution of causation should be made with extreme self-consciousness, and extreme care.[10] The particular strengths of the method should be brought to the fore. Cross-sectional surveys allow collection of detailed information about correlation, and multivariate analysis can tell to what extent socially important phenomena 'account' for each other, and to what extent certain classes of phenomena can be said to be distinct from one another. To work toward the specification of a scheme for classification of social phenomena is a respectable scientific enterprise.

CONCLUSION

About forty years ago, it was thought that study of 'attitudes' would move social science from a mixture of philosophy and moralizing to a science that could make exact predictions for future large-scale social events. One could ask large numbers of people what they thought about certain social objects that they themselves would not necessarily recognize as being important. One could then deduce social futures from the discovered aggregated mass viewpoints. Because of the relative ease with which it could be 'measured,' mere pro-con feeling (liking or disliking a social object) was substituted for an investigation of the *content* of mass views about a social object. While great advances were made in the technical ease with which such attitudes could be measured, it was gradually driven home through thirty years of criticism that public attitudes in the pro-con affective use did not predict other overt behaviour. LaPiere's study showed that innkeepers who were prejudiced against Chinese in pen-and-paper questionnaire behaviour were unprejudiced toward Chinese in the activity of accepting them as guests in their establishments. This was merely the first of scores of studies showing that attitudes as verbal statements of pro-con feeling had only the most tenuous (assumed predictive) connections with other behaviour.

In addition, it became clear that there were grave philosophical problems about the nature of the connection between attitude and behaviour. If attitude was construed as the 'motive' or 'will' aspect of a deed, was the relationship logical and therefore necessary (by definition, action is willed: else all would be behaviour); or was the relationship contingent, and therefore usefully investigated empirically? It became clear during the period of the great empirical failure of attitude that social scientists had rushed in where philosophers had long been fearfully treading. We simply did not understand what we meant in our investigations of the nature of the connection between attitude and behaviour, thought and action.

Having botched the conceptual work, social scientists appeared unable to perform technical assessments with any degree of appropriateness or exactness. Part of the problem stemmed from the first-mentioned theoretical difficulty of having chosen to regard attitude as only the affective element of an individual's stance toward a social object. Few social objects were in the front of most individual's consciousness. In other words, apart from wars and taxes, there are not many 'common values' that are of pressing policy importance. But when social attitudes were being measured, it was (and is) common practice to assume that all individuals have formed some view about whatever is being assessed. Further, most research failed to obtain any indication from an individual about whether or not a viewpoint, while held, was at all central to his or her concerns. Hence researchers have been, to an unknown extent, attempting to predict only vaguely specified behaviours from aggregated 'attitudes.' These measurements included unknown quantities of 'affect' formed on-the-spot, and/or were of only the most marginal importance to the actors concerned.

The theoretical proposal for this study is that a Bem-Kelman definition of attitude be adapted for survey methodology. Views and deeds will be held to create one another reciprocally. Further, we shall concern ourselves with stances that have some centrality for the individual subject. It is further proposed that these stances or ideologies of interest be regarded as *effects* as well as causes. We want to describe the social environments which have brought about these systematically different action-ideologies. In Bergman's terms, it is of considerable theoretical interest to describe the causes that bring about certain 'rationales.'

With so much centring on 'attitude,' and so-called advances, it is only civilized to add a few caveats. The attitude concept is, of course, only one of the many concepts of interest in the study of personality and individual differences. It has, perhaps, the most direct theoretical relevance to the prediction of behaviour. This claim would be difficult to establish, because there is no general consensus among scholars in the field as to what constitutes 'the literature' of the attitude-behaviour problems,[11] or as to what constitutes the core empirical literature of the major related social-psychological concepts. However, there is an increasingly strong trend toward what is often called an 'interactionist' position in the writings of an articulate minority of students of personality. This is the view that behaviour is the outcome of an interaction of fairly stable characteristics of the person with the characteristics of the situation. It is a corrective to a long-term tendency, as with attitudes, to see the (imputed stable) qualities of the person as the pre-eminent cause of behaviour choices. It is also a corrective to a tendency among some behavioural psychologists to view behaviour as solely the outcome of contemporary environmental presses. An article by Kenneth Bowers, published in 1973, called 'Situationism in Psychology' presents an early and thorough statement of the evolving viewpoint. Walter Mischel, who in his 1968 book amassed evidence against the attribution of cross-situational consistency in behaviour, has since provided very useful theoretical statements supporting an interactionist viewpoint (see, for example, Walter Mischel, 1973, 1977). The attribution theorists are by definition interactionists, but Daryl Bem and Andrea Allen have gone somewhat further by supporting empirically the contention that definitions of personality traits and descriptions of situations should be 'made to measure' for individuals and small groups rather than taken 'off the rack' and applied universally (see Bem and Allen, 1974). In theoretical terms 'classification will have to be in terms of the individual's own phenomenology, not the investigators' (Mischel, 1973). As Bem and Allen say, this kind of statement is bound to increase 'the déjà vu of any psychologist old enough to remember Kurt Lewin.' Essentially the same debate as the current one took place before the Second World War (Bem and Allen, 1974: 507). All of these theorists are open about the fact that this is 'recycled' theory. Hogan, DeSoto, and Solaro (1977) provide a useful review of old debts. It is interesting, they write,

> to watch the discipline of personality research recycle itself. Thus Bem and Allen (1974) return to Allport's (1937) thesis that the variables of greatest importance in the study of personality are those most important to the subject. Similarly Bowers (1973) reformulates Murray's (1938) view that overt behavior is a function of the interaction between traits (i.e., psychogenic needs) and situational contingencies (i.e., environmental press). Mischel (1977) also seems to return to a Murray theme: His statement that people are 'so complex and multifaceted as to defy easy classifications and comparisons on any single or simple common dimension (p. 253) sounds remarkably like Murray warning us about the overwhelming complexity of the human personality. (p. 262)

In essence, therefore, my own proposal is that attitude researchers who are interested in overt forms of behaviour, and who are using a survey methodology, adapt each of these theoretical 'advances' in general personality theory to their own use. The reward will be an improvement in clarity and strength of relationships between collateral life events and views and background factors. The present study is an attempt, assuredly less than perfect, to do this. The payoff is exemplary of future gains.

Finally, it is proposed that some appropriate modesty be adopted for the method of survey research. We should stop implying causation where we have no knowledge whatever of temporal sequence. We should stop spinning ad hoc psychoanalytic and developmental explanations for a-temporal correlations. And we should stop the self-serving confounding of statistical significance with theoretical importance.

2

Data collection and
scale development and validity

This chapter is a report on the reasoning behind and technical characteristics of the opinion measures which become flesh and blood in the later chapters. This discussion is given a place of honour here because decisions taken regarding the 'infrastructure' of quantitative research shape and limit findings about matters of substance. Technical decisions, controlling the range of potential findings of substance, must be exposed for the reader's evaluation. This is not highly technical material: it is an honest description of what was done and therefore reveals as many flaws as virtues. Just as there is no such thing as the perfectly run experiment, there is no perfect piece of survey research.

The chapter is in five sections: (1) a description of the survey and a discussion of reliability and validity goals; (2) a discussion of student power opinion measures; (3) a discussion of authoritarian-type measures; (4) a report on measures of 'mental health'; and (5) a report on results of concurrent validity testing.

RELIABILITY AND VALIDITY GOALS

The analysis is of data collected by the Determinants of Citizenship Orientation Project[1] in the spring of 1970. The survey was of a stratified random sample. The target sample, drawn from the records of the registrar at the University of Alberta using a computer-generated random sampling routine, comprised 1,200 individuals. The response rate was 79.8 per cent ($N = 958$), non-response being largely a result of the respondents' having withdrawn from university. The actual refusal rate was less than 10 per cent. Completed questionnaires were drawn almost equally from each of the six respondent categories: first-year, second-year, third-year, fourth-year (honours, education, and engineering), fifth-year (graduate and second degree education), and professional (law, medicine, dentistry, and library science) students. Only those students who were either native Canadians or naturalized citizens were sampled.

Questionnaire opinion measures and index sequences were formatted in the following sections for administration:

PART I: Childhood Background Survey, Demographic variables (sex, age, faculty, income, etc.)

PART II: Authoritarianism, Dogmatism, Tolerance-Intolerance of Ambiguity, Humanitarian Opinions, Student Power scales, Anomy

PART III: Self-Anchoring Striving scale, Machiavellian-Utilitarian outlooks, Rokeach Value survey

PART IV: Active Humanitarianism, Interest in Politics, Knowledge of Political Facts, Political Action (formal), Ideological Outlook Index, Interest in University Politics, University Life-Style Inventory, Political Party Identification, Civil Disobedience Orientation, Protest Activity, Tolerance-Intolerance of Non-conformists

PART V: Self-esteem, IPAT Anxiety scale, General Mental Health Index, Health Survey, Sensitivity to Criticism

Refinement of opinion measures included in the survey at the time of administration (henceforth to be referred to as 'postulated measures') was thought to be necessary on both theoretical and empirical grounds, despite the fact that postulated measures had been arrived at through a series of pre-tests.

For purposes of the discussion I take 'theoretical' to include considerations of face or content validity (does the scale, on a careful reading, appear to be a straightforward, coherent, and salient operationalization of the construct?) and concurrent, predictive, or construct validity (does the scale, when individual items are added together to form a sum score, enter into hypothesized patterns of relationship with other constructs?).

'Empirical' decisions are those taken on evidence of statistical homogeneity (item-item correlations within scales, item-scale correlations,[2] reliability coefficients, and dimensionality). High reliability of measurement is essential as, in general, the maximum correlation any variable can have with another is limited by the reliability with which both are measured. That is, when reliabilities are unknown, and happen in fact to be low, the researcher may find no relationship between constructs when there is in fact a relationship.

At the beginning of the refinement program, it was decided to work toward unidimensionality of measures. McKennell's statement that 'without homogeneity, measurement of one thing at a time, the meaning of any obtained correlations would be uninterpretable' (1970: 235) was taken as axiomatic. Factor-analysis was chosen as an appropriate scale-building technique: it would be used mainly as a data-summarizing technique, to search out clusters of items of semantic and topical similarity. Factor-analysis would also test the assumption of unidimensionality – and would establish the 'true' dimensionality of multidimensional measures.

But it is artificial to speak of reliability and validity as though they were two simple, readily realizable and clearly different concerns. Perhaps the only kind of reliability that is not also in part validity is a simple test-retest reliability coefficient. Test-retest reliability is an attempt to achieve virtually identical results through measuring the same trait by maximally similar methods and under maximally similar conditions. Abandonment of any of these stipulations – for example, changing the item set (as in split-half reliability) or changing the method – moves one into the region of validity. And despite the shading of one concern into another, the goals of the two aims of maximum reliability and maximum validity are not practically compatible. For maximum reliability of measurement, one must have long tests with high intercorrelations between items of similar difficulty: in practice the achievement of this aim results in tests consisting of very similar items. This in turn means that one has pared away variance which might have associated in a complementary fashion with other constructs. There is, however, a solution to the problem, and Guilford expresses the solution most clearly:

The solution to the incompatibility of goals of reliability and predictive validity is ... to use a battery of tests rather than a single test. Reliability should be the goal emphasized for each test; predictive validity the goal emphasized for the battery. Even in single tests some reliability should be sacrificed for the sake of well-graded measurements. It is strongly urged that, if possible, each test be designed to measure one common factor. It should be unequivocal, its contribution unique. In this way minimal intercorrelation between tests is insured, which satisfies one of the major principles of multiple regression. It was also shown that when tests are univocal, the various factors can be weighted in the best way to make each prediction. The univocal test will correlate less with a practical criterion than will a heterogeneous test, but what we lose in validity for the single test will be more than made up by forming batteries which cover the factors to be predicted in a more manageable manner. For the sake of meaningful profiles also, a battery of univocal tests has no equal. The use of single-test scores in a profile, however, calls for high reliability of each test. (1956: 482)

It is helpful to organize the opinion-scale measures of the survey into three broad types of measure: political and general orientations to the university, orientations to society, and orientations toward the self. The basic theme of this study is that university-political viewpoints are – and can be shown to be – part of a coherent 'ideology' which provides the student with an intellectual handle on the whole society. Further, it is thought that political opinions are cognitively based rather than being rooted in the individual's emotional needs or style. Therefore, it is helpful to present the measures organized in roughly the manner of their treatment in chapter 4 when the range and richness of student viewpoints is pursued. It can also be noted that measures originated in two separate projects. Finally, scale development and refinement procedures varied somewhat for each of the three major clusters of measures. The discussion will treat in turn each of the following:

1. Student viewpoints about 'student power' and the university experience in general. These scales, developed by Jerry Ezekiel and me in an earlier multistage project, and administered to the new sample, were named Rejection of Radicals and Radicalism, System Cynicism, Student Power, University Elitism, Contentment, Aimlessness, and Personal Alienation (see Sutherland, 1969; Ezekiel, 1971b.) Two measures of willingness to act, University Militancy and General Militancy, will also be discussed in this section. These were developed specifically for the new project.

2. Orientations to the society. Here are scales which propose to measure tendencies toward 'authoritarianism' – Dogmatism, the Short F-Scale, and Tolerance-Intolerance of Ambiguity – and scales which treat relatedness to other people and society – Faith in People, Anomy, Political Alienation, and Humanism. Measures of both this category and the first category can be thought of as typical scales measuring verbally expressed affect for some more or less clearly defined social object. Pre-tests for these measures were conducted under the Citizenship Orientation Project.

3. Orientations toward the self. Scales measuring aspects of 'mental health' or what may more modestly be called ease or difficulty in day-to-day functioning – Self-esteem, Depressive Affect, Sensitivity to Criticism, the Institute for Personality Assessment and Testing anxiety measure, and a short version of the General Mental Health Index. Each of these measures has an individual history in psychological testing. Note that the method of assessment is the same as for the other two groups (the subject chooses a response

indicating amount of agreement to a statement in standard Likert-type format); hence these scales should be thought of as measures of affect expressed toward the self as object. The Citizenship Orientation Project pretested these measures on Alberta samples.

The first step in refinement procedures was to assess the postulated forms of all measures. In preparation, more than 200 individual item-statements were allocated to their parent measures, and corrected for direction of expression. Simple sum scores, weighting each item the same within measures, were then calculated. Correlations were then obtained for items within scales and for each item with the sum of the postulated measure. Each scale could then be reviewed for reliability. The source and theory behind measures is discussed in the text, and the final versions of the scales are provided in appendix A.

STUDENT POWER AND THE UNIVERSITY EXPERIENCE

This group of scales proved to be very robust, which must be credited to the procedure by which they were developed. The procedure involved the student body in creation of the scales subsequently used to assess the sample's viewpoints.

Earlier, it was stated that the study of student activism in general had suffered because researchers did not adequately specify their dependent variable. It was hoped that our research[3] would clarify the status of 'the activist' and place 'student power' within a framework of viewpoints about the university and society in general. To this end, a procedure was developed to create objective scales of maximum relevance to the student community. In effect, groups of students were consulted about their detailed views of 'student power' and the university experience in general, and their elicited opinions were used as statements (followed by the usual response categories) in later closed-ended questionnaires. This situation is in contrast to the usual, in which subjects indicate agreement with the investigator's statements. The one exception among scales of this section is the measure of militancy, which originated with Dr Susan Hunter-Harvey. Because it held a strong a-priori interest, it was substituted for a weaker student-generated 'tactics' measure which covered much of the same ground.

The procedure was as follows. In the autumn of 1968, two exploratory questionnaires were administered to about 100 students. These included a number of Students for a Democratic University activists, graduate students in political science who were at the time working toward student representation on faculty administrative bodies, and four undergraduate classes composed of general arts and sciences students as well as pre-professional students.

An instrument to gather definitions of student power was the first to be administered. Given that any phrase would structure results to some extent, it was decided to concentrate upon, in Sampson's phrase (1967: 21), 'significant and meaningful participation in the processes of decision-making.' This is taken to be the common long-range goal of student power advocates, as argued in the Introduction.

In an attempt to operationalize this view, the student power stimulus questionnaire consisted simply of a line divided into seven units. Students were told that position 'one' reflected satisfaction with things as they then stood with regard to student participation in university decision-making. 'Seven' meant endorsement of what might be called the 50–50 student power objective, or equal participation with faculty and administration in all university decision-making which affects students. (Many students simply overrode the limitation by extending the line to a proportional representation position. The 50–50 goal became a mid-point here.) Each respondent was invited to circle one point on the line indicating 'how much' student power he favoured. He was then requested to articulate in a few sentences the *meaning* or opinion content of his chosen position, and to give a defence of his position. The opinion content and opinion defence provided the information needed to create the closed-ended statements. The function of the seven-unit line was only to focus attention.

Since one could not know beforehand whether opinions about student power would be held in isolation from other more general views of the university experience, a second questionnaire was administered. This was planned to collect opinions which would reveal something of the manner in which students oriented themselves to the university experience in general. It consisted of thirteen sentence-completion items,[4] such as:

The university is ...
The university should be ...
My role at university is ...
The role of the university is ...
My reasons for being in university are ...

Completed statements were separated into individual topic statements. Each prospective item was to treat one topic only. Where a statement seemed clearly expressed, and when the same statement was repeated time and again, original phrasing was retained. The process culminated in 500 individual statements typed individually on cards. These were then sorted into categories by four judges working at first independently, then together. Agreement that the total item pool could be summarized under nine 'idea type' headings was fairly readily reached. This sorting was regarded as a practical task and no effort was made to record agreement rates. The names applied to these hypothesized categories, or underlying dimensions, give a rough idea of the content of the statement pool: (1) advocated scope of student power; (2) strategies for achieving goals; (3) fear, dislike, or mistrust of radical students; (4) orientation toward democracy; (5) frustration or alienation; (6) sense of responsibility toward or commitment to the university; (7) statements concerning purpose and goals of the university in society; (8) cynicism or negative evaluations of worth and sincerity of authority figures and worth of the academic experience; and (9) paternalism, or statements indicating a view of faculty and administrators as benevolent parent substitutes.

At least one dimension – fear or dislike of radical students – was an unexpected discovery. Had the technique of student formation of measures not been used, the measure would not have been developed. The student body was ahead of the research group in thinking of radicals as an 'attitude object.'

The collection of items now had to be balanced for direction within categories, and categories balanced in number with one another. Once this had been accomplished, a re-sort of the shortened item pool was completed, yielding essentially the same structure.

The 273 remaining items were then typed into a pre-test questionnaire. Items were randomized, and the individual pages were collated randomly to minimize the effects of fatigue factor. The schedule was then administered to three classes ($n = 95$) at the university.

Responses to these statements could now be factor analysed, to assess the statistical pattern imposed upon the item pool by the student sample. Nine dimensions that were both interpretable and clearly different from one another emerged at the end of a lengthy overlapping analysis procedure. Again, names given to dimensions at this stage are perhaps sufficiently indicative of content: (1) student power, in which goals, strategies, and attitudes toward radical students merged; (2) cynicism; (3) system orientation or affirmation; (4) an assertion of the political competence of the peer group; (5) friendship satisfaction; (6) sense of being part of an educated elite; (7) aimlessness, or having simply arrived at the university with no clear goals; (8) alienation; and (9) a very general contentment with the university experience. Items that were redundant, or that behaved in an ambiguous fashion indicating that they could be interpreted in more than one way, were cut out. Therefore, these nine dimensions now contained 97 items: those with loadings greater than 0.4 on one or another of the factors, and on which distribution of responses indicated that the item tapped a real division of opinion. (An item with which 95 per cent of the population disagreed, or agreed, was regarded as a non-contentious platitude.)

Moving now into a third phase, we next administered these 97 items to a much larger sample. A mail-out technique was used on a target sample of 1,000 full-time students, the sample randomly chosen from the registrar's Home Address Coding Book; 428 usable questionnaires were returned. The sample is representative on criteria of faculty and sex. It is unrepresentative on the criterion of number of years at university: students who have been at the university for three or more years are over-represented. There is, of course, no way to assess representativeness of the distribution of responses on attitude variables.

Refinement and validation of measures were continued with data from the 428-member sample. (In subsequent references, these data will be called the 'first' study to avoid confusion with the project's 959-member random sample.) Results of a factor analysis of the 97 items were very close to dimensions emerging from analysis of responses to the pre-test questionnaire. However, there was one problem in that the first factor to emerge did not allow an unambiguous interpretation. Once again frequencies within response categories were checked. As often happens with preliminary factor analyses, it appeared that a lack of variation over a group of items had worked to obscure the basic structure of the data. Thirteen item-platitudes which less than 5 per cent of the sample had endorsed or opposed were removed from analysis.

A final factor analysis was now performed on the remaining 84 items: 15 factors emerged, the first 10 of which were readily interpretable. As these 10 factors had clear antecedents in all previous stages they were accepted as final measures. Names given factor-measures, in order of appearance, are: Rejection of Radicals and Radicalism, System Cynicism, Contentment, Aimlessness, Student Power Administrative, Student Power Academic, Alienation, University Elitism, Student Power Democracy, and Student Power Organizational.

A short version of each of these scales was included in the final project questionnaire. Scale items were selected for inclusion using two criteria. The first was item loading – that is, was the item a good indicator of the underlying factor dimension? Second, an attempt was made to represent the range of content within scales through choice of representative items. We now move to a discussion of these measures in the context of the new 959-member stratified-random sample of the Determinants of Citizenship Orientation Project.

Preliminary factor analyses of the total item pool showed that each of the factor measures maintained its coherence through the test of a new, large random sample. Items of the four Student Power scales, however, loaded together on one factor. Results for a final stage of factor analysis, in which items of each scale were factor analysed one scale at a time, are presented in appendix A. Brief scale descriptions are provided in the text below, along with the alpha reliability coefficient (calculated from the matrix of item inter-correlations from each scale). Statements making up the central measures Rejection of Radicals, Student Power, and Militancy are provided in the text; items of other scales are found in appendix A with their factor loadings. It will be noted that these analyses follow on the total-pool analyses.[5] Hence it was already established that items of one scale are much more highly related to one another than to items of any other scale. Inter-item and item-scale correlations can be found in Sutherland (1969, 1975). Coefficient alpha in effect summarizes the information of the item-item and item-scale correlations.[6] Factor scores were calculated at the end of this process. (See chapter conclusions.)

Rejection of Radicals and Radicalism (RRR)
The project version of this measure consists of five items which tap what might be called a general distaste for radical students per se and a desire to repress them. The 14-item version of the first study had, of all the scales developed in that study, proved both the most sensitive and the most theoretically suggestive. Within limitations of those data, a good argument could be made that orientations toward radical students acted to qualify the formation of other, more reasoned, opinions about student politics. Quarter (1972: 39–40) has suggested that the political self-concept is organized around the components (1) political identity or broad label, (2) the authority figures of that preference, (3) general beliefs, and (4) specific beliefs. In his scheme, one could think of the label as being 'for' or against student power, and of the radical contingent as being some of the authorities. Views of them are therefore of considerable importance. The other scales – primarily the Student Power scale – provide the belief content.

The measure Rejection of Radicals was a spontaneous result of the method by which the study was initiated. Measurement of such a dimension had not been planned. Indeed, respondents were thought to be sadly off the topic when they persistently gave their views of the radicals rather than a dispassionate discussion of their ideas about student power. At one point a number of statements approving of radicals were generated to match the negative, sample-volunteered statements. *None* of these items survived refinement procedures. These facts illustrate the operation of researcher pre-conceptions, even in a project in which the entire research strategy had been devised to minimize their force.

Scale items are (the plus and minus signs indicate the direction for scoring):

Radical students are a bigger threat to the ordinary student than are the faculty and administration. (+)

Student radicals' demands for student power are realistic, and should be supported by the student body in general. (−)

It would probably be best for the university if faculty and administrators took a hard line with student power advocates. (+)

Radical students are the greatest obstacle to change at this university because they irresponsibly antagonize faculty and administration. (+)

Generally speaking, the radical students have a pretty good idea of the way this university is run. (−)

Coefficient alpha = 0.79

Student Power

As mentioned earlier, this scale is formed from the four measures which had treated aspects of student power in the earlier study. Although the aspects were factorially distinct in their long versions, in the project data items loaded heavily together on the one factor. Items treat issues of participation in administration of the university, setting course content, the right to organize to press demands, and the 'rationale' for participation-democratization of the university. Readers familiar with the 'Issues Scale' developed by Quarter to reflect the issues at the University of Toronto 1967–69 (Quarter, 1972: 74–6, 104–8) will see strong similarities. Quarter's items are concerned with student participation in the university's decision-making process, and with the tactics that should be employed to gain a greater share for students in decision-making. In the present study, tactics were handled in the Militancy index. This was done because the measures reflect a conceptually separate means-end dichotomy, and because, empirically, items loaded on separate factors.

Student Power scale items are:

Students should have as much say in running the university as 'older, more experienced faculty and administrators.' (+)

Students should definitely have a voice in determining course content and required courses. (+)

University students should have the right to organize to protect their own interests. (+)

The university administration, like that of a city, province, or nation, should be controlled by those for whom it is administrating, that is, faculty and students. (+)

Students have a responsibility to be concerned, active, and informed participants in the running of the university. (+)

Students should have the right to strike if they are dissatisfied with conditions in the university. (+)

Decision-making in university affairs would take up too much of the student's time, and might stand in the way of important learning. (−)

If students had votes in the university's official governing bodies, they probably wouldn't know what to do with them. (−)

Coefficient alpha = 0.78

University Militancy

We move now to two militancy measures – General Militancy and University Militancy. These originated with Dr Susan Hunter-Harvey, and were pre-tested at the University of Alberta. University Militancy asks respondents whether or not, given they thought they had a legitimate grievance against the university, they would take part in a number of protest options. The postulated version included options of discussing the grievance with professors and engaging in armed violence. Only 3 per cent would refuse to talk to professors, and only 1 per cent were willing to engage in armed violence. Therefore these options, as they captured little or no patterned variance, were removed from analysis.

Options of this measure loaded on two factors. However, items were more strongly related to one another than to any other group of items. An oblique-solution factor analysis was performed, to discover the degree of relatedness of the two factors (see appendix A). The correlation between primary factors is 0.110.

A willingness to engage in violent demonstrations, plus an activity which would appear to be perceived as leading to violence (occupying buildings), seems to be distinct from peaceful options. This is an example of an index in which the options are of a-priori interest: one wants to identify those options which are of no relevance to the student population. Response frequencies to the University Militancy options are included as a matter of interest:

If you had what you thought was a legitimate grievance against the university, do you think you might:

Item Options:
... participate in non-violent demonstrations (yes, 63%; no, 29%)
... participate in a student boycott of classes (yes, 53%; no, 37%)
... raise or sign a petition to the administration (yes, 84%; no, 8%)
... participate in occupations of buildings (yes, 12%; no, 76%)
... participate in a violent demonstration (yes, 3%; no, 85%)

Alpha is 0.57, reflecting the low intercorrelation of items.

General Militancy
General Militancy is similar in form and options to University Militancy, yet the different context justifies inclusion of the parallel form. One will want to know the strength of association between inclinations to activity in the university and in the larger society. Here three items were omitted from the postulated version because of lack of patterned variation in responses. In this case, only 1 per cent of the sample thought they would neither discuss a grievance with friends, co-workers, or fellow students nor sign a petition opposing government actions. None would engage in armed violence. Following is the preamble, with options for action.

Now let's take a very general situation. Supposing you had a grievance against the national government. Let's just say that the party in control of the government was doing things that would likely harm your own well-being and/or that of your family. Following are a list of things people might do to oppose the government, and we would like you to check the list and answer 'yes' if you would consider doing this particular thing, and 'no' if you wouldn't consider doing this thing. Try to judge each separately with a 'yes' or 'no' answer.

Item Options:
... participate in a general strike, a national work stoppage (yes, 57%; no, 42%)
... participate in a potentially violent demonstration (yes, 10%; no, 88%)

... participate in a peaceful demonstration (yes, 84%; no, 15%)
... try to organize a group of people to oppose the government (yes, 66%; no, 32%)
... help raise a petition protesting the actions of the government (yes, 91%; no, 8%)
... join a political party opposed to the government (yes, 59%; no, 39%)

Alpha = 0.63

Again items load on two factors. The correlation between factors – whose items once more load according to extremeness of options – is 0.211.

At this point we turn from measures relating to the control of power in the university environment to more personal orientations of the student to the university. These measures, developed in the same procedure as the Student Power measure and Rejection of Radicals, owe most of the debt for their genesis to the sentence-completion procedures described earlier. Brief descriptions of these scales are provided below, along with the alpha reliability coefficient. Item content is listed in appendix A.

System Cynicism
The six items treat negative views of the worth of university course work, and negative opinions toward the motives and abilities of administrators and faculty. In the first study, this measure was shown to be significantly correlated with political variables and with the psychological functioning measures. It is thought that very critical orientations toward the university system may serve different functions in different psychological types, spurring the healthy on to political commitment, and merely being part of the general misery of the psychologically impaired. Alpha is 0.68.

Aimlessness
The four items of the Aimlessness scale tap whether the student simply arrived on the university scene without any clear academic or career goals. The scale is a useful discriminator, scores being significantly correlated with psychological distress. Alpha is 0.77.

Contentment
This measure's four items treat a very general satisfaction with the university experience. A finding from first data was that apolitical students are the least 'contented' – significantly less so than those who were either very strongly for or against student power. Alpha is 0.75.

University Alienation
This university-specific 'alienation' measure is composed of three statements expressing isolation and loneliness. Alpha is 0.58.

University Elitism
Perhaps the most interesting thing about the three-item University Elitism is the fact that the measure exists at all. The sentiments, it will be remembered, were volunteered by students. And there is a fair amount of agreement with the message of the scale, that university graduates are superior, despite the social strictures against voicing elitist sentiments. Alpha is low at 0.50.

ORIENTATIONS TO SOCIETY

We move now to the second group of scales. Well-known postulated measures included the California F-Scale, Dogmatism, and Tolerance-Intolerance of Ambiguity. Although the content of these scales is obviously overlapping, the three were included because of a lack of confidence in any one measure. Also in the group of measures were Rosenberg's Faith in People, Srole's Anomy, and about 20 items original to the project which had been written to measure 'humanitarian outlooks.' None of these measures was satisfactory in its postulated form, and a lengthy refinement process had to be carried out.

Some background on the major postulated measures will pave the way for a description of the refinement process. Measures to be described are the California F-Scale, Rokeach's Dogmatism, and Budner's Tolerance-Intolerance of Ambiguity (for work with Anomy and Rosenberg's Faith in People, see Robinson and Shaver, 1969).

California F-Scale
The California F-Scale ('F' for fascism) was developed by Theodore Adorno and colleagues to 'estimate the probability of Fascism in the United States. By their analysis of personality structures, [the researchers] seek to predict which types of persons will accept Fascist propaganda and become Fascists' (Shils, 1954: 43). Their work culminated in the publication of *The Authoritarian Personality* (1950). This project had a scope and sophistication which has yet to be duplicated in social science research. The method of detailed clinical interviews was combined with objective assessment through questionnaire research, on the same subjects, in the service of comprehensive theory. Overarching theory was Freudian, and lower-level work showed an astute and topical knowledge of the content of social ideology of the time.

'Authoritarianism' in this work was postulated as a syndrome of fairly distinct attitudes. Among the more important of the nine attitude-elements were authoritarian aggression (shown by overdoing respect for authority and in hostility to outgroups), authoritarian submission (shown by submission to authority figures, and desire for a strong leader), and destructiveness and cynicism (expressed through general hostility and vilification of the human) (Sanford, 1956: 269–75). As R. Brown notes (1965: 487), this social ideology is related to personality in an indirect way. It is true that the nine elements are *not* bound together by logic, but are contradictory. Their empirical co-occurrence in an individual signals presence of the disease process: the individual *needs* to hold these contradictory views to defend his own ego against overwhelming anxiety.

This 'authoritarianism,' then, is a complex phenomenon whose identification depends on the co-occurrence of at least several of the nine postulated facets. Adorno identified eleven important sub-syndromes, the most important of which was the authoritarian-submissive.

Despite this detailed specification in the beginning, and despite the addition of a comprehensive critique which re-emphasized the centrality of the notion of a 'syndrome' (Christie and Jahoda's *Studies in the Scope and Method of 'The Authoritarian Personality,'* 1954), subsequent work with versions of the California F-Scale have persistently treated it as one general variate. In application, survey researchers have simply lumped together any of the original items from any or all syndrome elements as *one* scale measuring 'authoritarianism.'

'Authoritarianism' so measured (one scale rather than a syndrome) is then interpreted in one of two manners. First, the researchers will often adduce the kind of psychoanalytic ego-defensive explanation that the original researchers used, although they have not designated a syndrome of attitudes and have not done their clinical work. Or researchers may regard the 'authoritarianism' manifested by the subject as a personality trait of 'authoritarianism.' A trait as a personality construct is very different from the original psychoanalytic notion of a person's ego-defensive use of a social ideology. A trait is a temporally well-established disposition which operates to homogenize the behaviour of the individual across situations. Bad-temperedness or neatness are traits. Authoritarianism treated as a trait slides into some notion of bossiness or bullying (see Sutherland and Tanenbaum [1977, 1980] for a more detailed discussion). This disregard of the originating syndrome idea, magical faith in the validity of the original items, and confusion of the status of the captured 'authoritarianism' explain the lack of productivity of what can be called the social psychology's most intensive and enduring research program – the study of authoritarianism in mass publics.[7] The desire to avoid these confusions dictated the approach taken to the California F-Scale in this work, and to the group of measures of social orientation as a whole.

A 12-item version of the F-scale had been administered in the questionnaire. It was similar to the 1952 Survey Research Centre F-Scale (Robinson and Shaver, 1969: 268). Specifically, it was decided that refinement should aim for a core version of authoritarianism which would treat desirability of discipline and obedience to legitimate authority figures such as political leaders, experts, and parents.

Dogmatism

The 20-item version of Dogmatism included in the survey was settled upon after pre-testing the 40-item Form E of Rokeach's Dogmatism. The scale was originally designed to redress flaws in early versions of the F-Scale: respondents' education had been found to correlate with an acquiescent response bias, which meant, in effect, that F could capture 'true authoritarianism' only in the educated who are not acquiescent. Rokeach felt the basic construct would be better tapped by designing a scale which would measure individual differences in openness or closedness of belief systems. With such a measure, he felt, one could measure 'dogmatism' regardless of the content of the particular belief system. (See Rokeach, 1960).

The trouble with Dogmatism, although some might say that it is a strength, is with the operationalization. To discover whether or not an individual holds his particular views in a dogmatic *manner* – regardless of the content or topic of those views – might logically dictate either that the component items be free of social referents, or that all possible social referents be included. The second alternative is in practice impossible, and adherence to the first would leave one with items about nothing at all. Therefore Rokeach adopted a tactic of writing items which would go beyond the specific belief content and penetrate the structure of *how* the belief was held. Rokeach created the item-statements of the measure by trying to approximate the thinking habits of persons whom he knew to be dogmatic. Topics were threatening issues like 'truth,' religion, and loneliness. He validated with known-groups also. That is, the measure successfully discriminated between persons previously designated as dogmatic by students and acquaintances and others not so designated.

Rokeach has himself acknowledged that Dogmatism is both factorially complex and subtle: items load on several dimensions of any factor structure, and most dimensions are not easily interpreted (see Rokeach and Fruchter, 1956; Kerlinger and Rokeach, 1966). The shared characteristic of items would seem to be a tinge of irrationality. It also seems fair to say, as with the F-Scale, that correlations of the measure with other non-desirable social opinions are built in through allusion to so many complex topics in the one measure.

Again it was decided that refinement should aim for a core version which would be something like (a) it is possible to know 'truth' with absolute certainty and (b) opposition is due to wilful wrong-headedness.

Tolerance-Intolerance of Ambiguity
Intolerance of Ambiguity is thought to be a tendency to perceive or interpret ambiguous situations as sources of threat, or stress, and therefore to deny them. Tolerance of Ambiguity is a tendency to see ambiguity as desirable – or at least not to be put off balance in an ambiguous situation. In the Budner (1962) formulation, ambiguity is thought to arise in problem situations which are novel, complex, or incapable of solution.

The item pool is not characterized by any of the obvious flaws that were thought to characterize those of both F and Dogmatism. That is, attitudes towards the social objects which would later be correlated with the measure are not a part of the measure. As well, items are balanced for direction by matching: an item such as 'People who insist on a 'yes' or 'no' answer don't appreciate how complicated things are' is matched by 'An expert who doesn't come up with a definite answer probably doesn't know too much.' Items are written in plain non-emotional language, rather than in the overblown nuanced language of the F-Scale and Dogmatism. It was therefore hoped that in so far as the three scales were aiming to describe the same tendency – an individual characteristic of premature (because not fact-based) attitude closure – Intolerance of Ambiguity would prove to be the most fruitful measure.

Project pre-tests of Budner's 1962 version of Tolerance-Intolerance of Ambiguity had resulted in worryingly low reliabilities (see Robinson and Shaver [1969: 318] for a description of Budner's technical development procedures and early reliability results). Despite this warning, a 12-item balanced version was included.

Scale refinement procedure
Of the three postulated measures, only F was at all satisfactory in terms of item intercorrelations and item-sum score correlations. One could see the possibility of retaining a five or six item core, with an average item inter-correlation of approximately 0.3.

However, item intercorrelations of the postulated short Dogmatism were not at all satisfactory, and Tolerance-Intolerance of Ambiguity simply did not exist for statistical purposes. Most item intercorrelations did not reach 0.05. It was abundantly clear that the postulated forms of these three measures would not be reliable enough for use.

As a matter of interest, individual scale factor analyses for the three measures were performed to test dimensionality. Six F items loaded on one factor. Dogmatism divided into three virtually unrelated factors, four items loading on the first factor. Tolerance-Intolerance of Ambiguity's 10 items divided their miserly amount of shared variance democratically over five factors: no pattern whatever could be discerned.

Therefore, a pool of all items having come initially from these measures, as well as all items from other scales which were at all similar in terms of statement topic, was formed. This item pool, which included some of Srole's Anomy and some items from Rosenberg's Faith in People, paranoia items from both Dogmatism and IPAT, religiosity items, all reflections on 'human nature,' idealism statements, humanism items, authoritarian submissiveness items, all of Tolerance-Intolerance of Ambiguity, and core Dogmatism and F, was then factor analysed. The item pool consisted of more than 100 statements. Again an item was retained on a factor if it loaded higher than 0.4 on that factor and no higher than 0.15 on any other factor in a structure (see note 5). This procedure was continued until it was established that each 'factor measure' described a group of items which were more strongly related to one another than to items not in that factor measure. The overlapping analyses were then followed with the necessary number of separate factor analyses of items which, judging from the overlap procedure, appeared to belong together. The second stage of analysis would test the saturation of each item on its factor-dimension and would yield the matrices from which the alpha reliability coefficient could be calculated.

In short, dimensions seem to have been formed in terms of content. There were many switches of items between scales. Most Tolerance-Intolerance of Ambiguity items did not load highly enough on any factor for retention.

Complete listings of all scales and indices arrived at by the procedure sketched above are provided in appendix A. Short descriptions are provided below, with coefficient alpha which assesses reliability of the measure.

A caution about scale names is in order: in work with such scales, there is always a danger of implying more by the name than is justified by item content. This error is both seductive and cumulative, because the construct 'name' rather than the complete body of item content is what we use when thinking about the relationships that the scale enters. An attempt has been made to use names which are apt, modest (free inasmuch as possible from undeserved 'halo' of meaning), and easy to remember. But this is no small task, and the reader is asked to judge subsequent work with scales by referring to their item content. Table A2 in appendix A displays Survey F, Closed-Mindedness, and Submissiveness correlations with other variables.

Survey F (Belief in Discipline and Obedience) Seven of the eight items of this scale are from the F-Scale, the remaining item espousing expertise coming from Dogmatism. The scale taps attitudes about the desirability of obedience: a kind of whole-hearted, unquestioning loyalty toward authority roles of the established order. Alpha is 0.76.

Closed-Mindedness This is a six-item scale formed from Dogmatism, Tolerance-Intolerance of Ambiguity, and the F-Scale. It expresses the view that there is one version of 'the truth,' which ought to be readily apparent to all. Alpha is 0.62.

Submissiveness (Lack of Confidence) The six items of this measure are evenly drawn from Dogmatism and Srole's Anomy. Three items express personal helplessness and three reflect on the terrifying nature of the world in general. Alpha is 0.63.

Pessimism (Negative Views of Human Nature) The six items express the views that 'human nature' guarantees both conflict and lack of progress. When scale items were factor analysed as a group, two factors emerged. The primary factors correlation is 0.225. The factors appear to be interpretable as judgments dealing with the present and the future. Alpha is 0.74.

Attitudes toward War and Force This three-item index suggests that the waging of war is inevitable, and can be justified. Alpha is low, at 0.52.

Religiousness Items say that religious faith, or belief in some supernatural power, is necessary to and indeed is definitive of 'man.' The three items are very strongly correlated, yielding an alpha coefficient of 0.82.

Alienation from People The index is composed of five items, each of which expresses or justifies a mistrust of people in daily life. Coefficient alpha is 0.65.

Nurturance The scale message is that the community has a responsibility to aid and to react compassionately toward unfortunate persons. Categories of persons represented in the nine items include criminals, drug addicts, the poor, immigrants, and children. Once again scale items loaded on two factors, separating 'innocent' economic misfortune from criminal references. The correlation between primary factors is 0.238, and alpha is 0.71.

Political Alienation This scale is retained despite an alpha of 0.25 because it is very close to a standard political efficacy measure, two of the items being drawn from Campbell's early Political Efficacy Scale. See Robinson, Rusk, and Head (1968: 460). The items express a sense of helplessness and distance from politics, government, and parliament. It is called alienation rather than efficacy here because of the direction of statements.

Alienation from People A sense of mistrust of people in daily life is expressed by the five items of this scale. Alpha is 0.65.

PSYCHOLOGICAL FUNCTIONING MEASURES

This third group of measures contains postulated versions of the IPAT Anxiety Scale, a short version of the General Mental Health Index, and Rosenberg's Self-esteem, Depressive Affect, and Sensitivity to Criticism. It treats the problematic area of what can be called 'the individual's relationship with himself.' Psychologists are more sophisticated in their application of scaling techniques than are other social scientists. As a result, these measures were a pleasure to work with in comparison with those of the previous group.

IPAT Anxiety Scale
This anxiety scale constructed by the Institute for Personality Assessment and Testing (IPAT) was developed 'as a means of getting clinical anxiety information rapidly, objectively and in a standard manner' (Cattell and Scheier, 1963: 5). The scale gives a clinically valid appraisal of free anxiety level, meaning that the measured anxiety is not perceived by the subject to be rooted in any particular situation or cause.

Cattell and Scheier claim that all known questionnaire items tapping personality dimensions can be summarized to measure about sixteen major personality dimensions. They further claim that five or six of these sixteen dimensions represent symptoms which a psychiatrist would immediately recognize as anxiety symptoms. That is, these dimensions meet a face or content validity test of anxiety.

These anxiety dimensions also cluster statistically, in experimental empirical analysis by correlation and factor analysis. Clustering has occurred in a dozen separate studies, testing a total of 3,000 persons. Further, scale scores tend to rank individuals in the same order as do psychiatric interviews by diagnosticians. The only unfortunate note is that psychiatrists' diagnoses correlate only to the order of 0.2 and 0.3. However, validity is more impressive when only subjects of known high anxiety are tested. Here the correlation between scale score and psychiatric diagnosis is high and the scale is 90 per cent successful in distinguishing extreme anxiety neurotics from normal persons.

Neither split-half nor test-retest reliability coefficients for the entire scale have gone lower than 0.8. Reliability is lower of course for the part scores on test dimensions, ranging from 0.26 to 0.60, indicating that one will find a good deal of fuzziness across dimensions. These dimensions are named Guilt Proneness, Tension, Unintegrated Self-sentiment, Ego Weakness, and Suspiciousness or Paranoid Insecurity.

Refinement work again began with examination scale intercorrelations and item-total correlations. Ten items which did not contribute to any cluster, and whose item-total correlation was less than 0.3, were removed from analysis.

The remaining 30 items were then factor analysed, and six interpretable factors emerged: these were clearly similar to those described by IPAT researchers.

However, two of these six factors were remarkably similar, in terms of content, to Rosenberg's Sensitivity to Criticism and Depressive Affect. Therefore, it was decided to bring these scale items into analysis with IPAT items. Self-esteem items were also brought in. It was hypothesized that Sensitivity to Criticism and Depressive Affect items would load on their similar IPAT dimensions, and that Self-esteem items would form a unique factor. This proved to be the case. It was decided that Sensitivity to Criticism items and Depressive Affect items would be left in IPAT, and that Self-esteem would be retained as a separate measure.

Another analysis was performed, and six factors again emerged. One of these dimensions was noticed to be remarkably similar in content to items of the Mental Health Scale; correlations of the magnitude of 0.85 between these IPAT items and Mental Health 'sister' items confirmed the judgment. As these items would serve gratuitously to inflate an Anxiety-GMHI correlation, they were removed from analysis. A final factor analysis was performed, and yielded five factors which were named Sensitivity to Criticism, Depression, Paranoid Insecurity, Irritability, and Tension. These 25 items were then summed, and it was discovered that the correlation between this 'little IPAT' and the 40-item postulated version was 0.975.

Factor scale scores were then computed for the five IPAT factors. To assess the relationships between these dimensions, an oblique factor analysis of these scores was then performed. Factors are related, but not so closely that they can be considered to be the same thing. The Sensitivity to Criticism factor is clearly dominant, leading one to suspect that IPAT taps aspects of an exaggerated concern with the self. The Sensitivity to Criticism items are likely the most direct statements, and thus the best indicators, of this self-concern and ensuing vulnerability to reactions of other people. A short description of each IPAT factor now follows, coefficient alpha being noted for each. Correlations between IPAT primary factors are presented in appendix A. Scale items cannot be presented, however, because of IPAT copyright restrictions. Table A3 in appendix A shows correlates of IPAT in comparison with correlates for Self-esteem, Mental Health, and Submissiveness.

Sensitivity to Criticism The six items specifically deal with the individual's disturbance or upset in the face of criticism, blame, or ridicule by others. Alpha is 0.72.

Depression The four items assess the individual's general hedonic tone, his feeling of being downcast, lonely, dejected. Alpha is 0.68.

Social ('Paranoid') Insecurity The five items express a kind of comprehensive insecurity focused on 'strangers' and 'people.' The term 'paranoid' seems too strong. Alpha is 0.60.

Irritability A lack of patience with other people, plus a general tendency to admit to excitability in interaction with other people, is expressed by the four items of the subscale. Alpha is 0.50.

Tension A general, unfocused feeling of being often in a state of overexcitement and turmoil is expressed by the five items of Tension. Alpha is 0.67.

Rosenberg's Self-esteem
In his development of the scale, Rosenberg conceived of it as tapping a 'favourable or unfavourable orientation toward the self' (1965: 5). The self-image is thus an attitude toward an object – one's self.

'High' self-esteem as measured by the scale reveals not conceit, but merely a healthy and wholesome positive orientation. The individual high on Self-esteem respects himself and considers himself worthy. 'Low' self-esteem, to take the other end of the scale, is predictive of low general mental health. The reason, according to Rosenberg, is that if an individual is wounded in his image of himself, his entire mental or psychological well-being will suffer.

Rosenberg's original scale included 10 items, several of which were virtually identical. The reliability of the original form has been high in every reported instance of its use (Robinson and Shaver, 1969: 98).

Self-esteem The six items tap a normal or healthy orientation toward the self. The measure does not extent to notions of conceit. Alpha is 0.74.

General Mental Health Index
This version of the General Mental Health Index was developed by Gurin et al. (1960) to capture a general notion of 'mental well-being.' Although both clinical and concurrent validity trials have shown satisfactory results, confidence (as with IPAT) is greatest at the polar extremes of the scale. More recent work with the GMHI suggests that it measures neurotic symptoms almost exclusively, in distinction from more severe psychosis and schizophrenia symptoms (see Schwartz, Myers, and Astrachan, 1975).

Mental Health Index Sixteen items were included in the project instrument. During refinement procedures, an additional item was removed from GMHI. This item – 'Do you ever drink more than you should?' – did not correlate with other items. Items are supposedly of two types: manifest nervousness or anxiety, and somatic indicators of underlying psychological distress. A factor analysis was performed, but emerging factors were not interpretable, the theoretical manifest-subtle dichotomy receiving no support. Coefficient alpha is 0.83. The average index-item correlation is 0.243.

CONCURRENT VALIDITY

As the university political variables are to bear the burden of the study, it is of considerable interest to review their validity. Concurrent validity is reviewed by scrutinizing the correlations between scales. But it is difficult to assess the importance of discovered correlations in a sample of the size of the survey ($N = 959$). Significance levels are not helpful. If figures appropriate for a 1,000-member sample are taken, tables of significance show that a correlation of 0.062 is statistically significant at the 0.01 level, and a correlation of 0.081 is significant at the 0.001 level. Therefore, we have a wealth of 'significant' correlations. The problem is to discern theoretically important clusters. Fortunately, the inclusion in the survey of a great number of diverse variables means that one can make contextual judgments in terms of relative strengths of correlations.

Correlations of Student Power, Rejection of Radicals, and University Militancy with the other measures are shown in table 2.1. From the earlier study, it is known that there is a strong negative relationship between Student Power and both Rejection of Radicals and Survey F. Radical students are a negative reference group for the rejectors of Student Power, and traditional

TABLE 2.1
Correlates of Student Power, Rejection of Radicals (RRR), University Militancy,
and System Cynicism (N = 799)

	Student Power	RRR	University Militancy	System Cynicism
RRR	−0.615	1.000	−0.478	−0.230
University Elitism	−0.148	0.127	−0.086	−0.064
Student Power	1.000	−0.615	0.480	0.312
Contentment	−0.047	0.071	−0.053	−0.372
Aimlessness	0.116	−0.111	0.101	0.322
System Cynicism	0.312	−0.230	0.234	1.000
IPAT	0.030	−0.067	0.043	0.262
Mental Health	0.083	0.143	0.032	0.203
Submissiveness	−0.039	0.060	−0.020	0.264
Self-esteem	0.006	0.011	−0.017	−0.252
Alienation from People	−0.096	0.082	0.044	0.371
Political Alienation	−0.127	0.193	−0.120	0.271
University Alienation	0.140	−0.128	0.135	0.402
Closed-Mindedness	−0.159	0.214	−0.123	0.216
Survey F	−0.437	0.536	−0.331	0.094
Religiousness	−0.173	0.248	−0.162	0.036
Pessimism	−0.230	0.252	−0.155	0.055
Nurturance	0.482	−0.428	0.279	0.062
War	−0.210	0.160	−0.073	−0.014
University Militancy	0.480	−0.478	1.000	0.234
General Militancy	0.268	−0.306	0.509	0.029

authority figures are a positive reference group. There will also be a strong
positive relationship between Student Power and System Cynicism, and
between Student Power and University Militancy. The desire to participate
in university decision-making will be associated with a negative evaluation of
the academic status quo and with a willingness to act militantly to win the
rights of participation.

One would not expect Student Power to be related to psychological functioning variables. Rather, it is expected that System Cynicism will be related
to these variables, and to the measures which tap attitudes toward the immediate environment and other people.

Taking Student Power first, it is seen from table 2.1 that the view that
students should be 'responsible and informed' co-participants in the running
of the university is associated with the following:

1 A lack of fear or dislike of the university's group of radicals. (RRR) $r = -0.615$

2 A refusal to condemn criminals, the destitute, etc. (Nurturance) $r = 0.482$

3 A willingness to engage in militant action in the event of perceived injustice in the university (University Militancy) $r = 0.480$

4 A rejection of the view that youth must assume a deferential attitude toward traditional authority figures. (Survey F) $r = 0.437$

5 A negative evaluation of the university's academic offerings, and of faculty and administrators. (System Cynicism) $r = 0.312$

6 A willingness to engage in militant action in the larger society. (General Militancy) $r = 0.268$

7 A rejection of the notion that there is a basic 'human nature' and that it is weak. (Pessimism) $r = -0.230$

8 A rejection of the idea that force and war are inevitable. (War) $r = -0.210$

Other relationships, while not as strong, confirm the emergent pattern: advocacy of student power is associated with variables which express concern for, and acceptance of, one's fellow man, and with rejection of variables which describe traditional hierarchical and authority relationships.

Perhaps most heartening in terms of research validity are the very strong correlations between Student Power, Nurturance, and Survey F. This is heartening because the respondent must agree with F items to get a high score, but must disagree with a large portion of Student Power and Nurturance items in order to obtain the associated *low* scores on these variables. This means that one is not tapping a simple acquiescent response bias.

The validity of University Militancy would seem to be good. It is positively correlated with Student Power ($r = 0.480$), System Cynicism ($r = 0.234$), Nurturance ($r = 0.279$), and its sister measure General Militancy ($r = 0.509$). Notable negative correlations are with RRR ($r = -0.478$) and Survey F ($r = -0.331$).

Rejection of Radicals is also sensitive. While establishing a similar network of relationships to those of F and Closed-Mindedness (see appendix A), correlates more strongly than do either of these with Student Power and University Militancy. It refers to a specific known group – the radicals – and establishes the group as a negative reference group for many students. This fact, of course, is noted in the impressionistic literature, which is studded with amazed references to the setting on fire, etc., of the leftists' long hair by 'jocks.'

The concurrent validity of the central scales measuring political preferences in the university environment has been reviewed. It has been shown that these scales correlate in predictable and substantively satisfying patterns. Further, the reliability with which the concepts are measured is satisfactory.

Factor analysis of scale scores

At the beginning of this chapter, it was stated that data were collected with three major types of measure: (1) university political scales; (2) scales tapping general orientation to the society, or 'social ideology'; and (3) scales assessing the individuals' psychological functioning. These researcher assumptions, which amount to preconceptions about how the individuals studied organize their ideas, can be checked empirically. Factor analysis of scale scores for the total group of 21 scales described in this chapter will pattern the scales' variance – establishing which scale belongs to which type, and to what extent a scale is representative of the dimension common to its scale types.

Oblique rotation was used, as it has greater flexibility in searching out patterns of variation, regardless of the correlation of these patterns with one another. It will reveal uncorrelated factors if they in fact exist. Further, oblique rotation allows calculation of correlations between clusters.

A summary of the primary structure matrix is presented in table 2.2. (Both the primary pattern and primary structure matrices are presented in appendix A.) It is seen that the variance in the total data set is statistically patterned into five (rather than three) dimensions or factors. Table 2.2 presents the most important loadings on each factor in capital letters. Minor loadings (as defined by the structure matrix) are listed beneath in lower case. Variables are listed in order of absolute magnitude of their factor loadings. The sign indicates the direction of scale score loading on the factor.

Factor I's highest loading – and therefore the variable most representative of the underlying dimension – is a stated propensity to act militantly in the university. Affect for student power goals, a lack of fear or dislike of radicals, and a willingness to act in the outside world have also loaded very highly on this factor. Interpretation as a 'student politics' factor would appear to be uncontentious. Minor loadings, and the direction of minor loadings, are supportive: these are a rejection of traditional authority figures, nurturant attitudes toward outgroups, negative views of the university system, and rejection of fundamentalist religion.

Factor II is equally clear-cut. Here reported high anxiety is the most representative variable. It is followed closely by negative views of the self, low mental health, and a lack of confidence or submissiveness. Factor II will

TABLE 2.2
Summary table for factor interpretation* (N = 799)

Factor I		Factor II		Factor III	
UNIVERSITY MILITANCY	+0.82†	IPAT	+0.83	NURTURANCE	-0.72
STUDENT POWER	+0.75	SELF-ESTEEM	-0.78	WAR	+0.60
RRR	-0.75	MENTAL HEALTH	-0.74	UNIVERSITY ELITISM	+0.60
GENERAL MILITANCY	+0.65	SUBMISSIVENESS	+0.74	PESSIMISM	+0.56
Survey F	-0.47	Alienation from People	+0.32	Survey F	+0.49
Nurturance	+0.42	Political Alienation	+0.29	Alienation from People	+0.45
System Cynicism	+0.32	University Alienation	+0.28	Closed-Mindedness	+0.42
Religiousness	-0.24	Aimlessness	+0.24	Student Power	-0.38
		System Cynicism	+0.21	RRR	+0.31
		Contentment	+0.20	Submissiveness	+0.20

Factor IV		Factor V	
CONTENTMENT	-0.77	RELIGIOUSNESS	+0.73
SYSTEM CYNICISM	+0.70	CLOSED-MINDEDNESS	+0.70
UNIVERSITY ALIENATION	+0.66	SURVEY F	-0.67
AIMLESSNESS	+0.56	POLITICAL ALIENATION	+0.54
ALIENATION FROM PEOPLE	+0.51		
		System Cynicism	+0.35
Submissiveness	+0.36	Pessimism	+0.33
Self-esteem	-0.30	Alienation from People	+0.30
IPAT	+0.25	Submissiveness	+0.29
Political Alienation	+0.22	RRR	+0.28
		General Militancy	-0.22
		Nurturance	-0.20

* I, Student Politics; II, Psychological Distress; III, Misanthropy; IV, Environmental Dissatisfaction (University); V, Social Negativism.
† The loading of the measure on the factor has been rounded to two decimal places. The primary pattern and structure matrices are presented in appendix A.

therefore be called the 'psychological health' factor. Minor loadings are again supportive. These are wary stances toward people, politics, and the environment; a lack of university-related goals; and a broad disaffection for the university.

Major loadings of factor III are negative views toward outgroups, an opinion that war is inevitable, a view that a university education justifiably sets one above others, and negative views of human nature. These suggest that factor III be named 'misanthropy.' Minor loadings indicate that a subscription to authority, dislike of people, a tendency to think in extreme categories, rejection of student power goals, dislike of radicals, and a lack of confidence are also representative of the dimension. 'Elitism' is also a tempting name.

Factor IV can be interpreted as fairly thoroughgoing lack of satisfaction with the university environment. Major loadings are a rejection of the notion that attending university is worthwhile or pleasurable; adoption of negative views of course work, professors, and administrators; a feeling of isolation in the university environment; a lack of goals; and suspicion of, or alienation from, people generally. One sees that three of the psychological health variables, loading in the distress direction, and Political Alienation are minor loadings. This factor will be named 'environmental dissatisfaction.'

Factor V's major loadings – Religiousness, Closed-Mindedness, Survey F, and Political Alienation – cause more than a moment's pause. One is tempted to call this factor 'authoritarianism,' but to do so would be misleading as only a few of the traditional elements of Adorno's authoritarianism are strongly represented. Further, it would appear to be an 'authoritarianism' without any clear negative focus – and it is intrinsic to traditional theory to think of 'authoritarianism' in relation to clear outgroups (Jews, Negroes, etc.). Minor loadings seem to indicate a complete 'grouchiness' toward life in general. These are dislike of the university system, negative views of human nature, dislike of people, lack of confidence, dislike of radical students, rejection of militancy, and a rejection of outgroups. The factor will be named 'social negativism.' Note that Survey F has loaded fairly strongly on three factors: the politics factor, the misanthropy or elitism factor, and the negativism factor. Nothing could illustrate better the complexity of attitudes toward authority figures, and the continued difficulty of knowing what to make of the F-Scale.

The matrix of correlations between primary factors is presented in table 2.3. Factors are named, rather than identified by number, for ease in discussion.

These correlations indicate that attitudes towards student politics are not related to psychological health, or to satisfaction with the university envi-

TABLE 2.3
Correlations between primary factors

	Student politics	Psychological distress	Misanthropy	Environmental dissatisfaction	Negativism
Student politics	1.000				
Psychological distress	0.014	1.000			
Misanthropy	−0.140	0.035	1.000		
Environmental dissatisfaction (university)	0.058	0.217	0.029	1.000	
Negativism	−0.144	0.130	0.155	0.116	1.000

ronment. A stance in favour of student politics, however, is negatively associated with misanthropy, and negatively associated with negativism. Psychological distress and environmental dissatisfaction are moderately related, whether 'causally' or not we do not know. There is no relationship between psychological distress and misanthropy, and none between misanthropy and environmental dissatisfaction. Negativism is slightly related to each of the other factors.

CONCLUSION

A short technical discussion follows on the topic of factor scores. The purpose is to assess the scope of improvement in intercorrelation magnitudes which can be realized routinely through technical adjustments. These magnitudes then provide a baseline for comparison with improvement brought about by other – i.e. conceptual – innovation.

Upon completion of the project reported above, factor scores based on the regression estimates approach were calculated for each scale. In factor scale calculation, each variable is weighted so that its contribution to the total scale score is proportionate to the amount of variance it has with the factor. Therefore, variables which load highly on the underlying dimension will make a larger contribution to the factor score than will variables with smaller loadings. In the case of two-factor measures, factor scores were calculated for each oblique factor, and these two scores were summed.

These new factor score scales were correlated with the scale scores which had been calculated by the summated rating procedure in which each item receives the same weight. In all cases except for the IPAT subscales and General Militancy the correlation of the factor score with the rough score was in excess of 0.99. Given that all scales except these IPAT subscales were composed of very tight unique factors, this result might have been expected.

However, there are also only minimal differences in correlations when factor scores rather than rough scores are used. For example, the correlation between Survey F and Rejection of Radicals when rough scores are used is 0.536. When the correlation between factor score versions of these same variables is taken, it is 0.545. In general, correlations between variables increase or decrease by this same margin – about 0.01.

Correlations between IPAT subscales are, of course, the exception. As calculated by the rough method, they are within a range from a minimum of 0.343 to a maximum of 0.528. When factor scores are calculated for each subscale taking the contribution to the factor of each of the 24 IPAT variables, correlations between the five subscales are, correctly, the correlations between oblique primary factors. These correlations are much lower. They range from below 0.100 up to approximately 0.300. Improvement in accuracy here is considerable, therefore.

Correlations will not be corrected for attenuation due to less-than-perfect reliabilities. The alpha coefficient is a conservative estimate of reliability. But a conservative estimate of reliability becomes a liberal estimate of correlation when correcting for attenuation. That is, if one accepts a modest reliability, the amount added to the correlation in correction may be unjustifiably large.

Let us close the chapter by taking note of the results of refinement procedures in the light of the closing recommendations of chapter 1.

Thus far, work has been with scales of verbally reported affect for social objects. Some of these measures originated with the milieu of the study – the scales measuring affect for student power and other aspects of the university experience. Other scales have been developed from standard measures. In both cases, an attempt has been made to work for strong intercorrelation of items within one-theme measures.

All measures resulting from the refinement procedures were then correlated with one another, to establish interpretive contexts for individual scales. It is seen that some relationships were as high as 0.6, which means that 36 per cent of the scales' variability is shared. Factor scores for scales were then computed, which resulted in minimal improvement in strength of intercorrelation.

The next step, then, is to find a strategy for sharpening relationships between variables. In chapter 1, it was suggested that this might be done by seeking increased relevance of the opinion at issue to our subjects. The usual method of increasing strength and precision in such research is to restrict prediction to the extreme scorers. We shall adapt this notion to the project at hand by sorting for only those individuals at extremes of individual criterion scales, and at extremes in terms of consistency. Once those individuals who are consistent in terms of their responses across the battery of criterion student politics scales have been located, we can work to link opinion stance to some specified behaviour stance (with reference to the same social object).

3

Words and deeds, or some kinds of behaviour and other kinds of behaviour

This chapter performs three tasks. First, it tests the power of the measures of attitudes toward student power which were developed in the previous chapter to predict actual compatible activity. Earlier, the argument was made that 'attitudes' and 'behaviours' should never have been measured as separate entities. Viewpoints which are focused upon a particular social object, and activities performed in a context dominated by that social object, exist together in a continuous process of reciprocal creation. Indeed, expressions of 'attitude' are a kind of overt behaviour, perhaps qualitatively different from 'other kinds' of behaviour mainly in that they occur outside the action context: this is the point of the second title above.[1] In the context of this study, therefore, it is probably most appropriate to think of the task of prediction as an attempt to assess the concurrent validity of self-reported verbal affect against the criterion of self-reported activities. This formulation is, however, pedantic and awkward. In any event, the problem is essentially the attitude-and-behaviour consistency test as discussed in the literature of the field. The text will therefore use both forms of expression.

Second, the chapter reports on the results of a number of avenues by which one might improve the amount of variance shared between the two domains of verbally and behaviourally expressed affect for participation by students in the running of the university. Commonly suggested tactics for improvement which have to do with scale validity are exhausted first. Attention is then turned to selecting the *subjects* for whom the attitudinal conditions (stipulated as a kind of criterion belief system) are appropriate. The improvement in the amount of variance which is shared between attitude and behaviour for only the 'appropriate' subjects is assessed. The outcome is to be the specification of analytical types on the criteria of both verbal and behavioural measures.

The specification of these types is the third task. The types are defined in terms of their minimal belief system relevant to student power, and in terms of their activities in the university environment. The attitude-action dimensions with regard to the issue of student power are used to create four types: active radicals, passive radicals, active conservatives, and passive conservatives. Although these types are of considerable intrinsic interest, they should also be thought of as analytic devices. Their creation provides a manageable and intuitively meaningful 'handle' on the patterns of relationships in the data.

The ultimate goal, then, is to provide a means for testing a central assertion of this study. The assertion is that an 'attitude' which is tempered and practised in the arena of overt behaviour is the 'true' attitude in terms of S-R learning theory: 'an implicit anticipatory response which mediates overt behaviours, and arises out of them through response reinforcement' (Scott, 1959: 328). There are two main tests. That is, it is held that the small belief system concerning student power is really the tip of an iceberg of 'ideology' in the sense made popular by Converse (1964b). The student power beliefs are thought to be part of a framework of beliefs (attitudes, opinions, ...) of wide range, considerable richness, and adequate logical constraint by which the individual interprets his or her world. These conditions should obtain most clearly for those individuals whose attitudes 'match' behaviour. This is the first test, pursued in chapter 4. The second test has to do with the personal and social antecedents of the criterion 'belief-behaviour system.' Beliefs are effects, as well as causes. It is therefore held that there will be a crisper and more readily interpretable pattern in the relationships between other factors and the belief system for those respondents in whom attitude has been reinforced by behaviour. Chapters 6 through 8 test this assertion.

ATTITUDE-BEHAVIOUR CONSISTENCY

In chapter 1 I alluded to a number of methodological tactics for improving the strength of relationship between attitudes and behaviours. One can think of these as falling under three main headings: traditional reliability-validity approaches, innovative validity approaches, and approaches which are centred on locating people who hold attitudes as opposed to measuring universally held attitudes in all the people. Under the first heading, for example, one would place the multi-trait multi-method tactic proposed by Campbell and Fiske (1967). Perhaps because of the amount of work involved in assessing each research concept by a number of maximally different methods in order to avoid method artefacts, the approach has more often been paid lip service than it has been seriously utilized.[2] The activities of which this is an exemplar slipped into the background with publication of major criticisms of 'personality' studies by Walter Mischel (1968) and A.W. Wicker (1969). Regardless of the degree of the research's technical finesse, they suggested, available evidence showed that cross-situational *inconsistency* of subjects was the rule rather than the exception. Behaviour was in fact not homogenized by stable aspects of the personality. Indeed, Wicker said, it is fairly rare in studies which assess both attitude and behaviour for a general attitude to correlate as much as 0.3 with an appropriate behaviour. Response to these two writers has been intense, virtually dominating the field of empirical attitude studies over the following decade. Responses to Mischel have tended to be logical-theoretical, the writers taking issue with a purely 'situational' view of behaviour creation. The general debate was outlined in chapter 1. Responses to Wicker, however, have tended to be centred on demonstrations, using empirical data, of plausible ways of increasing correspondence. If correspondence could be demonstrated empirically, the theoreticians would be forced to reinstate the basic premise of personality assessment 'that people have stable and identifiable response dispositions that can be mapped by test scores' (Hogan, DeSoto, and Solano, 1977: 257). Some of these tactics are ingenious, deserving of closer examination.

One could not exhaustively list all the studies exploring one or another innovative avenue for improvement of strength of correlation. The work has been so prolific that not even the professional reviews such as the *Annual Review of Sociology*, the *Annual Review of Psychology*, *Psychological Review*, and *Advances in Experimental Social Psychology* claim to have covered all contributions. Kiesler and Munson (1975) report turning up more than 1,500 relevant items for their 1975 report for the *Annual Review of Psychology*, for example. Instead, one can suggest exemplary applications of a particular tactic. In all of these applications, the amount of variance shared between domains is improved over the 0.3 threshold, sometimes dramatically so. Figures will not, however, be reported in the text because the bare numbers are essentially meaningless outside their design contexts.

Several of these new approaches depend on a multidimensional concept of attitude. Attitude as traditionally measured had come down to a one-dimensional measure of affect for or against a social object, couched in very general terms. Newer work holds that the predictive power of attitude can be improved – while maintaining measurement of one thing at a time – if several measures of attitude(s) are combined to jointly predict appropriate behaviour. Sometimes the additional 'dimensions' are thought of as covering views of the situation in which the act is to be performed. Other researchers, such as Fishbein, measure intentions to perform the behaviour. Still others assess subject norms and social norms toward the activity and the situation (see Frideres and Warner, 1980). At other times the supplementary scales are simply thought of as assessing a variety of possible perspectives toward the social object. Heise (1977), for example, says that improvement in prediction can be attained by including variables describing the social context. Liska (1974a, c) investigated the combined additive effects of attitudes on behaviour. In an examination of students' exam 'coping' behaviour, he found that using specific attitudes to predict specific behaviours works best. In a somewhat different approach, Crespi (1977) reviewed a successful instance of prediction and extracted the implications: prediction is most effective with specifically phrased multidimensional attitudes, he found.

There is a second sense in which attitudes are thought of as being multidimensional or, rather, multicomponent. This sense is not new, as it dates from an old conception of each 'attitude unit' as being composed of cognitive, affective, and conative components (see Hilgard, 1979; for empirical applications, see Ostrom, 1969; Kothandapani, 1971; Rosenberg, 1968). But there is a new emphasis on empirically ascertained 'consistency' and 'correspondence' of the components of the subject's attitude. That is, consistency is to be tested, rather than assumed. Working with the affective and cognitive components, Bagozzi and Burnkrant (1979) found that the two components were jointly effective in predicting *scaled* behaviours. Norman (1975) likewise took the view that the greater the consistency between the affective and cognitive components of an attitude, the more effective it would be in prediction of behaviour. The idea here, reminiscent of Heider, would seem to be that when an individual's impulses toward an object are harmonious, he or she is more likely to be able to express a coherent attitude toward an object in other overt behaviour. In their review of the three-component theory of attitude, however, Fishbein and Ajzen (1974) make a contrary argument from a practical perspective. In applications, the three components of attitude have always proved to be extremely strongly correlated among themselves. But highly intercorrelated variables are unlikely to lead to improved prediction of the dependent variable, they remind us, in either the additive or configurational (interactive) model. Instead, they say, attitudes toward objects are good predictors of multiple-act criteria that encompass a range of behaviours matching the level of generality of the definition of the attitude object. Davidson and Jaccard (1979) likewise find the degree of 'correspondence' between attitudes and behaviours important to prediction. The lesson, therefore, would seem to be that a multidimensional conception of attitude is sometimes useful, but that it is perhaps equally important to think of the scalar properties of a *range* of sampled behaviours. Bentler and Speckart (1979) also find that it is important to predict from one index or battery of indicators to another. The reason for this may be that item difficulty (perhaps the scarcity of the behaviour in question in the case of a one-behaviour problem) sets an upper limit for strength of correlation (see Barton and Parsons, 1977; Raden, 1977). One has a better chance with two groups of indicators.

There is still another sense in which attitudes are thought of as requiring multiple components/dimensions. This is the interaction argument, in which it is claimed that it is the configuration of attitude dimensions or components which is important. That is, the impact of one dimension or component is thought to be dependent upon the level of the other component(s). Liska (1974a), however, found only minimal support for an interaction effect in prediction of behaviour. Andrews and Kandel (1979) likewise test the 'contingent consistency hypothesis,' finding interaction effects for only some of the people. Susmilch et al. (1975), however, challenge the very utility of the multiple-regression test for interaction in non-experimental designs. In a second analysis of regenerated data originally reported by Acock and DeFleur (1972), they tested the ability of configurations of a variable complex to predict behaviour over and above the ability of the variables operating separately. They argue that main effects cannot be distinguished from interaction effects in situations where there are unequal numbers of observations in the cells of a design (p. 684; see also Kerlinger and Pedhazur, 1973: 414–15). When interaction terms are highly correlated with main effects, they say, whichever terms enter the regression equation first will be credited with all the explained variation the variables share. A simple additive model is most parsimonious, they contend.

There are a number of other attractive strategies for improving attitude-behaviour prediction which have to do with the quality of an attitude rather than with its components. For example, Fazio and Zanna (1978) find that those of their subjects who have had direct experience with an attitude object have an attitude which is better defined and more confidently held than do those who formed an attitude through more indirect means. Regan and Fazio (1977) likewise argue that attitudes formed as an inference from what the subject has actually done are strong because the subject has had clear grounds for inference as to what his or her attitude actually is. Attitudes formed through means like persuasive communication or inference from concatenations of other information are less likely to be clear enough to direct behaviour. This train of thought is similar in outcome to Campbell's earlier (1963) notion of thresholds. The idea is that attitudes as expressed verbally and by behaviour have different thresholds at which they are evoked. Affect is readily evoked verbally, as talk is cheap. Behaviour, being more costly to the individual, is rationed in a more conservative manner. Much so-called inconsistency is therefore really pseudo-inconsistency, in both formulations (see also Schwartz, 1968; Raden, 1977). The basic idea would seem to apply to behaviours which are clearly and legitimately conceived as episodic. Otherwise, in predicting from behaviourally formed attitudes or behaviourally expressed attitudes to continued behaviour, the correlation would include some element of autocorrelation.

Working from a similar desire to improve prediction by establishing some additional qualitative element of the attitude, Perry, Gillespie, and Lotz (1976) found that subjects for whom the attitude object was 'central' exhibited a higher level of attitude-behaviour consistency. They measured centrality of attitude by obtaining a separate ranking from the subject. Manis (1978) likewise suggests that researchers should seek to establish some additional attitudinal characteristic reflecting the salience or centrality or consistency. This is easier said than done when one is working with survey methodology. It is a short step from questions of attitude salience to a concentration on picking one's subjects.

The tactic of working only with subjects whose attitudes are well-formed and well-defined is of course not spanking new. In his 'Attitudes and Non-attitudes' study Converse (1970) reported on research on political viewpoints conducted between 1956 and 1960. But it is more recent that psychologists have suggested on theoretical grounds that prediction can be improved if researchers carefully cull out the specific public for the attitude or belief system of interest. In their 1974 review, Bem and Allen note (for an update, see Kenrick and Stringfield, 1980) that there is consistency between domains if the individuals in the sample agree with the researcher that sampled items belong in a common equivalence class. If subjects conceive of the problem or situation differently than does the researcher, regardless of how the researcher's definition evolved, there will be 'inconsistency.' As noted earlier this is a return to Allport's idiographic view of individuals: people differ from one another in terms of which traits are relevant as descriptions of them, as well as in amounts of any given trait. Bem and Allen's advice to the researcher is to find one's friends:[3] 'Separate those individuals who are cross-situationally consistent on the trait dimension and throw the others out, for by definition, only the behavior of consistent individuals can be meaningfully characterized on the investigator's construct; only their behaviors can be partitioned into the equivalence class under investigation. Perhaps a statistical metaphor will make this proposal seem less illegitimate:

Unless an individual's variance on a particular trait is small, it makes no sense to attach psychological significance to his mean on that dimension.' (1974: 512).

What is the gist of all this methodological advice generated by those who search to explain more than 9 per cent of the variability in behaviour by measured attitudes? In general, it would seem to be true that it is helpful to predict from groups of attitudes to samples of behaviour. The additive model is least problematic. Sometimes it is helpful to conceive of attitude as having several components, particularly if consistency between components indicates some degree of embedding of the attitude in the general belief framework. Generally, however, highly intercorrelated independent variables will not improve overall variance explained in the dependent variable. When all the possible technical improvements have been made, the researcher should separate out those individuals who agree with the researcher's definition of the salient aspects of the attitude object under study.

How effective will the measures of attitude toward student power prove in prediction of activities undertaken in the university setting? Chapter 2 described the genesis of the measure of affect toward 'student power' as a social object. The content of the Student Power scale (see p. 56) deals with the students' rights and ability to claim an ongoing equal role with administration and faculty in all aspects of university decision-making. The concurrent validity of this scale was demonstrated in the context of its correlations with twenty other attitude measures. It would seem to be an excellent candidate for prediction of political acts in the university setting.

But correlational analysis and a factor analysis of scale scores showed that Student Power shares a sizeable pool of variance with Rejection of Radicals and Radicalism and University Militancy. This result is interesting in view of the fact that item content is quite dissimilar. Student Power deals with legitimate group goals for roles, University Militancy with personal willingness to adopt a variety of action tactics, and Rejection of Radicals measures acceptance or rejection of the most visible group of students who are pursuing 'student power' goals.

Student Power, then, deals most explicitly with the substance of student demands for participation. It was conceived and designed to do so. But could the scale use a 'boost' by the inclusion of the other two measures in prediction of overt behaviour? It is tempting to think of the three measures in terms of the multiple-component theory of attitude. In this view, one could argue that Student Power assesses the cognitive component of attitude toward student power as a social object, Rejection of Radicals is a more pure assessment of affect or emotion, and University Militancy assesses the conative or behavioural element of the stance toward student power. It could then be hypothesized that all three elements should be similarly valenced in the subject before he or she would undertake compatible action. But this would be an undue capitalization on serendipity, as the researchers did not begin with an intention to test the multiple-component theory. The correspondence is merely pointed out for those readers interested in the theory. A legitimate argument for multidimensional assessment using the three scales can be made on validity grounds.

First, let us think of the possible weakness of the Student Power scale for prediction of activity in university affairs. In terms of face validity, for example, it might be possible for an individual to obtain a very high score on Student Power by answering the items from a position of cynicism about the competence and goodwill of academics and the administration. Similarly, some of the variance unique to the other two opinion measures would not relate to activity undertaken in support of student power. Thus an individual who was sensitive about the protection of his or her rights as an individual, or who simply liked action, could score high on University Militancy. A very low score on Rejection of Radicals could be obtained through general beaming benevolence toward all one's fellow creatures, or from obliviousness toward political objects in the university. In such cases, there would be no reason to think that high opinion scores should entail activity. Unique variance arising from such considerations must be pared off.

A positive argument that the pool of variance shared by the three measures will be particularly effective in predicting student power activities might proceed as follows. Let us take the ideas of the Student Power scale first. The possibility that an individual will act – in accordance with his approval of the idea of participation – will be moderated by his personal willingness to be at risk, as this willingness is tapped by University Militancy. 'Risk' is used here in the broadest sense, to cover everything from willingness to lose time from studies to willingness to risk physical injury. Why should low scores on Rejection of Radicals – that is, an acceptance of the visible radical group – be a condition for the syndrome? First, dislike generally leads to avoidance. A student who disliked the radical students would avoid activities typically involving radicals – political meetings and protest groups. It is also thought that undifferentiated, unequivocal judgments about entire groups are generally made from a standpoint of ignorance about that group. Thus students subscribing to the blanket condemnation of radicals, expressed by RRR, are probably reflecting upon a monolithic group perceived from afar. Further, RRR is strongly correlated with Survey F (a correlation of 0.548 between factor scales), which taps respect for, and deference toward, authority figures. Liking and respect for authority figures can decrease likelihood of action in two ways. First, the individual will not want to risk alienating authority. Second, he might feel that the decisions of the authorities would not be improved by student advice. In brief, liking for radical students will indicate some minimal acquaintance with their ideals, and a willingness to be associated with them.

It is therefore predicted that the three attitudinal measures will work together to improve prediction to behaviour over the power of any measure – including the Student Power scale – taken individually. Whether the joint effect will be best described by a simple additive model or an inter-active-configurational model can be tested later. Susmilch et al. (1975) cast doubt on the use of interaction hypotheses in survey analysis, however, as has been noted above.

A multidimensional approach to the attitude under study has been devised. What of the activities we wish to predict? As argued earlier, prediction will be most effective if attitudes are related to a selection of activities at a similar level of generality and difficulty as the statements of the verbal scales. Accordingly, data were collected on the individual's self-reported activity across a range of options (see Liska [1974a] for a number of references to favourable validity studies of self reports of behaviour). These options, all in the context of the university, concern (1) political discussion, (2) attendance at political meetings, (3) involvement in student council deliberations, (4) campaigning for student council candidates, (5) running for office, (6) approaches to the administration, and (7) protest activity. It is important that these activity options be open to both those pursuing traditional, systemic student politics and to those who are not. Protest activity is of course biased toward radical actors, as campaigning for council candidates is most appropriate to systemic actors (although radical students did capture the council at the university shortly after this study was conducted). The options of attendance at political meetings and contributing to council deliberations are where radical actors and systemic actors would 'visit' each others' arenas. Talking politics with friends, and contacting the administration, are fairly equally appropriate to any actor. One can argue, therefore, that the sampled activities are varied enough in kind so that student government type and radical alike will be sampled. These are the texts of the questions, with frequencies reported as a matter of interest:

... how often when you get together with friends ... would you say you discuss student politics and university affairs? very often = 210 (25%); fairly often = 446 (45%); hardly ever = 253 (26%); never = 36 (4%); never get together = 4 (0.4%)

TABLE 3.1
Correlations of opinions and activities for entire sample and 'consistent' subsample

	1	2	3	4	5	6	7	8	9	10	11
1 Discuss university politics with friends											
2 Attend student debates	0.355 0.156										
3 Addressed student council	0.138 0.150	0.290 0.382									
4 Campaigned for student council candidates	0.152 0.166	0.260 0.201	0.388 0.361								
5 Ran for office	0.059 0.044	0.189 0.111	0.198 0.275	0.257 0.275							
6 Tried to see administrator	0.099 0.114	0.106 0.060	0.179 0.170	0.100 0.138	-0.041 0.116						
7 Participated in social change group	0.133 0.027	0.259 0.383	0.246 0.351	0.163 0.259	-0.037 0.164	0.108 0.172					
8 Number of such groups	0.141 0.078	0.269 0.290	0.269 0.428	-0.207 0.323	0.065 0.196	-0.128 0.187					
9 Rejection of Radicals	-0.202 -0.152	-0.310 -0.444	-0.087 -0.186	-0.053 -0.159	0.016 -0.084	-0.011 -0.012	-0.260 -0.430	-0.286 -0.435			
10 Student Power	0.275 0.212	0.344 0.394	0.115 0.209	0.111 0.197	-0.036 0.111	0.012 0.009	-0.203 0.371	0.240 0.403	-0.607 -0.878		
11 University Militancy	0.158 0.122	0.283 0.416	0.071 0.212	0.092 0.190	-0.008 0.072	0.019 0.028	0.209 0.369	0.223 0.402	-0.495 -0.859	0.477 0.854	

NOTE The top correlation is for the whole sample, n = 799; alpha for acts = 0.64 (omitting items 6 and 8). The lower figure is for the opinion-consistent subsample, n = 219; alpha for acts = 0.68 (as above).

How often do you take time for student debates, or university-related political meetings? almost every time they are held = 35 (4%); occasionally = 310 (32%); hardly ever = 349 (36%); never = 258 (27%)

Have you ever sought out members of student council in order to express your views to them on some issue, or have you ever expressed your opinions from the gallery at student council meetings? yes = 118 (12%); no = 835 (87%)

During your time in university, have you ever worked for student council candidates, doing things like distributing campaign literature, making speeches, and so on? yes = 116 (12%); no = 839 (87%)

Have you ever wanted to run for an elected office here in university? ... Did you in fact run for that office? yes = 119 (12%); no = 836 (87%)

Have you ever, in any way, tried to contact a member of the university administration, say one of the vice-presidents or a dean or the president, about some question or problem (not things like changing course schedules, but something where it was entirely up to you whether or not you approached the member of the administration)? yes = 214 (22%); no = 741 (77%)

Have you ever in the past four years participated either as a member or active supporter or leader in any group supporting or protesting a particular political or social issue (such as student groups, protest demonstrations)? yes = 184 (19%); no = 772 (81%)
What kind/kinds of group/groups (university-specific = 141)
Number of groups respondent has participated in: five plus = 0; four = 21 (2%); three = 11 (1%); two = 38 (4%); one = 134 (14%)

Research reported above indicates that prediction is best if the activity options are sufficiently related to one another that they can be considered to form an index, or perhaps even a scale. Table 3.1 reports the correlations between these activities, and between the individual activities and the three opinion measures. Correlations for the whole sample, based on the 799 cases without missing data, make up the top number in each cell. For the time being, the bottom number can be ignored. It is seen that items intercorrelate in the 0.15 to 0.35 range generally recommended for formation of an index of suitable internal consistency. Alpha, computed by McKennell's (1970) approximate method, is 0.64. The weakest item is the activity of trying to see an administrator.

Table 3.1 also shows that the activities taken individually are slightly or moderately related to the attitude scales. The comparative strengths and

TABLE 3.2
Gamma for verbal scales and activities

	Student Power	Rejection of Radicals	University Militancy	Consistents
Discuss university politics	0.298	−0.236	0.292	0.496
Attend student debates	0.392	−0.344	0.382	0.551
Addressed student council	0.229	−0.149	0.172	0.307
Campaigned for student council candidates	0.124	−0.067	0.246	0.352
Ran for university office	0.106	−0.024	0.156	0.151
Tried to see administrator	0.003	−0.013	0.063	0.014
Participated in social change group	0.312	−0.390	0.507	0.673
Number of such groups	0.321	−0.397	0.501	0.662

directions of the correlations also support the claim that students of different ideological propensities will choose their activities accordingly. Students highly rejecting of radicals are least likely to attend political meetings or demonstrations of all the options. Student Power is somewhat better at predicting non-systemic activities, as is University Militancy.

Table 3.2 displays the relationships between the scales and activity options more explicitly. An ordinal level statistic, gamma,[4] is used to judge the degree of association between acts and ranks on the attitude scale. Here we trichotomize the frequency distribution of the three verbal scales Student Power, Rejection of Radicals, and University Militancy into ranks low, medium, and high. Gamma assesses the improvement in predicting activity from our knowledge of position on the verbal scale. Table 3.2 shows the gamma statistic of association for each of the samples' activities with each of the verbal scales. For the moment, the contents of the fourth column headed 'consistents' can be ignored. It is seen that knowing whether an individual is low, medium, or high on Student Power, for example, can improve efficiency by about 40 per cent in predicting to attendance at political meetings. Students high on RRR reject all activity, rejecting typically radical activities most strenuously. Student Power does somewhat better across the whole range. University Militancy is the best predictor of options requiring greater investment: campaigning and protest activity. Once again it is seen that the act of attempting to contact an administrator does not share variance with the three verbal opinion measures.

But having said that the activity options are sufficiently related to form an index, let us build one. The ability of Student Power, University Militancy, and Rejection of Radicals to predict that an individual will have engaged in a criterion activity is illustrated much more vividly by summing acts into a simple index. To form this simple activity index, an individual's score is incremented by one if (1) he discusses student politics with his friends 'very often,' (2) he attends student debates 'almost every time they are held,' (3) he has addressed student council, (4) he has worked for candidates, (5) he has run for office himself, and (6) he has participated in a university-situated protest demonstration. That is, the act of contacting an administrator is omitted, and the social change movement variable now includes only the instances of participation in a group whose genesis was in the university. An individual's score on this index can range from zero to six.

Table 3.3 shows the cross-tabulation of the new acts-summed index with each of the three trichotomized verbal scale scores. The score on the index is arrayed down the left, and refers to the appropriate row in each table. As can be seen from column totals for high, medium, and low categories of Student Power, RRR, and University Militancy, it was possible to more or less evenly trichotomize the frequency distributions of Student Power and RRR, but not of University Militancy because of the skewed frequency distribution for this variable (see appendix D, table D1): hence far fewer respondents are included in the high category for University Militancy.

Taking Student Power first, it is seen that of the students whose scores fell in the lowest third of the trichotomized frequency distribution, a majority (173 out of 310 or 55.8%) will not have performed any of the activities. As the acts index score increases, the number of students who score low on Student Power decreases: 28.7 per cent of these 'lows' obtained a score of one, only 10 per cent scored two, 4 per cent scored three, and just over 1 per cent scored four. None of the respondents in the bottom third of affect for Student Power scored five, and none obtained the perfect score. The picture is gratifyingly different for those students categorized in the top third of Student Power. Admittedly, a considerable number (103 out of 325 scoring high, or almost a third) endorse student participation in the running of the university as an ideal, but have a zero score on the activities index. Almost 25 per cent have a score of one, and a score of two on the activities index would seem to be a kind of watershed: 24 per cent (as opposed to 10 per cent of those low on Student Power) have scored two. Thirty-one individuals, or almost 10 per cent of the 'highs,' have scored three on activities index, nearly 6 per cent (19 persons) have scored four, 12 persons or nearly 4 per cent of those high on Student Power score five on activities, and one person has a perfect score. The group which is medium on Student Power also happens to be moderately active: more active than the

TABLE 3.3
Association of individual opinion measures with score on university activities index

Sum of acts	Student Power			Rejection of Radicals			University Militancy		
	Low	Medium	High	Low	Medium	High	Low	Medium	High
0	173 40.05r 55.81c	156 36.11 50.81	103 23.84 31.69	106 24.26r 32.19c	161 36.84 48.79	170 38.90 54.84	128 33.60r 62.44c	220 57.74 42.15	33 8.66 36.00
1	89 34.77 28.71	86 33.59 28.01	81 31.64 24.92	80 31.13 25.81	93 36.19 28.18	84 32.68 27.10	51 22.17 24.88	150 65.22 28.74	29 12.61 26.36
2	31 21.23 10.00	57 25.34 12.05	78 53.42 24.00	61 40.94 19.68	54 36.24 16.36	34 22.82 10.97	14 10.94 6.83	93 72.66 17.82	21 16.41 19.09
3	13 21.67 4.19	16 26.67 5.21	31 51.67 9.54	32 53.33 10.32	13 21.67 3.94	15 25.00 4.48	9 16.36 4.39	34 61.82 6.51	12 21.82 10.91
4	4 12.50 1.29	9 28.12 2.93	19 59.37 5.85	19 59.37 6.13	7 21.87 2.12	6 18.75 1.94	3 10.71 1.46	18 64.29 3.45	7 25.00 6.36
	–	2 14.29 0.65	12 85.71 3.69	11 78.57 3.55	2 14.29 0.61	1 7.14 0.32	–	6 46.15 1.15	7 53.85 6.36
6	–	1 50.00 0.33	1 50.00 0.31	1 100.00 0.32	–	–	–	1 50.00 0.19	1 50.00 0.91
Total (n) Total (%)	310 32.91	307 32.59	325 34.50	310 32.63	330 34.74	310 32.63	205 24.49	522 62.37	110 13.14

$N = 942$ $\chi^2 = 82.80$ $\gamma = 0.326$ $df = 12$

$N = 950$ $\chi^2 = 61.12$ $\gamma = -0.271$ $df = 12$

$N = 837$ $\chi^2 = 62.23$ $\gamma = 0.356$ $df = 12$

r = row percentage; c = column percentage

low scorers, and less active than those in the high category of the opinion scale.

Overall, then, the scale is quite effective in selecting those who will have behaved in affirmation of the ideas they espouse in response to the Student Power scale. The gamma statistic of association for scores on the six ranks of the activity variable with the three ranks of the opinion variable is moderate at 0.326.

When the activity score is regarded as the independent variable, it is interesting that not having acted (a score of zero) is not very useful for predicting the rank on the opinion score. A guess of 'low' would be marginally safe, as just over 40 per cent of those scoring zero have low affect for the opinions of Student Power, but still 24 per cent of zero scorers obtain high scores on Student Power. A score of one on activities is even less useful – individuals scoring one are arrayed almost evenly across the opinion spectrum. However, if we know that a student has scored two or more, then we can predict his rank on Student Power with some precision. A total of 254 students have scored two or more: of these, 55 per cent are high on Student Power, whereas about 20 per cent fall in the lowest third. Less than 2 per cent of all students have scored five or six on activities: of these none scored low on the opinion scale. About 5 per cent scored four. Again, it would be safe to assume that these persons would not fall into the lowest third. Such proportions of highly active students are usual. Peterson (1968) found that only about 2 per cent of students on a given campus can be classified as 'activist.'

The contingency table for summed acts and trichotomized RRR scores reveals roughly the same pattern (although reversed) as has been described for Student Power. The association, however, is not quite as high, gamma being −0.271 between the activities score and the three ranks of the opinion scale. As a person is increasingly active, he is less likely to express negative views of the radical students, and vice-versa.

The pattern is shown for the third time in the cross-tabulation of the activities index with University Militancy, which asks whether or not a respondent would perform certain protest acts. Here the association (gamma) between ranks is 0.356 and the high and low categories of the opinion measure are effective in selecting active persons: only 8 per cent of those classified as highly militant have scored zero on activities. (This apparent increased efficiency, however, is also due to the cutting points for trichotomization which were necessitated by the skewness of the measure.)

Once a pattern of relationships has been investigated by techniques appropriate to the level of measurement of the variables, it is more defensible to move to powerful summary techniques which make stronger statistical

TABLE 3.4
Predictive ability of individual activities
with opinions as dependent variables

Steps entered	Multiple regression
Dependent variable Student Power	
1 Attend student debates	0.344
2 Discuss university politics	0.380
3 Participate in social change groups	0.396
4 Tried to see administrator	0.398
5 Ran for university office	0.399
6 Campaigned for student council candidates	0.399
7 Addressed student council	0.399

Fraction of variance explained = 0.16 N = 795

Dependent variable University Militancy	
1 Attend student debates	0.284
2 Participate in social change groups	0.316
3 Discuss university politics	0.321
4 Ran for university office	0.324
5 Addressed student council	0.325
6 Campaigned for student council candidates	0.326
7 Tried to see administrator	0.327

Fraction of variance explained = 0.10 N = 795

Dependent variable Rejection of Radicals	
1 Attend student debates	0.311
2 Participate in social change groups	0.362
3 Discuss university politics	0.372
4 Campaigned for student council candidates	0.376
5 Tried to see administrator	0.379
6 Ran for university office	0.380
7 Addressed student council	0.380

Fraction of variance explained = 0.14 N = 795

assumptions.[5] Multiple regression can summarize the net power of the activities to pattern linear variance in the attitude scales, and, conversely, of the attitude scales to predict activity. Table 3.4 compares the three scales. The exercise is performed solely for summary purposes, and is not intended to test any hypothesis. The activities taken jointly explain about 16 per cent of the variability in Student Power scores, 10 per cent in University Mili-

TABLE 3.5
Additive and interactive multiple regression analysis predicting score on activities index;
dependent variable Summed University Political Activities

Independent variables	B^c	Std. error of B	Cum. R^2	F ratio[d]
Additive[a]				
Rejection of Radicals	−0.096	0.053	0.083	3.23
Student Power	0.287	0.055	0.124	27.27
University Militancy	0.016	0.019	0.131	0.20
Interaction terms[b]				
SP.RRR	−0.126	0.042	0.158	8.70*
SP.UMIL	0.058	0.033	0.165	3.09
SP.UMIL.RRR	−0.035	0.023	0.167	2.28

Constant = 0.884   df = 6; 790   Overall F = 26.48

a The three variables were entered together in the order named in the first stage of a two-
level regression.
b SP.RRR is the multiplicative term for the two variables, as is SP.UMIL. SP.UMIL.RRR is the
term for the three-way interaction. The remaining two-way interaction term, UMIL.RRR,
was also entered in the second stage, but did not make it into the equation because of an
insufficient tolerance.
c This is the unstandardized coefficient.
d This is the F for each variable in the final equation.
* Significant at 0.01.

tancy, and 14 per cent in scores on Rejection of Radicals. Thus the relationships are respectable, and arguably a slight improvement over the ubiquitous
0.3 threshold.

An even more concentrated summary of the relatedness of these acts and
attitudes can be presented. Table 3.5 shows the power of the three attitude
scales to explain variability in the index. A simple additive model is explored
first. We then explore the configurational-interactive model to see whether
the effect of one attitude is significantly dependent on the level of another.[6]
Interaction terms were calculated for each of the bivariate relationships, and
for the three variables together. A hierarchical stepwise regression was performed, with the main effects entered first. The hypothesis is that the impact
of one variable is dependent upon the level of another if the appropriate
interaction term explains variance over and above the accounted for in the
additive model. As we see, the main effects for Rejection of Radicals and

Student Power account for the lion's share of the variance (12.4 per cent), the main effect of University Militancy being trivial. The interaction terms jointly account for an additional 3.5 per cent of variance, with the contribution made by the interaction between Student Power and Rejection of Radicals reaching significance at the 0.01 level, itself accounting for most of the increment in the cumulative R^2. What should one make of this? Probably not too much. First, while it is gratifying that the opinion measures interact, the *amount* of improvement in explanation is fairly trivial. Second, as Susmilch et al. (1975) point out, interaction tests are inappropriate in non-experimental designs where numbers are unequal in the various cells. The variables which are entered first 'explain' most of the variance of the dependent variable. Indeed, when the interaction terms are entered first in a two-stage hierarchical regression, the three-way interaction term explains 10 per cent of the variance, all interaction terms together explain almost 12 per cent, and only Student Power of the main effects entered in the second stage makes a statistically significant contribution.

In summary, it appears that we have explored all avenues for improvement of the strength of relationship between attitudes and behaviours which are appropriate to the study design. The result is explanation of roughly 16 per cent of the variability in political behaviour by appropriate measures of attitude. That is, the multiple correlation is roughly 0.4, which is a modest improvement upon the typical result for research of this type. Surely the way has been paved for a less traditional approach. We now turn to an exploration of Bem and Allen's solution: to look for the *people* who agree with the stipulated definition of approval for student power and 'throw the others out.'

PICKING CONSISTENT PEOPLE

Here, the goal is to set conditions for a belief system that will allow selection of individuals. We are turning from attitudes per se to the persons who espouse sets of beliefs.

Thus, the goal is to set conditions for a syndrome of opinions. These conditions should operate to exclude undesired variance, and to retain variance which will relate to a corresponding syndrome of opinion-relevant activities. People whose attitude scores are in the highest thirds of Student Power and University Militancy, and in the lowest third of Rejection of Radicals, can be thought of as holding a set of coherent opinions favouring student power which would facilitate activity. Or, conversely, one can speculate that fairly intense 'practice' of university politics could lead to such an opinion syndrome. Similarly, persons whose scores are middling on all variables should exhibit less activity. Scores at the extreme negative pole are harder to interpret, because intense conservatives (in terms of university politics) might well concentrate upon certain compatible acts only.

The supposition that individuals who hold a more consistent syndrome of opinions will be more consistent in action level can be tested. The task of locating consistent individuals can be accomplished by cross-tabulating the trichotomized SP and UMIL with RRR controlled. There are 65 persons who: (1) are least rejecting of radicals, (2) most strongly express a propensity to action, and (3) most strongly endorse student participation goals. There are 77 persons who satisfy the opposite of the three conditions above. The question is: will prediction be improved for these individuals above the level of prediction possible in the whole sample?

The reader may now refer back to table 3.1. The bottom number in each cell gives the correlation between variables listed for this smaller sample of 'consistents,' which has a total of 219 members. It is seen that in most cases the correlations between activities, and between activities and the verbal scales, increases over what it is for the undifferentiated sample of 799 individuals. The average correlation between the activities is slightly improved, as revealed in the marginally stronger alpha coefficient for the 'consistent' group over the whole sample. The increased strength of correlation between the attitude scales is, of course, an artefact.

Next let us return to table 3.2, and look at the gamma statistic in the fourth column headed 'consistents.' This gamma is the association between the rank given to the individual on the consistency syndrome criterion[7] (one for consistent low, two for consistent moderate, and three for consistent high on student power stance) and each of the selected acts. Hence we see considerable improvement (in strength of association) over knowing only the position on each of the verbal scales taken individually. For example, knowing an individual's rank on the consistency typology reduced error to one-third on the variable 'participation in a social change group.' There is also a marked improvement on the variable 'discuss university politics.' Statistically, this comparison is probably the most 'legitimate' as gamma is appropriate for use with variables measured at ordinal level. There are the same number of ranks – three – in the attitude scales and the ranked affect for student power among consistents.

The individual's ranked affect for student power as calculated for only these consistent individuals can also be used to predict his or her score on the political activities index. Table 3.6 shows sharpened prediction over that possible with the whole sample, using the attitude scales individually (table 3.3). For the attitudinally consistent persons, knowing that a person is uni-

TABLE 3.6
Composite 'consistency' measure association with activities

Affect ranking	Score on university political acts							
	0	1	2	3	4	5	6	Total (%)
Low	49	15	7	5	1	0	0	
	63.64[r]	19.48	9.09	6.49	1.30	–		
	47.57[c]	31.25	21.87	25.00	12.50	0		35.16
Medium	41	20	9	5	1	1	0	
	53.25	25.97	11.69	6.49	1.30	1.30	–	
	39.81	41.67	28.12	25.00	12.50	14.29	–	35.16
High	13	13	16	10	6	6	1	
	20.00	20.00	24.62	15.38	9.23	9.23	1.54	
	12.62	27.08	50.00	50.00	75.00	85.71	100.00	29.68
Total (%)	47.03	21.92	14.61	9.13	3.65	3.20	0.46	

$\chi^2 = 47.58$ df = 12 $\gamma = 0.494$ Spearman's $r = 0.399$ $n = 219$

r = row percentage; c = column percentage.

formly low in approval of student power enables us to be correct almost two-thirds of the time in guessing that he or she will have performed no activities whatever. If we know that a student's rank is three, we can be correct four times out of five in guessing that that student will have performed one or more of the activities. In fact, 60 per cent of the 'highs' of the consistent group will have reported at least two of the acts. The gamma between attitude affect ranks and the ranks of the activity index is almost 0.5, indicating that the error has been reduced by one-half. The strongest gamma between acts and an individual attitude measure (University Militancy) reduces error by about a third. This is a worthwhile improvement.

Having once more paid our dues to the appropriate level of measurement, we can again move to a more powerful technique of analysis for a summary. Table 3.7 displays a stepwise multiple regression in which the activities are used to predict the rank of the individual on the 'consistency' measure. Only the students who are consistent across the three measures are involved in the analysis. Therefore, given that a student *is* attitudinally consistent, we find that level of activity 'explains' 28 per cent of the variability in ranks on attitudinal affect. Choosing our people thus results in substantial improvement over what is possible for the whole sample (return to table 3.4). Activities, to compare, explain 16 per cent of the variance in scores on the Student

TABLE 3.7
Predictive ability of individual activities with combined
attitudes ranking; dependent variable Consistency Student Power score

Steps entered	Multiple regression
1 Attend student debates	0.439
2 Participate in social change groups	0.482
3 Discuss university politics	0.508
4 Addressed student council	0.525
5 Tried to see administrator	0.528
6 Campaigned for student council candidates	0.528
7 Ran for university office	0.529

Fraction of variance explained $= 0.28$ $n = 219$

Power scale, that scale being treated as an interval-level variable. One is
tempted to say that the increase in explanation of positive affect for student
power as a social object, given that the person's belief system is coherent, is
in the order of 12 per cent. But to do so would be almost meaningless. The
total variance explained is not strictly comparable between table 3.4 and table
3.7, and not only because the dependent variables in the first instance are
closer to being proper interval-level measures. More important, the characteristics of the variance pools are completely different between the whole
sample and the small sample of individuals who are attitudinally consistent.
Here, we have a smaller amount of variance to explain, and that smaller pool
is more patterned because it has been constrained to be that way. That is, we
should not claim an artefact as an improvement. The utility of the 'consistency' condition will have to be explored in relation to other independent
variables. The most that should be claimed is that, in the consistent group,
the multiple correlation between acts and attitude ranks is above 0.5. A
worthwhile improvement has been established over the usual 0.3 threshold.
Variance explained is 25 per cent rather than 9 per cent. Later chapters can
investigate the implications, and suggest the nature of the pay-off should
more dramatic improvements be possible in the relationship between words
and deeds.

Parenthetically, table 3.7 also shows which of the activities account for
most of the variance in the three attitude ranks. The three activities (1)
attendance at student debates, (2) having participated in a group which was
working for social change, and (3) frequent discussion of university politics
with peers are the most opinion-relevant behaviours. They are, of course,

the most common activities. They are also, one might speculate, the kind of 'consciousness-raising' or educational activity in which an individual would be likely to adopt the radical platform. These are also the best predictors for the individual attitude scales, in analysis of the whole sample. By undertaking these kinds of activities, the student may also learn consistency, for or against the ideas of student power.

The last task of the chapter is a housekeeping activity. Analysis to this point has exhausted traditional options for improvement of the words-deeds relationship. It has established that additional substantial improvements can be realized if the researcher chooses the subjects whose views match the criterion definition. It now remains to stipulate the attitudinal and behavioural characteristics of opinion-activity types for the purposes outlined in the introduction to this chapter. Attitudinal conditions will be loosened somewhat,[8] because the tactic of trichotomizing scale frequencies, neat for heuristic purposes, does not always result in the best cutting point for the distribution.

SPECIFYING OPINION-ACTIVITY TYPES

There are four obvious possibilities for opinion-activity types: (1) those whose opinions meet the consistency criterion for being highly favourable toward student participation and who *are* active in political manners in the university; (2) those whose opinions meet the consistency criterion for being highly favourable towards student participation and who are *not* active in political manners in the university; (3) those whose opinions meet the consistency criterion for being highly unfavourable towards student participation and who *are* active in political manners in the university; (4) those whose opinions meet the consistency criterion for being highly unfavourable towards student participation and who are *not* active in political manners in the university.

The interpretation of these types requires some care. It is clear that the first group, which is highly favourable in opinionation toward student participation and which acts, clearly exemplifies a favourable total stance toward student power. The fourth group is highly unfavourable in opinionation, and does not act. This would seem to be a total stance in the same sense as that of the first group: the opinionation component, strongly against student participation, is 'consistent' with not acting.

'Consistency' on the part of the researcher might suggest that the groups which do not unambiguously match affect with activity be dropped from analysis. To do so would be an error. First, retention of these groups is necessary for comparison with 'perfect' groups (pro-student-power actors and anti-student-power non-actors) when correlates of the stance are investigated: if the perfect groups were compared only to each other and to the sample, we could not know if effects were due to opinion consistency, or to inclusion of the activity component in the typology, or to direction of ideology.

Second, it is not clear that a complete interpretation of the proper fit between the opinion criterion and the activity criterion can be specified at this point. That is, an opinion stance which is strongly against student partici-pation in the university does not necessarily entail that the individual refrain from activity in the university political arena. An individual could be against broad-based participation and act himself *if* he considered himself to be a member of an elite – perhaps of the traditional student government variety. Or he could think it his duty to act in order to put forward a conservative viewpoint. Thus those who oppose student power ideas, but who act, could be traditional student union activist types or ardent opponents of the student movement. (Notice that it is not possible, a priori, to authoritatively specify activities as being radical or in-system, as there is no reason that a radical should not run for student council and so forth.)

Third, there are a number of contextual questions to investigate. Most important, the non-acting individuals who possess the extreme and consistent network of opinions can be compared to their opinion-mates who do act, to locate factors that encourage or inhibit activity. For example, one can assume that the first group is formed of radical activists proper (to be established in chapter 5 onward). The second group is more difficult. It may prove to be a clientele from which future activists will be drawn – i.e., passive radicals may well become active in the natural course of their own development. But it may also be a group of individuals who will continue to be inactive for contextual reasons, such as low exposure to activity options because they are enrolled in 'removed' disciplines. Still another alternative is that these may be students who are prevented from activity by aspects of their own characters; that is, individual differences on variables like self-esteem might suggest that activists are a unique psychological type. The correlational evidence of this research may suggest useful hypotheses for test by other research methods.

As noted earlier, the criteria which have been used to demonstrate the usefulness of working for opinion consistency will be slightly loosened. The adjustment is dictated by the skewness of University Militancy's frequency distribution. University Militancy has been used until now with its frequency distribution roughly trichotomized, for ease in exposition and presentation of tables. Its distribution is now divided into high and low for purposes of stipulating final type groups:

High on opinion, high on activities (Acting Radicals): Rejection of Radicals is in the lowest third, Student Power is in the highest third, University Militancy is in the top half of the distribution, and the score on the summed university activities index is two or more. ($n = 82$)

High on opinion, but do not act (Passive Radicals): opinion configuration as for first type, but rank on the summed university activities index is zero. ($n = 39$)

Low on opinion, high on activities (Active Conservative): Rejection of Radicals score is in the highest third, Student Power is in the lowest third, University Militancy is in the low half of the distribution, and the score on the summed university activities index is two or more. ($n = 18$)

Low on opinion, do not act (Passive Conservatives): opinion configuration as for the third type, but score on the activities index is zero. ($n = 71$)

CONCLUSION

To review, the sample of 959 respondents has been skimmed of four distinct types as stipulated by their scores on opinion scales and an activity index, leaving a large residual group. The first type is formed of individuals who express strong affect for student power in both opinion and behaviour; these persons will be called 'pro-student-power actors' or 'active radicals.' The group which is high on verbally expressed affect for student power, but does not act, will be called 'pro-student-power non-actors' or 'passive radicals.' Those who meet the condition of action in the face of negative affect will be called 'anti-student-power actors' or 'acting conservatives.' The group which is consistently low on affect and action will be called 'anti-student-power non-actors' or 'passive conservatives.'

It is useful to think of these four types as being the 'cream' of the sample rather than as being even an approximation of an exhaustive typology. For the opinion components represent only the polar extremes of intensity of affect over three scales: there is a very large number of other plausible 'syndromes' which could be created from various combinations of ranks on these three scales. One could, for example, specify combinations of 'liberals,' 'action freaks,' and so forth. I have chosen to isolate analytic approximations of 'student activists,' active conservatives, and the two inactive types because their descriptive characteristics can be matched to the characteristics of types described in an existing body of research. Note then that individuals who remain in the 'residual' group, which is used throughout for comparative purposes, are not necessarily lacking in opinions and do not necessarily lack structure in their other opinions. They simply do not hold with the structured criterion student power ideology stipulated here. A good many, of course, could be individuals who have not formed a view one way or another, whether idiosyncratic or conforming to an ideology not described here. Regardless, all are cast in together. Together they serve as a baseline for comparison with the patterns we can establish by using subjects whose views fit the criterion belief system. Forthcoming work, then, is a conservative test of the improvement in sharpness and pattern that one can establish by setting opinion consistency and activity conditions.

So far, we have identified four more or less plausible political stances that one might take with regard to university politics and the student power movement. Chapter 4 will ascertain whether these stances can be interpreted and validated in the light of opinions and activities toward society and politics in general. Does the analytically established belief system have power and range, in other words? Our hypothesis is that the belief system an individual has vis-à-vis student politics is a fragment of a larger framework or ideology that interprets the wider society.

4

Additional dimensions of the belief system: political and social beliefs and activities

The radical and conservative types which have just been stipulated are to this point merely hypothetical. People have been selected from the sample because their opinions appear to be coherent on a priori grounds: their views on student participation in university decision-making, their responses to radical activists, and their personal willingness to adopt militant stances 'fit' together logically. It then emerged that when peoples' views are coherent in this respect, their level of affect for 'student power' broadly speaking is more strongly related to their activity level than it is for less coherent individuals. In other words, for attitudinally consistent people, attitudes and acts are more strongly correlated. The task of this chapter is to flesh out the four types into believable complete persons with plausible views on the politics and social characteristics of the world outside the university. It turns out that a coherent stance vis-à-vis student politics is part of a wide-ranging interpretive framework for political and social phenomena.

Many people find the term *ideology* provoking: ambiguous, ambitious, and pejorative all at once. It is, however, a useful term to indicate the sets of beliefs and preferences by which groups of people interpret their society and orient themselves to political matters. Philip Converse has already been alluded to for his writing on belief systems (Converse, 1964b). Two qualities by which we can describe belief systems are particularly relevant here: rich or poor articulation, and the degree of constraining power. A richly articulated system is one which contains a large number of elements. A system is constrained if, knowing that an individual holds one attitude, we can successfully predict that he holds other attitudes and ideas. Ideology in such a sense is what enables the individual to get a handhold on the world. The belief system organizes and gives valence to past experience and information from new political events which is flowing in at present, and further enables the individual to assume a 'readiness stance' toward future political and social events. Within this meaning, the student power belief system stipulated here has both range and power in the prediction of the broader characteristics of the individual relating to opinion and activity.

It does not matter much if, at this point, one thinks of the university-specific beliefs as the 'seed pearl' around which other views cohere, or, conversely, as logical deductions from longer-standing views about the wider society. For younger students being socialized into politics via student power rhetoric, it may be the former. Other students may simply deduce a position about student power from sets of views already held. Or a little of both may go on in a given individual at the same time. The point is simply that the students whose views on university politics are consistent also hold articulate and consistent opinions on a wealth of social and political events.

Why would one expect an individual's orientation to 'student power' to unlock an entire political-ethical world-view? One can argue as follows. The shared goal of student activists is the goal of democratic participation in decision-making of all the university's members qua citizens. The goal is an explicit challenge to the traditional practice wherein purely academic goals of excellence and accomplishment are given pride of place. Instead, each individual's feelings of self-respect and true human importance are to be the highest goals. Socialist, utopian, and general humanitarian policies are implied by acceptance of the egalitarian mode of living as the prime goal. One need not agree that the university is a fitting choice for such a hopeful transformation. It is important only to see the further political and ethical implications of an endorsement of 'student power.'

On the other side, in projecting the political and ethical continuation of the position opposing democratization of the university, one does not wish to paint conservatism as only an ethically repulsive desire to maintain the status quo. Conservatism can be seen as a pragmatic and intelligent respect for the established problem-solving mechanisms of the polity. But note that the 'conservatives' here (the anti-student-power group) are defined on the basis of being against a change rather than *for* differentiated aspects of the university as now constituted. One can expect this group to be similarly opposed to change in the wider society and to have a bias favouring more formal aspects of the status quo.

The first part of the chapter examines the variables that were used to construct the types, to gain a more exact idea of built-in qualitative differences between them. The discussion then turns to the types' stances on sets of measures of political and social ideology. Here we introduce indicators of political preferences, analyse the social opinion measures constructed in the last chapter, and investigate political and social activity. The chapter ends with a review of differences between the types on the third group of measures – psychological functioning – to assess the viewpoint that radicals' psychological health is better than that of other students. Once the types have been fleshed out through this process, it becomes interesting to match the viewpoints to social background and descriptions of upbringing (chapters 6 to 8).

STIPULATIVE VARIABLES FOR UNIVERSITY TYPOLOGY: REVIEW

In comparing the opinions and activities of the student political types, it is important to remember that the types are formed from an elite of sorts. The types have been selected from the entire sample because their opinions were consistent across three measures. Addition of an 'extreme' activity component (two or more activities being designated 'high' activity, so that the opinion-consistent individuals who had done only one act lose eligibility for inclusion) results in a further setting apart. The specification of the opinion-activity types apportions the sample as follows: (1) *passive conservatives*, who make up 7.4 per cent of the total sample, 33.9 per cent of those in a types group ($n = 71$); (2) *acting conservatives*, who form 1.8 per cent of the total sample and 8.6 per cent of those in a types group ($n = 18$); (3) *passive radicals*, who form 3.9 per cent of the total sample and 18.2 per cent of those in a type group ($n = 38$); (4) *acting radicals*, who make up 8.5 per cent of the entire sample and 39.2 per cent of those eligible for inclusion in a type ($n = 82$); (5) the *residual group*, which makes up 78.4 per cent of the sample ($n = 750$).

Figure 4.1 shows the positions of the political types graphed as standard scores on the variables by which the typology was stipulated: incidence of university-specific activity, University Militancy, Student Participation, and Rejection of Radicals. Passive conservatives and passive radicals begin from the identical position of no activity whatever, then take up 'shadow' positions relative to the respective acting type. And although acting conservatives and acting radicals were chosen from among the set of those who had completed at least two or more activities, the acting radicals have a higher absolute incidence of activity.

An activity-by-activity examination of proportions of the active types engaging in political activities in the university context does lend some additional information, however: table 4.1 shows that some activities are more typical of acting conservatives and others are more typical of acting radicals. Radical activists comparatively 'overdo' discussion of university-specific

Figure 4.1 Graph of scores of university political types on typology variables

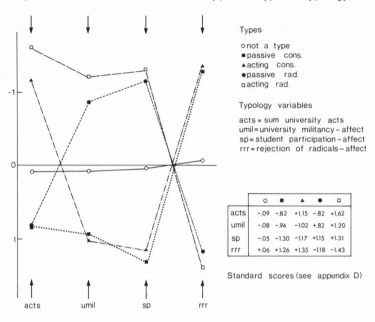

Types

o not a type
■ passive cons.
▲ acting cons.
● passive rad.
□ acting rad.

Typology variables

acts = sum university acts
umil = university militancy – affect
sp = student participation – affect
rrr = rejection of radicals – affect

	o	■	▲	●	□
acts	-.09	-.82	+1.15	-.82	+1.62
umil	-.08	-.94	-1.02	+.82	+1.20
sp	-.05	-1.30	-1.17	+1.15	+1.31
rrr	+.06	+1.26	+1.35	-1.18	-1.43

Standard scores (see appendix D)

matters, attendance at university debates and political meetings, use of student council as a forum for making their opinions known, and participation in campus-inspired demonstrations. Acting conservatives, in contrast, have a slight edge in incidence of campaigning for student council candidates and themselves running for student council offices – activities that would imply that acting conservatives are more traditionally oriented in their grasp of the university as a legitimate forum for political activity. And, although only wishing to run for a student council post is not summed in the activities index, frequencies are given here as a matter of interest: acting conservatives are somewhat more strongly tempted to participate in the traditional outlets for student activity than are acting radicals. Overall, the figures suggest that the acting conservatives tend to be drawn into the traditional aspects of university political life. Such an activity stance is compatibly linked with the content of their opinions: against broad-based student participation, censoring of the visible radical activists on campus, and low on propensity to take direct action on an ad hoc basis. We now move from *definitional* characteristics to non-definitional variables.[1]

TABLE 4.1
Percentages of university political types having engaged in
individual activities of summary indices

Activities	Passive conserv. (low SP, low acts)	Active conserv. (low SP, high acts)	Passive radicals (high SP, low acts)	Active radicals (high SP, high acts)	Resid. (not types)
University Context					
Discusses university politics 'very often' with friends	–	39	–	64	21
Attends university debates/ political meetings with regularity	–	72	–	95	34
Has contacted student council members/ has addressed council	–	56	–	39	10
Has campaigned for student council candidates	–	44	–	37	11
Has run for student council post	–	11	–	5	2
(Wished to, but didn't)	3	17	5	13	5
Has participated in campus-inspired demonstration	–	17	–	59	13
Non-university Political Context					
Discusses politics 'very often' with friends	11	50	8	60	23
Tried to contact member of Legislative Assembly (prov.)	18	44	34	63	29
Tried to contact member of parliament (fed.)	22	28	29	62	26
Paid-up party member	3	17	3	17	6
Has worked/campaigned for political party	8	44	13	41	15
Attends party meetings/rallies	33	83	39	84	49
Has participated in non-campus demonstration	1	5	–	23	3

SOCIAL-POLITICAL IDEOLOGIES OF THE TYPES

Here we begin to put political and social-ethical flesh on the bare bones of the university political types. We investigate their responses to the attitude scales developed in chapter 2, and describe their partisan political preferences and activities. An overview of the scheme of analysis follows.

General political preferences are indicated by (1) party identification, (2) an index of policy options, and (3) orientation toward civil disobedience. The attitude scales General Militancy, Nurturance, and Survey F also recommend politically relevant stances. The relationship of the individual to the general society is described by scores on Political Alienation, Closed-Mindedness, Pessimism, War, and Religion. His or her relationship to the special society of the university will be elucidated by responses to University Alienation, System Cynicism, Aimlessness, Contentment, and University Elitism.

The activity stance will be investigated through several indicators: 'Outside' Political Activity ('outside' meaning non-university), Social-Helping Activities, Informal Contacts, and Club Contacts. In addition, as a check on the opinion scales tapping kindly feelings toward one's fellow man, we have investigated the types' responses to a number of activity questions.

Expectations about radical types are quite straightforward. One can predict that radical students will be affiliated with 'left' political party options, will have 'left' policy preferences, and will advocate principled civil disobedience. Actors within the radical group will manifest a more consistent or developed ideology, that is, they will be more consistently and extremely 'left.' Student radicals who challenge university authority figures will exhibit the same questioning and challenging approach to the authorities of the larger society. In contrast, student conservatives who are supporters of the university's status quo will surely show a reluctance to interfere with the mechanisms of the larger society. But it is not possible to predict differences between the acting conservative group and the passive conservative group. There are two equally logical but opposite predictions one might make. It is possible that activity will make the views of these individuals more consistent; hence they will be more consistently and extremely conservative. But it is also possible that active participation within an essentially liberal society will pull their views toward the middle of the political spectrum. The types might therefore equally plausibly array from left to right: acting radicals, passive radicals, passive conservatives, active conservatives: or acting radicals, passive radicals, active conservatives, and passive conservatives.

Survey F and Nurturance allow the individual to describe his place in a social hierarchy. It is to be expected that conservative types – whether active or passive – will be more deferential toward traditional authority figures than will radicals, and that conservative types will be less accepting of unfortunates and misfits.[2]

For the change-oriented radical students, it is expected that the social picture will be flatter: they will tend to denigrate authority and to refuse to engage in ranking people. Again, this expectation flows from the basic stance. Radical students, feeling that their own human dignity allows them equal rights in making decisions that will affect them, will not accept the *source* of a decision as legitimating that decision. They will claim the right to challenge decisions. Radicals of either activity type should be higher than conservatives of either activity type on stated willingness to act in opposition to perceived injustice in the non-university community (General Militancy). This scale, in asking what protest acts an individual would perform, is a gauge of which protest options are perceived to be justifiable political activity. The reasoning is that conservative or status-quo types will tend to view almost any ad hoc action as unacceptable.

The overriding prediction for activity variables is that actors in the university context will also be actors in the context of the larger society, and that passive types will be shown to be passive across activities. That is, we expect to see a steady manifestation of an action style.[3] The political and social activity preferences of the two acting types will be congruent with the opinion stance: radicals will choose situationally suggested or informal political and social activities whereas conservatives will be more likely to act within socially pre-legitimated contexts in pursuit of determinate goals. The expectation for informal interpersonal contacts, club activities, and private humanistic action is that there will be little or no difference between active types.

MAJOR OPINION AND ACTIVITY STANCE INDICATORS

Let us now briefly describe each of the major opinion stance and activity stance indicators.

Party Identification Options for federal political party preference (not formal membership, which is a separate variable and which is included in an activity index), ordered from left to right, are New Democratic party, Liberal, Progressive Conservative, and Social Credit. (See Sutherland and Tanenbaum, 1975, for evidence bearing on the perception of a left-right continuum.) The Social Credit party was, at the time of this study, ending an uninterrupted reign in Alberta provincial politics of 35 years. Respondents were also given the option to write in a party, and to stipulate 'independent.'

Left-Liberalism This is an index of 26 then-current policy options, each option of which is scored in a left direction, with a score of two given for endorsing the 'good idea' category, a score of one for indicating uncertainty, and a score of zero for endorsing the 'bad idea' category. 'Leftness' or 'Rightness' of issues was stipulated by a panel of 26 Canadian political scientists at the University of Alberta in Edmonton. Many items, such as legalization of abortion or of homosexual activity between consenting adults, are more clearly of social rather than political importance, while others, such as guaranteeing French-language equality, involve fairly complicated historical and regional feeling. Yet the fact that the panel of judges were able to respond to issues in left-right terms suggests that use of the index to gauge a broad left-liberal criterion ideology is legitimate. In any event, types' positions on each of the issues taken individually will be briefly reviewed, so that any sense of outrage can be dissipated through a perusal of table 4.3. The range of the index is from 0 to 52.

Nurturance This scale's items pertain to the responsibility of the community to protect the unfortunate, and to refrain from intolerance.

Survey F This version of the F-Scale contains only items which advocate respect for and obedience to authority, and discipline. All other dimension-components of the traditionally delineated authoritarian syndrome loaded on other factors.

General Militancy The measure asks what action the respondent would take outside the university to redress grievances.

Civil Disobedience A lead question asks whether it is ever justified to disobey one's government's laws and orders. The following open-ended question asks the student to volunteer circumstances in which disobedience might be justified. Categories were then developed through a content analysis of responses.[4] (See table 4.4.)

Outside Political Activity Individual activity options of this index are listed in table 4.1. The range of the index is from zero to seven, with a score of one given to each option. These include intense discussion of politics with friends, being a paid-up member of a political party, having worked or campaigned with one of the parties, attendance at meetings and rallies, participation in a non-campus-inspired demonstration, and the act of having tried to contact a provincial politician or a federal member of parliament.

TABLE 4.2
Political party preferences of university political types

Political type	Political party preference									
	Lib.	NDP	PC	Soc.	Ind.	Other	None	Don't know	Missing data	Total
Not a type	350	62	167	36	78	20	19	7	11	750
	46.67^r	8.27	22.27	4.80	10.40	2.67	2.53	0.93	1.47	78.21
	82.16^c	66.67	77.67	87.80	71.56	71.43	70.37	77.78	100	
Passive conservatives	21	3	27	2	10	1	6	1	–	71
	29.58	4.23	38.03	2.82	14.08	1.41	8.45	1.41	–	7.40
	4.93	3.23	12.56	4.88	9.17	3.57	22.22	11.11	–	
Active conservatives	8	0	7	1	2	–	–	–	–	18
	44.44	–	38.89	5.56	11.11	–	–	–	–	1.88
	1.88	–	3.26	2.44	1.83	–	–	–	–	
Passive radicals	19	6	8	0	3	1	1	–	–	38
	50.00	15.79	21.05	–	7.89	2.63	2.63	–	–	3.96
	4.46	6.45	5.72	–	2.75	3.57	3.74	–	–	
Active radicals	28	22	6	2	16	6	1	1	–	82
	34.15	26.83	7.32	2.44	19.51	7.32	1.22	1.22	–	8.55
	6.57	23.66	2.79	4.88	14.68	21.43	3.70	11.11	–	
Whole sample	426	93	215	41	109	28	27	9	11	959
	44.42	9.70	22.42	4.28	11.37	2.92	2.82	0.94	1.15	

$\chi^2 = 86.08$ df $= 32$

r = row percentage; c = column percentage.

Social/Helping Activity Options for this index, listed in table 4.4, are each given a score of one, again yielding a range of zero to seven. Options are: having served with the United Community Fund (a federation of charities which holds a once-yearly fund-raising drive); having worked as a volunteer for a service club or church organization; having served as a volunteer with a youth organization; participation in the Miles for Millions march as either a sponsor or walker; and having served with any or all of the Alberta Youth Corps, the Company of Young Canadians, and the Canadian University Students Overseas – broadly similar full-time youth service organizations at provincial, federal, and international levels respectively. Frequencies for having wanted to join these last three noted organizations are reported as a matter of interest, but no points were given for having had an unfulfilled desire.

Informal Contacts This index is of informal contacts, and can be thought of as tapping the sociability of the individual. Summed in the direction of increasing numbers of contacts, constituent items are: how often the respondent 'gets together' with friends and with relatives; frequency of student-initiated calls on professors in their offices; how well the student feels he knows classmates; whether the student has ever invited someone who is new on campus, or a foreign student, to his home or to a social activity. A 'never' option being scored zero in each case, the index has a range of 0 to 19.

Club Contacts The index sums the number of university clubs to which the respondent belongs, number of outside clubs, and number of offices held. The possible range is 0 to 18.

OPINION STANCES OF POLITICAL TYPES

Party of political preference
The Liberal party is overwhelmingly the students' favoured party, with almost 47 per cent of the entire sample professing identification with it (see the row proportions of table 4.2). Differences of 5 per cent or more between a type's proportion in a category and the proportion of the whole sample in that category will be noted. Taking the types in order, we see that passive conservatives are heavily Progressive Conservative and Independent in comparison with the other three types and sample proportions. Acting conservatives do not disproportionately prefer any one party, although the New Democratic party would seem to be under-favoured. Passive radicals oversubscribe to the Liberal party, and have a fairly heavy New Democratic party subscription. Acting radicals are mainly New Democratic party[5] and Liberal

party members, and also have a fairly heavy representation of 'Independent' and 'other.' The main revelation of an overview of column proportions would seem to be the distributions of New Democratic, Independent, and other parties: all three are very heavily concentrated in the fourth or acting radical type. As well, New Democrats have an overall higher proportion of individuals who could make it *into* a type by virtue of their opinion 'consistency.'

In sum, the two conservative-opinion types are fairly solidly with the old-line parties, Progressive Conservative and Liberal. Passive radicals move slightly further left to the Liberal party and the NDP. Acting radicals are furthest left in party preference. New Democratic party members would seem to have arrived at a higher level of consistency – more have made it into a consistent opinion type than have any other party group – and would seem most 'consistent' in terms of the act-attitude relationship.[6] Findings for party preferences, then, are straightforward. The figures do not suggest, for example, that either passive radicals or conservatives are under any sort of cross-pressure with regard to a possible action-hampering conflict of their political party loyalty with their views on student power.

Left-Liberalism index
Scores of the four types on the Left-Liberalism index of policy options reaffirm the information given by proportions of the types identifying with the political parties. Figure 4.2, on which scores are transformed into standard scores and plotted, shows that acting and passive conservatives are close together at the 'right' extreme of the pole, that passive radicals are much more 'left' with regard to general social and political issues than are the conservative types, and that the acting radicals have the most 'left' position on the index.[7]

When the proportions of each of the types thinking a position is a 'good idea' are examined issue by issue, several interesting facts emerge (see table 4.3). First, the sample is fairly well agreed on a number of central social and political issues. Very few university students in 1970, no matter what position they have adopted on student power, would think that stopping old age pensions was a good idea. There is also fairly general agreement that taxing the wealthy more heavily than at present would be a good idea, and that it is a good idea for Canada to recognize 'Red China.' About one-third, across the board, would approve of 'hiving off' the national transport industries, and there is high agreement that legalization of abortions would be a good idea. Further, there is a majority of each type in favour of taxing churches

Figure 4.2 Positions of types of politically relevant opinions and political and social activities

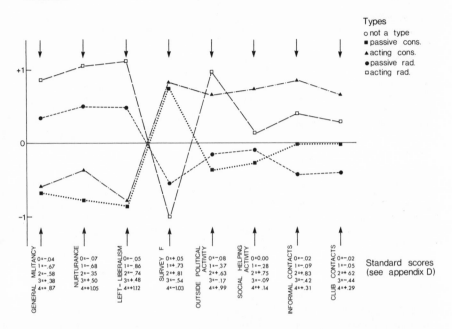

Types
o not a type
■ passive cons.
▲ acting cons.
● passive rad.
□ acting rad.

Standard scores
(see appendix D)

and church property and in favour of restricting profits of corporations, with most acting radicals in favour of these policies.

Other issues distinguish between types in two ways. Some issues create only two groups. For one example, while the highest proportion of active radicals (93 per cent) and the lowest proportion of passive conservatives (56 per cent) favour a guarantee for French language rights, we find that the issue does not distinguish between active conservatives and passive radicals. In two other cases, the two radical types are close together, having roughly equal proportions favouring restriction of American investments in Canada and improvement of Indian housing conditions. Elsewhere, the two conservative groups are closer together than radicals on the issue of allowing the police a freer hand with student protestors, and concerning possible legalization of the sale and use of marijuana. A similar pattern is evidenced on the remaining eight issues – more acting radicals take up the left position than individuals of any other type, but the three other types cluster in various combinations.

TABLE 4.3
Percentages of university political types favouring individual issues of left-liberalism scale

Issue item	Passive conserv.	Active conserv.	Passive radicals	Active radicals	Resid.	Judges' direction
Stop old-age pensions	4	6	–	2	3	R
Tax wealthy more heavily	68	89	74	88	72	L
Sell Air Canada/CNR						
to private business	27	33	31	26	27	R
Legalize abortions	79	72	84	94	83	L
Tax churches/						
church property	58	61	61	87	61	L
Restrict profits						
of corporations	51	50	55	74	56	L
Help United States						
in Vietnam war	16	33	–	5	11	R
Take Canada out of NATO	28	17	45	70	34	L
Legalize sale/use						
of marijuana	25	28	68	87	44	L
Free medical care	68	61	90	96	82	L
Restrict American						
investments	61	50	84	88	81	L
Improve Indian						
housing conditions	59	59	82	82	72	L
Nationalize oil industry	31	22	42	66	42	L
Restrict labour's						
rights to strike	73	67	21	18	46	R
Give police freer hand						
with student protestors	54	50	8	–	27	R
Refuse entry to U.S.						
dodgers/deserters	48	50	16	6	28	R
Restrict coloured						
immigration	24	11	–	2	15	R
Free university education	39	50	74	90	53	L
Permanently abolish						
death sentence	28	44	61	79	46	L
Make adult homosexual						
activity legal	48	67	71	96	67	L
More liberal						
divorce laws	66	78	89	99	84	L
Canada to recognize						
Communist China	66	83	90	94	82	L
Guarantee French						
language parity	56	78	79	93	74	L
Guaranteed						
annual income	63	72	84	92	79	L
Cut back welfare programs	49	44	26	13	39	R
Take harder line re						
Quebec/separatists	78	72	47	33	61	R

Other issues, however, appear to distinguish more clearly between types. That is, a higher proportion of acting radicals than of passive radicals favour the 'left' direction on the policy option, and a higher proportion of passive conservatives than of active conservatives favour the 'right' direction on the option. These issues seem to be mainly egalitarian-tolerance recommendations for social policy. Thus, the smallest proportion of passive conservatives is in favour of liberalizing divorce legislation, with 66 per cent thinking liberalization a good idea. The proportion favouring liberalization increases to 78 per cent for acting conservatives, 89 per cent for passive radicals, and 99 per cent for active radicals. This pattern of step-by-step increase is repeated on the two issues concerning homosexual activity and a guaranteed annual income (again table 4.3). Active radicals have the highest proportion of members favouring legalization of homosexual activity between adults, the provision of free university education, and permanent abolition of the death sentence. Proportions of acting conservatives and passive radicals are ordered midway. Most passive conservatives, and least active radicals, approve both of taking a harder line with Quebec and 'the separatists' and of decreased expenditure on welfare programs. Again active conservatives and passive radicals are in between.

In summary, options of the Left-Liberalism policy index believably describe the views of the student body. The sample is both agreed and liberal on a number of basic issues. However, illiberality with regard to taking a harder line with Quebec and the separatists (61 per cent thinking such a stand to be a good idea) coupled with the even higher proportion (74 per cent) affirming the need to guarantee French language rights is a completely believable reflection of western Canadian viewpoints.

The finding that radical actors are indeed more consistently left than radical non-actors in regard to policy preferences supports the theoretical position of this work. Action and opinion reciprocally create one another.[8] Where activity is more intense, one finds an increased coherence and intensity of appropriate views. As suggested earlier, the active conservatives qualify this finding: they are more *liberal* than passive conservatives on several policy issues. It may be that public activity implies or creates (or both) a certain liberal commitment to improving life chances of disadvantaged groups. Perhaps activity brings the individual into closer contact with mainstream moral norms. In the university these norms tend to be left wing and humanitarian. It could be that the active conservative would be pulled 'left' on topical moral issues, but not on most clearly economic issues. This problem can be pursued using the opinion scales which tap orientations to the underprivileged.

TABLE 4.4
Percentages of university political types on civil disobedience variables

	Passive conserv.	Active conserv.	Passive radicals	Active radicals	Resid.
Should a person always obey his government's laws and orders, or should he only obey when he is sure the laws and orders are just and right? ($N = 959$)					
Should always obey	68	44	22	5	37
Only when 'just and right'	32	56	78	95	63
Under *what circumstances* do you think individuals are justified in defying or not obeying the laws of their nation? ($n = 696$)*					
1 Trivial, ad hoc reason	20	7	8	18
2 For individual's own freedom or safety	30	27	26	31
3 To protect the rights of any group	10	14	17	12
4 When the law is against a *group*'s morality or religion	20	–	9	10
5 When the law is against the judgment of the *individual*'s conscience	20	52	40	30

* 263 refusals and/or missing observations.

Civil disobedience

Proportions who think that one should always obey the government are given in table 4.4. It is interesting that although only about 40 per cent of the entire sample thinks obedience must always be given, almost 70 per cent of the passive conservatives hold this view. Acting conservatives are also fairly stern on this indicator, with 44 per cent thinking that one should always obey. Passive radicals, by a large majority (78 per cent), think one should obey only when laws are just and right. Acting radicals are virtually unanimous in the view that one should obey the laws only when they are 'just and right.'

'Circumstances justifying disobedience' shows the expected patterning of responses: radical types are more likely to give a theoretical justification for civil disobedience. The base number of conservative actors is too small (10) for the calculation of percentages. The small proportion of *passive* conservatives who think it possible to justify disobedience tend not to have come to a principled stand, but slightly over-choose the trivial and individual safety categories. Radicals comparatively over-choose the last category, for which an answer qualified if it drew upon the classic principle of the rights of the individual conscience.

Other major opinion scales
Standard scores on the major opinion scales are plotted on figure 4.2. Conservative types are very close together on General Militancy and on Survey F. However, the positions of the two *radical* opinion types – actors and non-actors – are fairly different. Radical actors are higher on stated willingness to act, as one would expect, and lower on Survey F or deference toward authority figures.[9]

Thus, the less respectful an individual of radical opinion stance is toward authority figures, and the more acts of engagement or protest he deems legitimate, the more likely he is to engage in politically relevant activity himself. But why should conservative actors be politically active even though their militancy and Survey F scores are, respectively, as low and as high as those of *non*-acting conservatives – and, for that matter, much more extreme than those scores which we have just said to be inhibiting of activity in those of radical opinion? One can suggest a simple answer: conservative students are not hampered by the 'rebellion-respect' aspects of militancy and authority because it would not occur to them to think of their own activity as anything but supportive of the system and of duly-constituted authority. And, in fact, the conservative student's choice of activity is system-supportive, as was seen from the types of university activities they over-chose.

The ordering of the types on the Nurturance measure is what one would expect from the findings on the tolerance-type issues of the Left-Liberalism index. Radical actors, with the highest mean score, are most tolerant toward social misfits and unfortunates and most likely to wish to give aid rather than punishment. Passive conservatives are the most harsh. The action component, then, does appear to exert a pull in the liberal direction: conservative actors have a more kindly orientation toward out-groups than do passive conservatives, and acting radicals are still more protective than are passive radicals.

In oblique introduction of the next topic, one may ask how important a simple non-ideological liking for one's fellow man might be in drawing an individual into political activity. Milbrath (1962) finds that 'sociality' is highly correlated with activity in his sample of Washington lobbyists. Our measure of Nurturance is politically loaded: that is, while the conservative may well empathize with, and himself personally aid people whom he sees to be in distress, he cannot intellectually endorse statements which imply government provision of automatic aid (because of his own views on self-help and maintenance of a disciplined society in which 'deserving' does not subsume 'needing'). The notion that individuals are drawn into political and social-helping activity in part as an aspect of general sociability can be indirectly assessed by examining characteristic activity choices of the types.

ACTIVITY STANCES OF POLITICAL TYPES

Non-university Political Activity
Positions of the types on indices dealing with activity are plotted in standard scores on figure 4.2. The passive types score below the sample mean of Outside Political Activity and below the mean of the residual group, and radical actors have a slightly greater intensity of activity than acting conservatives.[10] Table 4.1 displays the information in somewhat more detail. It is apparent that radical actors are very much more likely to contact a federal politician and to have participated in a demonstration. Equal proportions of actors engage in mainstream political party activity, including taking up party membership, working and campaigning, attending party meetings and rallies. Discussion of politics is much more evenly distributed when the topic is not the university: there is only a 10 per cent discrepancy here for frequent discussion in favour of the acting radicals, in contrast with a 25 per cent discrepancy on the variable indicating intensity of discussion of university politics with peers. Thus radical actors would appear to have a more individualistic view of how politics can be conducted – a preference for direct contact with politicians and direct action. However, they would appear to make equally intense use of traditional outlets for political energy as do the acting conservatives. Their 'extra' behaviour, then, seems to be innovative and personal.

Social/Helping
There is a provocative reversal of the ordering of the types on apolitical (or less clearly political) options. The activities of the Social/Helping index are the arena of action of the conservative actor: or, perhaps better, this is *not* the arena for active radicals. Those activities of the Social/Helping index which are most often taken up (shown in table 4.5) are mainstream system maintenance activities. The radical might view them as counter-productive to his political stance. For although the acts of campaigning for money for the city's major charities, working for service clubs and church organizations, working with youth organizations, and participation in the fund-raising Miles for Millions marches are indeed helpful co-operative activities, involvement can also imply a basic satisfaction with the political and social system. Full-time volunteer service with the Alberta Youth Corps, CUSO, and the Company of Young Canadians is infrequently reported. Only the radical actors have had sufficient commitment to serve with these organizations. A higher proportion of radical actors report having been tempted to join (not added into the score).

TABLE 4.5
Percentages of university political types having engaged in
individual activities of social/helping index

Activities	Passive conserv.	Active conserv.	Passive radicals	Active radicals	Resid.
Served with United Community Fund	23	47	14	22	17
Worked for service club/ church organization	38	65	33	38	40
Worked with youth organization	16	53	31	32	29
Participated in Miles for Millions	44	67	53	59	56
Served with Alberta Youth Corps	–	–	–	6	2
(Wanted to, but didn't)	12	27	28	39	26
Served with Canadian University Students Overseas	–	–	–	3	1
(Wanted to, but didn't)	28	39	53	63	44
Served with Company of Young Canadians	–	–	–	–	0.5
(Wanted to, but didn't)	5	6	33	54	16
Totals	($n = 71$)	($n = 18$)	($n = 39$)	($n = 82$)	($n = 749$)

While it is understandable that both radical types should comparatively under-choose the acts of the Social/Helping index, it is somewhat less obvious that conservative actors should engage in these activities with enthusiasm. That is, low scores of conservative actors on Nurturance suggest that they do reject, in the abstract, precisely those groups of people to whom they devote actual time and energy in helping. Even though the opinion-only stance of the conservative actors should predict withdrawal or punitive behaviour (and does in fact imply withdrawal for the numerically much larger passive conservative type), acting conservatives are the world's 'nice guys' when it comes to the actions of the Social/Helping index. Similar results are found from the Informal Contacts index, which taps respondent-initiated social contacts, and the Clubs index, which is a simple count of numbers of memberships and offices held in both university and non-university organizations (see figure 4.2). Of all groups, acting conservatives have most informal contact with the people of their immediate environment: they are most linked in to their world. They *are* most sociable. They also score higher on club contacts than do other groups. And, while the absolute difference beteen the activity-intensity of the two passive types is not large, it can be noted that passive radicals are least linked in to the environment.

Private humanitarian
It is pertinent also to take an overview of the types' non-public helping or humanitarian behaviour. A number of personal acts thought to indicate general kindliness are reported in table 4.6. These include giving blood, donating money, aiding stranded motorists, graciously making small loans to friends, and, finally, behaving in a civilized manner towards unlovely losers. The last is assessed by an item that asks whether the respondent has been approached for money by an inebriate, and collects the reaction. There are two tendencies to note: first, despite the opinion stance, acting conservatives do behave nicely toward their fellow men in private situations where they are not to be suspected of aiming for the applause of their peers (unless one suspects a social desirability bias on the deeds, in which case one must ask why it did not operate on *opinion* scale items as well). Acting conservatives give blood rather more often, donate money equally with liberal types, and are helpful toward stranded motorists (a common and unpleasant task in Alberta winters). Their friends find them approachable for small loans, they are most likely to comply, and least secretly resentful of having been asked for the loan. Both radical and conservative types of actor not only initiate more contacts with people, they are also more often the object of an approach. Friends are more likely to ask favours of them, and the item which asks whether the respondent has ever been approached for money in the downtown section by 'someone who had obviously been drinking' suggests that they are approachable. More happens to the active type, seemingly no matter what kind of event is in question.

Although so few persons have been approached for money by an inebriated gentleman that no real weight can be placed on responses, there are a few hints for further research. The categories, derived from content analysis of self-descriptions of behaviour, suggest systematically different response emphases in this conflict-filled situation. The non-punishing conservative tends to ignore or refuse the drunken supplicant, the radical escapes through the token sum. Also, persons belonging to *both* acting types will sometimes devote some constructive energy to the situation by offering an address or some information about an appropriate helping agency. They attempt to deal with the person as well as with the situation. These very particular action stances (in distinction from broad questions about how one feels about deviants, etc. in general) are provocative enough to suggest that development of

TABLE 4.6
Percentages of university political types engaging in
private 'humanitarian' activities, plus qualitative indicators

Acts	Passive conserv.	Active conserv.	Passive radicals	Active radicals	Resid.
Given blood during last five years	52	61	47	50	50
Donated money to charities	62	72	68	69	63
Always try to help stranded motorists	6	17	5	12	6
(No opportunity)	17	17	24	27	17
Friends do request small sums of money	72	94	76	90	76
Respondent always complies	21	44	30	40	26
Does not resent requests	39	77	40	67	48
Totals	($n = 71$)	($n = 18$)	($n = 39$)	($n = 82$)	($n = 749$)
Has been approached for money by 'a drunk'	49	72	53	67	58
Response:*					
1 Threatens	13	8	11	4	9
2 Ignores	16	31	17	6	21
3 Refuses	41	39	39	28	41
4 Gives token sum	13	8	17	28	12
5 Gives as requested	6	–	11	18	7
6 Offers address/aid	–	8	–	14	4
7 Offers meal	3	–	6	2	3
8 Supervises meal	9	8	–	2	2
Totals	($n = 32$)	($n = 13$)	($n = 18$)	($n = 51$)	($n = 426$)

* The percentages in the lower half of the table are based on the proportion of persons who have been approached.

similarly attitude-object specific and behaviour-object specific indicators could be a rewarding tactic in survey research. Such a tactic might obviate one dilemma of this research: what the acting conservative is really like. Is he described by his opinions, which seem to be punitive? Or is he described by his activities, which suggest a basic jollity and a helpful approach in personal behaviour? Indeed, if the only persons who hold punitive and misanthropist attitudes of *The Authoritarian Personality* genre either *do not act* in any of the standard manners in the public forum (passive conservative), or act in such a way as to be incongruent with their punitive beliefs (acting conservatives), why should we care what anyone merely thinks?

RELATIONSHIP TO SOCIAL ENVIRONMENT

The topics of the socially focused attitude scales are basic to political recommendations. It is expected that conservative students will express approval of established authority and traditions, and will express doubts that 'human nature' will allow much improvement. Conversely, radicals' libertarian views are founded on greater faith in the ability and worth of people in general.

The six non-university social orientation measures we work with share a nuance of simple-minded negativism, misanthropy, and traditionalism. A rational individual endorsing the sentiments of these scales should assume a stance of withdrawal from public life, on the grounds that events are taking what is basically an unalterable course. Active types sought to be less despairing than their complementary non-active types.

Political Powerlessness/'Alienation' This index expresses a sense of futility on the part of the individual regarding the possibility of personal impact on parliamentary democracy.

Closed-Mindedness A belief that there is one version of 'the truth,' that it is possible to know it, and intolerance of those who do not adhere to this truth are scale topics.

Pessimism This taps negative views of human nature in the present, and expresses the view that there can be no future change because of the 'inborn' weaknesses of human nature.

War This scale expresses the view that war and the use of force in the regulation of human affairs are both necessary and justifiable.

Religiousness A strong recommendation that an unquestioning belief in a superior power is necessary for a 'complete' existence is indicated.

The second battery of university-specific scales tells how the individual feels about himself in the immediate context of 'the university.' It indicates how he evaluates the university experience both for gross emotional impact

(University Alienation and Contentment) and in somewhat more differentiated terms (System Cynicism). One would, of course, expect conservative students to have a more positive general evaluation of the environment than radical types, who, by definition, are working for change.[11]

University Alienation This is a personal expression of loneliness within the 'impersonal' university environment.

System Cynicism The scale expresses negative views of the motives and abilities of administrators and faculty and of the worth of course work.

Aimlessness A sense of having drifted into the university rather than having come because of academic goals or preferences is expressed by this scale.

Contentment A very general sense of satisfaction with the total university is expressed.

University Elitism A conviction that the university graduate is superior to people who have not acquired a university education, and thereby deserves a privileged position in society, is the gist of this scale.

See figure 4.3. Taking Political Powerlessness/Alienation first, it is found that passive radicals are more alienated than are active radicals. Active radicals are least likely to feel that the individual is powerless to make an impact on the governmental system.[12] The mean score for acting conservatives hovers about the sample mean: one might have expected them to hold very affirmative views about the larger society. Their response, however, is consistent with a general tendency to endorse statements which point to the complexity of society, thereby casting doubt that any one individual would have much impact.

On Closed-Mindedness we see the passive conservatives with highest scores, considerably higher than for conservative actors. Acting radicals are likely to express the more tolerance of diversity of belief. Conservatives are most likely to feel that 'human nature' dictates the way things are, and the way things will be (Pessimism). They are most accepting of the need of wars, and most likely to think that religious belief is necessary for a full existence. On each of these last three scales passive radicals occupy an ambiguous position: they are less likely to accept the negative than are conservatives, but not so affirming in stance as the acting radicals.

Figure 4.3   Positions of types on relations of self to society and the university

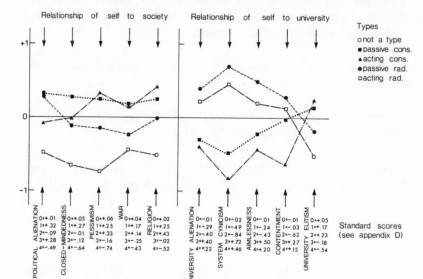

Turning to university-specific measures we see that conservative types are indeed more satisfied with the university. They are most likely to affirm the worth of the total university experience. Acting conservatives are still more positive than passive conservatives: conservative actors have the lowest scores on University Alienation, are least damning about the motives and abilities of administrators and faculty (System Cynicism) and of the worth of course work (also System Cynicism), and have the highest diffuse affection for the university (Contentment). It can also be seen that they are more likely than any other students to feel that they came to university in pursuit of some goal, rather than having simply drifted into the experience. They are also the most elitist of all students, most convinced that a university education improves the quality of a person. Passive conservatives, in comparison, are less affirmative: their scores on Alienation are minimally higher, they are somewhat more cynical about the worth of the academic experience, slightly less likely to feel they have come in pursuit of a goal, and minimally less elitist about the degree. They are notably less likely to express contentment: they are not enjoying themselves as much as are the acting conservatives.

The plot of the scores of radical student types on these university-specific variables is almost exactly a mirror of the plots for conservative types. As predicted, the *passive* radicals' scores are at the extreme. They feel most lost and alone on campus, and most denigrating of the faculty and administration, are most likely to feel they are on campus for no good reason, and feel least diffuse warmth for the entire experience. They are higher on University Elitism than are active radicals, another manifestation of their less-developed ideological position.

Findings on these last two batteries of scales, which assess the individual's view of this social environment and of his place in that environment, pose a problem which will be investigated subsequently. Why should certain syndromes of opinions be shared by acting and passive radicals (political indicators) while the passive radicals' less-specifically political opinions move in the direction of opinions held by the conservative groups (social and efficacy type indicators)? Yet taking a conservative view does *not* in itself preclude activity. Might views of the society be mediated by views of the self per se? Do actors of both types have a stronger and more positive self-image than do passive types?

PSYCHOLOGICAL-FUNCTIONING VARIABLES

Does the radical student activist enjoy better 'psychological health' than the conservative activist or the politically apathetic student? Keniston (1967), Bay (1967), and Hampden-Turner (1970) feel that he does. Speculating about psychological health, Keniston writes 'many of the person characteristics of activists – empathy, superior intellectual attainments, capacity for group involvement, strong humanitarian values, emphasis on self-realization, etc. – are consistent with the hypothesis that, as a group, they are unusually "healthy" psychologically' (1967: 129). But Lipset (1968a) points out that almost all the analyses which conclude that left-wing militants exhibit superior psychological attributes are based upon comparisons with the student body as a whole, not with activists of conservative persuasion. He suggests that activists of other ideologies would share the healthy traits. In support, Mussen and Wyszynski say that the politically active individual appears to have 'free energy' (not used up in coping with personal anxieties) which he can expend in concern with humanity in general (1952: 80). A fair amount of empirical work challenges the 'superiority' claim. Doress (1968), taking right, moderate, and left activists, found no evidence that left activists exhibit superior psychological characteristics. Nor did Kerpelman (1969) find differences between right-left and acting–non-acting groups on a measure of emotional stability. Trent and Craise (1967) found no differences between Free Speech Movement arrestees and the general student body on a measure of manifest anxiety.

It is important to be clear about the meaning of 'psychological health.' Bay and Hampden-Turner, certainly, and perhaps Keniston also, have a very broad definition in mind, in the psychoanalytic tradition. Bay and Hampden-Turner seem to accept virtually any measure of authoritarianism as a valid indicator of a neurotic tendency. Bay thinks that 'conservative views, among students or adults generally, are likely to be less rationally, less independently motivated, compared to more radical-liberal views' (1967: 88). The frequency of neurotic motivations will be the higher 'the further away the active person is from the left side of the political spectrum.' Thus, in Bay's formulation, the holding of certain sets of punitive and elitist views, these being measured by instruments like the F-Scale, is evidence of neuroticism or mental ill-health. But neuroticism is also evidenced by the holding of 'conservative views' per se, which must include politically conservative preferences which are recognizable on the left-right continuum. These conservative views will have ego-defensive motivations.

Although it is not possible to test whether conservative views have their genesis in ego-defensive needs in cross-sectional survey research, it is possible to form an argument and see if available evidence is contradictory or confirming. The problem would seem to be as follows: it is true that persons of conservative political viewpoints disproportionately adopt negative views of human nature in general, and hold suspicious views of others' motivations. Psychoanalytic theory holds that such negative views of others would be ego-defensively based. Anxiety which would well up and overwhelm the individual (caused by unpalatable 'truths' about the self) is handled by transforming reality and believing ill of others rather than of the self. *If* illiberal political views are based in punitive social views which are in turn based in emotional needs of the individual, *then* it ought to be true that conservatives would have higher scores on measures which indicate some difficulty in day-to-day psychological functioning. But if conservatives do not suffer undue emotional distress, one can suppose that their political and social viewpoints are reflections of social teachings rather than reflections of emotional inadequacy.

The view that conservative views are mediated by psychological needs related to the self-image, and the Lipset view that all activists will be psychologically superior, can be tested at the same time. To assess psychological health, we shall use the third group of measures that tap opinions about the self, assessing anxiety and psychologically based somatic distress. These indicators do not focus upon subjects other than the self, and they engage values only in so far as they relate to the self.

On the grounds that it may be the extra energy for involvement that we are explaining let us predict that both groups of activists will show less psychological distress than the opinion-mates who do not act. Who should show least good psychological adjustment? Presumably those who have exerted the energy to scan the issues and emerge with a consistent set of views, but who do not carry through into activity. Passive radicals should show worst overall psychological adjustment because their ideology is clearly a call to action which they do not fulfil.

Indicators are the General Mental Health Index, Anxiety (IPAT), Rosenberg's Self-esteem, and Submissiveness. Because morbid reporting on the state of the organism may measure only the propensity to whine, there are added some less-subjective auxiliary measures of physical health, and four questions about classmates and studies. After Scott (1968b), this tendency to 'do one's time' with more or less pleasure, more or less good grace, is called 'hedonic tone.' A short description of each variable touched upon in the discussion of general hedonic tone follows.

General Mental Health Index This is a short version of the index developed by Gurin to capture a general 'mental well-being.' GMHI, here scored in the directon of *ill* health, correlates with 'objective' indicators of bad physical health: 0.375 with an evaluation of one's health being 'poor' in the past year, 0.125 with numbers of serious adult illnesses (after the age of 15), 0.277 with numbers of minor chronic health problems, 0.289 with numbers of non-routine visits to a doctor in the past year, 0.143 with numbers of times hospitalized in the past five years, and 0.084 with numbers of operations in the past five years. (For other evidence bearing on the validity of GMHI-type items, see Robins [1969], Langner [1962], and Tousignant, Denis, and Lachapelle [1974]. The last reports on five surveys.)

IPAT Anxiety Scale This is a 25-item version of Cattell's measure of free anxiety level.

Rosenberg's Self-esteem This scale measures a healthily favourable attitude toward the self as object.

Submissiveness A feeling of personal inadequacy to cope in a complex world is the underlying dimension of this scale. Items are factorially distinct from dimensions which place 'the blame' on any focus other than the self.

Enjoyment of Routine Four items deal with the student's involvement and satisfaction with other students, professors, and course work. The reasoning was that a very negative self-view would likely also be manifested in an inability to enjoy immediate others. Items are: (1) How well would you say that you know your classmates in general? (2) Thinking generally about your work here at university, how happy would you say you are with the things you are studying? (3) And how about your fellow students and colleagues? Do you find interacting with them to be a rewarding experience? (4) And how about your professors? Do you generally find them to be stimulating and exciting, or not? Responses in each case are scored on a four-point scale from 'very' (high) to 'not at all.'

Perception of Physical Well-being Expectation for political types on 'objective' indicators of physical health was that active individuals might enjoy physical health superior to that of the average student or that ideologues who do not act might be objectively disadvantaged in terms of physical energy. Accordingly, students were asked to evaluate their health over the past year, response categories being five points from 'very good' to 'very poor.' Further, they were asked to list serious childhood (before the age 15 years) illnesses, serious adult (after the age 15 years) illnesses, minor but enduring complaints (unexplained pains, trouble with eyes, etc.). In each case, plagues were simply summed and coded from one through six and above. The final item asks for the number of times the student has been hospitalized in the past five years.

Dramatized Anxiety The question – 'Have you ever felt as though you were going to have a nervous breakdown?' – supplements the treatment accorded clammy hands, bad appetites and nerves, and butterflied stomachs of IPAT and GMHI. Responses are 'yes' and 'no.' In an open-ended follow-up the student was asked to specify 'what it was about.'

Standardized scores on interval self-opinion scales for the four types are plotted in figure 4.4. All scores except for Self-esteem are in the 'distress' direction. First, it can be noted that scores for the residual group, passive conservatives, passive radicals, and *acting* radicals cluster fairly closely together. Any 'trend' difference discernible between these three types would indicate that passive conservatives show slightly *less* evidence of distress overall than the radical groups. If any one group can be said to show superior psychological functioning, it is the small group of eighteen active conservatives. But this finding should be interpreted with great caution because of the

Figure 4.4 Hedonic tone: opinions of types about the self

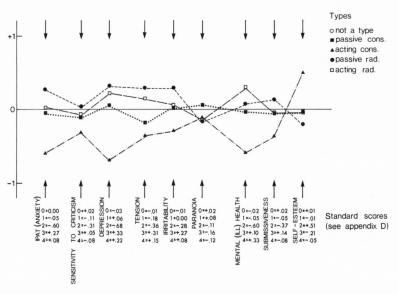

Types

o not a type
■ passive cons.
▲ acting cons.
● passive rad.
□ acting rad.

Standard scores
(see appendix D)

small number in the group and because differences of this magnitude would not be clinically meaningful.

To proceed in somewhat more detail: the first position on figure 4.4 represents scores for IPAT-sum, followed by scores on IPAT subscales Sensitivity to Criticism, Depression, Tension, Irritability, and Paranoid Insecurity. Mean group scores for IPAT-sum show passive radicals suffering from somewhat higher levels of anxiety, passive conservatives and active radicals hovering about the mean, and active conservatives suffering somewhat less anxiety. Anxiety as measured by IPAT, therefore, would not seem to be an action-boosting characteristic. The overall differences in IPAT would seem to be largely contributed by the variance on Depression – here the spread between groups is greatest. This subscale taps a loneliness-sadness-dejection dimension. It is worth noting that Paranoid Insecurity contributes almost no variance: it would seem that the variable (as measured here) is not engaged with any particular political style.

GMHI fares about the same for magnitude of differences: here acting conservatives report fewest manifest and somatic symptoms of nervousness, acting radicals most. GMHI 'anxiety' as body consciousness would again seem to favour conservative groups in so far as one wishes to attend to these trends. Nor is speculation that submissiveness is part of the conservative's

Figure 4.5   Hedonic tone of the types: enjoyment of routine and perception of physical well-being

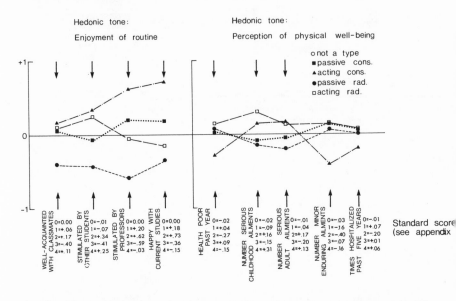

make-up supported. Here the small group of acting conservatives is slightly less intimidated by the world, the other three groups hovering about the mean, with passive radicals just slightly more submissive. Self-esteem returns the same pattern: acting conservatives have healthier views of the self, passive conservatives and acting radicals are at the mean, and passive radicals are just slightly less accepting of themselves.

Let us turn to hedonic tone as indicated by enjoyment of university routine and perceptions of physical well-being (see figure 4.5). Again differences are not great, but the pattern is the same as for the more opinion-type scales. Acting conservatives have most fun, they are best acquainted with classmates, enjoy other students and professors most, and are happiest with their studies. Passive radicals are estranged from their colleagues, and are least satisfied with their studies. Passive conservatives and acting radicals are about average, the acting radicals showing somewhat more approval for peers but less for professors and their current studies. Indicators of physical well-being thus show no large differences: an action stance is not supported by clearly superior physical health, whether objective or merely in the mind of the actor.

One final indicator of ease/enjoyment of personal functioning remains: this is the question about perceived imminence of a 'nervous breakdown'

TABLE 4.7
Dramatized anxiety: 'Have you ever felt as though you were
about to have a nervous breakdown?' (percentages)

		Yes	No
Not a type	(739)	24.8^r	75.2
Passive conservatives	(70)	18.6	81.4
Active conservatives	(18)	27.8	72.2
Passive radicals	(37)	21.6	78.4
Active radicals	(81)	43.2	56.8
Whole sample	(945)	25.8	74.2

$\chi^2 = 15.516$ df = 4

'Causes' of the threatened breakdown*
(percentages based on affirmation of breakdown imminence)

		1	2	3	4	5	6	7
Not a type	(183)	9.8^r	16.4	23.0	8.2	12.6	22.4	7.7
Passive conservatives	(13)	–	23.1	30.8	15.4	15.4	7.7	7.7
Active conservatives	(5)	20.0	–	20.0	–	–	–	60.0
Passive radicals	(8)	12.5	12.5	–	–	12.5	50.0	12.5
Active radicals	(35)	5.7	17.1	14.3	14.3	8.6	20.0	20.0
Whole sample	(244)	9.0	16.4	21.3	9.0	11.9	21.7	10.7

$\chi^2 = 32.434$ df = 24

* 1 = don't know, not able to verbalize; 2 = generalized depression, general dismay, fear
of the future; 3 = work overload at university, failure of paper, exam; 4 = problems with
the parental family; 5 = problems with love relationship, marriage; 6 = combination of
worries over university work with personal problems; 7 = a physical health problem, or a
specific tragic personal event (e.g. one student lost his wife and son in a car crash).
r = row percentage.

which was referred to above as dramatized anxiety. Table 4.7 shows proportions of types and of the residual group who have felt severely traumatized.
As the table indicates, slightly more than one-quarter of the whole sample
have felt on the verge of a nervous collapse. Of the types, only acting radicals
are markedly discrepant: 43 per cent of acting radicals answered 'yes' to the
breakdown question. Passive radicals, although somewhat higher on the
free-floating anxiety of IPAT, are considerably less likely than acting radicals
to suffer the feeling of intense, focused anxiety of imminent breakdown.
Likewise passive conservatives are less likely than acting conservatives to
suffer this focused, dramatized anxiety – although the small number of act-

ing conservatives counsels caution in making such a statement. One conclusion can be drawn, however: acting radicals are considerably more likely than the average student to have felt that a nervous collapse was imminent, and to acknowledge the experience.

To conclude: on several established indicators of psychological health/distress no evidence whatever is found to substantiate the claim that student radicals are superior in psychological 'health.' Nor is there any evidence for the claim that conservative political viewpoints are mediated by 'deep' inner, psychological inadequacies. Trends in the data would indicate that acting conservatives are slightly superior in psychological attainment, and other groups are not distinguishable from the average. Results for physical and sociability indicators of hedonic tone support these findings. Booth and Welch (1978) report very similar results from a study conducted on adults in metropolitan Toronto. They found that the health status of activists was very similar to that of inactives. Activists did, however, manifest just slightly more stress. Bradburn (1969) found from a panel study, however, that 'positive affect' increases with the degree to which an individual is involved in the world. Interestingly, he finds that lack of participation is not related to 'negative affect.' In his formulation, participation is a source of satisfaction, but a lack of participation does not cause conscious dissatisfaction. It would seem reasonable to conclude that politically pertinent attitudes, in this university sample, are not serving irrational personality needs. Further, one can conclude that the 'extra' energy for public activity does not arise from any kind of super psyche or superior health. Indeed, the largest group of active students, the radicals, perceive and report at least an average amount of self-disorder.[13]

SUMMARY OF DIFFERENCES

We now summarize differences between the constituted university political types with regard to the total political-social world-view. Most of the variables reviewed distinguish between types in a theoretically plausible manner. Most predicted differences between types are statistically significant,[14] although some differences are not substantial. Let us review substantive findings.

It is found, first, that there is an activity 'pay-off' in the sense that the addition of an action component to an opinion-type reveals subsequent qualitative differences in the broader political stance. This is perhaps most interesting in the context of the difference between acting and non-acting pro-student-power (radical) types: persons who take up the same university idea stance, but who also act in support of their views, show a more clearly defined and thoroughgoing commitment to other sets of 'left' preferences, opinions, and activities than do university non-actors. Radical actors, in comparison with passive radicals, are more humanitarian, have more respect and liking for their social and personal settings, are less respectful of traditional authority figures, and are more likely to recognize and follow through the opportunities for personal action and self-expression. They do not feel powerless in their environment, which is the key difference Keniston sees between passive and active radical students.

Conservative actors are also qualitatively different from passive conservatives. Addition of an activity component to the status-quo opinion stance appears to soften the orientation regarding broader social and political issues. The acting conservatives are more forgiving of out-groups, more likely to show independence in deciding civil disobedience could be justified, more positive and contented in the immediate university environment, and the most likely of *any* of the types to show behavioural evidence of enjoyment of contacts with other people – if one can accept intensity as suggesting presence of some reward.

The major qualitative differences between acting types are those which one would expect from the conservative and radical positions that they hold on university politics. Conservative actors are more strongly right-wing on party identification and policy preference than radical actors. They also engage in system mainstream and supportive types of activities. But although active conservatives hold rather social Darwinian and punitive views of the role of the underprivileged in the social order, they engage in far more social-helping types of *activities* than do members of any other type, and reveal themselves to be friendly and human on a number of private humanitarian-type *behaviours*. Acting radicals are somewhat higher on activity overall: the 'extra' political activity is innovative and individualistic. Both types of actors share a generally positive orientation toward the potential of activity, and toward other people: the difference would seem to be that the conservative actor is less autonomous in choice of action forms. There are strong differences on views of civil disobedience. A picture, however, is built up of acting conservatives as enjoying greater inner calm and satisfaction. This provocative finding should perhaps be taken with a grain of salt because of the small size of the sample of conservative actors.

It should also be explicitly noted that the problem mentioned at the end of the previous chapter, when it was not yet possible to interpret membership in the class of acting conservative unambiguously, has been resolved. Acting conservatives, in the context of the university political opinionation and activity which defined them and the other types, are activists of the traditional student government type. Hence their opinion and activity stance vis-à-vis the wider society consistently reveals 'conservative' opinion and in-system activity options.

The detail and convincing nature of the substantive differences support the major theoretical claims of this study. First, attitudes which are forged in the area of action do appear to be qualitatively different from unpractised views. Second, it is clear that a stance in the context of university political affairs – for or against broad-based student participation in the university – is one part only of a broad and coherent political view-point. Translated into method, this means that it is possible, by means of stringent use of cutting points and a consistency criterion, to 'artificially' constitute types from opinion measures and activity measures. Bem's advice to 'throw the others out' is well taken.

5

Empirical studies of student activists

It would not be much of an exaggeration to say that there are as many kinds of literature about student protest as there are academic disciplines and literary genres. There are historical studies of student politics in all countries, through the ages. All tendencies in historical scholarship are represented, including what is called 'psycho-history.' There are macro-sociological examinations of social structures, which seek to find a cause for student protest in systemic shifts. There are less broad sociological analyses, which attribute protest to characteristics of the institutions of higher learning as they evolved in the 1960s. There are studies at the psychological level, both empirical and theoretical, representing all tendencies within the discipline of psychology. There are the political writings of the students themselves, and of their gurus. There is much poetry, some of it extremely scurrilous, some plaintive, some funny. There are the moral writings about the functions of the university by faculty members, most of whom had completely forgotten how to conduct political activity and political bargaining when challenged by students. As though provided in a spirit of helpfulness, there are case studies of individual protest events which extract the strategic lessons. And, based on these, there is the odd game-theoretical account.

Of these riches, only one narrow genre is directly relevant to our study. This genre is, of course, empirical studies of individual students which isolate factors associated with attitudinal or behavioural stances toward student power. The movement is taken as a given, and the interest is in explaining why some students took part while others did not. The main purpose of the present chapter is to summarize these relevant studies, so that the results can be compared to our findings. This is a very narrow focus given the breadth of the whole literature. To aid the reader who might wish to explore somewhat further afield, therefore, some brief remarks follow which identify notable landmarks in the wider literature. Citations for these works are to be found in the bibliography. A critique of the work that is relevant to the present research then follows. The core of the chapter is a variable-by-variable summary of this narrower literature.

LANDMARKS OF THE BROAD LITERATURE

Lewis Feuer's book, *The Conflict of Generations* (1969b), is undoubtedly the most cited of the historical studies. Feuer argued that the universal fount of student protest was to be found in the Oedipus complex. This theme served to unify his massive compilation of the characteristics of student political movements around the world, over almost the last one hundred years. His chapter on the Berkeley free speech movement has provoked a great deal of abuse. Seymour Martin Lipset has ranged as widely as Feuer, providing historical and macro-sociological comment on the student movement (Lipset, 1960, 1968b). He has also written a number of useful reviews of empirical sociological and psychological studies (Lipset, 1968a, 1969, 1972, 1973) and has conducted projects himself (Lipset, 1965). He has been the source of much good sense. One example is his advice, largely unheeded, that analysts should make careful distinctions between sociological- and psychological-level variables so that the two could be related explicitly to one another.

Lipset's writings are, on balance, sympathetic to the movement and to student activists. Edward Shils's are not. The student movement is peripheral to Shils's major contributions to sociology, but his essay 'Plenitude and Scarcity' (1969) is a major contribution, matching both Feuer's and Lipset's contributions in scope and power. Shils characterizes not an ideology but a 'mood' of student protest as feeding on the works of writers Marcuse, Louis Althusser, R.D. Laing, Foucault, Norman Brown, Fanon, Paul Baran, and Ernest Mandel, among others. Many scholars have noted what they call an authoritarian streak in this 'mood.' Shils identifies this tendency most precisely in a central paradox in the view of the most impassioned of the leaders. They were *utterly sure* that 'dispassionately acquired knowledge is an impossibility' (1969: 45). The radicals of the 1960s were thus opposed in principle to the use of quantitative methods in the social sciences, holding that their use simply masked service of 'the system.' These quantitative studies were characterized as 'positivist.' Although Shils adamantly opposed the movement, he was more calm than most critics because he believed that it was doomed: 'The present state of possession will ebb. Widespread enthusiasm has never persisted before in human history, and it is not likely to do so in the future. Most students will return to their studies and will re-enter the body of moderates, variously diligent, variously interested in their studies, variously deep and original. Some student consultation in the government of academic institutions will occur and it will be, as the student radicals fear it will be, "incorporated," into the governing system of most universities' (p. 56).

The author of another first-rate theoretical contribution, Samuel Friedman (1973), is less sure of the ephemeral nature of the outcome. Speaking only of the American student movement, Friedman sees the source of discontent in what he calls the 'alienation of intellectual labour' (p. 292). Intellectual labourers are people who put their minds to subjects not of their own choosing, for salaries. This class is growing in numbers, even as the individuals comprising it lose in importance. Its unrest will therefore find its outlets in other social movements, as they form, he thinks.

Richard Flacks is probably the best known of the structural analysts who unequivocally favour the student movement. Flacks was himself a student activist. In his essay 'Young Intelligentsia in Revolt' (1972), Flacks provides a valuable history of the development of the American student movement, and an analysis of its prospects for the future. He then saw the movement as doomed to failure unless it broadened its base of support, but he felt that there were signs of such a broadening. Besides this higher-level analysis, Flacks has also conducted a considerable amount of empirical research, making him something of an oddity among his contemporaries.

Each institution has also its own history, and its own chronicles of incidents of protest. An exhaustive collection of these reports has never been compiled, although quantitative comparative scholars have attempted controlled national comparisons (see, for example, Backman and Findlay, 1973). There are a good many edited compilations of individual case studies of protest events. Among those dealing with American protest are Lipset and Wolin (1965), Foster and Long (1970), Becker (1970), and Bell and Kristol (1968). The movement's outcroppings in Britain are described in Cockburn and Blackburn (1969), and more recently in Marsh (1977). The Canadian scene is described in Reid and Reid (1969). There are also a few edited collections of student writings, of which Harris (1970) is an example. Nagel (1969) also contains writings by students, but covers Western Europe as well as North America.

A more recent contribution to this broad type of analysis is a collection edited by Light and Spiegel (1977). The editors say their book is either the last of the 1960s era, or the first of the next wave of protest. The collection is unique in its emphasis on tactics – of students, faculty, and university authorities.

Quantitative studies, those which the student activists would call 'positi-
vistic,' divide into two broad categories. There are those in which analysis is
at a sociological level, as opposed to the psychological studies of individual
differences between students. The major theme of the first type of study was
that protest was importantly related to institutional quality.[1]

Remarkably little of this vast literature deals with Canadian institutions or
events. Writing in 1976, Simpson and Phillips presented the following list as
exhausting the publications in English: McGuigan, 1968; Reid and Reid,
1969; Roussopoulos, 1970b; Quarter, 1972; Lehtiniemi, 1972; and Bissell,
1974. Of these, three are edited collections. The Roussopoulos reader is the
most disciplined: it presents province-by-province analyses of the strength of
the 'New Left.' The McGuigan reader presents some historical material on
English Canadian and Quebec radicalism, as well as a collection of impres-
sions of student protest by scholars of the international movement. The Reid
and Reid book is an eclectic collection of analysis, theory, and cases of protest (including some high school events). There exists only the merest handful of published empirical studies of Canadian students. The Simpson and
Phillips article is one such, conducted at the University of Toronto. Quarter's
1972 book is also based on data collected on Toronto students, as is another
later article (see Quarter, 1974). Lehtiniemi's data are also drawn from
Ontario. In addition to these, we find also an empirical study by Geschwender, Rinehart, and George, conducted at the University of Western
Ontario (see Geschwender et al., 1974).

Distinguished Canadian comment of the Lipset-Shils-Flacks genre is
equally sparse. There are the studies by Bissell and Roussopoulos, noted
above. In addition, there is a little known piece by James Laxer (1969) in
which he discusses the Canadian left and its dependence upon American
sources, and analyses some of the confusions and incongruities which result.
Also of great value is an overview by Kenneth Westhues, published in a
collection of studies on social movements in contemporary Canada (Clark,
Grayson, and Grayson, 1975). In a field replete with complex analyses of
why the movement happened at all, Westhues presents a straightforward and
convincing account. Protest came about in part because of a discrepancy
between what students expected of the university and what they got, particularly at the multiversities. Universities expanded dramatically during the
early 1960s, which altered the character and quality of the education they
dispensed. But the students who arrived in their hordes were expecting the
kind of education their parents had received, or which was portrayed in the
contemporary media. Expecting therefore a great deal of personal attention,
students were appalled by the demeaning rituals of mass registration and

mass attendance at classes (Westhues, 1975: 402–6). These factors made youth easily mobilized, aided by the contingent structural conditions. Ignition of protest of course depended upon the specific causes and events as they unfolded. Which individuals took fire depended upon their personal characteristics.

Having paid respects to the broader literature, we can now turn to those studies which are more directly relevant: empirical studies of the personal characteristics of students. This is in itself a vast literature, with a long history. Some of the earlier work is clearly superior to more current contributions, just as Deutscher found in studies of prejudice (Deutscher, 1969). One example is a short research report by Krout and Stagner published in 1939. Called 'Personality Development in Radicals,' it avoided the worst excesses of studies conducted thirty years later, which attributed radicals' views to their superior mental health and conservative ideology to deep-seated personality defects. It is interesting to note that the preoccupations of the 1930s were attitudes toward breast-feeding and bowel movements, rather than premarital sex, drug use, and 'openness.' The Bennington study (see Newcomb, 1958) is perhaps the most familiar of the pre-1960s studies of student attitudes toward society and politics. It has probably never been matched for quality.

In fact, it is difficult to be too hard on the literature flowing out of the 1960s movement. Kenneth Keniston, a long-time scholar of alienated students and student activists (see Keniston, 1960, 1968: Keniston and Lerner, 1971), has characterized empirical research on student activism as a 'widening puddle.' His image is chosen to contrast with the conventional view of scientific research where early work forms a base upon which later findings build. He is well qualified to make the judgment: he has located and abstracted research on activism since the Second World War, turning up more than 300 data-based articles and books, both published and unpublished (Keniston et al. 1973). The comparability of any two of these studies, he says, is usually very tenuous. There is no steady trend of improvement in either methods or theoretical focus.

The most obvious cause of the lack of comparability of studies is the wide range of research criteria used to identify 'activists' and 'protest.' Activity indicators vary from letter-writing and petition-signing through to sitting-in and participating in violent protests culminating in arrest. The foci of these acts range from restrictive dormitory regulations of the institution, through racial and war policies, to practices of the polity and society. Whether dealing with opinionation or behaviour, few researchers specify whether their criteria select only anti-systemic stances and strategies, or whether these criteria also locate within-system activists. Therefore truly revolutionary protestors have been confounded with within-system activists.

Indeed, much of the research actually omits behavioural indicators, dealing solely with attitude. But still, findings are presented as pertaining to 'activists.' Attitudinal criteria have been as wide-ranging as the acts that qualify students as protestors. Many have dealt with student attitudes toward marijuana, or sexual mores, ignoring the rest of the broad ideology which, as summarized somewhat unsympathetically by Westhues, amounted to 'a rejection of industrial capitalist social orders, of "establishments" of whatever kind, of the cult of consumer goods, and of the quest for upward mobility. The ideology promised instead a new alienation-free society, to be accomplished through the democratization of universities, an end to racism and the Vietnam War, a return to nature, and through "turning on" to the world of psychedelic drugs' (1975: 389).

Others closer to the centre of the movement and the Port Huron Statement, Tom Hayden and Bettina Aptheker for example, have also told us repeatedly that the overriding goal of the student movement is full citizenship for students in every aspect of university procedure (see Shoben et al., 1970; Sampson, 1967). The fact that students wanted to take over university governments was therefore staring researchers in the face. It inspired a good deal of faculty hysteria, and a good deal of comment by journalistic-type commentators. Still, only a handful of researchers took such a definition as the dependent variable when investigating correlates of attitudinal affect for student power.

Despite the non-comparability of the dependent variable, a very few studies have been accepted as comprising 'the literature.' Consensual magic has operated so that a handful of the early studies (roughly 1964 to 1968) are repeatedly paid homage. Probably the most famous studies, done on prestigious American schools but not markedly more sound methodologically than many others, are those of Block, Haan, and Smith; Braungart; Flacks, and later Flacks and Mankoff; Peterson; Solomon and Fishman; Somers; Watts and Whittaker; and Westby and Braungart. Such studies of the role of individual differences developed a theme of the student activist as uniquely privileged in both personal and background resources. Then about 1968 it was deduced that the base of the student movement had itself broadened and changed (Dunlap, 1970; Mankoff and Flacks, 1971) and the activist student could no longer be distinguished from his fellows by his resources. 'The literature,' though valid for the past, had apparently been rendered irrelevant to the present by social fiat. During this same 'middle period' in activism research – 1969 to 1971 – Kerpelman was, unfortunately, almost completely ignored. Kerpelman (1969) included in-system activity indicators (in addition to radical or protest indicators) in his research, and controlled for direction of ideology in relating activity to independent variables. He was able to show that it was activity per se, whether radical or conservative, that correlated with characteristics hitherto thought to identify only left activists. But the main trend of activism research was not to be deterred by any distinction so elementary and so sensible. The focal question has continued to be whether or not 'student activists' are distinguishable from their peers by resources of talent, psychological functioning, and advantage vis-à-vis ascribed position in the social structure. Many studies explain findings of no differences by recourse to the fact that data are drawn from 'non-quality' institutions. By so doing, their findings add to the 'accepted wisdom' in the area. That is to say, the process of broadening the student movement's base is accepted and more or less charted across types of institutions. 'Evidence' at the psychological level is interpreted by recourse to variables of another level, about which there is no evidence. Certainly the accuracy of the early study findings is seldom seriously challenged.

In summary, therefore, research on student activism is characterized by non-comparability of studies, a lack of definition of the criteria of membership in the activist group when 'known groups' are selected for research, a general lack of distinction between opinions and activity let alone provision of designs to enable control of one or the other, and a lack of distinction in independent variables between psychological and sociological factors. There is also a heavy dependence on purely bivariate analysis. Most harmful of all, there is a complete disregard for elementary sampling rules. Keniston calls activism research 'firehouse' research, because the researchers have raced out to capture the flavour of protest at a moment's notice. Research has been a search for *any* characteristics which might differentiate the local known protestors or activists from the unexamined group of 'other students.'

Although it goes a long way, the decision to study 'known groups' does not do away with all sampling concerns. In almost all activity studies, the activist is selected because of *one* criterion act – signing an anti-war petition, being arrested in the Free Speech Movement sit-ins, peace marching, etc. – which is assumed to reflect an indubitable commitment. There is almost never a recognition that the criterion act is itself merely a sample of action possibilities, perhaps tangentially relevant to the verbal focus of discussion, 'student power,' to which findings are related. Control groups are more often suspect than not: introductory sociology classes are a favourite.

Controls are even sometimes robbed of their like-criterion-group members when they have been chosen randomly, or matched according to a few criteria like faculty and sex. Seemingly innocuous control groups which can be charged with having contrast-enhancing characteristics are sometimes chosen, as when members of a campus hobby club become the comparison group for highly political known groups. Questionnaire completion rates for the 'relevant' populations are often as low as 44 per cent, even in studies as fine as that of Smith, Haan, and Block. Sample numbers are therefore often very small. This problem is magnified when proportions and percentages are reported throughout, giving a spurious weightiness to 'one-quarter of right-wing students' as opposed to 'two out of eight right-wing students.'

Lipset (1973) is the most vigorous critic of the lack of distinction between psychological and sociological factors: his example is the fact that early studies find activists to be disproportionately Jewish *and* to have disproportionately undergone a warm, highly interactive, and intellectually stimulating upbringing. Lipset says that we must work *within* cultural and socio-economic contexts to locate processes of action-enabling socialization (p. 97). This general lack of controls in analysis strategies has meant that we have gained almost no insight into how sociological statuses translate into personal qualities. Where a few researchers have undertaken multivariate analyses, results have indicated that the early emphasis on socialization characteristics needed qualification.[2]

Even when the most flawed studies are screened out, a considerable body of work remains. Findings from relevant North American studies are therefore summarized below, in tabular form. A study is included if it is of a 'known group' (even so general a 'known group' as a class of sociology students) or of some approximation to a representative sample of a student body,[3] if the activity or attitudinal criterion which serves as the independent variable is operationally defined, and if the independent variables have been used elsewhere in approximately the same guise. In these tables, 'activist' means left activist only, unless it is otherwise specified. Some unpublished studies clearly deserved citation. In such cases, I have relied upon Keniston's abstract for the direction of the finding. These are of course noted as unpublished in the bibliography. Although the literature has been criticized, the studies cited here are quite similar in quality to the most famous early studies. A review of independent variables will therefore establish points of consensus where they exist. Independent variables are divided into three main groups: (1) family background variables, (2) socialization variables, and (3) the student's own characteristics. We shall touch on each in turn.

FAMILY BACKGROUND OR ATTRIBUTED CHARACTERISTICS

See table 5.1. It would appear that there is little consensus on the effect of the major background variables. One exception is findings about the mother. Where she is highly educated, and/or holds a high-status occupation, results indicate that the family background is associated with left activism. Another exception is parental religion. Families which are Jewish or which do not take any conventional religion seriously would also appear to prompt activism.

Findings for the other status variables are so mixed that it would appear that we simply do not know about their effects on activity. Perhaps we do know that low income and grade-school education of the father are not strong advantages but we might have guessed this. Also, it is probably true that being female is not a predictor of political activity.

Variables which do relate consistently to behavioural activism are those describing an interesting quality of 'advantage': the mother who brings additional resources of stimulation and knowledge into the home, and a religion which is connected with political liberalism in the case of Jews. One expects that the non-religiousness of non-Jewish activist parents indicates that the family has been moving away from tradition-oriented modes of thought for at least the parental generation. Protest activity, therefore, would not conflict with the home moral-political atmosphere.

SOCIALIZATION CHARACTERISTICS IN THE LITERATURE

See table 5.2. The child-rearing practices of parents of student activists have not been so widely investigated as comment would lead one to believe. The conclusions about the 'family climate' which has spurred activism have most often been inferred from objective family status variables like parental education and income.[4] Commentators have assumed, perhaps correctly, that upper-middle-class liberals have a distinctive method of rearing children. Few studies employ multivariate techniques that make it possible to control effects of social-structural variables. Those that do – Braungart (1971b), L.E. Thomas (1971), and Aron (1974) – find that socialization variables are not independently strong predictors of activism.

Socialization characteristics for which findings are reported include: birth order of the student; various indicators of permissiveness, warmth or closeness to parents, and methods of punishment; and conflict, either parent-parent or parent-child (it is not always obvious which is being reported).

TABLE 5.1
Attributed characteristics in empirical activism studies

Variable	Criterion	Study and finding
Father's occupation	Activity: differences found	A. Astin (1968), H. Astin (1970), Flacks (1967), Gergen and Kenneth (1971), Smith, Haan, and Block (1970), Watts and Whittaker (1966), Weissberg (1968): high-status occupations for activists' fathers, low or farm occupations for non-activists' fathers
	Opinion: differences found	Fenton and Gleason (1969): blue collar fathers for student power supporters. Somers (1965): professional fathers for Free Speech Movement (FSM) supporters
	Activity: no differences	Cowdry et al. (1970), Dunlap (1970), Kornberg and Brehm (1970), Lewis and Kraut (1972), Wood (1971)
	Opinion: no differences	Kornberg and Brehm (1970), Lewis and Kraut (1972), Sutherland (1969), Turner (1972)
Mother's occupation	Activity: differences found	A. Astin (1968), Flacks (1967): activists' mothers have high-status occupations. Donovan and Shaevitz (1970): activists' mothers employed (with girls sample). Farley (1968): activists' mothers employed (for men only). Weissberg (1968): activists' mothers employed. Wood (1971): activists' mothers in people-oriented occupations
	Opinion: no differences	Turner (1972)
Father's (or 'parental') education	Activity: differences found	Flacks (1967), Gergen and Kenneth (1971), Mankoff and Flacks (1971), Smith, Haan, and Block (1970), Watts and Whittaker (1966), Watts, Lynch, and Whittaker (1969), Weissberg (1968), Wood (1971): activists' fathers or parents of high education attainment
	Activity: no differences found on father's education	Dunlap (1970), Lewis and Kraut (1972), Tygart and Holt (1971)

	Opinion: no differences found on father's education	Lewis and Kraut (1972), Meier and Orzen (1971), Sutherland (1969), Turner (1972)
Mother's education	Activity: differences found	Dunlap (1970), Flacks (1967), Tygart and Holt (1971), Wood (1971): activists' mothers high education status
	Opinion: differences found	Everson (1970): attitude militants' mothers high education. Somers (1965): FSM supporter's mothers high education
	Opinion: no differences found	Turner (1972)
Parental income	Activity: differences found	Allerbeck (1972), H. Astin (1969), Aron (1974), Flacks (1967), Gergen and Kenneth (1971): activists' parents of high income
	Opinion: differences found	Henry (1971): liberal opinion holders' parents of high income
	Activity: no differences found	Auger et al. (1969), Baird (1970), Clarke and Egan (1971), Dunlap (1970), Friedman et al. (1972), J. Goodman (1968), Tygart and Holt (1971), Wood (1971). The Baird finding is for 60 institutions, two studies conducted in 1964, 1965
	Opinion: no differences found	Somers (1965), Surgeon (1969), Sutherland (1969)
	Activity	Simpson and Phillips (1976): higher family income students favoured strike (sample of sociology students)
Parental social class	Activity: differences found	Braungart (1971b): conservative activism and low social class (Young Americans for Freedom). Westby and Braungart (1966): left activists from upper middle class, right activists from lower middle or working class

TABLE 5.1 (continued)

Variable	Criterion	Study and finding
Parental religious preference	Activity: differences found	H. Astin (1971), Clarke and Egan (1971), Gamson et al. (1967), Gergen and Kenneth (1971), Dunlap (1970), Flacks (1967), Mankoff and Flacks (1971): activists of Jewish background. Auger et al. (1969), Clarke and Egan (1971), Doress (1968), Dunlap (1970), Gergen and Kenneth (1971), J. Goodman (1968), Mankoff and Flacks (1971): activists' parents disproportionately non-religious. Braungart (1971b): right activists high religious status
	Opinion: differences found	Everson (1970): protest supporters of Jewish origin. Gales (1966): FSM supporters disproportionately Jewish, or non-religious. Meier and Orzen (1971): females favouring 'legitimate activism' come from Protestant families
	Activity: no differences found	Aron (1974): activism not related to secular background in multivariate analysis
Ethnicity	Activity: differences found	Braungart (1971a): SDS members low-status. Westby and Braungart (1966): right activists from British and North European backgrounds
	Opinion: differences found	Flacks (1967), Kahn and Bowers (1970): disproportionate southern and eastern European origins of left students
	Activity: no differences found	Tessler (1970)
Gender	Activity: differences found	H. Astin (1969), Blackstone et al. (1970), Clarke and Egan (1971), Geschwender et al. (1974), Kornberg and Brehm (1970): males more active
	Opinion: differences found	Everson (1970), Fenton and Gleason (1969), Lehtiniemi (1972), Sutherland (1969): women more radical than men. Kornberg and Brehm (1970): males support sit-in

Activity: no differences found	Baird 60-institution (1970), Auger et al. (1969), Braungart (1974), Gold et al. (1971), Wood (1971), Smith, Haan, and Block (1970): no differences on left activists, but dissenters predominantly male, 'constructivists' predominantly female
Opinion: no differences found	Gold et al. (1971), Meier and Orzen (1971)
Activity	Simpson and Phillips (1976): male students favour strike (sample of sociology students)

TABLE 5.2
Socialization characteristics in empirical activism studies

Variable	Criterion	Study and finding
Birth order (first or only child)	Activity: differences found	Paulus (1967), Solomon and Fishman (1964): activists and demonstrators disproportionately eldest child
	Activity: no differences found	Lewis and Kraut (1972): self-reported high-school activity
Permissiveness	Activity: differences found	Flacks (1967): positive definition of permissiveness; activists' parents supportive, firm but not severe. Block, Haan, and Smith (1969): negative definition of permissiveness (absence of control); dissenters' (alienated) parents were permissive, activists' parents firm
	Activity: no differences found	Aron (1974), J. Goodman (1968), Lewis and Kraut (1972), L.E. Thomas (1971): applied to right and left activists. Blume (1972): liberal and conservative activists (Young Democrat and Republican Club presidents)
Family warmth 'Closeness'	Activity: differences found	Braungart (1971a), Donovan and Shaevitz (1970): radicals characterize both parents negatively. Gurin (1971), Spreitzer and Snyder (1971): radicals 'less close' to parents. Jansen et al. (1968): liberal activists report more parental displeasure than conservative leaders. Smith, Haan, and Block (1970): left activists (women and dissenters report more flawed parental relationships than other students.) Cowdry et al. (1970): when opposition to Viet Nam war controlled for parents, students' closeness and similarity to father predicted opinion-consistent action. Doress (1968), Jensen et al. (1968), Lewis and Kraut (1972): activists less influenced by parental views. J. Goodman (1968), Keniston (1967): Goodman's stable activists closer to mother than to father, once-only activists most attached to mother of any group; Keniston's 'alienated' radical most attached to mother
	Opinion: differences found	Fenton and Gleason (1969), Surgeon (1969): student power supporters, leftists distant from parental influence

Discipline intensity, type	Activity: differences found	Block et al. (1969): activists' parents used isolation, withdrawal of privileges, low on obedience demands, physical punishment; conventionalists more often physically punished (but recall parents more fondly)
Family conflict, interaction	Activity: differences found	Braungart (1971a): conservative families harmonious. Braungart (1971b): SDS parents' marriages unhappy. Doress (1968): non-activist students' families less conflictual. Freeman (1969): male demonstrators report intense political discussion in home (criterion self-defined). Katz et al. (1968), Lewis and Kraut (1972), Westby and Braungart (1966): activists report more strife between parents. Lehtiniemi (1972): student decision-makers more active in protests (sample of sociology students)
	Opinion: differences found	Smith, Haan, and Block (1970): family conflict associated with left ideology; mother-conflict moderately associated with left beliefs (activist and dissenter types)
Division of parental authority	Activity: differences found	Braungart (1971b): non-democratic family structure associated with conservatism. Flacks (1967), Westby and Braungart (1966): power shared

'Permissiveness' is used to denote a variety of ideas. Among them are an *absence* of disciplinary structure within the family, or a disciplinary structure characterized by rational flexibility rather than by rules. The variable 'democratic family structure' is also fairly generally discussed, and can also mean non-authoritarian parents, joint decision-making between parents, or parent-child consultation. And so on. In other words, the variable titles should be taken *cum grano salis*.

Researchers of student activism base their expectations about family dynamics on the general socialization literature. These can be reviewed fairly briefly for each general topic.

Altus (1966) notes that Galton was the first data-collector on sibling rank, finding that eminent men are disproportionately first-born. Since then, research tends to report first-borns as disproportionately possessing success-producing characteristics. An exception is the suggestion that emotional development of first-borns may be inferior (e.g., Douglas, 1964; Schachter, 1963; Macfarlane et al., 1954).

Explanations for the advantage seemingly conferred by birth primacy focus upon the idea that the first child enjoys more interaction with parents (Bossard and Boll, 1956a; Clausen, 1966; Sampson, 1965). McArthur (1956) found first-born children to be conscientious, studious, and serious, and to aim at adult-approved activities. Complementarily, McCandless (1969) found first-borns to be more likely to volunteer to take part in experiments or other volunteer activities, and to be more 'affiliative' – to have their behaviour guided by a need to find love. Schachter (1963) also found first-borns to be more driven by affiliative needs. Hence, we might expect that the first-born will be more oriented to political concerns than later-born children, as an appropriately 'adult' sphere of interest, and be ready to join groups and work in concert with others.

With regard to characteristics which might increase the likelihood of development of a coherent political ideology, Sears, Maccoby, and Levin (1957) found greater 'conscience' development in first-borns. Parents set more bounds for the first-born's behaviour, punishment is more likely to follow and more likely to be related to misdemeanours, and the father is more involved. The 'just' connection between fault and punishment might encourage the child to see the world as rational and organized. The superior 'conscience' development of first-born children may be particularly relevant to student politics as distinct from politics in general, for it can be argued that student politics is notably a 'moral' politics, dealing in issues of racial discrimination, misused power in Vietnam, freedom of speech and restrictions of freedom of speech, and the unfairness of either regulation or administrative over-response to their breaking. Economic issues are raised, but mainly to cry out against the unfairness of privilege.

An aptitude for information processing might also help develop political ideas. First-borns, whether or not superior in intelligence, are more successful academically. See Clausen (1966), Schachter (1963), Social Science Research Council Work Group (1965), and Douglas (1964).

Even as judged by their siblings and playmates, first-born children exhibit a sense of mastery; as cited by McCandless (1969), Sutton-Smith and Rosenberg (1966) found that older children are seen as bossy and demanding, and are likely to be bullies. In contrast, also judged by their peers, younger children whine, wheedle, sulk, and ask for help. As children are added to the family, older children 'help' rear siblings (Bossard and Boll, 1956a), and there is greater use of authoritarian behaviour control by parents, more physical discipline, fewer explanations of rules, and lower parental aspirations for the children (Elder and Bowerman, 1963). It is little wonder that younger children become supplicants.

With reference to family decision-making practices, the directions taken by the general socialization literature are also pertinent. For example, Strodtbeck (1958) found that the less the mother and son are dominated by the father, the greater the disposition of both to believe that the world can be rationally mastered. Straus (1962) reports that boys from families in which authority was shared were highest in school achievement, and were optimistic and satisfied with their parents. There is some evidence that an overpowering mother creates special difficulties: Kohn and Clausen (1956) report that maternal dominance is a frequent correlate of schizophrenia and other forms of psychological distress. Langton (1969) reports on a maternal-dominance variable in studies of American elementary school children, Caribbean secondary school children, and American secondary school children. Overall, maternal dominance appears to be related to authoritarianism, low efficacy, and low political interest in lower-class families (most strongly at the elementary level). Among the most highly educated families, however, maternal dominance increases male political involvement. Maternal dominance, in a study by Hess and Torney (1967), affected male childrens' interest and efficacy negatively, but did not affect female children. It may be that social class should be routinely controlled.

Indeed, the Flacks result associating permissiveness in upbringing with activism, which has dominated both the literature and popular commentary, may well be spurious. The association may come about as the result of a

TABLE 5.3
'Students' own' characteristics in empirical studies

Variable	Criterion	Study and finding
Faculty of enrolment	Activity: differences found	H. Astin (1970): protest activists in English, not in engineering; campus leaders in law, pre-professional programs. Auger et al. (1969): activists major in humanities, social sciences, architecture, social work, graduate studies; under-represented in business, engineering, library science. Braungart (1974), Clarke and Egan (1971), Doress (1968), Gamson et al. (1967), Gastwirth (1965), Gergen and Kenneth (1971), Gurin (1971), Kornberg and Brehm (1970), Solomon and Fishman (1964), Wood (1971): activists disproportionately drawn from arts and humanities, not from vocational schools. Blackstone and Roger (1971): London School of Economics dissenters from sociology. Paulus (1967): Activists from arts and letters, student government leaders from social sciences
	Opinion: differences found	Cohen and Watson (1971), Gales (1966), Jameson and Hessler (1970), Somers (1965), Sutherland (1969), Turner (1972): militant attitudes related to humanities, social sciences majors. Everson (1970), Fenton and Gleason (1969): graduate students and engineering students most likely to be opposed to student power goals. Feldman and Newcomb (1970): rank order faculties on liberalism index: social sciences, humanities, natural science and business, education, engineering, household economics, and agriculture. Henry (1971): students in academic courses more liberal scale than those in vocational courses. Mankoff (1970): social sciences and humanities enrolment predicts radical ideology. Meier and Orzen (1971): males in humanities favour 'legitimate activism.' Brown (1973): engineering students under-represented in strike support
Year of study	Activity: no differences	Braungart (1974), Clarke and Egan (1971), Wood (1971)
	Opinion: differences found	Fenton and Gleason (1969), Henry (1971), Jameson and Hessler (1970): attitudes favouring student power, student protest activity, and liberalism increase during course

Age	Activity: differences found	H. Astin (1969, 1970): student government leaders and anti-protestors oldest, protestors next, random student sample youngest. Blackstone and Roger (1971), Kornberg and Brehm (1970), Watts and Whittaker (1966): activists younger. Lyonns (1965): experienced demonstrators older than first-time demonstrators
	Opinion: differences found	Brown (1973): younger students support protest. Fenton and Gleason (1969): anti-student-power students older than those favouring student power. Henry (1971): age-liberalism association (control for year erases)
	Activity: no differences	Auger et al. (1969), Wood (1971)
Degree aspirations	Activity: differences found	H. Astin (1969): largest proportions of protestors aiming for doctorates
	Opinion: differences found	Henry (1971): liberalism increases with number of degrees aspired to
Career aspirations	Activity: differences found	A. Astin (1968), Baird (1970), Blackstone and Roger (1971), Cowdry et al. (1970), Doress (1968), Flacks (1967), Gamson et al. (1967), Gurin (1971), Katz (1968), Smith, Haan, and Block (1970), Solomon and Fishman (1964): activists' career goals tend to social service, people-oriented occupations, including teaching, not narrowly vocational; anti-groups, conservatives favour professions, government, business. Lewis and Kraut (1972), Solomon and Fishman (1964), Weissberg (1968): activists have most indefinite plans
		(Developmental Studies) Demerath et al. (1970): voter-registration volunteers became more vague with time spent on project. Fendrich and Tarleau (1973): ten years later, former activists found in academic, social service, creative occupations; student government members in business and professions, some in government and some few in academia
	Opinion: differences found	Everson (1970): militant students disproportionately plan to enter clergy, social work, and teaching. Meier and Orzen (1971); also Quarter (1972): students favouring 'legitimate activism' have uncertain career plans. Surgeon (1969): using self-characterization of political stance, found conservatives had vocational (government, business) goals in college, liberals had academic goals, leftists wanted self-discovery (future as artists, writer, or unknown)

TABLE 5.3 (continued)

Variable	Criterion	Study and finding
	Activity	Simpson and Phillips (1976): uncertain students favour strike as did graduate students (sample of sociology students)
Grade levels (academic achievement)	Activity: differences found	Gamson et al. (1967), Gastwirth (1965), Flacks (1967): activists more intellectual, higher grades. Paulus (1967): student government leaders lowest grades; activists, controls higher averages and higher verbal ability (self-reported grades)
	Opinion: differences found	Fenton and Gleason (1969): students favouring student power had low averages. Gales (1966), Henry (1971), Somers (1965), Surgeon (1969), Sutherland (1969): change-oriented students have higher grades. Meier and Orzen (1971): students favouring 'legitimate activism' have higher grades
	Activity: no differences found	Aron (1974), Baird (1970), Clarke and Egan (1971), Doress (1978), Weissberg (1968), Wood (1971): self-reported grades. Watts and Whittaker (1966): used registrar's data to compare Free Speech Movement arrestees with average
	Opinion: no differences found	Braungart (1974)
	Activity (with ideology controlled)	Kerpelman (1969): both right and left activists higher than non-activists on intelligence (test). Spreitzer and Snyder (1971): activism per se associated with high average grades
	Activity and Opinion	Rogers (1972): no reliable differences between intellectual abilities of different ideological preferences; political activists more capable on behaviour criterion
University careers	Activity: differences found	Demerath et al. (1970): voter registration volunteers disproportionately change majors. Gamson et al. (1967): once-only protestors drop in and out again, change majors. Keniston (1967): cites unpublished studies which show dropping out not associated with activism

Marital status	Opinion: differences found	Henry (1971): the sooner student plans marriage, the more conservative are his/her views
	Activity: no differences found	Clarke and Egan (1971), Smith, Haan, and Block (1970), Wood (1971)
Religious affiliation	Activity: differences found	A. Astin (1968), Blackstone and Roger (1971), Doress (1968), Lyonns (1965), Paulus (1967), Tessler (1970), Watts, Lynch and Whittaker (1969), Watts and Whittaker (1966), Weissberg (1968): activists are non-religious or not affiliated with an organized religion. Gurin (1971), Solomon and Fishman (1964): activists associated with no affiliation or with liberal (non-fundamentalist, non-Catholic) denominations. Westby and Braungart (1966): conservative activists attend church or synagogue regularly, SDS do not
	Opinion: differences found	Fenton and Gleason (1969), Jameson and Hessler (1970), Jansen et al. (1968), Kornberg and Brehm (1970): change-oriented students non-religious or unaffiliated. Jameson and Hessler (1970): conservatives members of established denominations, radicals not. Meier and Orzen (1971): students favouring 'legitimate activism' alienated from organized religion. Turner (1972): Jewish students favour protest, Protestants disapprove, and Catholics intermediate
	Activity: no differences found	Aron (1974), Baird (1970), Kornberg and Brehm (1970), Lewis and Kraut (1972)
	Opinion: no differences found	Lewis and Kraut (1972): used Christie's New Left Scale

relationship between political liberalism in parents and 'liberal' child-rearing practices. That is, left activists may be a subset of those raised as little 'liberals.'

In the middle class at least, psychological methods of punishment are thought to be superior to physical methods. Psychological punishment is usually taken to mean withdrawal of parental love (or the threat of it), or perhaps the withdrawal of privileges, as opposed to physical force. Martin Hoffman (1962) theorizes that use of physical punishments which openly confront the child with superior parental power develop a fear of authority in the child. Sears et al. (1957) found that withdrawal of love was associated with higher development of conscience (self-policing), but only if this technique were employed by a 'warm' mother. McCandless (1969) adds that the 'love' method can be too successful, immobilizing the child with guilt.[5]

Few conclusions seem justified on the basis of the narrower literature summarized in table 5.2. It appears that left activists are disproportionately first-born, and have been reared in highly interactive families not characterized by calm or harmony. Conservative activists seem to recall childhood and parents with more warmth than do left activists.

ACTIVISTS' OWN CHARACTERISTICS

The final set of variables to be discussed are those which describe the student himself at the time of study, and tell us something of his planned future. These variables include faculty of enrolment, year at university and age, number of degrees aspired to and career plans on graduating, academic success in terms of grades, and, finally, marital status and religious status (see table 5.3).

Conflicting results are noted for age, grades, year of study, and marital status. Conflicts across studies with regard to age of activists may be caused by characteristics of the institutions: i.e., the average age of the student body will vary across institutions according to the proportionate enrolment of graduate students.

Student reports of grades are almost invariably used. Kirk and Sereda (1969) have studied the accuracy of these self-reports. Slightly more than 20 per cent of students in their University of California sample took considerable liberties, 43 per cent made precise reports, and the remainder took a small percentage leeway if it made up the difference to a higher letter grade. The authors found that tendency to inflate grades was associated with an intellectual, aesthetic, complex, and autonomous thinking origin. Such characteristics are often associated with activism (see, for example, Hampden-Turner, 1970).

In summary, it would seem that student activists are found to be most frequently enrolled in the humanities and social science faculties, to be vaguely oriented toward social service and intellectual occupations, and to be lacking in religious commitment. It can be noted that in 1969–70 maintaining a religious commitment was in itself a conservative choice. Yankelovich (1972) reports from a large national random sample in the United States that only 35 per cent of students polled believed that belonging to an organized religion was 'important' in life. The figure for a similar opinion question in this study is 34 per cent agreement.

A believable, if minimal, core portrait of the activist has now been distilled from pertinent empirical research. The following chapters accomplish two purposes. First, they investigate whether the analytical aggregates defined in this work – the types – resemble the known groups of student activists as described in this literature. Success will support the utility of the analysis strategy of working from extremes of attitudinal strength and consistency. The second purpose is to isolate personal characteristics and conditions that can be said to increase the likelihood that the individual will participate in public affairs.

6

Identifying the types:
parental characteristics

Empirical studies of student activism have centred on discovering adjectives to modify 'student activist.' Researchers have tried to identify the antecedents to activism in family background and socialization experiences, and in the psychological and maturational characteristics of the individual activists.

One main purpose of this chapter is to duplicate this endeavour for the background characteristics of our stipulated types. Can one draw qualitatively different portraits of the four types? Will the picture that emerges for the active radicals of this study resemble that for activists described elsewhere? But such description is not the only goal. The types – acting radicals and conservatives and passive radicals and conservatives – are specified using characteristics of activity and opinion. We can therefore search for factors which modulate the quantity of 'activity output' within opinion-ideology groups. We can also look for patterns of attributes which distinguish between the types in terms of their beliefs – that is, which distinguish between conservative and radical groups.

In broad terms, it is expected that the student activists will be seen to be acting from a basis of values and expectations for conduct that have been transmitted to them in the home. Because we have no direct data on parental values, we must impute these values from the shorthand of objective descriptions of their places and roles in society. Such guesswork is, however, well documented in the broad political science literature that captures the social and background antecedents of partisanship. The conservative actor is expected to emerge from a 'traditional' family background. The 'traditional' family is thought of as one where the males alone exhibit competencies outside the home. Women perform supportive, auxiliary, and mothering activities. The father's earning power is sufficient for the comfort of the family. Radical activists are expected to emerge from 'modern-liberal' households.

In such homes, the family is making a conscious effort to adjust to the society-wide changes taking place in the last half of the twentieth century – indeed, to anticipate some of these changes. Many of these changes involve encouraging women to be active outside the home. In both kinds of families, the children internalize attitudes that approve of the family's use of its opportunities. In both kinds of families, high status is an important activity-enabling factor. First, it gives confidence. Second, the associated advantages of high status facilitate the development of attitudinal consistency, which in turn is important to action. (For independent evidence that there are class differences in the degree to which adolescents' attitudes are structured, see Berg and Mussen [1976].)

It is important to emphasize that we should not expect to find gross status differences between types, however. If one were working with a sample drawn from the mass population, one might expect to find substantial income and occupational discrepancies between members of one or another political partisan group. But a sample of university students is disproportionately drawn from the upper strata. That is, on average, the university-attending individual comes from a fairly well-to-do background. The average income of a university student's family is dramatically higher than for the average family in the city. The fathers are overall disproportionately professionals, the parents highly educated and of 'Anglo' origin.[1] Instead of gross status differences, therefore, we are searching for patterns of characteristics which will suggest qualitative differences between subgroups of the higher socio-economic strata.

The parental social context is described here by status, religion and ethnicity, and locale of rearing. Specifically, students have supplied information on the following parental characteristics: both father's and mother's occupation, education, religious preference and ethnicity, family income, and location within Canada at time of the student's birth and rearing. As gender is also set at birth, it is treated in this chapter as well as in later chapters.

Following a short description of the way in which each of these background variables was measured, expectations for distinctions between the types are discussed. Results of bivariate cross-tabulation analyses are then reported. The procedure isolates factors that appear to be associated with increased activity, that is, that are true of one or the other of the active types but not of passive types. The impact of these likely activity-enhancing characteristics upon activity per se will then be assessed by separating radicals from conservatives, and examining the effect of background factors within ideology groups.[2] Regression analysis provides coefficients which assess the impact of individual independent variables, holding all other independent

TABLE 6.1
Mean activity scores of types

Type group	University political acts*	Non-university political acts	Social helping	Total
Passive conservatives	0.00	1.56	1.06	18
Active conservatives	2.39	3.11	2.17	71
Passive radicals	0.00	1.87	1.26	38
Active radicals	3.00	3.66	1.51	82
Not a type	0.89	2.01	1.35	750
Whole sample	0.99	2.14	1.35	959

* One of the criteria for membership in a types group. An individual must have a score of two to qualify for an 'active' group and a score of zero for a 'passive' group. See chapter 3.

variables constant. The activity to be explained is represented by three indices: the university political activities index, the non-university activities index, and the index of social-helping activities. Each serves in turn as the dependent variable. Table 6.1 shows the average score for each group on these activity indices. We now move to the independent variables.

ATTRIBUTED CHARACTERISTICS

Father's occupation was obtained by an open-ended question which asked the student for a specific description. Each occupation was assigned a unique code from among the 320 occupational titles accepted by the Canadian census. Using Bernard Blishen's scheme (1958), these titles were then subsumed into the categories (1) professional, (2) semi-professional, (3) owner-manager (large), (4) owner-manager (small), (5) white collar, (6) skilled worker, (7) semi-skilled worker, (8) unskilled worker, and (9) farmer or rancher. Blishen's view that the division is hierarchical is not at issue here, as the categories are used nominally. School teachers are included with the professionals, and semi-professional describes occupations like social worker, journalist, and the higher-ranking personnel in computing installations. For a record of other decisions, see appendix B.

Mother's occupation was obtained through two questions. First, it was necessary to know whether the mother had worked during the student's childhood (defined as the first fifteen years of life). A second question asked the student to write in a description of the mother's occupation. The father's occupational categories were too detailed, and were therefore collapsed into (1) professional and semi-professional, i.e., high-status occupations, (2) owner-managers, white collar and clericals, i.e., medium-status occupations, and (3) skilled and unskilled, i.e., low-status occupations.

Father's and mother's education were measured separately. The student checked one of ten categories ranging from no schooling to an advanced university degree. There was a separate category for trade or technical school, and for teaching certificates from one of the provincial 'normal' schools. The categories can be thought of as nominal, or the series can be used as a rough continuum for amount of educational attainment.

Ethnicity was assessed by four questions. These asked for country of birth of mother and father separately, and for the country from which most of the father's and mother's ancestors had come. Responses to each question were allocated to one of 24 discrete geographical categories. These categories were recoded to accord with popular gross status attributions: (1) Canada, (2) United States, Great Britain, and France, (3) a European nation which is neither a founding nation nor a Slav nation, and (4) Slav nations.

Income was referred to as 'parent's income.' Responses were rounded and coded in units of one thousand dollars.

Religious preference was obtained separately for mother and father, the student writing in the denomination. Responses were first coded in more than 40 individual categories. These were then recoded to (1) Anglo-Protestant or liberal Protestant and British-associated denominations such as Anglican, Presbyterian, Methodist, United Church, (2) European Protestant denominations such as Lutheran, Baptist, Moravian, Greek Orthodox, (3) evangelical Protestant denominations such as Pentecostal, Church of God, Jehovah's Witnesses, Assembly of God, (4) Roman and Greek Catholic churches, (5) Jewish, (6) other non-Christian faiths, and (7) no religious affiliation, atheist, agnostic.

'Rootedness' was assessed by two questions. One asked for the student's province of birth, and a second asked where the student had resided for the first fifteen years of life.

Gender was obtained by asking the student to check either male or female.

EXPECTATIONS FOR BACKGROUND CHARACTERISTICS

According to Skinner's behaviour theory, the more a form of behaviour meets with reinforcement, the more likely that it will be repeated in future. Of course an individual's behaviour consists of both verbal behaviour and other activity. Therefore one can expect that the more 'attentive' he is, and the more consistent or coherent the context is, the more likely it is that an individual will acquire one or another of the 'off-the-rack' social ideologies. In a sense, certain sentiments and activities have greater 'survival value' in the setting. (Just which sentiments and acts are pertinent within each social sub-setting is empirically contingent upon the particular history and its interpretations, and is not a matter for a priori deduction.) A great deal of research supports this view of ideology as learned in social settings,[3] and as learned most effectively where settings present fewest complexities for the individual. For example, Olsen (1962) took a sample of liberals and conservatives and assessed their consistency (attitude crystallization) on international relations, domestic politics, racial integration, moral problems, and religious beliefs. He found that people in status-ambiguous situations – such as never-marrieds over forty years of age – tend not to have acquired criterion ideologies (consistent attitudes). Similarly, DiPalma and McClosky (1970), discussing the correlates of social adaptation, note that almost any impediment to social interaction or communication reduces the probability that an individual will encounter and acquire mainstream norms. We shall assume that politics is peripheral to most people, and that students, being young, are doubly handicapped vis-à-vis political learning in that they do not have a store of adult experiences to draw upon. Hence it is hypothesized that the rare consistency in viewpoint, as well as increased activity, will be related to what we call 'patterns of consistency' in environment – membership in thoroughgoing 'traditional' or 'modern-liberal' families.

Specifically, it is predicted that activism among conservative students will be associated with factors which in a mutually reinforcing way describe membership in a small-'c' conservative economic elite. Students will come from high-status traditional families: fathers will have prestigious occupations, high income, and high education. Ethnic status and religious preference of both parents will be mainstream. The mother will have at least an average education, but will not work outside the home. Conservative activists will be mostly males. They will have been born and raised in Alberta.[4]

Radical activists will come from high-status families which are modern-liberal in orientation. Fathers will have high overall status, as predicted for conservatives. Mothers will be highly educated, but will be more likely to have an occupation, and that occupation will be of high status. Parents will be less church-oriented than parents of other types and, when affiliated, will adopt 'liberal' denominations. No predictions are made for ethnicity, but it is predicted that activists will be disproportionately likely to be well-rooted in Alberta. The reasoning is that it is easier to act within a familiar environment. Women from such backgrounds will be as active as males. Results of bivariate analysis follow.

TABLE 6.2
University political type by gender (percentages)

University political type	Male	Female	Total
Not a type	58.4	41.6	750
Passive conservatives	59.2	40.8	71
Active conservatives	77.8	22.2	18
Passive radicals	62.2	37.8	38
Active radicals	54.9	45.1	82
Total (%)	58.7	41.3	100.0

FINDINGS IN CROSS-TABULATION ANALYSIS

Gender

Gender is investigated first. Women are perhaps slightly over-represented in the active group of radicals, relative to their proportion of the total sample. See table 6.2. Passive conservatives are distributed as for the sample. Active conservatives appear to be disproportionately male, as expected. Passive radicals have a slight over-representation of males. But these are merely trends.

Parental occupation

A cross-tabulation of father's occupation by types reveals no differences between types aside from a trend toward over-representation on professional fathers and under-representation on farm fathers for the active radicals. Nor are there any differences between types and the group of students that did not qualify for opinion consistency.

We turn now to the mother's work history. Just over one-third of sample mothers worked during the first fifteen years of the student's life. Active conservatives are least likely to have had a working mother; more than two-thirds of their mothers have never worked outside the home. Comparisons are just less than 50 per cent for active radicals, 52 per cent for passive radicals, and 61 per cent home-centred mothers for passive conservatives. (The result is significant at the 0.01 level.) The variable appears to be more sensitive to the belief dimension than to activity levels, however.

Moving to occupations of mothers, it is found that a larger proportion of mothers of active radicals pursued a high-status occupation. Forty-seven per cent of mothers of active radicals were professionals and semi-professionals, in comparison to 40 per cent each for passive radicals and conservatives. Only one mother of an acting conservative was in this category. Differences between types, however, do not reach significance at the 0.05 level.

Parental education
No differences are found in the average educational attainment of the mother or father for each of the types (F test). A cross-tabulation reveals one trend: there is a tendency for active radicals to have more than their share of mothers with some amount of university education.

Parental income
There are no differences.

Ethnicity
A close examination of ethnic background of the four types, paying particular attention to the possible impact of parental and ancestral categories which might indicate discontinuities in acculturation, reveals no differences. The only matter of interest is that the small group of active conservatives is found to have 100 per cent Canadian-born mothers, whereas the average figure is 72 per cent (also the overall figure for Canadian-born fathers).

Rooted in Alberta
At the time of the survey the provincial Social Credit party was within a year of the end of its uninterrupted 35-year reign. This was a conservative party, and one might expect that long familial exposure to its norms would teach conservative political norms. One might also expect that long-term residence in the province would facilitate development of political views and enable activity *regardless* of the family's ideological direction, simply because less energy would be needed for mapping the political environment. Taking province of birth first, it is seen that there are only small fluctuations about the sample norm of 69 per cent of the student body having been born in Alberta. Seventy-eight per cent of the sample have spent the first fifteen years of their lives in the province. But if one layers the two place variables, it is found that only 51 per cent of the sample were both born and raised in the province. This is true of 57 per cent of active radicals, 61 per cent of passive radicals, 62 per cent of passive conservatives, and 67 per cent of active conservatives. Differences are not significant, and trends support both theoretical notions: long-time residence is associated with increased conservatism and increased likelihood of activity. Any impact of this variable would, of course, be mediated by the type of occupation held by the father, as occupational choice is associated with geographical mobility.

TABLE 6.3

Denominational affiliations of parents and of respondents (percentages)

Religious category*	Mothers	Fathers	Students
No religion	2.8	8.9	35.3
Anglo-Protestant	40.4	37.7	23.8
European Protestant	24.9	24.5	10.6
Evangelical Protestant	5.5	4.8	4.6
Catholic	24.2	21.4	17.9
Jewish	0.8	0.9	0.7
Other non-Christian	0.3	0.2	0.2

$N = 959$

* Category contents are: 0, no religious affiliation, atheist, agnostic, etc.; 1, Anglican, Presbyterian, United Church, etc., i.e. liberal Protestant and British denominations; 2, Baptist, Lutheran, Moravian, Greek Orthodox, etc., i.e. European Protestant denominations; 3, Pentecostal, Church of God, Jehovah's Witnesses, Assembly of God, etc., i.e. evangelical Protestant denominations; 4, Roman and Greek Catholic churches; 5, Jewish; 6, other non-Christian faiths. Where figures do not add to 100, the missing amount is due to missing data.

Religious affiliation

Affiliations of students, and of their mothers and fathers, are described in table 6.3. The proportion claiming 'no religion' increases quite dramatically across the one generation. Cross-tabulation of the parental religious preferences by type group are presented in tables 6.4 and 6.5. It would appear that European Protestant churches and evangelical denominations are over-represented in the parents of passive conservatives, Anglicans and Catholics appear to be slightly over-represented among active conservatives, Catholics are somewhat over-represented in the passive radicals group, and Anglicans are over-represented among parents (mothers) of active radicals. The finding is significant at the 0.03 level for both parents.

Summary for bivariate analysis

The results of cross-tabulation analysis have provided only partial support for the hypothesis that active types would have been socialized into ideology and activity by virtue of membership in clearly structured traditional or modern families. There were no differences between types on status via the father (which might have been expected given the higher overall status of a university sample). There were no differences on ethnic origin, beyond the finding

166 Patterns of belief and action

TABLE 6.4
Mother's religious affiliation* by type (percentages)

University political type	No relig.	Anglo- Prot.	Eur. Prot.	Evang. Prot.	Cath.	Total
Not a type	3.1	40.5	25.6	5.1	24.8	
Passive conservatives	0.0	38.2	32.4	14.7	14.7	
Active conservatives	0.0	44.4	5.6	11.1	38.9	
Passive radicals	2.7	37.8	21.6	2.7	35.1	
Active radicals	3.8	48.1	22.8	2.5	22.8	
Total	2.8	40.8	25.5	5.6	24.4	100.0

$N = 949$; $p = 0.03$
* Jewish category omitted because the number of individuals is too small.

TABLE 6.5
Father's religious affiliation* by type (percentages)

University political type	No relig.	Anglo- Prot.	Eur. Prot.	Evang. Prot.	Cath.	Total
Not a type	9.4	38.0	24.7	4.6	22.3	
Passive conservatives	4.3	37.7	36.2	11.6	10.1	
Active conservatives	11.1	44.4	5.6	5.6	33.3	
Passive radicals	10.8	37.8	18.9	2.7	29.7	
Active radicals	8.8	42.5	25.0	2.5	21.3	
Total	7.8	40.2	26.0	5.9	20.1	100.0

$N = 944$; $p = 0.03$
* Jewish category omitted because the number of individuals is too small.

that active conservatives tend to have all-Canadian parentage. There were mixed differences on the 'rootedness in Alberta' variable. But it did appear that more parents of active students were members of higher-status religious denominations than of passive students. Further, it appeared that there was some support for the hypothesis that the mother has a special role in creating (or exemplifying) the family ethos: mothers of radicals tended to be more likely to have maintained a higher-status occupation during the child-rearing years.

In attempting to establish a pattern of background characteristics which might distinguish between 'traditional' and 'modern' families, we have been interested in merely identifying variables which discriminate between types. While bivariate analysis is a useful preliminary tactic, multivariate analysis can test directly for which variables have the greatest impact upon the activity scores.[5] The problem of level of measurement for nominal variables can be met by forming dichotomous (dummy) variables according to whether or not the attribute is possessed. These background variables will be examined for their effect on each of the activity indices.

There are three basic questions for exploration. First, do different parental attributes affect activity depending upon the ideological stance of the student? Second, can we locate background factors which increase activity overall? Third, is prediction most efficient and more meaningful substantively within ideology groups and within the attitudinally consistent sample? In short, one can investigate whether different backgrounds exist for, and facilitate activity within, ideological groups,[6] *and* whether prediction is most efficient within samples chosen for extremes of opinion consistency.

ATTRIBUTED CHARACTERISTICS IN REGRESSION ANALYSIS

Parental income was retained as a continuous variable. The following dichotomous variables[7] were formed to describe parental attributes: male gender/not male gender, professional father/not professional father, farm father/not farm father, highly educated father/not highly educated father, working mother/not working mother, professional mother/not professional mother, highly educated mother/not highly educated mother, Canadian parents/not Canadian parents, one foreign-born parent/not one foreign-born parent, Alberta born and raised/not Alberta born and raised, secular father/not secular father, Anglo-Protestant mother/not Anglo-Protestant mother, Catholic mother/not Catholic mother.

We can now use stepwise multiple regression[8] to evaluate the impact of these selected variables on students' activity scores. Stepwise multiple regression selects the strongest (in terms of amount of variability accounted for) predictors of the dependent variable in turn. Tables 6.6, 6.7, and 6.8 present results for university activities, non-university activities, and the social-helping activities. Within each table, results for the two subsamples of the ideology types are presented first: a subsample of both radical types (the 38 passive radicals together with the 82 active radicals) and a subsample of both conservative types (the 18 active conservatives together with the 71 passive conservatives). We then move to factors most strongly predictive of activity for the subsample of all four types together and then to results for the undifferentiated sample. In these tables, the overall F assesses the likelihood that the solution for the entire table is significant, that is, whether or not the results could have been obtained through sampling error. The 'significance' of the individual coefficient is best assessed by comparing the size of the unstandardized B coefficient to the standard error of that coefficient. Where the standard error is more than half the size of the B coefficient, one cannot be sure that the sign attached to B, or the magnitude of B, is stable. The tables have been selected for presentation in the light of these two guidelines.

The difficulty of finding moderately graceful English for speaking of results leads one to talk of 'advantages' and 'disadvantages' for activity, and 'factors which facilitate activity.' One is of course justified only in pointing to effective predictors of activity.

Predicting university activities

Taking summed university political activities as the first dependent variable for discussion (table 6.6), we see that only one background attribute – the possession of a highly educated father – is unambiguously significant in the subsample of radical students. This one factor explains 6 per cent of the variance in summed university activities. The large standard errors of the other three factors makes assessment of their import chancy: however, the simple r and the B coefficient are similarly ranked in magnitude and are of the same sign. Although the effects of these variables are slight, effects are also consistent and persistent. Therefore, an interpretation might be as follows: were one wishing to predict political activity among a sample of left-opinionated young people using the variables so far considered, one could say that the possession of a highly educated father is a moderate advantage for activity. Having two Canadian-born parents (as opposed to having parents who have come from, perhaps, a quite dissimilar culture) and a professional mother are perhaps very slight advantages for activity, and having a farmer father and therefore a farm background oneself is a slight disadvantage for activity. The factors which emerge as aiding radical activism, then, describe a high-status or accomplished urban family.

Most important, it must be emphasized that these four factors are the only ones out of the entire group of parental attribute background factors that have a systematic and measurable effect on the summed university activities variable, that the contribution of all but father's education is under some cloud, and that all together account for only less than 12 per cent of the variance in university activities. That is, parental characteristics in total, as we have measured them, have only slight impact in determining the activity intensity in university of a politically radical student. The gender-neutral

TABLE 6.6
Parental attributes predicting university political activities:
dependent variable Summed University Political Activities Index

Independent variables	Cumulative R^2	Pearson's r	B	Std. error B
Radical University Ideology Students				
Highly educated father	0.068	0.261	0.872	0.350
Farm father	0.097	−0.209	−0.701	0.407
Canadian parents	0.114	0.163	0.405	0.303
Professional mother	0.122	0.083	0.357	0.372
Constant = 1.607 df = 4; 106 Overall F = 3.67 p = 0.008				
Conservative University Ideology Students				
Catholic mother	0.079	0.281	0.802	0.302
Anglo-Protestant mother	0.112	0.060	0.354	0.254
Highly educated mother	0.137	−0.114	−0.410	0.259
One foreign parent	0.157	−0.201	−0.442	0.324
Male gender	0.176	0.186	0.291	0.221
Constant = 0.174 df = 5; 73 Overall F = 3.14 p = 0.013				
Four Types				
Farm father	0.019	−0.139	−0.551	0.297
Canadian parents	0.029	0.108	0.322	0.230
Constant = 1.284 df = 2; 188 Overall F = 2.84 p = 0.061				
Whole Sample				
Highly educated father	0.023	0.150	0.436	0.095
Male gender	0.033	0.102	0.258	0.081
Working mother	0.041	0.077	0.282	0.112
Catholic mother	0.044	0.053	0.258	0.106
Anglo-Protestant mother	0.048	0.045	0.161	0.093
Constant = 0.567 df = 5; 857 Overall F = 8.68 p = 0.0001				

word 'student' is used advisedly, for it will be noted that the variable of sex was entered here and had no systematic impact: in regard to university political activities, being female is neither a significant disadvantage nor an advantage among those of radical views.

Let us now assess the impact of background variables upon university activities among the conservative subsample. Here one sees a few factors explaining a considerable portion of what is really a very small pool of variance due to the fact that slightly under one-quarter of those who belong to this ideology designation have in fact acted in university politics. (In comparison, there is a preponderance of active radicals among the radical ideologues, which means that there is more variation to be explained.)

Background factors which predict university political activity, given that the student is of conservative persuasion with regard to university-relevant matters, involve religion and mother's education. Within conservatives, it is an advantage for activity to have a Catholic background, rather than a Protestant denomination. It is disadvantageous to have one parent from a 'discontinuous' culture and to have a mother who is more highly educated than is the sample norm. These factors together explain almost 16 per cent of the variance in university activities. They sketch a traditional high-status household which may be more church-oriented than the norm. It is provocative that the influence of the mother for activity goes in the *opposite* direction for the radical students' group. For the radical or liberal student, an accomplished mother is a slight *advantage* for activity: for the conservative ideology student, a *disadvantage*. One might speculate that an over-educated mother might create challenges and inconsistencies in an otherwise father-ruled high-status home, causing some tensions in the student's conservative world view and impeding opinion-actualizing activity. Or perhaps she simply creates discontinuities in the pattern of socialization into ideally traditional values.

What happens to one's ability to predict activity intensity from background attributes if one removes the ideology restraints? There are really two ideology restraints to remove, of course, the first being the stipulation of substance of ideology – conservative or radical – and the second being the stipulation that the student belong to a types' group – that his opinions and actions in the context of university politics be interrelated and 'consistent.' Lifting the control for direction of affect decreases our ability to locate significant predictions. Only the factors of urban origin and Canadian parentage predict action, accounting for about 3 per cent of the variance in activity level. This is a considerable loss of predictive power. In analysis of the whole sample, many variables account for little variance – their individual contributions being, however, significant because of the increased sample size. The depressive effect of the accomplished mother on conservative activity is, however, cloaked. Male gender enters as an overall advantage for activity.

Predicting non-university activities
Moving to outside or non-university political activity, and assessing regression results for the subsample of radicals, one sees that possession of a highly educated father is again (table 6.7) the strongest parental-attribute advantage

TABLE 6.7
Parental attributes predicting summed non-university (outside) political activities:
dependent variable Summed Non-university Activity Index

Independent variables	Cumulative R^2	Pearson's r	B	Std. error B
Radical University Ideology Students				
Highly educated father	0.036	0.190	0.890	0.380
Alberta born and raised	0.057	−0.162	−0.442	0.325
Secular father	0.078	0.134	0.962	0.557
Working mother	0.096	0.074	0.561	0.382

Constant = 2.885   df = 4; 106   Overall F = 2.81 p = 0.029

Conservative University Ideology Students				
Male gender	0.072	0.268	0.761	0.311
One foreign parent	0.100	−0.170	−0.654	0.425

Constant = 1.49   df = 2; 76   Overall F = 4.22 p = 0.018

Four Types				
Highly educated father	0.021	0.146	0.616	0.280
Working mother	0.042	0.113	0.605	0.305
Alberta born and raised	0.052	−0.123	−0.350	0.248

Constant = 2.497   df = 3; 187   Overall F = 3.44 p = 0.018

Whole Sample				
Highly educated father	0.019	0.141	0.581	0.121
Male gender	0.032	0.106	0.338	0.104
Working mother	0.042	0.091	0.404	0.143
Canadian parents	0.050	−0.085	−0.284	0.104
Catholic mother	0.052	0.040	0.163	0.120

Constant = 1.862   df = 5; 857   Overall F = 9.46 p = 0.0001

for activity. Having a secular or non-religious father also encourages activity in the larger political sphere if one is a radical. A mother who worked regularly during the formative first fifteen years is also an advantage (although not significant) for activity. It would seem that, for radicals, the more 'modern' (or the less traditionally oriented) a student's family is, the more likely it is that he will become active in the usual political avenues.

For the conservatives' subsample, the non-university political activity score is significantly affected only by gender: among conservatives it is an advantage to outside political activity to be male. The gender factor alone explains almost 10 per cent of the variance in the dependent variable. Com-

TABLE 6.8
Parental attributes predicting summed social-helping activities:
dependent variable Summed Social-Helping Index

Independent variables	Cumulative R^2	Pearson's r	B	Std. error B
Radical University Ideology Students				
Highly educated father	0.052	0.228	0.235	0.356
Male gender	0.083	−0.155	−0.502	0.212
Secular father	0.106	−0.173	−0.606	0.359
Highly educated mother	0.123	−0.106	−0.738	0.315
Professional father	0.137	0.214	0.675	0.405
One foreign parent	0.152	−0.064	−0.446	0.310
Professional	0.167	−0.033	0.451	0.334

Constant = 1.750   df = 7; 103   Overall F = 2.94 p = 0.007

Conservative University Ideology Students				
Catholic mother	0.041	0.202	0.810	0.344
Canadian parents	0.078	0.199	0.362	0.254
Male gender	0.111	−0.175	−0.588	0.264
Parental income	0.133	0.155	0.019	0.011
Highly educated mother	0.157	−0.073	−0.555	0.315
Anglo-Protestant mother	0.182	0.029	0.420	0.284

Constant = 1.051   df = 6; 72   Overall F = 2.67 p = 0.021

Four Types				
Male gender	0.028	−0.167	−0.521	0.163
Professional father	0.048	0.131	0.489	0.202
Highly educated mother	0.071	−0.090	−0.545	0.193
Parental income	0.093	0.122	0.014	0.007
One foreign parent	0.113	−0.105	−0.477	0.234
Secular father	0.131	−0.140	−0.532	0.298
Catholic mother	0.142	0.122	0.283	0.191

Constant = 1.592   df = 7; 183   Overall F = 4.32 p = 0.0001

Whole Sample				
Male gender	0.022	0.147	−0.342	0.073
Secular father	0.038	−0.116	−0.487	0.127
Highly educated father	0.044	0.084	0.175	0.091
Catholic mother	0.048	0.072	0.178	0.085
Working mother	0.053	−0.062	−0.275	0.106
Farm father	0.058	−0.067	0.209	0.094
Professional mother	0.061	0.048	0.292	0.135
Highly educated mother	0.063	0.002	−0.154	0.106

Constant = 1.597   df = 8; 854   Overall F = 7.24 p = 0.0001

ing from a family in which the immigrant experience is recent appears to be a slight disadvantage for conservative activity.

When the ideology control is removed, the result resembles the picture for radicals, but somewhat less variance is accounted for.

Moving to the whole sample, we find that many effects, though statistically significant, become substantively confusing. Variance accounted for is again reduced. One can well see how aggregating groups in which variance is systematically distributed in opposite fashions produces this noncommittal result.

Predicting social-helping activities

Many of the same factors describe both the radical and conservative ideology student who is active in this broadly non-political genre of activity (table 6.8). Catholic religious background is a strong advantage, as it was for university political activity. Among conservatives, this type of activity belongs more to the females, as one would expect. And again, having a highly educated mother is a slight disadvantage. Two Canadian-born parents, as opposed to one or both parents immigrating to Canada from any other country, constitute an encouragement for activity.

For radicals, only one factor is positively associated with the social-helping activity score: a highly educated father. Male sex is a disadvantage, which again means that this kind of activity is the female's speciality, and having a secular father is a disadvantage. A working mother constitutes a disadvantage. Substantively, these factors suggest that among radicals a traditional church-oriented background will foster the 'constructivist' genre of activity.

Because the predictors work in the same direction for both groups in predicting social-helping activity, effects are still clear when the ideology control is removed. The social-helping actor is female, and comes from a traditional (non-secular) high-status family. Prediction is less powerful for the whole sample, but, substantively, results are very similar.

CONCLUSION

It appears that, for students of radical ideology, a 'modern' or non-traditional family background does in fact facilitate the political types of activity, as was anticipated. Among conservatives, both types of political activity as well as social-helping activities are fostered by a traditional father-centred and church-oriented family background: it is also a considerable advantage to be male (gender among radicals is an advantage only in the social-helping activities, and then 'femaleness' is the advantage). Peripherally, one may note that the effect of possession of *any* religious background among radicals is depressive of political activity: among conservatives it makes a difference which religion forms the background, a Catholic background being supportive of activity. A highly educated father is the most important advantage for political activity for radicals, and high education in the mother is also a slight advantage for activity. For conservative students, high education in the father does not enter as either advantage or disadvantage, and high education in the mother enters as a disadvantage. One might speculate that the prevailing liberal ethos in higher education tends to confuse and perhaps contaminate the conservative stance. Hence the highly educated mother would be in an ambiguous position and might be unable to socialize her child thoroughly in the traditional conservative mould. In a word, and not a very elucidating word, the conservative background that facilitates activity is a traditional background, the radical background that facilitates activity is distinguished by more 'modern' aspects such as a working mother and secular father. Flacks's (1967) conclusion that radical activists are acting on values inculcated by the family would seem to be at least equally true of both kinds of actor. Social-helping activity is clearly a different type of activity from political activities, and is facilitated by possession of the more traditional background, regardless of ideology stance.

Analysis within subsamples has given support for the view that background attributes will have different 'meaning' for activity within contrasting ideology groups. The control for direction of ideology is most productive for activity which is ideologically relevant, improving the predictive power of the independent variables. More important, it yields patterns of results which can be given substantive interpretation. Results of analysis with the whole sample are weak and difficult to interpret in comparison but are statistically significant because of the large sample size.

We move now to discuss factors of childhood socialization which facilitate activity. Later, the match between the 'objective' factors utilized in the present chapter and the more interpretive socialization variables can be examined.

7

Socialization characteristics of political types

We move now to the questions of whether the political types experienced qualitatively different upbringings, and to the possible effects of different child-rearing practices upon the propensity for action of the types.

The field of socialization research has been enormously prolific over the past twenty years. In general terms, socialization research considers the way in which society teaches its values and manners to succeeding generations. Childhood learning has been thought to be particularly important and durable because this experience is writ upon a blank slate. Renshon (1977) notes that this 'primacy principle' actually contains three related assumptions. These are that early childhood attitudes, values, and behaviour are 'fundamental,' that they will endure through life, and will structure the acquisition of subsequent orientations and behaviour.

Accordingly, political scientists have assumed that a careful examination of childhood experiences would reveal patterns of early learning which could be shown to transmit fairly detailed orientations toward the political and social systems from one generation to another. Indeed, it has often been further claimed that a study of socialization agencies and processes could explain both stability and change in the social system. With regard to stability, it was argued that certain 'habitual' patterns of child-rearing would set up habits of response in the child which he would generalize from the family situation to larger spheres of action. But systemic change would result should the family consciously alter its theories of child-rearing. This was thought to have happened with the middle-class adoption of the permissive Spock approach, popularly alleged to have empowered the radical university students of the sixties. Particular practices within particular family settings were thought to have created the set of psychological characteristics that distinguished the student activist. With this view, the study of family socialization is of pressing importance, because socialization would explain variation in the approach of the individual to the political system which could not be explained by class and status alone. That is, socialization processes would be found to mediate between parental attributes (which place rough boundaries on the individual's hopes and prospects) and later-acquired attitudes and orientations toward political and general life roles.

But an alternative view has more recently been formed. This view holds that socialization variables will be less powerful than factors that are contemporaneous with the activity. For example, Braungart (1971b), L.E. Thomas (1971), and Aron (1974) find that typical socialization variables are not very strong predictors of student activism. A cogent discussion of why this should be true is provided by Kavanagh (1972b). Kavanagh criticizes those 'highly speculative inferences' of socialization researchers which involve 'a large number of connecting links and unproven assumptions about transfers from childhood to political adulthood. The assumptions include: socialization → political beliefs → individual behavior → aggregate pattern of behavior. Moreover, there is also the assumption that these connections are made in predictable ways. As many other experiences and learning agencies intervene between childhood and adulthood, and as socialization is a developmental process, we can afford to be less deterministic in our view of childhood orientations' (1972b: 29). Kavanagh suggests, as does Brian Barry (1970), that it is a mistake to see political culture as exclusively the product of values and influences arising from outside the political system itself. 'This is implied in Almond and Verba's concentration on the family, school and workplace as casual factors, and political culture and behavior – e.g., sense of competence and efforts to influence the government – as dependent variables' (1972b: 35). Kavanagh further notes that there is a marked decline in the degree of political trust shown by children as they mature, and that studies of adults record cynicism and mistrust. Origins of some of this mistrust will be found in later unfavourable experiences of the political culture, he says, arguing that 'the performance of the system is vitally important in developing citizens' evaluations of it' (ibid.). Searing et al. (1973) present empirical data to support essentially the same argument.[1]

Even very basic truisms have come under attack. Gender differences in adoption of political roles have pretty generally been accepted as arising from early training into gender-appropriate roles.[2] But Anthony Orum et al. (1974) conclude that sex differences in political expression do not emerge in childhood. Such differences, they think, may or may not emerge as children grow to adulthood and are affected by situational and structural characteristics. Useful reviews of other trends in socialization research are presented by

DiRenzo (1977), L.W. Hoffman (1977), Niemi and Sobieszek (1977), Sears (1975), and Zigler and Seitz (1978).

In summary, mainstream socialization theory argued that childhood experiences importantly affect mature personality and political orientations. These aggregate to impinge on the structural characteristics of the political system. More recent theory has held that the importance of childhood learning for later political behaviour (and thus importance for the political system) is minimal. Sociological variables like class, and temporally recent experiences, will be far more important in their effect on politically relevant behaviour and attitudes. The task of the present chapter is to examine the relation of socialization characteristics to activity. Findings for socialization variables can later be evaluated in the context of findings regarding the effect of attributed characteristics (chapter 6) and findings for contemporaneous choices and characteristics of the individual (chapter 8).

The variables to be related to activity are firmly within the tradition of the socialization literature. The emphasis is on the perceived warmth of the childhood family, the family power structure, the intensity and type of discipline, parental conflict, and global judgments of sense of happiness and effectiveness within the childhood family. As well, we treat intensity of early religious training, the birth order of the respondent, and his or her recollection of whether there was an explicitly political content to family teaching. Most of these variables are vulnerable to the charge that they represent the student's reconstruction of reality. Brief descriptions of the variables follow.

Parental warmth and discipline were assessed by four questions. 'Warmth' of the childhood family is tapped by asking how 'close' the student recalls feeling to mother and father when a child (up to fifteen years of age). Intensity of discipline is assessed through the question: 'How strict were your mother and father with you when you were a child?' Type of punishment was obtained by inviting the respondent to check as many as were applicable of alternatives 'withdrawal of affection,' 'physical means,' 'withdrawal of privileges or material goods, allowances,' and 'never punished.'

Family power distribution was also obtained by a series of questions. Whether or not the family was a co-operative enterprise is assessed by asking: 'Who would you say made most of the decisions in your childhood family?' with response categories being 'mother,' 'father,' and 'mother and father together.' Amount of between-parent conflict is tapped in a question asking the respondent for a judgment of how often parents argued. Child power is assessed in a separate sequence. First was a question asking how much 'influence' the respondent

usually had on parents' decisions. Next came frequency of childhood complaint about the decisions that parents made. Following from this question
was: 'If you did complain, how much difference did it usually make in your
parents' decisions?' The first question of the child power sequence involves
a global judgment of the respondent's centrality or importance in the childhood family. The second indicates a feeling that one's viewpoints were
important, as well as a feeling of freedom to speak out. The third reveals a
sense of having been dealt with more or less seriously, as opposed to having
been consistently brushed to one side, or having been given an inflated view
of one's importance. Overall, the problem is whether or not any type disproportionately shows memories of the presence (or absence) of a co-operative
and interactive family that conferred importance on the child.

Overt political socialization was measured by one question which asked: 'How
often would you say your parents discussed politics and community affairs
when you were a child?' Response options were 'very often,' 'fairly often,'
'hardly ever,' and 'never.'

Childhood church-going is the intensity with which a family pursued its
denominational affiliation. A question asked for frequency of church attendance until age fifteen of the respondent, the mother, and the father.
Response options ranged from 'more than once per week' to 'never.'

Birth order of the respondent was obtained by asking the student to rank
himself or herself as first, second, third or later of children in the family.
'Only child' was also an option.

Global judgment of childhood happiness was represented by a question which
asked: 'How happy would you say your childhood was?' Options were 'very
happy,' 'fairly happy,' 'only a little happy,' and 'not happy at all.'

EXPECTATIONS FOR SOCIALIZATION VARIABLES

The overall expectation is the same as for the family background characteristics: a similar mechanism will be seen to be operating to increase activity of
both the conservatives and the radicals. This is what might be called a
coherent-supportive background, that is, an upbringing in which the social-
ideology 'messages' transmitted to the family through its various roles and
status are mutually reinforcing and even redundant. Such messages eventually create intra-familial 'understandings' of the environment. These learned
messages, being both clear and shared, provide a basis from which the indi-

vidual feels secure in acting. In a sense, the total structure of the family is in 'good synch' with the group of social institutions which are (contingently) transmitting mutually reinforcing beliefs and attitudes. This 'rationalized' structure of the family experience is thought to create the sense of security and power that enables later activity. Most important, therefore, it is expected that the family associated with later activity will show evidence of consistent structure: the active individual will recollect experiencing discipline, fairly intense interaction, and parental discussion. These variables will be more important for activity than those indicating warmth and harmony alone. That is, what parents do – how they act – will affect learning of co-operative and combative skills.

Moving to specific variables, it is therefore expected that both active types will recall more discipline than passive types. Conservative actors will recall childhood feelings of warmth and closeness to parents, while active radicals will have been endowed with a critical bent and the psychological freedom to apply it to parents: they will report negative parent-child relationships.

The distribution of power between parents, and between parents and child, is more problematic. Theory has held that attitudinal conservatism is created by father-centred and repressive backgrounds, whereas radicals are created by democratic family situations where power is shared. But the theory seems flawed. In the case of radicals, a family style is thought to affect both the content of beliefs and the activity style, and in the case of conservatives, it explains only the content of beliefs. The problem is, should a harsh upbringing not keep the conservative inactive, cowering in some psychological corner for the rest of his life? And for the radicals, how does the experience of power in childhood create specific liberal and humanitarian views? Indeed, as indicated earlier, some commentators on student power have argued that the experience of power in the childhood family directly created a generation of self-obsessed, petulant, ignorant would-be dictators. (See Friedman [1973] and especially Shils [1969] for unmatchable eloquence against the movement.) Therefore, it is thought that activists of both stamps should recall the parents as sharing power. The family in which one parent dominates will teach neither co-operative nor combative skills and hence will not be associated with activity.

Expectancies with regard to the type of punishment experienced are more straightforward. Anaclitic theory (Merelman, 1969: 759) suggests that psychological punishment in a warm family encourages the development of an 'internalized' moral sense, or conscience. A technique like withdrawing affection is said to encourage the child to think through the situation that has led to his punishment. Physical punishment merely suggests to him that the spanking is simple payment for the crime. The developed moral sense, in turn, increases likelihood that a political ideology will be formed, because the child has grown accustomed to reasoning in a complex and morally informed manner. Formation of coherent views is then associated with activity (Merelman, 1969: 759–60). Alternatively, the link from the mode of punishment to activity may be through self-esteem rather than through the developed conscience. Physical punishment in the middle-class family (in which non-ritualized physical contact is almost completely abandoned early in childhood) may be experienced as shocking, shaming, and violating. Decreased self-esteem is associated with passivity. Psychological punishment, in contrast, grants the child the status of adversary. Whatever the causal link, both theories suggest that active types will prove to have been punished by methods granting most equality or status to the child. These status-granting methods would be withdrawal of affection or of privileges, which may be the option involving least emotion: a kind of rational cost levied against transgression of family rules. Conversely, passive types will prove to have been disproportionately physically punished.

Both active types should recall more overt political socialization than their complementary passive types. In keeping with the hypothesis of the previous chapter, which said conservatives are from traditional families and radicals are reared in modern families, it is expected that active conservatives will have attended church more frequently than passive conservatives, and active radicals will prove to have had the most secular backgrounds of any of the types. Birth order of radicals will be disproportionately first or only child; there are no particular expectations for conservative actors. With regard to childhood happiness, it is thought that active conservatives will recall the most happy times, and that active radicals will be most critical.

FINDINGS IN CROSS-TABULATION ANALYSIS[3]

Parental warmth and discipline
In fact, it is passive radicals rather than active radicals who come closest to the conventional image of the dissident individual who has been permissively reared: passive radicals report a 'normal' (as sample figures) amount of warmth, and somewhat *less* discipline than other types. Active radicals report less warmth, and a normal amount of discipline. They have been disproportionately disciplined by psychological means, implying that parents have granted them more status in childhood.

Moving to conservative types, actors have experienced slightly less parental warmth than passives, a similar intensity of discipline, less physical punishment, and more psychological punishment.

Family power distributions
There are some interesting tendencies among the family-power variables. Passive conservatives tend to recall little or no parental conflict in the childhood home, one in which the father made most decisions, and they hardly ever complained as children – if they did, they felt it was to no effect. They felt unimportant overall. *Acting* conservatives, however, recall a fair amount of parental conflict in a family situation in which *both* parents made decisions. They felt influential in the family, but similarly to passive conservatives they hardly ever complained, and if they did, felt it was to no effect. Passive radicals perceived a fair amount of parental conflict, within families which were either co-operative or mother-centred, and they felt influential, complained fairly often, and to some effect. Active radicals report more parental conflict, were in families where decisions were taken jointly, and they felt fairly influential, complaining frequently and feeling these complaints made some impact. The summary, for ease of exposition, has exaggerated beyond legitimate inference.

Perhaps it is true that a truly interactive and democratic *parental* relationship, observed by the child, creates a personality with a talent for political activity. This appears more important than parental actions that seek to confer importance and status directly on the child (or which are identified by researchers as evidence of conferred importance). Passive conservatives felt themselves to be *least* powerful and considered as children, the acting conservatives *most* so. Yet they report *equal* parent-child consultation with actors showing more parent-parent consultation. This suggests that the relationship between consultation and conferred importance is not so straightforward as has been thought. Again the acting group of the radical ideologues have seen more parental conflict, other variables being more or less equal.

Overt political socialization
Both active types are more likely than either passive type to remember talking politics 'very often' in family situations. About one-fifth of active types remember political discussion 'very often' whereas less than 6 per cent of each of the passive types have such a memory.

Childhood church-going
True to expectation, active conservatives attended most often during childhood, followed by passive conservatives. Active radicals attended least often. Passive radicals fall between. Church-going may encourage activity among conservatives, providing an early grounding in ideologically continuous social involvement. It may *discourage* activity among radicals in so far as a

conventionally religious upbringing may indicate lack of family support for a radical ideology.

Birth order
Results confirm expectations: active radicals tend disproportionately to be first or only children. Active conservatives, however, tend disproportionately *not* to be first-born or only children. Perhaps the less traditional the family, the smaller the family is kept, and the more traditional the family, the larger the family becomes. But any selective 'empowering' of children for later activity through parental attentiveness to a first child would appear to be operating only within the radical ideology group.

Childhood happiness
The hypothesis about recollection of a happy childhood is also supported: active conservatives are more positive than passive conservatives or radical types, and active radicals recall childhood most dismally. It is probable that these memories are strongly coloured by the student's current ideology. Conservatives are popularly supposed to glorify parents and childhood, and are found to do so by other researchers. Radicals are thought to be capable of disengaged analysis and therefore are critical and fault-finding. But it is also possible that conservatives' parents have put more emphasis upon family life than have radicals' parents, resulting in an objectively more pleasant childhood for those of conservative ideology.

Summary
The analysis has indicated some tendencies for types to remember and evaluate their childhoods differently. It would seem that it is the passive radicals rather than the radical actors who have undergone the permissive and mother-centred upbringing similar to that of Keniston's alienated dissidents (1968). Similarly, it is passive rather than active conservatives who report a father-dominated and conflict-free home. The importance of these trends is, however, difficult to assess through bivariate analysis. Multiple regression analyses, as in the previous chapter, can isolate the more important of these factors in terms of their impact upon activity.

SOCIALIZATION VARIABLES IN REGRESSION ANALYSIS

Variables to be treated as dichotomous are: male gender/not male gender, first or only child/not first or only child, felt 'very close' to mother/did not feel 'very close' to mother, felt 'very close' to father/did not feel 'very close' to father, parents argued frequently/parents did not argue very frequently, father dominated family decision-making/father did not dominate family decision-making, was psychologically punished/was not psychologically punished. Retained in *continuous* form are: rate of church-going as a child (infrequent coded high), recollections of childhood happiness (negative coded high), mother strict (negative high), father strict (negative high), childhood complaining frequency (infrequent direction coded high), frequency of family political discussion (infrequent discussions coded high).

We now move to regression results for the four groups of interest, that is, the subsample of conservatives, the subsample of radicals, the subsample that contains all four university political types, and the entire sample.

Questions are: (1) whether the socialization factors at hand affect activity differently if the ideological stance is different, (2) whether some of the same factors that increase activity within an ideological stance also have an impact upon activity intensity in the whole sample,[4] and (3) whether predictive ability has been improved by selecting the opinion-consistent students of the types' sample and by controlling for ideology. The dependent variables are once more the interval-level activity scores for university political activity, outside political activity, and social-helping activity. Results are presented for each of these indices in turn in tables 7.1, 7.2, and 7.3, reporting analyses for each sample of interest.

Predicting university activities
Let us begin with the effect of socialization factors upon university political activities among the radical students (see table 7.1). Only two variables have a sure impact upon the activity score (size of the standard error less than half that of *B*): having had a strict mother and having been the first-born in the family. Thus, given that one is of radical-liberal political orientation, recollections of a firm rather than a lax mother are associated with *increased* activity. Being a first or only-born child is also associated with increased activity. Other factors, although not significant, show effects in the same direction as cross-tabulation analysis. This finding suggests that relationships, though weak, are not spurious. Among radicals, there is an association of later activity with memories of more inter-parent conflict and less happy childhoods. There is also a factor of overt political socialization by the family associated with increased activity. To sum up: among radicals, later university-related political activity is associated with being the first or only child in a family which was disciplined, and which contributed to the political education of the child. Tendencies suggest a combative family, rather than a 'warm' one.

TABLE 7.1

Socialization factors predicting university political activities:
dependent variable Summed University Political Activities Index

Independent variables	Cumulative R^2	Pearson's r	B	Std. error B
Radical University Ideology Students				
Mother strict (neg. high)	0.047	−0.219	−0.686	0.304
First born in family	0.079	0.204	0.764	0.310
Parents fought frequently	0.107	0.114	0.426	0.324
Family discussed politics (infreq. high)	0.124	−0.116	−0.325	0.186
Childhood happiness (neg. high)	0.143	0.117	0.329	0.216

Constant = 2.927   df = 5; 105   Overall F = 3.51 p = 0.006

Conservative University Ideology Students				
Childhood happiness (neg. high)	0.050	−0.224	−0.306	0.199
Male gender	0.086	0.186	0.544	0.227
Father dominated family	0.129	−0.196	−0.363	0.243
Felt close to father	0.154	−0.068	−0.404	0.234
Mother strict (neg. high)	0.176	−0.122	−0.293	0.211
Father strict (neg. high)	0.206	0.193	0.360	0.211
Family discussed politics (neg. high)	0.221	−0.136	−0.228	0.166
Church-going as child (infreq. high)	0.238	−0.128	−0.102	0.082

Constant = 1.67   df = 8; 70   Overall F = 2.73 p = 0.001

Four Types				
First born in family	0.032	0.180	0.616	0.220
Psychologically punished	0.063	0.168	0.671	0.300
Parents fought frequently	0.080	0.135	0.365	0.236
Family discussed politics (infreq. high)	0.095	−0.129	−0.339	0.147
Father dominated family	0.114	−0.105	−0.443	0.237
Felt close to father	0.126	−0.135	−0.390	0.241

Constant = 1.882   df = 6; 184   Overall F = 4.44 p = 0.0001

Whole Sample				
Family discussed politics (infreq. high)	0.024	−0.154	−0.258	0.053
Male gender	0.036	0.102	0.271	0.082
Psychologically punished	0.045	0.092	0.336	0.112
First born in family	0.051	0.079	0.199	0.084
Felt close to mother	0.055	−0.049	0.146	0.081
Childhood complaining (infreq. high)	0.059	−0.074	−0.116	0.065

Constant = 1.701   df = 6; 856   Overall F = 8.98 p = 0.0001

Within the conservatives' ideology group, memories of a happy childhood are most strongly predictive of later university activity, but the standard error is fairly large. Male gender facilitates activity. Memories of a *less* strict, non-dominating father and a more strict mother, of more frequent church-going as a child, and of overt political socialization also figure slightly. The negative relationship of 'closeness to father' suggests that a distanced father figure is relevant to the activity-enabling conservative family. Perhaps discipline flowed from the mother – as the strictness variables indicate – simply because the children were her charge. To sum up: the conservative family associated with later activity shares with the radical-activity-enabling family only the characteristic of having been comparatively heavily disciplined – and by the mother in both cases. Other characteristics of the activity-enabling conservative family suggest a traditional family (males being more likely to act, and church-going being important as a predictor) which bestowed considerable happiness on its members. This is a more detailed portrait than exists for radicals, and has a stronger influence on activity levels.

What happens to the power of the socialization factors to predict university activity when one removes *both* constraints: the stipulation that the individual belong to a type as well as the ideology control? In work with the whole sample, less of the larger variance-pool is accounted for, and again factors which had worked in different directions or with differing intensity within the samples of conservatives and radicals have their effects obscured. (These are the different impacts of reported happiness, gender, being first or only child, and church-going.) Numerically more variables account for less variance than for the ideology samples and for the consistent (types) subsample.

Predicting non-university activity
The non-university activities index used as the dependent variable (table 7.2) in the sample of radicals reinforces rather than adds to the picture offered by the university activity index. Among radicals, non-university political activity is associated with a somewhat *lower* frequency of childhood complaining (than is the norm among those now of radical ideology, at least), with memories of a *less* happy childhood, and with recollection of overt political socialization. There are tendencies for a family with somewhat more conflict between parents, and for having been first-born, to be predictive of later activity.

For conservative students, family socialization factors predicting non-university political activity are overshadowed by the impact of gender. That is, among families of conservative students, males have been disproportion-

TABLE 7.2
Socialization factors predicting summed non-university (outside) political activities: dependent variable Summed Non-university Activity Index

Independent variables	Cumulative R^2	Pearson's r	B	Std. error B
Radical University Ideology Students				
Childhood happiness	0.031	0.176	0.391	0.231
Childhood complaining (infreq. high)	0.059	0.174	0.556	0.265
Family discussed politics (infreq. high)	0.078	−0.097	−0.314	0.198
First born in family	0.097	0.106	0.577	0.328
Parents fought frequently	0.115	0.130	0.508	0.352

Constant = 1.152   df = 5; 105   Overall F = 2.74 p = 0.023

Conservative University Ideology Students				
Male gender	0.072	0.268	0.922	0.311
Father dominated family	0.117	−0.147	−0.742	0.314
Felt close to mother	0.143	−0.143	−0.596	0.313
Family discussed politics (infreq. high)	0.168	−0.075	−0.329	0.225

Constant = 2.703   df = 4; 74   Overall F = 3.73 p = 0.008

Four Types				
Childhood happiness (neg. high)	0.159	0.159	0.474	0.173
Family discussed politics (infreq. high)	0.212	−0.101	−0.356	0.161
Father dominated family	0.251	−0.123	−0.490	0.257
First born in family	0.282	0.116	0.440	0.239

Constant = 2.48   df = 4; 186   Overall F = 4.02 p = 0.004

Whole Sample				
Family discussed politics (infreq. high)	0.018	−0.135	−0.326	0.069
Male gender	0.032	0.106	0.385	0.106
Childhood happiness (neg. high)	0.044	0.088	0.220	0.081
Father dominated family	0.047	−0.035	−0.186	0.110
Parents fought frequently	0.049	0.078	0.174	0.118

Constant = 2.323   df = 5; 857   Overall F = 8.93 p = 0.0001

ately enabled to be active (this is *not* true for radical students, where gender is not a predictive factor). Recollections associated with outside activity are of *not* having been close to the mother, and the father as not dominating family decision-making. Weaker relationships suggest that, among conservatives, later propensity for action is – as for radicals – associated with increased frequency of overt political education. Again the family process predictive of later activity would appear to be fairly democratic (as between parents), and firm but not repressive in effect in parent-child relationship.

Removing only the control for direction of ideology coincidentally increases the amount of variance that can be accounted for by socialization factors. This is because factors which facilitate activity within ideological groupings are not directly contradictory. In the case of political discussion, the effect is in the same direction in both groups. Results are substantially obscured in analysis with the whole sample, appearing as a patchwork of minor effects.

Predicting social-helping activities
Breaking the order of presentation and beginning with the conservative sample, let us see what factors increase the likelihood that social-helping types of activities will develop (table 7.3). Fittingly enough, frequent church-going as a child is the factor more predictive of later intensity of action in these less-political activity options. Other factors significant (among conservatives) are political discussion and less closeness to the mother.

Among radical students, the family processes which predict social-helping activity would likewise appear to be more traditionally oriented. Frequent church-going is again an important predictor, within a mother-disciplined family. Childhood happiness is here *positively* associated with social-helping activity. Tendencies show that the radical student now active in the social-helping area remembers having complained comparatively little. It would seem safe to say that once more social-helping activity is predicted by a clutch of variables which paint a more 'traditional' family, close to the conservative action-enabling family, as also occurred in analysis of the parental-attribute factors.

Analysis within the whole sample works out better for the social-helping activities than for the two previous indices. This would be because findings for both ideology groups run in the same direction: social-helping acts are predicted overall by a traditional, happy, church-going, and disciplined rearing. Action generally is predicted by increased discipline, by discussion and exchange between parents, and by the experience of being the first or only child. Male gender figures as an advantage for political acts in the whole sample, but not in the opinion-consistent sample, suggesting that females are roughly equally likely to act politically once they have formed coherent opinions (i.e. radical) but that among the non-opinionated, males will be more likely to be drawn into activity.

TABLE 7.3
Socialization factors predicting summed social-helping activities:
dependent variable Summed Social-Helping Index

Independent variables	Cumulative R^2	Pearson's r	B	Std. error B
Radical University Ideology Students				
Church-going as child (infreq. high)	0.041	−0.202	−0.149	0.079
Mother strict (neg. high)	0.072	−0.200	−0.413	0.212
Childhood happiness (neg. high)	0.100	−0.176	−0.262	0.138
Childhood complaining (neg. high)	0.116	0.113	0.237	0.172

Constant = 2.638 df = 4; 106 Overall F = 3.49 p = 0.01

Conservative University Ideology Students				
Church-going as child (infreq. high)	0.092	−0.304	−0.251	0.089
Family discussed politics (infreq. high)	0.122	−0.163	−0.356	0.188
Felt close to mother	0.149	−0.065	−0.445	0.261
Mother strict (neg. high)	0.177	−0.222	−0.352	0.224

Constant = 3.72 df = 3; 75 Overall F = 4.38 p = 0.007

Four Types				
Childhood church-going (infreq. high)	0.056	−0.237	−0.167	0.059
Mother strict (neg. high)	0.082	−0.200	−0.327	0.153
Male gender	0.098	−0.167	−0.317	0.164
First born in family	0.155	0.112	0.298	0.158

Constant = 2.539 df = 4; 186 Overall F = 6.027 p = 0.0001

Whole Sample				
Church-going as child (infreq. high)	0.045	−0.212	−0.158	0.027
Male gender	0.061	−0.147	−0.258	0.073
Family discussed politics (infreq. high)	0.069	−0.095	−0.115	−0.048
Mother strict (neg. high)	0.072	−0.093	−0.132	0.075
Childhood happiness (neg. high)	0.076	−0.091	−0.093	0.053

Constant = 2.65 df = 5; 857 Overall F = 14.11 p = 0.0001

CONCLUSION

We can summarize the predictors of activity within radicals and conservatives groups. Jointly applicable factors predicting later activity are limited to those that indicate the presence of a disciplinary structure in the family. Within both groups, increasing activity is positively associated with memories of a strict mother. Parental warmth, in terms of closeness to father or mother, enters only as a negative predictor. For the ideology groups, therefore, propensity to act is *increased* by comparatively firm discipline in the childhood family. Nor do results point to the presence of a very high 'child power' factor as facilitative of later activity.

For radicals only, being first-born is a predictor of greater action propensity; in conservatives, being born *male* is a predictor of greater action propensity. An unhappy childhood predicts political action among radicals, as does parental conflict. Conservative political action is predicted by a happy childhood and a co-operative family. We know that a high level of education in the father and mother, and professional accomplishment in the mother, are predictors of radical activity: it may be that the radical actor's family stimulates the child by presenting combat between equals, whereas the family of the acting conservative, more traditional in outline, passes on its benefits in the form of stability and security.

Once more it seems fair to conclude that the 'return' for the investment of forming the opinion-consistent group, and then controlling for ideology, has been justified in substantive terms.

8

Students' own characteristics and activity

Are the members of the groups of the four types significantly and systematically distinguishable from one another according to the student's current characteristics? For example, researchers have established that an 'academic ecology' exists. Radical and liberal students – those who favour change and protest – study in the social sciences and humanities departments, while apathetic and conservative students, including the anti-protestors, are located in applied studies and the professions. Will the four types of this research resemble members of the known groups described in the literature? The 'own characteristics' to be reviewed serve to locate the individual in the university-peer environment: faculty of enrolment, year of study, and success in terms of grades and scholarships won. We have also recorded the student's decisions on a few fundamental issues: how many degrees to aspire to, what occupation to follow on graduation, and whether to forego or maintain a commitment to organized religion. These 'own' and semi-voluntary characteristics[1] describe the individual 'on the hoof.'

The broad expectation is that political activity by radicals will increase with secularization and with factors that link the individual to the liberal arts-humanities peer culture. Seymour Martin Lipset has claimed that 'academic ecology' is all-important in the formation of students' opinions and activity propensities (1968a). The claim is consistent with our view that the number of reinforcing messages received by the individual is crucial for ideological learning. Students who are not part of the social sciences or humanities are much less well placed to receive the large numbers of consistent and even redundant messages which instil the belief system. Political activity by conservatives should increase as the number of ties to traditional aspects of the larger culture increase, and with maturational characteristics and evidence of personal accomplishment.

It is also expected that the variables of this chapter, which are temporally closer to the individual, will have a major impact upon the propensity for activity. Further, prediction of activity should be easier for radicals than for conservatives, because opinion content is most appropriately matched to activity for radicals.

Specifically, variables for treatment in this section are (1) age, (2) number of years at the university, (3) faculty of enrolment, (4) grade-point average of the previous year, (5) number of degrees aspired to, (6) whether a scholarship has been won, (7) marital status, (8) present work status, (9) whether the student has changed educational direction during his years at university or (10) has interrupted his education for a year or more, and (11) what career plan has been formulated (or whether there is a career plan). These variables tap life direction and chronological maturity in the university career, and are related to intellectual ability.

PREDICTIONS FOR STUDENTS' OWN CHARACTERISTICS

Age is an important variable. Were passive groups to resemble the active ideology-mates in all but age, being much younger, age could provide almost a total explanation of activity. That is, passive students could be thought to be in a pre-activity stage of their development. Hence a prediction of 'no differences' on age must be made for consistency with our hypothesis that active and passive radicals are found in qualitatively different settings, and are therefore qualitatively different from one another.

Year of study is more problematic: the literature indicates that liberalism increases with years of exposure to arts and humanities faculties, but our interest concerns factors which will increase activity. No prediction will be made.

For faculty of enrolment, it is predicted that radical actors will be disproportionately enrolled in arts and humanities and in graduate studies. Conservatives will have given more attention to vocation-oriented and professional faculties.

Both types of actor will show evidence of commitment to academic values: actors will drop out less often, change academic orientation less often, aspire to more academic degrees, have higher grades, and disproportionately hold scholarships.

The remaining life-style variables are marital status, career commitments, and religious commitment. In keeping with the popular view that conservatives set up families and radicals set up communes, it is predicted that the radical group will contain the largest number of single persons and that

TABLE 8.1
Faculty of enrolment for university political types

	Arts	Science	Ed., Phys. Ed., House-hold Econ.*	Professional faculties	Graduate faculties	'Women's,† nursing	Engineers	Commerce	Total
Not a type	14.7ʳ	14.4	32.1	9.7	9.7	5.9	7.5	6.5	78.4 (750)
	77.5ᶜ	79.4	80.9	71.9	68.9	83.0	86.2	80.3	
Passive conservatives	4.3	14.3	31.4	14.3	20.0	2.9	5.7	7.1	7.3 (70)
	2.1	7.4	7.4	10.4	13.2	3.8	6.2	8.2	
Acting conservatives	11.1	11.1	22.2	5.6	33.3	5.6	11.1	–	1.9 (18)
	1.4	1.5	1.3	1.0	5.7	1.9	3.1	–	
Passive radicals	13.2	21.1	36.8	10.5	5.3	7.9	–	5.3	4.0 (38)
	3.5	5.9	4.7	4.2	1.9	5.7	–	3.3	
Acting radicals	27.2	9.9	21.0	14.8	13.6	3.7	3.7	6.2	8.5 (81)
	15.5	5.9	5.7	12.5	10.4	5.7	4.6	8.2	
Whole sample	14.8	14.2	31.1	10.0	11.1	5.5	6.8	6.4	
	(142)	(136)	(298)	(96)	(106)	(53)	(65)	(61)	(957)

$\chi^2 = 48.040$ df = 28 $p = 0.01$

* The household economics component is only 2.2 per cent of the population ($n = 21$) and was grouped with the education faculty because most household economics students cite secondary school teaching as their intended occupation.
† Includes Dental Hygiene, Rehabilitation Medicine, Community Medicine, Medical Laboratory Science, and Library Science.
r = row percentage; c = column percentage.

conservatives will be most often married. No predictions are made about activists within groups. Career aspirations will be in keeping with faculty of enrolment. Conservatives will have planned their futures. Radicals – active radicals in particular – will be vague as to the future. The radicals will be secular in their approach to life, and conservative students will be most likely to have maintained a religious affiliation. Active types should, as noted, be at the extremes.

In keeping with previous practice of showing proportional distributions of types on key variables, differences will first be investigated through cross-tabulation and in some cases through mean scores. A regression assessment of the impact of selected characteristics upon propensity to act will follow.

FINDINGS IN BIVARIATE ANALYSIS

Age
The average ages of the groups were tested for differences. The average age of the whole sample is 22½ years. Passive conservatives are a full year older as a group (23½) and active conservatives average 24 years of age. Passive radicals are a matter of months younger on average than active radicals, the actors approaching 23 and the passive group about 22½. These differences are not statistically significant (*F*-test).

Year in university
Because the sample is stratified by year of study, the average year of study for the whole sample is just more than three. Acting conservatives have been longest at university, with an average of four and one-half years each. Next are passive conservatives, with just more than three and one-half years of study behind them, closely followed by acting radicals with three and one-half years of study. Passive radicals on average have attended for slightly less than two and one-half years. Acting conservatives have therefore been on campus longest, and passive radicals have had least time on campus. Using analysis of variance and an *F*-test for differences between means, it is found that these differences are significant at the 0.0001 level.

Faculty of enrolment
Table 8.1 is cumbersome, but some emphases of 5 per cent and more are apparent in enrolment preferences. Taking sample proportions as baseline, we see that acting conservatives have more graduate students than they 'should.' Passive conservatives are under-represented in the arts, and over-represented in graduate studies and the professions. The main difference

between these two groups, then, would seem to be in the comparative concentration of professions in the passive group. These students would be mature and probably of above-average ability. These two factors would encourage opinion-consistency.

There would certainly appear to be qualitatively different enrolment patterns between the two radical ideology groups. Passive radicals are over-represented in science and education studies. Acting radicals, in contrast, are under-represented in these two areas. It would seem unlikely that passive radicals, although holding appropriate opinions, could be spurred into action in large numbers given more years at university and more exposure to opportunities for activity. Their faculties of concentration are faculties which are less central to the traditional activist base.

Grade-point averages
There are serious problems in comparing grade-point averages of groups whom we know to differ in faculty of enrolment, because grades are influenced by faculty marking habits. In addition, graduate students and professional students would be good students by definition: they have had to qualify for entrance to their respective schools. Therefore one expects types' groups which have heavy representation from older students, graduates, and professionals, most markedly the two acting types, to show evidence of academic success. Any first rough comparison, pending regression analysis, is most legitimately applied to differences between the passive groups. We shall look first at results from cross-tabulating types by self-reported grade-point average for the previous year (table 8.2).

Both acting types are well represented in the top two-fifths of the grades distribution. Passive conservatives are fairly average on grades, with perhaps a slight tendency to good grades: 24 per cent are in the top fifth of the distribution. Non-acting radicals lack star quality: only 11 per cent qualify for the top fifth. But it should be noted that they are not markedly unsuccessful: the group would merely appear to contain fewer students of very high academic capacity. The mean grade for each group is useful for summary presentation. Grades are rather high overall: the average for the entire sample is 65.7 per cent. Acting conservatives have highest grades, with a group mean of 69.4. Next are acting radicals, one percentage point lower at 68.4. The average grade of passive conservatives is 67 per cent, and passive radicals trail with a mean grade of 62.4 per cent. Alone among types, their mean grade is less than that for the whole sample. (Using analysis of variance and the F-test, $p = 0.07$.)

TABLE 8.2
Previous year's grade-point average* of university political types

	Low	Medium low	Medium	Medium high	High	Total
Not a type	21.2^r 80.1^c	19.6 79.2	21.8 84.7	20.2 76.4	17.2 71.8	78.5 (739)
Passive conservatives	19.1 6.6	22.1 8.2	16.2 5.8	19.1 6.7	23.5 9.0	7.2 (68)
Acting conservatives	5.9 0.5	29.4 2.7	5.9 0.5	29.4 2.6	29.4 2.8	1.8 (17)
Passive radicals	23.7 4.6	21.1 4.4	18.4 3.7	26.3 5.1	10.5 2.3	4.0 (38)
Acting radicals	20.3 8.2	12.7 5.5	12.7 5.3	22.8 9.2	21.6 14.1	8.4 (79)
Whole sample	20.8 (196)	19.4 (183)	20.2 (190)	20.7 (195)	18.8 (177)	(941)

$\chi^2 = 23.374$ df $= 16$ $p = 0.1$

* The approximate fifths of GPA represent the best attempt to apportion frequencies of the continuous percentage distribution.
r = row percentage; c = column percentage.

Intensity of academic orientation

Table 8.3 reviews three factors of academic orientation: winning scholarships, shifting across faculties, and dropping out. It is seen that actors – most notably acting conservatives – are somewhat more likely to hold awards. Contrary to popular wisdom, radicals do not drop in and out again. In fact, any tendency to do so points to passive conservatives.

A change of faculty during the university career was deemed a major redirection. Nineteen per cent of all students in the sample have changed faculty. Again actors are roughly as the sample, less than a fifth having changed faculty. Passive conservatives, as suggested above, are fairly high in subject continuity even though they tend to drop out for a period. In contrast, almost a third of passive radicals have undergone a major redirection. This is quite remarkable, as these non-acting radicals tend to be in their early years of study. Passive radicals, then, are not only at the beginning of a university career, they are at an unsettled beginning in terms of what they

TABLE 8.3
Academic orientation variables for university political types

	Scholarship winning	Change of faculty	Taken period out
Not a type	14.4	18.3	35.1
Passive conservatives	13.0	14.1	46.5
Acting conservatives	33.3	16.7	38.9
Passive radicals	13.2	31.6	34.2
Acting radicals	17.3	18.3	34.6
Whole sample	14.7	18.5	35.9
p	0.2	0.2	0.5

TABLE 8.4
Number of degrees aspired to by university political types

	One degree	Two degrees	Three degrees	Total
Not a type	44.0 [r]	40.4	15.6	
	83.7 [c]	76.9	68.5	78.2 (725)
Passive conservatives	36.8	45.6	17.6	
	6.6	8.1	7.3	7.3 (68)
Acting conservatives	17.6	29.4	52.9	
	0.8	1.3	5.5	1.8 (17)
Passive radicals	59.5	32.4	8.1	
	5.8	3.1	1.8	4.0 (37)
Acting radicals	15.0	50.0	35.0	
	3.1	10.5	17.0	8.6 (80)
Whole sample	41.1	41.1	17.8	
	(381)	(381)	(165)	(927)

$\chi^2 = 52.603$ df $= 8$ $p = 0.001$

r = row percentage; c = column percentage.

should be doing at university. Non-acting conservatives are much more likely to be committed to a particular discipline. None of these trends reach significance as assessed by chi-squared.

Findings of the number of degrees aspired to (see table 8.4) fit the emerging view of passive radicals as somewhat less than enthusiastic scholars.

Many more passive radicals than members of any other group intend to leave after one degree. Of the whole sample, about two-fifths intend to take one degree only, the same proportion intend to take two degrees, and the remaining near-fifth aspire to three degrees. The other group which showed some academic indecisiveness, passive conservatives, is much closer to the sample baseline in its aspirations. In contrast, both acting groups are oriented toward academic life, acting conservatives perhaps most so. Clearly, passive types are less ambitious academically than active types. Figures for 'not a type' in table 8.4 show that as the number of degrees aspired to *increases*, so does the likelihood that the respondent will qualify for types' membership. That is, intention for long study is associated with formation of coherent sets of opinions about the university. Still, passive radicals are even less ambitious than those who do not qualify for types' membership by virtue of their opinion 'inconsistency.'

Firming-up of life pattern
Occupational plan is treated as a dichotomy: having settled upon a choice as opposed to not having done so (table 8.5). This method is followed because of lack of variance in occupational choice. The great majority of all students who have formulated a career plan are settled upon a profession. Sixty-seven per cent of all students intend entering a profession, 19 per cent have not formulated any plan, and the remaining 14 per cent's ambitions range freely over the occupational map, from rodeo rider to taxi driver. (See appendix B on coding of occupational choice.) Differences between types, then, are differences in proportions not having a plan. We would expect passive radicals to be planless because of their youth and unsettled status, but find *both* radical types are somewhat planless,[2] in comparison with conservative types and the whole sample. A third of active radicals have not settled upon an area for their life work. Just slightly fewer passive radicals have not yet formulated career plans. Only one active conservative is planless, and passive conservatives are lacking plans to only the same extent as the whole sample.

Conservative actors are indeed the most marrying kind of all students: almost one-half are married (see table 8.5). Next most often married are passive conservatives. Equal proportions – about a fifth – of each radical group is married, which is rather surprising as passive radicals are both *younger* and more preponderantly *male* than acting radicals. And radicals are not in fact bypassing marriage as an institution. (Only four students out of the entire sample checked the 'cohabiting' option for marital status.)

The final variable for treatment in this section is whether the student claims 'no religion' as a status (table 8.5). Conservative students are, as

TABLE 8.5
Life pattern variables for university political types

	Has no occupa-tional plan	Is now married	Claims 'no religion'
Not a type	16.8	25.4	37.4
Passive conservatives	18.6	36.6	29.4
Acting conservatives	5.6	47.1	12.5
Passive radicals	29.7	21.6	45.7
Acting radicals	33.7	22.5	52.7
Whole sample	18.7	26.3	37.9
p	0.001	0.06	0.01

expected, disproportionately likely to have a religious affiliation. Active conservatives are the most likely to have maintained the affiliation. Passive conservatives are second most likely, passive radicals following in third place, and only a minority of active radicals are affiliated.

Summary for bivariate analysis
Acting conservatives are mature students who tend to be enrolled in graduate faculties, to be oriented toward academic careers, to be married, and to have maintained a religious preference. Passive conservatives are less academic in orientation, are enrolled more often in arts and professional faculties, but otherwise resemble the conservative actors fairly closely. Passive radicals are younger, less-experienced students who are not academically inclined. They are over-represented in science and education faculties relative to their ideology-mates. Active radicals are planless, single, and secular, and have fairly clear academic orientations relative to passive students. There would appear to be a clearer difference between radical types than between conservatives. Finally, it seems unlikely that the passive radicals form a clientele for activity, situated as they are in fringe disciplines.

OWN CHARACTERISTICS IN REGRESSION ANALYSIS

Multiple regression analysis will allow assessment of the impact of these individual attributes upon the activity scores. Dichotomous variables formed for non-interval variables are: male gender/not male gender, in arts faculty/not in arts faculty, in graduate faculty/not in graduate faculty, in education faculty/not in education faculty, in professional faculty/not in professional faculty, has changed faculty of enrolment/has not changed faculty, has taken time out from university/has not taken time out, has formed a career plan/ has not formed a career plan, works full or part-time/does not work, is now married/is not married, respondent secular/respondent not secular. Continuous variables entered are: higher degree goals (actual number), last year's grade-point average, years in university, year of birth (last two digits of year).[3]

The set of dummy and continuous variables will now be analysed with the dependent variable being, in turn, each of the activity scores university political activity, outside or non-university political activity, and social-helping activity.[4] Results will once more be presented for each of the samples of interest: radicals, conservatives, the four types together, and the entire sample.

Predicting university activities

With the subsample of radical ideology students (table 8.6), let us take the 'own characteristic' variables in prediction of proclivity to act in university politics. It is seen that the first five significant variables cumulatively explain almost 40 per cent of the variance. It was expected that this set of variables – which is closer to the student – would be more likely to predict his or her activities. Of most importance to the prediction of university-related activity, given that the student holds a consistently pro-student participation position, is the factor 'higher degree goals.' It alone explains more than 20 per cent of the variance. Thus activity in the university increases most notably with commitment to a lengthy academic career. The next most important factor, explaining an additional 9 per cent of the variance, is number of years already spent at university. These two factors, commitment to a long university career and a longer history in university, together explain 31 per cent of the variance. Having changed faculties follows with a negative impact upon propensity for action. The remaining two significant variables are faculty definers: being enrolled in a professional faculty and being enrolled in an arts faculty, in contrast to all other enrolment options, are associated with increasing activity. The pattern of factors associated with *radical* activity in the university, then, portrays a long-term student, with high degree aspirations, who has remained in his or her faculty of original choice. This faculty is more likely to be a professional one or general arts.

These characteristics do not have nearly so great an impact within the sample of students of consistent anti-student-power ideology. Higher degree goals is most important, but accounts for much less of the variance in university activities. The next most important variable is the religion variable.

TABLE 8.6
Students' own attributes predicting university political activities:
dependent variable Summed University Political Activities Index

Independent variables	Cumulative R^2	Pearson's r	B	Std. error B
Radical University Ideology Students				
Higher degree goals	0.223	0.472	0.843	0.184
Year in university	0.311	0.415	0.371	0.092
Has changed faculty	0.348	−0.115	−0.766	0.307
In professional faculty	0.366	0.250	0.787	0.387
In arts faculty	0.383	0.068	0.585	0.318
Respondent secular	0.395	0.042	−0.381	0.263

Constant = −0.710   df = 6; 104   Overall F = 11.32 p = 0.0001

Conservative University Ideology Students				
Higher degree goals	0.082	0.285	0.512	0.202
Respondent secular	0.108	−0.147	−0.488	0.252
Works part/full time	0.130	0.146	0.278	0.233
Male gender	0.151	0.186	0.410	0.240
In professional faculty	0.171	−0.113	−0.603	0.348
In graduate faculty	0.194	0.117	0.523	0.366

Constant = 0.523   df = 6; 72   Overall F = 2.88 p = 0.014

Four Types				
Higher degree goals	0.137	0.371	0.810	0.171
In graduate faculty	0.158	0.058	−0.888	0.372
Works part/full time	0.171	0.149	0.337	0.223
In arts faculty	0.181	0.178	0.593	0.314
Year in university	0.195	0.178	0.152	0.084

Constant = −0.815   df = 5; 185   Overall F = 8.969 p = 0.0001

Whole Sample				
Higher degree goals	0.076	0.276	0.438	0.062
In arts faculty	0.087	0.117	0.359	0.121
Year in university	0.092	0.144	0.130	0.038
In graduate faculty	0.102	0.057	−0.484	0.157
Is now married	0.109	−0.023	−0.246	0.097
In education faculty	0.111	−0.140	−0.121	0.093

Constant = −0.0911   df = 6; 856   Overall F = 17.86 p = 0.0001

Among conservatives, increased university activity is associated with an ongoing religious commitment. Also important is male gender and enrolment in a professional school, the last with negative impact. The acting conservative is an employed male student with stable religious convictions who is not in a professional faculty. These variables cumulatively account for just less than 20 per cent of the variance.

We turn now to prediction of non-university activities by these same factors. The effect of removing the ideology controls is discussed below for all three indices of activity.

Predicting non-university activity

For the radicals, maturity and stronger commitment to the academic life are again the important personal characteristics facilitating outside or non-university political activity (see table 8.7). These factors of commitment to academic life have, however, a much smaller impact upon the non-university political activity score. Less than one-half as much variance – about 15 per cent – is explained by years at the university, higher degree goals, and change of faculty (again having a negative impact).

Among conservatives, factors which are significantly associated with increasing non-university political activity are higher degree goals, a change of faculty, and having taken a break from university. The factor of having dropped out of school for a time thus positively predicts activity among conservatives. Perhaps having taken time out indicates increased maturity and confidence among conservatives.[5] Parenthetically, there is a correlation in the conservatives' sample of 0.302 between having taken time out from university and increasing political activity. There is a slight negative correlation of −0.104 between these same variables within the radical group. One might speculate that conservatives were drawn into activity *during* their year out. Radical outside political activity may well depend more upon peer support from within the university environment, hence the slight negative correlation between dropping out and non-university political activity. To summarize: variables indicating personal maturity are the most important predictive factors for outside political activity for both radical and conservative groups.

Predicting social-helping activities

Taking the radical sample first (table 8.8), four variables are important. Enrolment in a graduate or education faculty, maintaining a religious affiliation, holding to one area of study, and aspiring to more than one degree are the factors having significant impact. These variables – which together account for about 20 per cent of the variance – describe a mature and successful individual with religious beliefs from within the left-wing ideology group. Factors predicting conservative social-helping activity are very similar (table 8.7): holding a religious preference, working, and not being in a professional faculty. It is worth recalling that the faculty variable is rather

TABLE 8.7
Students' own attributes predicting summed non-university (outside) political activities:
dependent variable Summed Non-university Activity Index

Independent variables	Cumulative R^2	Pearson's r	B	Std. error B
Radical University Ideology Students				
Year in university	0.066	0.257	0.254	0.109
Has changed faculties	0.108	−0.145	−0.810	0.394
Higher degree goals	0.138	0.247	0.423	0.212
Taken time out from university	0.153	−0.120	−0.574	0.345
Is now married	0.172	0.137	0.634	0.407

Constant = 1.693   df = 5; 105   Overall F = 4.37 p = 0.001

Conservative University Ideology Students				
Higher degree goals	0.184	0.429	0.867	0.204
Has changed faculty	0.229	0.267	0.801	0.396
Last year's GPA	0.254	0.085	−0.022	0.011
Taken time out from university	0.284	0.244	0.507	0.286

Constant = 1.36   df = 4; 74   Overall F = 7.34 p = 0.001

Four Types				
Higher degree goals	0.093	0.305	0.637	0.158
Works part/full time	0.103	0.141	0.339	0.246
In arts faculty	0.111	0.122	0.423	0.326

Constant = 1.146   df = 3; 187   Overall F = 7.75 p = 0.0001

Whole Sample				
Higher degree goals	0.061	0.248	0.518	0.073
Year of birth	0.072	−0.135	−0.391	0.103
In arts faculty	0.081	0.089	0.436	0.144
Last year's GPA	0.085	0.039	−0.079	0.042

Constant = 3.502   df = 4; 858   Overall F = 19.87 p = 0.0001

strongly associated with gender in both samples. The dummy variable denoting membership in the education faculty correlates −0.214 with the dummy variable for male sex in the radical group and −0.522 in the conservative groups. The *faculty* effect is therefore stronger than is the effect of gender with faculty controlled. Overall, it is seen that the factors that are positively associated with social-helping activity hold in both ideology orientations once more. They again indicate that traditional roles and values are associated with this genre of activity.

TABLE 8.8
Students' own attributes predicting summed social-helping activities:
dependent variable Summed Social-Helping Index

Independent variables	Cumulative R^2	Pearson's r	B	Std. error B
Radical University Ideology Students				
In graduate faculty	0.049	0.222	0.879	0.342
In education faculty	0.101	0.178	0.655	0.243
Has changed faculty	0.138	−0.154	−0.524	0.238
Respondent secular	0.171	−0.205	−0.522	0.208
Higher degree goals	0.204	0.135	0.317	0.152

Constant = 0.901   df = 5; 105   Overall F = 5.37 p = 0.0001

Conservative University Ideology Students				
Respondent secular	0.185	−0.430	−1.25	0.274
Works part/full time	0.215	0.114	0.426	0.259
In professional faculty	0.238	−0.179	−0.619	0.358
Higher degree goals	0.246	0.068	0.255	0.176
Last year's GPA	0.266	−0.026	−0.014	0.009

Constant = 1.97   df = 5; 73   Overall F = 5.28 p = 0.001

Four Types				
Respondent secular	0.074	−0.271	−0.693	0.164
Works full/part time	0.110	0.177	0.370	0.165
Higher degree goals	0.130	0.108	0.326	0.113
In education faculty	0.155	0.168	0.464	0.188
Has changed faculty	0.167	−0.061	−0.317	0.198

Constant = 0.790   df = 5; 185   Overall F = 7.40 p = 0.0001

Whole Sample				
Respondent secular	0.078	−0.279	0.621	0.075
Male gender	0.087	−0.147	−0.274	0.075
Higher degree goals	0.103	0.048	0.265	0.054
Year in university	0.110	−0.046	−0.089	0.027
Year of birth	0.119	−0.067	−0.031	0.008
Is now married	0.126	−0.048	−0.231	0.094
No career plans	0.132	−0.106	−0.214	0.092

Constant = 3.097   df = 7; 855   Overall F = 18.51 p = 0.0001

Removing ideology constraints

There are perhaps fewer major differences in emphasis between the factors predicting activity among conservatives and among radicals than for previous sets of variables. In general, activity is predicted by chronological and intellectual maturity. The emphasis on enrolment in the arts faculty is unique to radical political activity, as is maintenance of a religious preference to conservative political activity in general. (It relates to social-helping activity in both cases.) Therefore, removal of the ideology constraint does not modify the pattern of predictors to the same extent as with previous sets of independent variables. The strength of relationship merely finds the intermediate position between the individual prediction of the two subsamples. Analysis within the whole sample does little to alter the pattern of variables entering equations, but does notably decrease the amount of variance accounted for by independent variables. Still it is chronological and intellectual maturity that predicts activity. Entry of marital status is a departure, however. For the whole sample, being married occurs as a factor negatively associated with intensity of activity.

Summary
For students taking a pro-student-participation position (the sample of radicals), the factors most strongly predictive of university political activity are those which indicate greater commitment to the university and a steady commitment to one particular field of study. Among conservative students these factors do not operate to increase activity nearly to the same extent, although we find that conservative actors are older, settled, and talented students. Rather, the factors that predict activity within the conservative subsample emphasize the portrait established in chapter 6 – a male with traditional values.

The student political types are now filled out intellectually and psychologically, and are dressed in their street clothes. We have their addresses and telephone numbers, as it were, through the information on their parents' and their own characteristics. It is the task of the following chapter to compare these data to the portraits established in chapter 5 for students elsewhere. Following this evaluation, the costs and benefits of the analysis strategy will be weighed.

9

Conclusion

The voice of any particular citizen can have little measurable impact on such large social choices as the policies of the government or the outcome of an election. [Sidney Verba and Norman Nie, *Participation in America* (1972)]

People like me don't have any say about what the government does. [Political Efficacy Scale item Positive alternative: disagree]

A bubble of confusion in the heart of quantitative political science is neatly captured by placing these two statements side by side. In the first, Verba and Nie acknowledge reality: any one citizen's views are of little importance. The second statement is a standard item from a standard measure of political efficacy. The 'right' thing to do as a citizen is to disagree with this statement. Here we have the political scientist presenting an aspect of the unrevised democratic myth to the citizen, without qualm or qualification. In the myth, the 'ideal' citizen should see himself as a participant in shaping the destiny of the nation. He should guard his own dignity, and that of others. He should seek knowledge about the affairs of government, trust in the decency and fairness of his fellow citizens and the political system as a whole, trim his personal interests to harmonize with the common good, and participate vigorously with a view to influencing public policy. When he or his candidate loses, the good citizen should shake his head ruefully, acknowledge that it was a fair fight, and resolve to work harder next time.

The empirical evidence is, of course, disappointing to the myth-endorsing political scientist. As described by survey findings, the average citizen sees himself as helplessly subject to the destiny of the nation and the wishes of the powerful. He vaguely wonders what 'they' are going to do, or do next, and wishes that they would do it. Very often he is out of date on who 'they' are. In fact, not only is the average citizen found to be inefficacious, he is found also to be anomic, low in information, alienated, submissive, cynical, and low in sense of citizen duty (see, for example, Berelson, 1952; Mussen and Wyszynski, 1952; McClosky, 1958, 1964; Rosenberg, 1962; McDill and Ridley, 1962; Erbe, 1964; DiPalma and McClosky, 1970; Levy, 1970; Sniderman and Citrin, 1971; and the F-scale literature references in Sutherland and Tanenbaum [1980]). In the lowest classes, the mix is volatile: there are suggestions of sado-masochism.[1] And all this because the citizen is realistic about his role, and resigned. The analysts are a little condescending: they know individual members of the mass public are not powerful, but do not think the mass public should know it.

Empirical research also chronicles the merits of elites. A very few extraordinary people are found to exhibit the characteristics of the ideal citizen. Just how few depends on the criteria set by the researcher for knowledge of issues or levels of activity. These few are variously called the 'leaders,' the 'political stratum,' 'the gladiators,' 'the activists,' 'the notables,' or 'the politically informed.' Without exception, positive personality traits and all-round good characteristics are attributed to those with high levels of knowledge and high activity. (See, for example, Dahl, 1961; Prothro and Grigg, 1960; Rose, 1962; Stouffer, 1963; McClosky, 1964; Jackman, 1972; Budge, 1970; and Budge et al., 1972. Milbrath and Goel [1977] present a summary of research findings.)

With these sorts of references piling up for members of the elite and the mass public, it is not surprising that some political scientists drew the logical conclusion: that it is fortunate that the elite is the elite, and that the mass public refrains from exercising its ignorance. Elite traditions provide stability, and the apathy of the disinterested provides, as well, an element of flexibility for the whole system. Robert Dahl (1956b, appendix E) and Harry Eckstein (1966), for example, both see dangers in an increase of participation by non-elites, because of the concentration of 'authoritarian' characters in this stratum, and because of the lack of mass consensus on democratic procedural norms. From here, it is a short but significant step to McClosky's statement: 'Democratic viability is ... saved by the fact that those who are most confused about democratic ideas are also likely to be politically apathetic and without significant influence. Their role in the nation's decision process is so small that their 'misguided' opinions or non-opinions have little practical consequence for stability' (McClosky, 1964: 376).

What are the implications of the present study for this grim little theory? Let us spell out a few of its assumptions. One is that opinions of the mass publics have been reliably and validly measured. A second is that opinions and attitudes are clearly casual for activities. A third is that individual acts bear the imprint of their 'motives' and have attitude-congruent 'consequences' (presumably when aggregated) for the system. In other words, attitudes cause behaviours and these (and all their bells and whistles) aggregate into systemic consequences. In chapters 1 and 3, a theoretical argument was made that attitude and behaviour should be considered as existing in a relation of mutual causation. In later chapters, we have seen some technical benefits accruing from such a conception. About the third assumption we can say little, beyond pointing out that the standard systemic options for political participation are so ritualized that personal style could have little impact (see also Sutherland and Tanenbaum, 1980). But we can address the implications of this theory – which is a fear of broadened participation and a related fear of the conservatism of mass publics – fairly directly through the substantive findings of the present research. To do so is the primary task of this conclusion.

Just as members of the political elite have been found to exemplify 'good' characteristics, so have radical activists generally been described as monopolizing the 'good' personal and socialization characteristics. But what if one could show that the 'good' characteristics are associated with *activity* within ideological groups, rather than with any particular content or quality of viewpoints? If this were the case, one could argue that just as those who are sociable and informed are drawn into the business of the community, so does participation per se educate and increase healthy self-confidence. Attitudes are forged in the arena of action. One hopes, therefore, to persuade the reader that the personal traits and activities, if not the opinions, of the active types are about equally attractive. There are a couple of stages involved in this task. First, it must be shown that the four types as described in this research are believable in the context of others' research. This established, one can argue that participation is in itself educative, and that fears of broadening participation in decision-making are at least partly misplaced. Findings of chapters 4 to 8 are then reviewed for factors associated with increased activity. When these tasks have been attempted, we turn to the technical-cum-methodological aspects of the project. The costs and benefits are weighed. A final section assesses the 'generalizability' of the entire analysis strategy.

COMPARISON OF TYPES TO FINDINGS OF THE LITERATURE

The most detailed portrait available from others' work is that drawn for the radical activist. We can begin with the core portrait as outlined in chapter 5.

There was little consensus on the effect of the major background variables. It did, however, appear that left activists' mothers were disproportionately highly educated and/or a member of a high-status occupation. Left activists' backgrounds also appeared to be Jewish or non-religious. With regard to socialization factors, it appeared that left activists are disproportionately first born, reared in highly interactive families, and recall somewhat more conflict than do most people. Finally, student activists are disproportionately located in humanities and social science faculties. They tend to be oriented to social service and intellectual occupations if they have plans for the future, and tend not to maintain a religious affiliation. Table 9.1 presents a summary of this work's findings on the variables. The acting radicals are described by the characteristics listed in the left-hand column. Acting radicals are found to have more than their share of mothers with professional occupations; to be disproportionately first-born; to recall a conflict-filled, democratic, rather unhappy, and secular childhood; to be located disproportionately in arts (and the professions); and to be planless if talented scholars. This is an excellent likeness. There are no surprises in this emerging portrait: we find nothing that contradicts the centre of gravity of results of other research. There is only one qualification or adjustment to the portrait: there is a tendency for acting radicals to be less 'rooted' in the province.

The case is quite different for conservative activists. Much less empirical research has focused on the conservative, although there is a good deal of speculative libel (see Hampden-Turner, 1970, for a summary). In general, researchers have assumed that conservative students and conservative activists represent a polar type to the radicals. Researchers have seldom specifically studied representative groups of ideologically conservative activists. In the present research, however, an individual type who is highly active but strongly opposed to student power has been specified. The column at the extreme right of table 9.1 lists the characteristics describing these students. First, let us take the 'non-surprising' findings, marked with a (+). Conservative actors are disproportionately male, their mothers are unlikely to hold professional occupations, they attend church, they are most frequently married, and they have planned out their futures. Now let us review the characteristics that are somewhat more surprising to find defining these students. These characteristics are marked by a (!) to indicate that the result is not commonly reported in the literature: it is a qualification, as it were, to what is found elsewhere. The active conservatives have fewest highly educated mothers, they are more likely to have parents who belong to a higher-status Protestant denomination or to the Catholic church, and they are most 'rooted' in the province. They are more likely to be second or later born; they were disciplined psychologically rather than physically; and they recall explicit political socialization in a harmonious, happy home. At present, they are disproportionately graduate students, talented scholars, and aiming for three degrees. Again there is nothing in this portrait that directly contradicts evidence from other research, although the complete portrait contradicts the inferred or deduced characteristics.

The second column of table 9.1 lists the characteristics which stand out (comparatively) as describing the passive radicals. One can briefly indicate their flavour. These individuals tend to remember a family in which the mother made the decisions and a somewhat unhappy childhood. They are now disproportionately enrolled in the sciences and education, are comparatively new to the university, have lower grades (lower than the conservatives, which is supposed to be surprising), lack career plans, and have changed faculties at least once. To me at least, this is quite a convincing portrait as well. These students, while liberal in viewpoints, don't 'get it together' to become active because they are in departments that are peripheral to the activist base. They are also less talented students, struggling harder in the university.

The characteristics that are emphasized for passive conservatives are listed down the third column. They are unlikely to have mothers who worked outside the home, their parents are disproportionately members of lower-status religious denominations, and they are long-term residents of the province. They just tend to recall that the father made most of the family's decisions, and that they occupied a less central status in the childhood family (than conservative actors). At present, they are disproportionately in professional training, least likely to be working during the school year, and most likely to have dropped out of university for a year or more. Again the factors distinguishing them from the active conservatives sum up a convincing 'excuse' for inactivity: they have been raised in lower-status families and were socialized to be less assertive, and are now attempting to establish themselves, with fewer resources of talent or background.

In summary, therefore, the portraits of the types achieve a good match with the literature where evidence is available. Where no comparisons are possible, the results for this research are coherent and convincing.

We can also review the attitudinal characteristics of the types. Although scales used here are non-standard, one can review characteristics for their consistency and plausibility. Tables 9.2 and 9.3 present a tabular summary of the findings about the political and social viewpoints of the types and their attitudes about themselves. These findings are drawn from chapter 4.

Acting radicals are again at the extreme left of the table. The sign $(+)$ represents results which one should have expected, given the general thrust of the literature. The $(!)$ indicates somewhat less mundane information. In

TABLE 9.1*
Summary of findings, chapters 6 to 8

Acting radicals	Passive radicals	Passive conservatives	Acting conservatives	Ranks[†]
Attributed Characteristics (social locations of the types): bivariate summary				
Proportion of males roughly as sample (55% male) (+)			Disproportionately male (78% male) (+)	n.s.[‡]
More professional occupational (+) mothers		Tied second	Fewest professional (+) occupational mothers	0.005
More working mothers	Second	Fewest working mothers	Third	0.01
More mothers with high education (+)	Third	Second	Fewest mothers with high education (!)	n.s.
Parents disproportionately in status denominations (+)		Parents disproportionately in non-status denominations	Parents disproportionately in status denominations, Catholic (!)	0.03 df = 16
Least 'rooted' in province (!)	Third on 'rooted' variable	Second most rooted in province	Most 'rooted' in province (67%) (!)	n.s.
Socialization Characteristics (childhood family dynamics)				
Disproportionately first-born (+)	Second	Third	Disproportionately not first-born (!)	0.02
Recall parents unfavourably (+)				n.s.
Disproportionate psychological discipline (+)			Disproportionate psychological discipline (!)	0.01
Recall most parental conflict (+)				0.02
Recall explicit political socialization (+)			Recall explicit political socialization (!)	0.02
Family decision-making shared (+)	Families disproportionately mother-dominated	Father dominated decision-making	Family decision-making shared (!)	n.s.

Least central childhood status (+)	Radicals lowest on happiness (+)	Recall less central status in childhood than act. cons.	Recall childhood influence happiness, central status (!)	0.01
Disproportionately non church attenders (+)		Second highest church attenders	Disproportionately church attenders (+)	
Students' Own Characteristics (post-childhood identity)				
Disproportionately in arts, professions (+)	Disproportionately in sciences, education	Disproportionately in professional studies	Disproportionately in graduate studies (!)	0.01 df = 28
	Shortest period in university (!)		Longest period in university (!)	0.01
Disproportionately aim for three degrees (+)			Disproportionately aim for three degrees (!)	0.05
Disproportionately high grades (+)	Lowest grades (?)		High grades (!)	n.s.
Rank second in scholarships (+)			Disproportionately hold scholarships (!)	n.s.
Tied most working	Second	Fewest working	Tied most working	0.05
	Disproportionately change faculties (!)	Disproportionately take time out from university (!)		n.s.
Likely to lack career plans (+)			Disproportionately well-planned for future (+)	n.s.
Most secular (48%) (+)	Second (42%)	Third (28%)	Fewest secular (2%) (+)	0.05
Tied third	Tied third	Second	Most frequently married (+)	0.06

* (+) following an item indicates direct support in the empirical literature; (!) indicates qualified findings reported in empirical literature; (?) indicates a finding that is contrary to empirical literature.

† Ranks denote types from highest to lowest on the dummy variable. Significance is χ^2 with four degrees of freedom unless otherwise noted. 'Not a type' included in analysis.

‡ See note 2 at end of book.

TABLE 9.2
Political-social attitudes and activities: bivariate summary*

Acting radicals	Passive radicals	Passive conservatives	Acting conservatives	Ranks†
Disproportionately NDP, Liberal (+)	Disproportionately Liberal	Disproportionately Progressive Conservative	Disproportionately few NDP (+)	0.001 df = 32‡
Most left policy preferences (+)	Second most left	'right' policy preferences (actors 'moral' liberals)		0.0001
Most on Nurturance (+)	Second	Lowest	Third (!)	0.0001
Lowest on F-scale (+)	Second lowest	Highest on F-Scale (+)	Second (+)	0.0001
Highest on Non-university Political Acts (+)	Lowest	Third		0.0001
Second on Social-Helping Activity (!)		Lowest on Social-Helping	Highest on Social-Helping Activity (!)	0.001
Second on Club Contacts	Second on Club Contacts	Lowest on Club Contacts	Highest on Club Contacts (!)	0.0001
Second on Informal Personal Contacts (!)	Fewest Informal Personal Contacts (!)		Highest on Informal Personal Contacts (!)	0.0001
Second on Humanistic Deeds (+)	Second		Highest on Humanistic Deeds (!)	0.01
Least Political Alienation (!)	Tied highest on Political Alienation			0.0001
Lowest on Closed-Mindedness (+)	Third	Highest on Closed-Mindedness	Second	0.0001
Lowest on Pessimism	Third	Second	Highest on Pessimism (+)	0.0001
Lowest on War (+)	Second	Tied highest on War		0.001

Lowest on Religion (+)	Third	Second	Highest on Religion (+)	0.0001
Second on University Alienation	Highest (!)	Third	Lowest on University Alienation (+)	0.001
Second on System Cynicism	Highest (!)	Third	Lowest on System Cynicism (+)	0.0001
Second on Aimlessness	Highest (!)	Third	Lowest on Aimlessness (+)	0.001
Third on Contentment	Least (!)	Second	Most on Contentment (+)	0.02
Least elitist (+)	Second	Highest on University Elitism (+)		0.001

* For (+), (!), (?) see table 9.1.
† Denotes 2-tailed T-test (SPSS) except as noted.
‡ Chi-square.

TABLE 9.3
Summary for psychological and physical states of types

Acting radicals	Passive radicals	Passive conservatives	Acting conservatives	Ranks
Opinions about the Self: Bivariate Summary				
Tied second on Anxiety	Highest	Tied second	Lowest on Anxiety (?)	n.s.
Worst on GMHI	Second	Third	Best on GMHI (?)	n.s. (0.07)
Tied second on Submissiveness	Highest	Tied second	Lowest on Submissiveness (?)	n.s.
Tied second on Self-esteem	Lowest (+)	Tied second	Highest on Self-esteem (?)	n.s.
Enjoyment of Routine, Physical Well-being: Bivariate Summary				
	Least well-acquainted with classmates (+)			n.s.
Tied most stimulated by other students (+)	Least stimulated (+)		Tied most stimulated (!)	0.01
Third most stimulated by professors	Least stimulated (+)	Second	Most stimulated by professors	n.s.
Third least happy with studies	Least happy with studies (+)	Second	Happiest with studies	n.s.
			Best health	n.s.
Tied for most childhood illness			Tied for most childhood illness	0.01
Tied for most serious adult illness			Tied for most serious adult illness	n.s.
			Least minor illness	n.s.
			Hospitalized least	n.s.

* For (+), (!), (?) see table 9.1.

keeping with their views, left activists are disproportionately likely to endorse left party preferences and options, they are highest on compassionate attitudes toward the unfortunate, and least approving of authority, war, and religion. They are least pessimistic about 'human nature' and least likely to hold that there is one version of 'the truth.' They are, in keeping with their high activity in the university setting, most active in the political activity outside the university. They are second-most active – following the active conservatives – on all the non-political activity options, including small daily kindnesses to others. They are distinguished in viewpoints from their passive opinion-mates by comparatively less alienation from both the political system and the university environment. Passive radicals are most disenchanted of all the types with the university experience and setting.

Active conservatives are characterized by the expected opinion content, but are less expectedly more active than radicals in *all* the non-political options. They are sociable and helpful in the extreme. Overall, they appear to be set apart from the passive students who share their views on university politics by slightly *less* 'conservative' attitudes and more affection for the university experience and setting. Once again these results are utterly plausible, in terms of both internal coherence and external touchstones.

It is with regard to the individual's opinions about himself or herself that results from this research diverge from expectations of other researchers. It is found here that acting radicals are not characterized by superior mental or physical health. If any one type has an edge, it is the passive conservatives.

We can now turn to the question of the autonomy of these effects. Findings reviewed to this point are derived from bivariate analysis, and one must ask whether effects would be diminished or erased in multivariate analysis. The multiple regression analyses of chapters 6, 7, and 8 weighed the effects of each factor with other factors controlled. We can review these findings, which indicate the autonomous effect of each variable, other variables controlled, within each group of factors. The separate question of the autonomy of the *groups* of factors themselves – background, socialization, and the students' own characteristics – will be addressed later.

Table 9.4 summarizes the results of the multivariate analyses, with regard to factors which appear to facilitate activity within ideological groups. Factors listed in the first column under each of the headings are those whose effects were strongest and clearest. Factors listed between lines and slightly to the right are those variables whose standard errors were approximately one-half the unstandardized B coefficient. There are no surprises with regard to factors aiding university activity or outside political activity within the samples of radicals and conservatives. Quite different factors emerge as encouraging

TABLE 9.4
Variables emerging as activity facilitators when ideology controlled: multivariate analysis summary

Radical university ideology students	Conservative university ideology students
University Activity	
Highly educated father	Catholic mother
Strict mother	Male gender
Professional mother (trend)	Highly educated mother a disadvantage (trend)
First-born status	Strict mother
Less happy childhood (trend)	Not close to father (trend)
Explicit political discussion	Higher degree aspirations
Higher degree aspirations	Presence of religious affiliation
Professional faculty (trend)	
Advanced year of study	
Arts faculty (trend)	
Not changing faculty	
Non-university Activity	
Highly educated father	Male gender
Secular father	Democratic family decision-making
Complained in childhood	Canadian parents (trend)
Working mother (trend)	
Advanced year of study	Higher degree aspirations
Less happy childhood (trend)	Change of faculty (graduate school)
Explicit political discussion (trend)	Explicit political discussion (trend)
Not changing faculty	
First-born status	Taken time out of university
Higher degree aspirations	
Parent-parent conflict (trend)	

Social-Helping Activity

Not male gender	Highly educated father (trend)	Catholic mother	Canadian parents (trend)
Not secular father		Not male gender	Not highly educated mother (trend)
Not highly educated mother	Professional father (trend)		Anglo-Protestant mother (trend)
More church-going		More church-going	Explicit political discussion (trend)
Strict mother	Happier childhood (trend)		
	Less childhood complaining (trend)		Less close to mother (trend)
In graduate faculty		Not secular	
In education faculty		Works part/full time	
Not changed faculty		Not professional faculty	
Not secular			
Higher degree aspirations			Higher degree aspirations (trend)

activity within the ideology-preference groups, but the gist is the same as that indicated in bivariate analysis. Interestingly, types appear to converge on social-helping activity: similar characteristics seem to push the individual in this direction regardless of the overall political make-up. Parenthetically, we can note that the genres of political and social-helping activity are quite different from one another.

It seems, in short, to be true that those students with some background benefits are more likely to become active in politics. It seems also to be true that identification of an action component in the subject's past allows the researcher to predict to coherent and thoroughgoing sets of viewpoints which are compatible with the 'seed' views. In short, it is plausible to argue that activity in concert with others to influence the conduct of public affairs leads to improvement in coherence of the belief system.

The Port Huron Statement, which is a founding document of the student movement, was just such a demand for the right to act in concert with others, to influence the conduct of public affairs. The demand was for participation per se. This view of democracy, which has less to do with the character of outcomes than with the development of human excellence, is of course far older than the 'functional apathy' theory with which this chapter began. Carole Pateman (1970) and Peter Bachrach (1967) identify the central theme as stemming from classic democratic theory as expressed by John Stuart Mill, Rousseau, and Kant. This theme is that 'man's development as a human being is closely dependent upon his opportunity to contribute to the solution of problems relating to his own actions' (Bachrach, 1967: 97).

Geraint Parry (1972: 3) has remarked that we do not have a participant society, even though we have a norm that participation is desirable. The extent to which the society is and can be participant will be touched upon later. Let us think for a moment about our norm or value that participation is desirable. It is possible to suggest that, as a society, we are very ambivalent about political activity, rather than whole-heartedly in favour of it. The existence of the functional apathy theory is a powerful manifestation of ambivalence. Ambivalence about the norm also surrounded the response of faculty and administration to student demands for participation. Student claims to roles which would develop brotherhood and confer dignity struck many ears as mere rhetoric. That students wanted participation 'just for the sake of it' was a fairly frequent condemnation by committee-weary faculty members. Some permanent traces of a contemporary debate in the academic community remain in the scholarly literature. Translating demands for 'participation,' for example, David Braybrooke wrote that 'to demand to participate is ... to demand to play a recognized role in a joint human activity.' He also explained that a 'broad and vague' demand for participation such as that made by students was not meaningless: 'vagueness is indispensable to demands to participate ... the demands require a vague term. People want more to say, or more to do; but they often do not know specifically just what to say or what to do, or when, or in what capacity. The demand to participate is thus a demand that groups and activities be re-organized to give people recognized roles which they do not now have and which they may not be able, at this point in time, to specify. The absence of this specification, when it is absent, does not make the demand any less serious' (Braybrooke, 1975: 78).

One does not have to hold that the university is the most fitting institution for an experiment in democracy to regret that our participant norms are so befuddled. Why does this confusion and ambivalence exist about the value of political activity, and the ability of the system to withstand broader-based participation? The nervousness is caused, one can suggest, by a mistrust of the motives and qualities of those individuals who want to express themselves in public life. We want only 'uncommon people' to guide our affairs. We do not want malevolent nincompoops to take over our institutions while we are watering our gardens. But what if there is nothing special to fear, beyond the contingencies perpetrated by the existing elites? Such is my interpretation of the substantive findings of this research about active students. Neither the left nor the right of the political spectrum could find cause for alarm in the personal characteristics or qualities of either the left or the right activists as they are described in this research. Findings about students who are both opinion-consistent *and* active in a complementary manner, compared with findings for students who are opinion-consistent only, reveal patterns of broader ideologies, more consistent views on issues, more humanitarian behaviour in personal matters, and lack of psychological distress symptoms. Passive individuals are less attractive and accomplished. Activity, at least to some extent, *causes* 'uncommon people' to develop out of ordinary individuals.

The interpretation goes beyond the cross-sectional data, as do all interpretations or 'recognitions' of pattern. Still it is in keeping with both classic democratic theory and with more recent interpretations of evidence. Carole Pateman's *Participation and Democratic Theory* (1970) is a distinguished presentation of the same argument. Pateman bases her argument in Rousseau, Mill, and G.D.H. Cole, bringing empirical evidence to bear on her central theme. This theme is that participation is educative, and that exclusion from participation stunts human potentialities. Hence opportunities for participation should be created in areas of immediate consequence to the individual

(Pateman, 1970: 20–40). Evidence is reported from Easton and Dennis (1969), and from Almond and Verba (1963), who adduce that early opportunities to participate in the family create an increased sense of competence or efficacy.

Almond and Verba also find that opportunities to participate in the workplace are associated with increased levels of efficacy. Verba, in his *Small Groups and Political Behaviour* (1961), collected findings from small-group experiments which also support the view that increased consultation, involvement, and activity enhance the self-image. Related research on management methods also shows that conditions of both real and manipulated participation increase the individual's sense of efficacy. Examples are Blauner (1960), Lipsitz (1964), Blumberg (1968), McGregor (1960), Likert (1961), and Mayo (1945).

Pateman also notes some results which qualify enthusiasm. There is some worker neglect of participation opportunities at British firms which make wide provision for participation, John Lewis and Scott Bader. With regard to workers' self-management in Yugoslavia, she notes that opportunities to participate are most intensively taken up by male, skilled workers (1970: 73). But the basic point remains: some careful research shows a moderately strong probabilistic link between participation and human pride in self-development. Regardless of outcome, people thrive in 'the relations of mutual recognition and reciprocity that constitute (or should constitute) the activity itself' (Braybrooke, 1975: 80). Finally, one by no means intends to imply that 'the system' has *nothing* to fear from broadened participation. One is not insisting on the citizen's fundamental rights to be co-opted, to be incorporated into the traditional outcomes. Broadened participation may well alter substantive outcomes.

Potential for participant society
Earlier, a word was promised about political take-up of opportunities to participate. Two sets of findings from the broader empirical political science literature form a backdrop for the discussion. First, there is a well-documented association of high educational attainment, high income, prestigious occupation, high levels of interest in public affairs, etc., with higher levels of political participation in the general population (see, for a summary, Milbrath and Goel, 1977: and in Britain, Budge, 1970, and Budge et al., 1972). Second, it has been almost equally well established that politics (the processes and outcomes of the handling of 'public goods') is so peripheral to most people that fewer than 5 per cent will develop even loose networks of opinions which bear consistently upon the same attitude object (see, for a

'classic' example, Campbell et al., 1960).[3] A sample of university students is made up of individuals with the characteristics that distinguish the highly participant and well-informed members of the mass public. It is possible to argue, therefore, that a study such as ours of opinion and activity in a highly educated group indicates the upper limits of the potential take-up of opportunity for participation. It was conducted at a historical moment when one attitude object had great salience, and the opportunities to participate were plentiful: indeed, people were recruited into activity.

Results of this study indicate that more of the same kinds of education will not be all that is needed to increase participation. Only about 20 per cent of the students satisfied the rather loose criteria for having formed a consistent set of beliefs. About half of these were highly active, defined as having undertaken two or more appropriate activities. About 12 per cent of the whole sample had taken part in the traditional student council activities and 19 per cent reported having participated in some kind of demonstration. (Coincidentally, this is the exact proportion of demonstrators found by Braungart and Braungart [1974] in their random sample of students at Pennsylvania State University.) While we may not wish to see the population demonstrating in the streets, the lesson can still be extracted: only a small proportion of the well educated will reach sophisticated levels of opinionation about any particular attitude object, and fewer still will reach high levels of participation. Thus to develop what might be called 'participatory citizenship' to higher levels would require dramatic innovations: maybe structural (an opening of opportunities to participate perhaps along the lines of the Guild Socialism of G.D.H. Cole), maybe education in politics[4] (inclusion in school curricula of pragmatic courses explaining how to get what from whom, to paraphrase Lasswell), maybe in cultural norms; maybe all three and, besides, something as yet undreamed of.

Having discussed the major substantive message that I would like my work to support, I can now weigh its technical-methodological recommendations. Following this discussion I turn to one final substantive problem: the mechanism that I have called 'coherent learning' which appears to operate in both active types.

METHODOLOGICAL IMPLICATIONS

The research strategy isolated analytical aggregates which show consistent similarity to the known groups of activism research. As well, chapters 6 to 8 showed that the analysis strategy and its criteria for consistency and activity could improve predictive power over less-controlled modes of analysis.

TABLE 9.5
Comparison of ideology groups, consistent subsample, and whole sample for amount of variance explained/number of variables/significance of equation*

Sample	University activity			Outside activity			Social-helping		
	1	2	3	1	2	3	1	2	3
Radicals	12[a]/4[b]/0.01[c]	14/5/0.01	40/6/0.0001	10/4/0.03	12/5/0.02	17/5/0.001	17/7/0.01	12/4/0.01	20/5/0.0001
Conservatives	18/5/0.01	24/8/0.001	19/6/0.01	10/2/0.02	17/4/0.01	28/4/0.001	18/6/0.02	18/4/0.01	27/5/0.001
Consistent subsample	03/2/0.06	13/6/0.0001	20/5/0.0001	05/3/0.02	28/4/0.004	11/3/0.0001	14/7/0.0001	12/4/0.0001	17/5/0.0001
Whole sample	05/5/0.0001	06/6/0.0001	11/6/0.0001	05/5/0.0001	05/5/0.0001	09/4/0.0001	06/8/0.0001	08/5/0.0001	13/7/0.0001

* 1 = parental attributes, 2 = socialization factors, 3 = own attributes. Figures taken from Tables 6.6–6.9, 7.1–7.4, 8.6–8.9.
a Percentage of variance accounted for by whole table (rounded).
b Number of variables required to account for this amount.
c Figure of significance (overall F) for whole table (rounded).

One would like to know whether or not the condition that subjects hold consistent opinions has 'paid off' in the technical sense that more powerful explanations for increases in activity levels have been forthcoming. The question is, baldly: How much more lawful does the phenomenon of political participation become if it is ascertained beforehand that the subjects hold consistent beliefs on the (criterion or stipulated) topic of interest? One would also like to evaluate the decision to regard activity as qualitatively different in antecedents (really correlates in survey research) depending on the ideology of the subjects. The question here is: How much more lawful does the phenomenon of political participation become if one conducts analyses within ideology groups (roughly subcultures which are relevant to the transmission of the characteristics being studied)?

That simple term 'how much' unfortunately poses a problem. It is supremely difficult to find legitimate ways to assess the improvement brought about by imposing the controls in analysis for, first, opinion consistency, then for direction of ideology. Many strictures warn against comparing magnitudes of variance-accounted-for from subsample to subsample, because of the different characteristics of the variance pools. The constructive core of these warnings is a caution against putting undue importance on the fragile false precision of numbers generated in defiance of a good many assumptions.

Yet this is what we need and want to do: compare results for the radicals, conservatives, and consistent subsamples and the whole sample. An explanation of some phenomenon is evaluated according to several criteria. How logical the explanation is, and how well it fits with current knowledge is important, as is the orthodoxy of the evidence-collection, including the use of statistical evidence. But the seeming importance of the so-called explanatory factors is the nub of the matter. To take an example from a more compelling literature, the detective is less interested in the presence of traces of drugs in the blood of the victim in cases where there has been extensive damage to the head. Perhaps I can be forgiven for a number of small murders if I am modest about magnitudes. Table 9.5 is presented as a rough summary of the kinds of rules of thumb social scientists work by. The table presents the summary figures for each of the equations for the regression analyses of chapters 6, 7, and 8. These summaries are for the four samples (radical students, conservative students, the types, and the whole sample) in which attempts were made to explain the variation in activity levels (for the three types of activity) by recourse to facts about the subject's parents, socialization factors, and the subject's own attributes. The reader has been cautioned: the cumulated R^2 figures should only be ranked for 'goodness' and then only in very broad categories. 'Goodness' has two components: (1) the amount of variance accounted for by the final equation, and (2) the number of variables required to account for the variation.

It may be recalled from chapter 3 that it was thought that the radical students were the most likely subjects for a powerful explanation of university political activities. The ideological definition is most appropriate to this group, the activity is most clearly 'entailed' by the ideology, and the activity is probably the most accessible within the environment.

Table 9.5 shows that this is so. The most variance – 40 per cent – is accounted for in the university political activity of radical students by a combination of six of their 'own' characteristics. Overall, the table shows that the control for ideology (i.e., analysis within the conservative and radical opinion groups) improves the amount of variance-accounted-for in all but one instance. This is where socialization factors predict more of the variability in outside political activity in the subsample which contains all the types.

Further, with only one tie, it is seen that when analyses are conducted within the whole sample (i.e., removing both the stipulation that subjects hold consistent views and the direction-of-ideology control) more variables are required to account for less of the variability in activity level. Equations are highly 'significant' in part because of the large number of subjects involved. Controls for ideology and consistency have generally resulted in a 75 to 100 per cent improvement in these terms over explanatory power in the unpartitioned sample. It seems clear, therefore, that the strategy of (1) insisting upon opinion being well-formed before we look for the lawful correlates of opinion, and (2) controlling within the opinionated sample for the direction of the ideology, has paid off in terms of power of explanation.

Only one major methodological question remains, one that has important substantive implications. This question is the (rough) degree of autonomy of the three categories of explanatory factors: parental attributes, socialization factors, and the students' own attributes.

Table 9.6 summarizes the results of an exercise designed to answer the question: Are the groups of factors used to represent parental characteristics, socialization characteristics, and the students' own characteristics autonomous in their effects *as groups*, or do effects overlap? That is, we have said that in absolute terms students' own characteristics are most important in accounting for university political activity levels of radical students. But it might be that all students with the appropriate personal characteristics were *also* raised by highly educated mothers in democratically organized families (hence to talk about factors other than parental attributes would be redundant in terms of variance-accounted-for). Logically, one should take *all* vari-

TABLE 9.6
Variation explained added by socialization factors given parental attributes
and by own characteristics given both previous categories*

Sample	University activity	Outside activity	Social-helping
Radicals	$12^a/22^b/50^c$ $(0.001)^d$	10/21/30 (0.02)	17/19/29 (0.03)
Conservatives	18/33/45 (0.001)	10/18/36 (0.03)	18/26/43 (0.002)
Consistent subsample	03/18/32 (0.0001)	05/14/21 (0.008)	14/20/27 (0.0001)
Whole sample	05/09/17 (0.0001)	05/08/14 (0.0001)	06/13/18 (0.0001)

* Variables presented in each of the regression analysis tables of chapters 6 to 8 are entered in stages with the significant parental attributes being entered together as a group first, then the socialization factors, then students' own characteristics. (The solution is stepwise within stages.)
a Variation (per cent) accounted for by parental attributes.
b Variation added by socialization factors (cumulated) controlling for important parental attributes.
c Variation added by own characteristics (cumulated), controlling for important parental attributes and socialization factors.
d Significance of whole equation.

ables from each group, entering them in a regression equation in stages with activity dependent. But to do so would involve technical mayhem, because the size of the conservative sample in particular is too small to bear analyses with such large numbers of variables in the equation. Accordingly, the variables which emerged as the most important of their category in stepwise regression analyses are entered in groups, the dependent variables being each of the activity variables. The question is whether a good deal of improvement is brought about in our ability to explain levels of activity by knowing about socialization characteristics *as well* as about parental attributes, and by knowing about students' own characteristics as well as about their parents' characteristics and their upbringings. This is an obvious and minimal developmental ordering entailed by time, and no specific causal imputations are made.

Overall, it is seen that explanations of activity level through socialization factors and through the students' own characteristics are important in themselves. That is, groups of factors are fairly autonomously related to activity levels. In terms of substance, this means that although the increased activity of students with conservative ideology is associated with a rearing by parents in certain social locations, it cannot be taken for granted that these social locations are perfectly related to certain childrearing practices, or that the student then necessarily grows along certain lines in the university career. To put the case mildly, there is a great deal of indeterminancy from one level of description to another. Thus parental attributes explain 10 per cent of the variation in the outside political activity of conservative students, socialization factors add a further 8 per cent to the explanation of activity levels, and knowledge of the students' own characteristics adds a further 18 per cent to the total of 36 per cent of the variation explained. It will be noted that other researchers (see chapter 5) have not found socialization factors to be so autonomous, but then they were working with less homogeneous groups.

The reader is reminded of the earlier hypothesis that activity would find its 'best' explanation in factors temporally closest to that activity. It seems that students' own characteristics overall explain more variability than do socialization factors, and that effects of the student's own characteristics are most autonomous vis-à-vis university activities for the sample of radicals. These figures should not be taken too seriously in themselves. But they can be regarded as rough evidence for the contention that the findings from chapter to chapter describe fairly autonomous variance domains, and therefore are worth taking seriously in terms of substance.[5]

COHERENT LEARNING: THE PROCESS FACILITATING BELIEF-SYSTEM FORMATION AND ACTIVITY

The pieces are now in place for a discussion of the explanation of the underlying advantage enjoyed by those who are highly participant. In earlier chapters, it was shown that the likelihood that an individual will be active, and the frequency of political activity, increased as evidence builds up describing personal and social privilege. But there was a quirk: whether a characteristic is an advantage in terms of boosting activity or a disadvantage seems to depend upon the ideological direction of the individual's beliefs. For example, being the child of a mother who held a high-status occupation is slightly associated with increased activity in radicals but with decreased activity in conservatives. In short, what is a 'good' characteristic in one group can show up as a 'bad' characteristic in another. It was then the task of the 'coherent learning' notion to explain how this could be. And although the explanation goes considerably beyond the kind and extent of evidence available in this study, I offer it as one that may be usefully invoked and investigated in future research.

The factor that appears to characterize the qualities of actors (whether conservative or radical) is that their characteristics cumulate into something we can recognize as a pattern. This can be explained in somewhat more detail. First, let us simply accept that pattern or lawfulness exists in both persons and in their social settings: everything is *not* possible. In a minimal definition, Skinner has defined personality as 'a repertoire of behavior imparted by an organized set of contingencies.' (1976: 164). The sociologist W.I. Thomas had much earlier (Thomas and Znaniecki, 1918) argued that the content and characteristics of attitudes described the imprint of culture on the individual. We can also accept that for an aspect of culture to leave its residue, the individual must have been exposed to it. A person will have as many 'selves' as he has had central roles in central settings in terms of his own life.

The political aspect of personality, or the political 'self' (selves), must then be the ideological direction espoused and the frequency of political activity. This will be a repertoire of behaviour like any other, imparted by an organized set of contingencies. The degree of organization of the political personality will have to do with the synchronization of the individual's roles: will the individual's 'reality testing' of his many contexts teach him to organize his ideas in keeping with one or another of the elite criterion ideologies? For these ideologies exist to be bought ready-made: their content is a contingent fact – that is, a fact to be established empirically. Indeed, Converse has recommended that social scientists accept provision of such description as a primary task.

The lesson of the present research is that coherent learning takes place in coherent settings – where contingencies are organized into 'sets.' Where there is no organization in 'the environment' there will be no apparent organization of ideas. Indeed, the phrase 'the environment' suggests a spurious unity: the individual plays many roles from situation to situation, over time. The ideas drawn from experiences will be summaries to the extent that the contingent reinforcers – the rewards – reinforce similar behaviours and viewpoints across situations, so that some pattern emerges with high survival value. This could be simply the patterning in the person of some directed thrust in views which is compatible with one of the main contemporary belief systems. 'Survival value' might then mean that the ideas are comfortably 'voicable' in the person's main social contexts.

At the risk of being tedious, an example of how this might work can be provided. A stereotype is best for the purpose. Imagine that one is born to a father who is a successful businessman in a small but respectable enterprise. One's mother in this fiction is happy in her role as wife, mother, and director of consumption. Views expressed at the dinner table are small 'c' conservative. No particular child-rearing practice is absolutely entailed by the social location: the culture and contingencies of the family translate the earnings of the father into its own currency. But the social status will set rough boundaries for what can happen, to and for the child. Our intuitions about what sorts of social facts go with each other tell us, for example, that such a family would not allow its children to stay up at night until they fell asleep of their own accord. We expect some rules to operate. Similarly, both the parents' characteristics and the quality of upbringing the individual has undergone will set only rough boundaries for what he will make of himself. True or not, one has the impression of a moment of flexibility vis-à-vis one's future at the moment one 'chooses' one's university discipline, for example. The person of our example at age eighteen can choose to do a degree in commerce, business administration, economics, or even fine arts.

Imagine that he chooses business administration or commerce. The conversations he hears while he relaxes with his friends may well repeat the conversations he has been accustomed to hear at his own dinner table. Gradually he will learn a set of views: he may even learn how to place current issues so that they can be deduced from the main principles of small-'c' conservatism. He may 'go out' for student council at the urging of his friends.

But now pretend for a moment that the student chose to enrol in fine arts in that moment of flexibility. His peers and mentors, if they have any politics at all, will regret Mammon and the society which barely allows them a living. They will wish that the state were *more* generous in its support of the 'hangers-on.' These are new views for our imagined student: he may learn not to voice them at the family dinner table. The old views and the new views alike remain somewhat unpractised. Bits and pieces are acquired, but a belief system does not develop which has constraint and range: at least not so readily as in the first case. The student may 'go out' for a demonstration against a fee increase, still not 'learning' very much. It will be rarely that an individual consciously undertakes the revision and reconciliation of the various views. If he does, it may be the task of half a lifetime.

In general, probably very little that we hear or do adds up to much. The riches of one's apprehension of one's various environments brings a kind of confetti blizzard of ideas. Summaries of experience which are durable over time are hard won. Relatively little of the detail of life can be fitted into any one of these summaries or 'theories' by the individual. Or it may be done in a proliferation of little 'theories.' For this reason, or, rather, from this assumption or perspective, I offer the 'coherent learning' formulation in preference to a cross-pressures explanation. It stands in roughly the same relation to cross-pressures theory as does attribution theory to cognitive dissonance theory. The difference is primarily that both cross-pressures and dissonance theory posit a motivational state of discomfort in the individual.[6]

This discomfort is 'caused' by ostensibly conflicting needs and objective information. In the case of dissonance theory, the discomfort triggers a virtually random choice between equally attractive alternatives. It is then assuaged by post-decisional selection of only comforting information. In cross-pressures theory, the dilemma is 'solved' when the individual avoids or opts out of any decisions and the conflicted area.

Cross-pressures theory posits that when an individual is in a position where his reference groups conflict in matters of value and opinion, then that individual will find himself in a poignant quandary about his own views. An example of conflict would be when the person's educational attainment is high, but his occupation is of low status. The person will take longer to make up his mind on any conflicted issue, and will be less likely to choose and fulfil a course of action. The 'coherent learning' explanation would posit, in contrast, that the individual concerned would simply not have learned to hold opinions on the matter on which his reference groups 'disagree.' Too many different things may have been said for any one sentiment to have had the benefit of recognition: all the ideas are casual strangers. Or perhaps nothing has been attended to. The 'coherent learning' notion has therefore the advantage of simplicity. One does not think of the individual as suffering routinely at each opportunity for self-expression. Most of the time, he will be merely innocent of knowledge. Among the small group of ideologues will be mainly persons whose political learning has been clear sailing, as it were, and a few others who have worked their way into and out of conflicted states. In summary, it is from the meeting of an organized environment and the receptively organized personality – and vice-versa – that political activity springs. The organized environment is one that as a contingent matter is repeatedly, across settings, suggesting some social ideological option that is well formulated – Fabian socialism, Marxism, the Social Gospel, New Left views, Old Left views, Friedmanism, Burkean conservatism, Douglas's A plus B Theorem, or even the student power belief system.[7]

The relative autonomy of the three domains of explanatory factors seems to be of some relevance to the coherent learning explanation. If the domains of parental attributes, socialization factors, and the student's own characteristics were found to be very heavily overlapping in explanatory power, then one would be led to think that the detailed outcomes of one's life (as indicated by the student's own characteristics) were largely determined by background and socialization factors. But in fact we see that factors that are temporally closest to the activity in question explain a different subset of the variance in the activity score. See again table 9.6, which reviews the autonomous nature of the groups of factors. This suggests that so long as an individual is alive to his experiences, investing in his roles, then he is in a profoundly developmental stage in terms of new opinions and new competencies.[8] An important caveat is that our research may not have captured the particular variables that *would* have predicted (correlated) across the groups of factors. That is, social statuses may as a matter of fact powerfully determine child-rearing practices which in turn powerfully determine the detail of later 'choices' about what to do in life. We might have been studying the wrong variables.

RECOMMENDATIONS

This last unhappy notion brings me to the recommendation for future research with which all books end. To me, the most important work must be to study how closely and in what ways social statuses and contexts translate into the contemporary beliefs and actions of the individual. In chapter 1 it was promised that this research would tell us about the 'causes' of belief systems in terms of social locations and the person's characteristics. To some extent, this was done. But we have also found that many of the commonly used variables of political sociology do not neatly describe the environments in which the learned opinions 'precipitated out.' The gross context variables of income, education, and occupation must in future be related to more detailed descriptions of cultural settings. These settings must in turn be related to the content of preferences, and to typical personal styles (traits) of conduct.[9] Perhaps most important, such links must be established on the basis of prior theory: the riches of the mind will always provide convincing pattern after the fact.

Having started with very detailed descriptions of environments, we should further assume that discovered 'laws' are of restricted generality. We should therefore only aggregate groups as it becomes clear that characteristics and processes are shared. The characteristics on the basis of which groups are formed for analysis will be course vary between academic disciplines: to control along the divisions which define the subcultures which are relevant to the transmission of the characteristics under study would appear to be an obvious guideline.

While it would be nice to end on a full-throated high note, it is important to review both the positive and negative lessons to be taken from this research. The entire book is a recommendation about methodology. But the case studied had the exaggerated characteristics of all good examples. The attitude object was of considerable salience. It was possible to devise several indicators of opinions, and to collect information on a range of relevant behaviours. Opportunities for opinion-consistent activities were readily available, indeed difficult to avoid. 'The movement' provided a political milieu. (In effect, this is what social movements do: they provide roles for actors who are not in the elite political stratum in the ordinary course of events.) The subjects were easily captured for interview.

One is struck, in this research, by how *little* real consistency there appears to be in people's beliefs. What does the strategy of cross-examining for consistency mean for more heterogeneous populations contemplating less immediately salient problems? Probably it means that the researcher should be clear in his own mind as to what he is doing: (1) is he looking for incidence of agreement among the population with a criterion sentiment, *or* (2) is he trying to find out what the population itself believes? In the first case, the consistency method would be useful. In the second, he should start with homogeneous groups, interview them to ascertain their views, and aggregate upwards only when it is justified.

Next, what of the tactic of building the activity component right in to the 'stance' or 'attitude' toward the social object? This seems to suggest some problems. For example, what about situations where there is no immediate opportunity for an appropriate behaviour? Shall we conclude that only systemically provided activity is relevant – voting, campaigning, and so forth – and that views which do not mesh with these should be ignored? Probably not. One can conclude, however, that researchers should be clear about whether they are studying viewpoints as (1) causes of action, or (2) residues of experience which help the individual to interpret the world, not necessarily having any implication for action, *or* (3) activity-seasoned stances which encourage the individual to move forward into *new* activity. It is to the last of these that this book is most relevant. Another way of saying much the same thing is that we should not only be clear about whether we are using viewpoints as dependent or independent variables, we must also specify the nature of the non-attitudinal causes or effects. Political scientists simply must force themselves to consider the lack of handholds on the political system when working with alienation, efficacy, etc. as *political* attitudes. If they are concerned about non-voting, let them say so. If they are worrying about riot potential, let them say so.

This is tedious work indeed, and it is important not to exaggerate the potential pay-off. On the plus side, the return on the analysis and investigation strategy has been considerable. An 'ideology of student power' has been defined which extends into every other important aspect of the world-view. It has been shown to stop at the boundary of what is usually termed 'personality factors' or personal emotional needs. Thus, actors of both ideological extremes have been revealed as kindly and thoughtful people. Their ideologies have been shown to be associated with structured environments in completely believable manners, just as Bergman said. Last, contemporaneous factors have been shown to account for great amounts of the variability in the action level of the defined political personality.

On the other side, there have been few strong surprises in the course of this work. If there has been good sense, it has come at enormous cost. In terms of the money to finance a survey of this magnitude, the cost was high. In terms of the time spent drawing often unrevealing tables in an attempt to comply with the cannons of best current practice, while not bending the questions to fit the readily available answers, the cost was great. In assessing the cost-benefit ratio of survey research, one must surely admit that the costs outweigh the benefits. What it does offer is the representative sample, which allows us to discover the islands of consistency, and to guess about the size of the unmapped terrain. I do not anticipate that we will ever report on specific environments turning out specific kinds of persons with the precision of a bottle factory.

But probabilistic kinds of knowledge must be possible as a matter of scientific faith and of our common-sense observation of how things go together. We grow in humanity as we take moral responsibility for our social settings. The discovery of islands of consistency in human affairs allows us to see in what ways we ourselves are causes.

APPENDIXES

A

Individual items for scales of chapter 2, tables relating to concurrent validity

Scales are presented here in the same sequence as in chapter 2. These factor analyses are of the items of each scale, one scale at a time. It will be recalled that they follow analysis of the total item-pool which established that items of each scale are more strongly related to one another than to items of another scale. The loadings at the right indicate the amount to which a statement is correlated with the dimension of variance common to all the statements on the factor. As usual, it can be squared to interpret the amount of the item's variability which is loaded on the dimension. These are the weights used to calculate factor scale scores.

STUDENT POLITICS AND OTHER UNIVERSITY-SPECIFIC MEASURES

Rejection of Radicals

Radical students are a bigger threat to the ordinary student than are the faculty and administration. (+)[1]   0.776

Student radicals' demands for student power are realistic, and should be supported by the student body in general. (−)   0.723

It would probably be best for the university if faculty and administrators took a hard line with student power advocates. (+)   0.704

Radical students are the greatest obstacle to change at this university because they irresponsibly antagonize faculty and administration. (+)   0.702

Generally speaking, the radical students have a pretty good idea of the way this university is run. (−)   0.625

---

1 The (+) and (−) indicate the direction of the 'correct' response for the cumulative score.

Student Power

Student should have as much say in running the university as 'older, more experienced faculty and administrators.' (+)   0.713

Students should definitely have a voice in determining course content and required courses. (+)   0.672

University students should have the right to organize to protect their own interests. (+)   0.609

The university administration, like that of a city, province, or nation, should be controlled by those for whom it is administering, that is, faculty and students. (+)   0.603

Students have responsibility to be concerned, active, and informed participants in the running of the university. (+)   0.598

Students should have the right to strike if they are dissatisfied with conditions in the university. (+)   0.597

Decision-making in university affairs would take up too much of the student's time, and might stand in the way of important learning. (−)   0.589

If students had votes in the university's official governing bodies, they probably wouldn't know what to do with them. (−)   0.543

University Militancy[2]

If you had what you thought was a legitimate grievance against the university, do you think you might:

participate in non-violent demonstrations?   I 0.763, II   0.217

participate in a student boycott of classes?   I 0.715, II   0.285

raise or sign a petition to the administration?   I 0.697, II −0.128

participate in occupations of buildings?   I 0.265, II   0.797

participate in a violent demonstration?   I 0.014, II   0.836

Correlation between factors = 0.110

---

2 Oblique rotation produces two factor matrices, the primary pattern matrix and the primary structure matrix, rather than just one. According to Rummel, primary pattern emphasizes differences between factors (as does orthogonal rotation), whereas structure loadings emphasize interrelatedness of factors. The primary structure loadings can be interpreted as product-moment correlations of the variable with the oblique factor (Rummell, 1967, 1970). The primary structure loadings are reported here for the two factors emerging for these items in oblique solution. (For primary pattern loadings, and item correlations, see Sutherland, 1975.)

General Militancy

Now let's take a very general situation. Supposing you had a grievance against the national government. Let's just say that the party in control of the government was doing things that would likely harm your own well-being and/or that of your family. Following are a list of things people might do to oppose the government, and we would like you to check the list and answer 'yes' if you would consider doing this particular thing, and 'no' if you wouldn't consider doing this thing. Try to judge each separately with a yes or no answer.

participate in a general strike, a national work stoppage	I 0.190, II	0.788
participate in a potentially violent demonstration	I 0.129, II	0.724
participate in a peaceful demonstration	I 0.492, II	0.427
try to organize a group of people to oppose the government	I 0.721, II	0.223
help raise a petition protesting the actions of the government	I 0.775, II	−0.078
join a political party opposed to the government	I 0.424, II	0.305

Correlation between factors = 0.211

System Cynicism

The student in this university is just a ⅟16 inch hole in an IBM punch card. (+)	0.716
University courses don't deal with the important questions, they deal with the trivia that surround these questions. (+)	0.699
University administrators just don't give a damn about how their decisions affect students' lives. (+)	0.647
University lectures are usually dry and boring. (+)	0.600
Many faculty members won't take radical stands on issues because they are afraid of losing their jobs. (+)	0.535
A university student probably learns more from discussions with fellow students than he does from faculty. (+)	0.540

Aimlessness

I guess the main reason that I'm in university is that it was the 'thing to do.' (+)	0.820
I came to university mainly because it was expected of me. (+)	0.768
My reasons for coming to university were poorly defined, and are subject to constant re-examination. (+)	0.745

Upon graduating from high school, I didn't really know what I wanted to do,
so I came to university. (+)   0.730

Contentment

Had I known more about what the university would really be like, I would still
have been anxious to come here. (+)   0.797

For a variety of reasons, the university experience has not been very pleasant for
me. (−)   0.789

Being in a university community is generally depressing. (−)   0.729

Attending university is one of the most rewarding experiences in one's
life. (+)   0.717

University Alienation

The size of the university has not interfered with my being able to make friends
with other students. (−)   0.785

I feel lost and alone much of the time on campus. (+)   0.725

The university is too impersonal. (+)   0.707

University Elitism

If university graduates weren't somehow superior to other people, they wouldn't
have gotten through university. (+)   0.735

People who go to university work hard for what they get, and therefore belong
'on the top' relative to the rest of society. (+)   0.746

University graduates aren't really better than other people; other people probably
didn't get the breaks. (−)   0.605

ORIENTATIONS TO SOCIETY

Survey F (Belief in Discipline and Obedience)

What youth needs today is strict discipline, rugged determination, and the will to
work and fight for family and country. (+F)   0.764

Obedience and respect for authority are the most important virtues children
should learn. (+F)   0.742

Young people get rebellious ideas, but as they grow up they should get over
them and settle down. (+F)   0.618

There is hardly anything lower than a person who does not feel a great love,
gratitude, and respect for his parents. (+F)   0.596

If people would talk less and work more, everybody would be better off. (+F)   0.595

Most of our social problems would be solved if we could somehow manage to get rid of the immoral, crooked, and feeble-minded people. (+F)   0.571

What this country needs most, more than laws and political programs, are a few courageous, tireless, devoted leaders, in whom people can put their faith. (+F)   0.468

In this complicated world of ours, the only way we can know what is going on is to rely on leaders or experts who can be trusted. (+Dog)   0.418

Closed-Mindedness

There are two kinds of people in this world: those who are for the truth, and those who are against the truth. (+Dog)   0.711

A good job is one where what is to be done, and how it is to be done, is always clear. (+I of A)   0.600

The sooner we all acquire similar values and ideals, the better. (+I of A)   0.591

Of all the different philosophies that exist in this world, there is probably only one which is correct. (+Dog)   0.566

An expert who doesn't come up with a definite answer probably doesn't know too much. (+I of A)   0.563

People can be divided into two classes, the weak and the strong. (+F)   0.564

Submissiveness (Lack of Confidence)

It seems to me that other people find it easier to decide what is right than I do. (+Anomy)   0.648

It is only natural for a person to be rather fearful of the future. (+Dog)   0.635

I would like it if I could find someone who would tell me how to solve my personal problems. (+Dog)   0.622

Everything changes so quickly these days that I often have trouble deciding which are the right rules to follow. (+Anomy)   0.605

Fundamentally, the world we live in is a pretty lonesome place. (+Dog)   0.568

It is hardly fair to bring a child into the world with the way things look for the future. (+Anomy)   0.541

Pessimism

In the future, mankind will probably be able to eliminate war and other social problems. (−)   I 0.865, II 0.221

Human nature being what it is, there will always be war and
conflict. (+F)   I 0.765, II 0.474

Man will someday become a less selfish creature. (−)   I 0.810, II 0.147

Human nature is basically evil. (+)   I 0.234, II 0.812

Aggressiveness, destructiveness, and cruelty are inborn human
tendencies. (+)   I 0.120, II 0.805

When you come right down to it, it's human nature never to do anything
without an eye to one's own profit. (+)   I 0.361, II 0.629

Primary factors correlation = 0.225

Attitudes toward War and Force

The evils of war are greater than any possible benefits. (−)   0.751

There can be no progress without war. (+)   0.750

While the use of force is wrong by and large, it is sometimes the only way to
advance a noble ideal. (+Dog)   0.611

Religiousness

Mankind's existence is not complete without the idea of a greater, supernatural
power. (+)   0.907

Man's life can never be full or complete if religion is absent. (+)   0.898

Every person should have complete faith in some supernatural power whose
decisions he obeys without question. (+F)   0.786

Nurturance

The best way to deter men from crime is to make them suffer. (−)
                                                           I 0.695, II 0.348

Drug addicts should be regarded as victims of a disease rather than as criminals.
(+)   I 0.698, II 0.004

Physical punishment, like whipping or beating, is the best way to maintain discipline in our jails. (−)   I 0.687, II 0.177

All criminals are victims of circumstance, and deserve to be helped rather than
being put in jails. (+)   I 0.589, II 0.257

One should never punish children too harshly. (+)   I 0.487, II 0.226

It is just as well that the struggle of life tends to weed out those who cannot
stand the pace. (−)   I 0.251, II 0.661

Most people who don't get ahead just don't have enough willpower. (−)
                                                           I 0.240, II 0.644

The economic needs of individuals are the responsibilities of themselves and their families, and are not the responsibility of the community in general. (−)   I 0.416, II 0.571

Our country should permit the immigration of foreign peoples, even if it lowers our own standard of living. (+)   I 0.057, II 0.644

Primary factor correlation = 0.238

Political Alienation

Sometimes politics and government seem so complicated that a person like me can't really understand what is going on. (+)   0.760

Voting is the only way that most people can have any say about how the government runs things. (+)   0.734

Generally, those elected to Parliament soon lose touch with the people. (+) 0.269

Alienation from People

Do you think most people would try to take advantage of you if they got a chance, or would they try to be fair? (Faith in People)   0.707

These days a person really doesn't know whom he can count on. (+Anomia)   0.705

Generally speaking, would you say that most people can be trusted, or that you can't be too careful in dealing with people? (Faith in People)   0.703

Most people really don't care what happens to the next fellow. (+Anomia Dog)   0.620

I doubt the honesty of people who are more friendly than I would expect them to be. (+IPAT)   0.498

PSYCHOLOGICAL FUNCTIONING MEASURES

Self-esteem

I feel that I have fewer good qualities than most people. (−)   0.712

All in all, I am inclined to feel that I am a failure. (−)   0.703

At times I think I am no good at all. (−)   0.695

I feel that I am a person of worth, at least on an equal plane with others. (+)   0.675

I wish that I could have more respect for myself. (−)   0.668

Generally speaking, I think that I have a lot to be proud of. (+)   0.554

General Mental Health Index
1. Do you ever have any trouble getting to sleep or staying asleep?
2. Have you ever been bothered by nervousness, feeling fidgety or tense?
3. Are you ever bothered by headaches or pains in the head?
4. Do you have loss of appetite?
5. How often are you bothered by having an upset stomach?
6. Do you find it difficult to get up in the morning?
7. Has any ill health affected the amount of work you do?
8. Have you ever been bothered by shortness of breath when not exercising or working hard?
9. Have you ever been bothered by your heart beating hard?
10. Do you ever have spells of dizziness?
11. Do your hands ever tremble enough to bother you?
12. Are you ever bothered by nightmares?
13. Do you tend to lose weight when you have something important bothering you?
14. Are you troubled by your hands sweating so that you feel damp and clammy?
15. Have there been times when you couldn't take care of things because you just couldn't get going?

Response categories are uniformly 'very often,' 'fairly often,' 'hardly ever,' and 'never.' 'Very often' is scored high, and an overall high score indicates ill health. See table A6 for correlations between items.

Institute for Personality Assessment and Testing Anxiety Measure
Because of copyright restrictions, items for the subscales cannot be reported. The correlations between the subscales are shown in table A1.

COMMENT ON SURVEY F CORRELATES (TABLE A2)

Table A2, in which correlates for Survey F. Closed-Mindedness, and Submissiveness are shown, supports the hypotheses of relationships as suggested by the 'traditional' F dimensions (see Sutherland and Tanenbaum, 1980). Taking Survey F correlates in order of absolute size of the correlation, findings can be stated as follows.

There is a relationship between a tendency to advocate obedience to traditional authority figures (Survey F) and the following:
1 A rejection and fear of that group of students who are challenging university authority figures. (RRR) $r = 0.536$

TABLE A1
Correlations between Anxiety (IPAT) primary factors

	Sensitive to criticism	Irritability	Depression	Paranoia	Tension
Sensitive to criticism					
Irritability	0.158				
Depression	0.279	0.185			
Paranoia	0.212	0.197	0.159		
Tension	0.299	0.117	0.145	0.103	

TABLE A2
Correlates of Survey F, Closed-Mindedness, RRR, and Submissiveness

	Survey F	Closed-Mindedness	Submissiveness
RRR	0.536	0.214	0.060
University Elitism	0.245	0.235	0.022
Student Power	−0.437	−0.159	−0.039
Contentment	0.032	−0.050	−0.240
Aimlessness	0.004	0.076	0.269
System Cynicism	0.094	0.216	0.264
IPAT	0.112	0.123	0.566
Mental Health	0.003	0.050	0.388
Submissiveness	0.288	0.253	1.000
Self-esteem	−0.099	−0.171	−0.522
Alienation from People	0.272	0.342	0.408
Political Alienation	0.353	0.274	0.323
University Alienation	0.019	0.068	0.229
Closed-Mindedness	0.536	1.000	0.253
Survey F	1.000	0.536	0.288
Religiousness	0.405	0.320	0.143
Pessimism	0.362	0.319	0.263
Nurturance	−0.495	−0.327	−0.050
War	0.243	0.138	0.097
University Militancy	−0.331	−0.123	−0.020
General Militancy	−0.279	−0.188	−0.122

2 A tendency to think in black and white terms. (Closed-Mindedness) $r =$ 0.536

3 A rejection of the notions that one should withhold judgment of and should extend nurturance to immigrants, criminals, and the destitute. (Nurturance) $r = -0.495$

4 A rejection of the idea that the peer group (students) should share in decision-making in the university. (Student Power) $r = -0.437$

5 A tendency to prescribe belief in religion or 'a supernatural power.' (Religion) $r = 0.405$

6 A tendency to believe that there is an innate 'human nature' and the mistrust of it is evil or at best weak. (Pessimism) $r = 0.362$

7 A tendency to feel that the individual is of little importance in political decision-making. (Political Alienation) $r = 0.353$

8 A rejection of the possibility that the individual might himself become engaged in opposing university authorities. (University Militancy) $r = -0.331$

9 A lack of confidence, a tendency to feel helpless and lonely in isolation. (Submissiveness) $r = 0.288$

10 A feeling of justified or 'earned' superiority toward persons who have not attended university. (University Elitism) $r = 0.245$

11 A view that war and force are necessary. (War) $r = 0.243$

12 A dislike and mistrust of other individuals – a tendency to adopt a stance of wariness, which fits well with the associated view of human nature. (Alienation from People) $r = 0.272$

13 A professed unwillingness to take a stand in the general political environment despite perception of an injustice. (General Militancy) $r = -0.279$

Relationships which are not strong are equally interesting. Table A2 shows that Survey F is not associated with a negative orientation toward the immediate university environment, nor is it strongly associated with the psychological functioning variables Mental Health, IPAT, and Self-esteem. This is an important disclaimer, because it is generally assumed that the high authoritarian individual is psychologically impaired. He is thought to bask in the reflected glory, power, and security of authority to make up for his basically insecure personality.

The strong association of Submissiveness with psychological distress, and the moderate association of Submissiveness with F suggests that the usual finding of association between authoritarianism and impaired mental health may be largely due to the inclusion in F versions of items which themselves tap impaired mental health (i.e. Submissiveness-type items). Table A3 shows

245 Items for scales of chapter 2

TABLE A3
Correlates of IPAT, Mental Health, Self-esteem, and Submissiveness

	IPAT	Mental Health	Self-esteem	Submissiveness
RRR	−0.067	−0.143	0.011	0.060
University Elitism	−0.018	−0.000	0.013	0.022
Student Power	0.030	0.083	0.006	−0.039
Contentment	−0.219	−0.186	−0.252	−0.240
Aimlessness	0.227	0.133	−0.248	0.269
System Cynicism	0.262	0.203	−0.252	0.264
IPAT	1.000	0.475	−0.572	0.566
Mental Health	0.475	1.000	−0.427	0.388
Submissiveness	0.566	0.388	−0.522	1.000
Self-esteem	−0.572	−0.427	1.000	−0.522
Alienation from People	0.285	0.180	−0.269	0.408
Political Alienation	0.266	0.126	−0.219	0.323
University Alienation	0.274	0.215	−0.289	0.307
Closed-Mindedness	0.123	0.050	−0.171	0.253
Survey F	0.112	0.003	−0.099	0.288
Religiousness	0.112	0.031	−0.107	0.143
Pessimism	0.112	0.020	−0.098	0.268
Nurturance	0.062	0.093	−0.029	−0.050
War	−0.020	−0.035	0.041	0.097
University Militancy	0.043	0.032	−0.017	−0.020
General Militancy	−0.066	−0.000	0.063	−0.122

the similarity between submissiveness and the psychological functioning scales. Their patterns of intercorrelation with the social and political scales, and with each other, are quite alike.

The oblique factor analysis reported in tables A5 and A6 makes the same point about the relatedness of the individual scales. See table 2.2 in text for a summary of the primary structure matrix.

TABLE A4
Primary pattern P of 21 major scales (oblique factor analysis)

	I	II	III	IV	V
RRR	−0.6962*	−0.0856	0.1897	−0.0802	0.1662
System Cynicism	0.3285	0.0264	−0.0164	0.6433*	0.3207
Contentment	0.1215	−0.0489	0.1063	−0.7878*	0.1332
Aimlessness	0.0734	0.1309	0.1169	0.5444*	−0.1348
University Elitism	0.0985	0.0104	0.6084*	−0.1614	0.0570
Student Power	0.7157*	−0.0079	−0.2949	0.1061	0.0547
Survey F	−0.3434	0.0140	0.3500	−0.0020	0.5642*
Political Alienation	−0.0719	0.2029	0.0831	0.1220	0.4808*
Self-esteem	0.0545	−0.7474	0.0364	−0.1366	−0.0351
Religiousness	−0.1534	0.0343	−0.1933	−0.1502	0.7484*
Pessimism	−0.1041	0.1151	0.5097*	0.0084	0.2229
Nurturance	0.3115	0.1223	−0.6752*	0.0047	−0.0676
University Militancy	0.8182*	−0.0057	0.0307	0.0461	0.0058
General Militancy	0.6542*	−0.0478	0.1082	−0.0730	−0.1277
Mental Health	0.0620	0.7622*	−0.0384	−0.0297	−0.0757
University Alienation	0.0407	0.1427	−0.1835	0.6212*	0.0890
Closed-Mindedness	0.0110	0.0011	0.3148	0.0794	0.6485*
Submissiveness	−0.0571	0.6777*	0.1416	0.1913	0.1480
Alienation from People	0.0179	0.1931	0.4048	0.4366*	0.1690
War	−0.0621	−0.0347	0.6132*	0.0478	−0.1342
IPAT	0.0110	0.8141*	−0.0263	0.0636	0.0629

* Loadings greater than 0.4 are asterisked to help identify the factor.

TABLE A5
Primary structures of 21 major scales (oblique factor analysis)

	1	2	3	4	5
RRR	−0.7529*	−0.0848	0.3082	−0.1144	0.2757
System Cynicism	0.3222	0.2126	0.0067	0.7051*	0.3491
Contentment	0.0409	−0.1976	0.0852	−0.7727*	0.0339
Aimlessness	0.1099	0.2372	0.1062	0.5648*	−0.0467
University Elitism	−0.0047	0.0059	0.5990*	−0.1291	0.1197
Student Power	0.7554*	0.0222	−0.3844	0.1437	−0.0832
Survey F	−0.4742	0.0946	0.4863	0.0571	0.6697*
Political Alienation	−0.1431	0.2941	0.1787	0.2205	0.5448*
Self-esteem	0.0356	−0.7797*	−0.0074	−0.2993	−0.1506
Religiousness	−0.2426	0.0899	−0.0587	−0.0699	0.7275*
Pessimism	−0.2059	0.1627	0.5633*	0.0683	0.3329
Nurturance	0.4185	0.0949	−0.7250*	0.0219	−0.2009
University Militancy	0.8157*	0.0181	−0.0825	0.0939	−0.1031
General Militancy	0.6525*	−0.0670	−0.0076	−0.0572	−0.2202
Mental Health	0.0877	0.7453*	−0.0325	0.1300	0.0052
University Alienation	0.0918	0.2837	−0.1523	0.6597*	0.1458
Closed-Mindedness	−0.1224	0.1143	0.4162	0.1650	0.7051*
Submissiveness	−0.0775	0.7429*	0.2024	0.3570	0.2888
Alienation from People	−0.0354	0.3250	0.4481	0.5112*	0.3053
War	−0.1269	−0.0208	0.6013*	0.0388	−0.0290
IPAT	0.0211	0.8354*	0.0129	0.2482	0.1707

* Loadings greater than 0.4 are asterisked to help identify the factor.

TABLE A6
GMHI item intercorrelations

	1	2	3	4	5	6	7	8	9	10	11	12	13	14	15
1															
2	0.433														
3	0.261	0.317													
4	0.261	0.287	0.325												
5	0.250	0.288	0.270	0.365											
6	0.180	0.211	0.128	0.107	0.111										
7	0.255	0.290	0.363	0.352	0.269	0.110									
8	0.166	0.178	0.216	0.213	0.176	0.120	0.314								
9	0.187	0.215	0.262	0.214	0.179	0.101	0.298	0.448							
10	0.195	0.266	0.339	0.281	0.270	0.121	0.268	0.275	0.284						
11	0.252	0.373	0.207	0.239	0.208	0.090	0.240	0.309	0.290	0.337					
12	0.257	0.327	0.266	0.262	0.211	0.133	0.241	0.218	0.259	0.290	0.311				
13	0.207	0.295	0.231	0.373	0.237	0.120	0.235	0.177	0.218	0.231	0.241	0.339			
14	0.194	0.331	0.210	0.187	0.196	0.112	0.160	0.191	0.247	0.244	0.337	0.297	0.278		
15	0.200	0.326	0.225	0.197	0.205	0.200	0.368	0.254	0.275	0.222	0.216	0.215	0.169	0.274	
Sum	0.548	0.645	0.565	0.566	0.512	0.378	0.572	0.514	0.545	0.567	0.582	0.578	0.547	0.541	0.531

Average item intercorrelation = 0.243 $\alpha = 0.83$

B

Occupation, education, and income tables

Bernard Blishen's listing of occupations was used for coding occupational titles (Blishen, 1958, 1967). His titles were taken in order, each being assigned a unique code in the sequence, working down from the most prestigious.

Recoding followed Blishen's scheme for occupational strata (see table B1). Some codes were added: (a) farmer, (b) rancher, (c) Canadian University Service Overseas, (d) travel.

Other relevant coding decisions were:

1 Where a response was vague, codes were assigned after consulting income and education questions.
2 Blishen's denotation Owners and Managers was interpreted as Owners and/or Managers. Decisions following from this were:
   a) School superintendents – both public school and technical – were coded as Owners and Managers, Education and Related Services.
   b) Bank Managers were coded Owners and Managers, Finance, Insurance and Real Estate.
   c) Owners and Managers, Local Administration, includes a few persons who listed their occupation as Hospital Administration.
   d) Owners and Managers, Miscellaneous Services, includes service station owners/managers, and restauranteers.
   e) Owners and Managers, Provincial Administration and Federal Administration, includes civil servants in well-paid positions (over $10,000).
3 Working down alphabetically through the rest of the occupational categories, decisions made were:
   a) 38, Authors, Editors, and Journalists was enlarged to include TV scriptwriters and non-technical TV personnel.

b) 58, Health Professionals, other, was interpreted to mean persons such as trained speech therapists.

c) Professional Occupations, Not Elsewhere Specified, includes clinical psychologists and occupations for which a university degree is necessary, but which are not clearly designated elsewhere.

TABLE B1
Distribution of fathers' occupation for whole sample

Occupational category	n	Percentage
Professional	159	17.0
Semi-professionals*	35	3.7
Owner-manager (large)	160	17.1
Owner-manager (small)	128	13.6
White collar	67	7.1
Skilled	106	11.3
Semi-skilled	32	3.4
Unskilled	60	6.4
Farmer or rancher	191	20.4
Total	938	100.0

* Includes occupations such as social worker, journalist, and computing personnel.

TABLE B2
Distribution of working mothers' occupation for whole sample

Occupational category	n	Percentage
Professional and semi-professional (high-status occupations)	112	33.3
Owners-managers, white collar and clerical workers (medium-status occupations)	156	46.4
Skilled and unskilled (low-status occupations)	68	20.2
Total	336	100.0

TABLE B3
Father's occupation by income

Parental income in fifths	Father's occupation									
	Profes-sional	Semi-profess.	Owner-manager Large	Small	White collar	Skilled	Semi-skilled	Unskilled	Farmer/rancher	Total
1	8 / 5.5r / 5.3c	1 / 0.7 / 2.9	9 / 6.2 / 5.8	7 / 4.8 / 5.6	8 / 5.5 / 12.3	27 / 18.5 / 26.0	7 / 4.8 / 22.6	27 / 18.5 / 48.2	52 / 35.6 / 32.5	146 / 16.6
2	18 / 8.0 / 11.9	8 / 3.6 / 23.5	27 / 12.0 / 17.5	31 / 13.8 / 24.8	32 / 14.2 / 49.2	37 / 16.4 / 35.6	16 / 7.1 / 51.6	16 / 7.1 / 28.6	40 / 17.8 / 25.0	225 / 25.6
3	19 / 11.7 / 12.6	7 / 4.3 / 20.6	32 / 19.6 / 20.8	40 / 24.5 / 32.0	9 / 5.5 / 13.8	22 / 13.5 / 21.2	3 / 1.8 / 9.7	6 / 3.7 / 10.7	25 / 15.3 / 15.6	163 / 18.5
4	42 / 22.8 / 27.8	11 / 6.0 / 32.4	45 / 24.5 / 29.2	32 / 17.4 / 25.6	7 / 3.8 / 10.8	14 / 7.6 / 13.5	4 / 2.2 / 12.9	4 / 2.2 / 7.1	25 / 13.6 / 15.6	184 / 20.9
5	64 / 39.5 / 42.4	7 / 4.3 / 20.6	41 / 25.3 / 26.6	15 / 9.3 / 12.0	9 / 5.6 / 13.8	4 / 2.5 / 3.8	1 / 0.6 / 3.2	3 / 1.9 / 5.4	18 / 11.1 / 11.2	162 / 18.4
Total	151 / 17.2	34 / 3.9	154 / 17.5	125 / 14.2	65 / 7.4	104 / 11.8	31 / 3.5	56 / 6.4	160 / 18.2	880 / 100.0

$\chi^2 = 270.69$ with 32 degrees of freedom. $\gamma = -0.42100$.

r = row percentage; c = column percentage.

TABLE B4
Income by parents' social class

Parents' social class	Parental income in fifths					Total
	1	2	3	4	5	Total
1	0	0	1	1	13	15
	0.0^r	0.0	6.7	6.7	86.7	
	0.0^c	0.0	0.6	0.5	7.9	1.7
2	3	16	30	61	101	211
	1.4	7.6	14.2	28.9	47.9	
	2.0	7.2	18.2	32.4	61.6	23.7
3	56	145	104	112	43	460
	12.2	31.5	22.6	24.3	9.3	
	37.1	65.0	63.0	59.6	26.2	51.6
4	52	45	21	12	4	134
	38.8	33.6	15.7	9.0	3.0	
	34.4	20.0	12.7	6.4	2.4	15.0
5	40	17	9	2	3	71
	56.3	23.9	12.7	2.8	4.2	
	26.5	7.6	5.5	1.1	1.8	8.0
Total	151	223	165	188	164	891
	16.9	25.0	18.5	21.1	18.4	100.0

$\chi^2 = 495.47$ with 16 degrees of freedom. $\gamma = -0.67580$.

r = row percentage; c = column percentage.

TABLE B5
Educational attainment of respondents' parents

Education categories	Father	Mother
1 No schooling	0.7	0.7
2 Some grade school	16.5	10.0
3 Finished grade school	16.2	16.4
4 Some high school	23.6	23.5
5 High school diploma	10.0	19.0
6 Trade/business school	8.3	8.1
7 Teacher's training college ('Normal School')	1.2	8.3
8 Some university	5.6	4.8
9 University degree	11.7	7.6
10 Advanced degree	5.6	0.7

C

Standard scores on variables for the political types

The standard scores for the political types on the variables discussed in chapter 4 are calculated by dividing the difference from the sample mean of each group (type) mean by the sample standard deviation. These scores are intended to indicate the general relative patterns of the various types on the variables; it is evident that many of the differences are small. Table C1 tabulates the scores plotted in the figures in chapter 4 together with the appropriate means, standard deviations, and numbers in groups. Note that the number in parentheses following the total for the entire sample is the total number of missing cases for that variable. Thus the given sample size plus the number of missing cases should be 959, which is the total sample size. The five groups are discussed in detail in chapter 3; in brief: group '1' is Passive Conservatives with 71 cases, group '2' is Acting Conservatives with 18 cases, group '3' is Passive Radicals with 38 cases, and group '4' is Active Radicals with 82 cases; group '0' is the residual group of 'non-types' whose members did not satisfy the opinionation consistency criteria. There are 750 in this group.

TABLE C1
Standard scores, means, standard deviations, and group sizes of the political types
(0 = Residual 'non-type' group; 1 = Passive Conservatives group; 2 = Active Conservatives
group; 3 = Passive Radicals group; 4 = Active Radicals group)

Group	Standard score	Mean	Standard deviation	Group size
Sum of University Political Acts				
0	−0.09	0.89	1.05	750
1	−0.82	0.00	0.00	71
2	1.15	2.39	0.61	18
3	−0.82	0.00	0.00	38
4	1.62	3.00	1.09	82
Entire sample	1.62	0.99	1.21	959 (0)
University Militancy Affect				
0	−0.08	−0.11	1.30	628
1	−0.94	−1.40	0.70	71
2	−1.02	−1.53	0.76	18
3	0.85	1.27	1.18	38
4	1.20	1.80	1.57	82
Entire sample	0.00	0.00	1.49	837 (122)
Student Power Affect				
0	−0.05	−0.05	0.85	733
1	−1.30	−1.30	0.75	71
2	−1.17	−1.16	0.56	18
3	1.15	1.15	0.46	38
4	1.31	1.31	0.50	82
Entire sample	0.00	0.00	0.99	942 (17)
Rejection of Radicals Affect				
0	0.06	0.07	0.84	741
1	1.26	1.27	0.52	71
2	1.35	1.35	0.52	18
3	−1.18	−1.18	0.53	38
4	−1.43	−1.42	0.54	82
Entire sample	0.00	0.01	0.99	950 (9)
General Militancy Affect				
0	−0.04	−0.07	1.54	727
1	−0.67	−1.06	1.42	71
2	−0.58	−0.93	1.59	16
3	0.38	0.59	1.35	37
4	0.87	1.36	1.17	81
Entire sample	0.00	−0.01	1.58	932 (27)

255 Standard scores for political types

TABLE C1 (continued)

Group	Standard score	Mean	Standard deviation	Group size
Nurturance Affect				
0	−0.07	−0.10	1.45	736
1	−0.68	−1.07	1.69	71
2	−0.35	−0.55	1.22	18
3	0.50	0.79	1.42	38
4	1.05	1.66	1.30	81
Entire sample	0.00	0.00	1.57	944 (15)
Left-Liberalism Affect (summary index)				
0	−0.05	35.14	7.00	730
1	−0.86	29.00	7.94	69
2	−0.74	29.94	6.32	17
3	0.48	39.16	4.67	38
4	1.12	44.00	4.94	82
Entire sample	0.00	35.54	7.56	936 (23)
Survey F Affect				
0	0.05	0.06	0.95	733
1	0.73	0.74	0.81	71
2	0.81	0.81	0.95	18
3	−0.54	−0.54	0.93	38
4	−1.03	−1.03	0.68	81
Entire sample	0.00	0.00	0.99	941 (18)
Sum of Outside (Non-university) Political Acts				
0	−0.08	2.01	1.48	750
1	−0.37	1.56	1.14	71
2	0.63	3.11	1.61	18
3	−0.17	1.87	1.55	38
4	0.99	3.66	1.50	82
Entire sample	0.00	2.14	1.54	959 (0)
Sum of Social-Helping Activities				
0	0.00	1.35	1.07	750
1	−0.28	1.06	1.05	71
2	0.75	2.17	1.20	18
3	−0.09	1.26	0.89	38
4	0.14	1.51	1.23	82
Entire sample	0.00	1.35	1.09	959 (0)

TABLE C1 (continued)

Group	Standard score	Mean	Standard deviation	Group size
Informal Contacts (summary index)				
0	−0.02	9.17	2.31	711
1	−0.09	9.00	2.37	69
2	0.83	11.18	1.63	17
3	−0.42	8.21	2.56	38
4	0.31	9.94	2.34	78
Entire sample	0.00	9.22	2.35	913 (46)
Club Contacts (summary index)				
0	−0.02	1.25	1.52	734
1	−0.05	1.20	1.41	71
2	0.62	2.22	1.52	18
3	−0.44	0.61	0.86	38
4	0.29	1.71	1.71	80
Entire sample	0.00	1.28	1.52	941 (18)
Political Alienation Affect				
0	0.01	0.02	1.15	743
1	0.32	0.38	1.12	71
2	−0.09	−0.10	1.54	18
3	0.28	0.33	1.16	38
4	−0.49	−0.57	1.09	81
Entire sample	0.00	0.00	1.17	951 (8)
Closed-Mindedness Affect				
0	0.05	0.05	0.99	742
1	0.27	0.27	1.08	70
2	−0.01	−0.01	1.03	17
3	−0.12	−0.12	1.04	37
4	−0.64	−0.64	0.74	81
Entire sample	0.00	0.00	1.00	947 (12)
Pessimism Affect				
0	0.06	0.10	1.52	740
1	0.25	0.40	1.45	71
2	0.33	0.52	1.73	18
3	−0.16	−0.24	1.58	38
4	−0.74	−0.16	1.52	82
Entire sample	0.00	0.00	1.57	949 (10)

TABLE C1 (continued)

Group	Standard score	Mean	Standard deviation	Group size
War Affect				
0	0.04	0.05	0.99	746
1	0.17	0.18	0.97	71
2	0.14	0.15	0.91	18
3	−0.25	−0.23	0.85	38
4	−0.43	−0.42	0.88	81
Entire sample	0.00	0.01	0.99	954 (5)
Religion Affect				
0	0.02	0.02	0.99	750
1	0.25	0.25	1.15	71
2	0.43	0.42	1.07	18
3	−0.02	−0.03	0.98	38
4	−0.52	−0.53	0.84	82
Entire sample	0.00	−0.01	1.01	959 (0)
University Alienation Affect				
0	−0.01	−0.00	0.98	743
1	−0.29	−0.29	0.96	71
2	−0.40	−0.40	1.10	18
3	0.40	0.40	1.13	38
4	0.22	0.23	1.01	81
Entire sample	0.00	0.00	1.00	951 (8)
System Cynicism Affect				
0	−0.02	−0.04	0.95	741
1	−0.49	−0.50	0.89	71
2	−0.84	−0.85	0.61	18
3	0.72	0.69	1.13	37
4	0.46	0.44	0.97	78
Entire sample	0.00	−0.02	0.99	945 (14)
Aimlessness Affect				
0	−0.01	−0.01	0.98	739
1	−0.24	−0.23	0.98	71
2	−0.43	−0.43	0.90	18
3	0.50	0.50	1.18	38
4	0.20	0.21	0.95	82
Entire sample	0.00	0.01	0.99	948 (11)

TABLE C1 (continued)

Group	Standard score	Mean	Standard deviation	Group size
Contentment Affect				
0	0.01	0.14	0.98	743
1	0.03	0.04	0.95	71
2	0.62	0.62	0.77	18
3	−0.27	−0.27	1.17	38
4	−0.15	−0.17	1.12	81
Entire sample	0.00	0.00	0.99	951 (8)
University Elitism Affect				
0	0.05	0.05	0.99	740
1	0.17	0.18	0.96	71
2	0.23	0.23	0.95	18
3	−0.18	−0.17	0.87	38
4	−0.54	−0.53	0.99	82
Entire sample	0.00	0.01	1.00	949 (10)
IPAT (Anxiety) Affect				
0	0.00	−0.02	2.84	729
1	−0.05	−0.15	2.90	69
2	−0.60	−1.73	2.84	18
3	0.27	0.75	2.95	38
4	0.08	0.23	2.90	78
Entire sample	0.00	−0.01	2.86	932 (27)
Sensitivty to Criticism (IPAT Component Scale)				
0	0.02	0.04	0.98	729
1	−0.11	−0.09	1.12	69
2	−0.31	−0.30	0.81	18
3	0.05	0.06	1.06	38
4	−0.08	−0.06	1.01	78
Entire sample	0.00	0.02	0.99	932 (27)
Depression (IPAT Component Scale)				
0	−0.03	−0.03	0.98	729
1	0.06	0.06	0.96	69
2	−0.68	−0.68	1.13	18
3	0.33	0.34	1.20	38
4	0.22	0.23	1.10	78
Entire sample	0.00	0.00	1.01	932 (27)

259 Standard scores for political types

TABLE C1 (continued)

Group	Standard score	Mean	Standard deviation	Group size
Tension (IPAT Component Scale)				
0	−0.01	−0.01	0.97	729
1	−0.18	−0.19	1.12	69
2	−0.36	−0.36	0.56	18
3	0.31	0.30	0.95	38
4	0.15	0.14	1.12	78
Entire sample	0.00	−0.01	0.99	932 (27)
Irritability (IPAT Component Scale)				
0	−0.01	−0.02	0.87	729
1	0.00	−0.01	0.80	69
2	−0.28	−0.25	0.95	18
3	0.27	0.23	0.94	38
4	0.08	0.06	0.87	78
Entire sample	0.00	−0.01	0.87	932 (27)
Paranoia (IPAT Component Scale)				
0	0.02	0.02	1.00	729
1	0.08	0.08	1.00	69
2	−0.11	−0.11	1.02	18
3	−0.16	−0.16	0.98	38
4	−0.12	−0.12	1.02	78
Entire sample	0.00	0.00	1.00	932 (27)
Mental (Ill) Health Affect				
0	−0.02	27.47	5.74	727
1	−0.05	27.29	6.01	69
2	−0.60	24.18	4.77	17
3	0.10	28.17	5.09	36
4	0.33	29.50	5.54	80
Entire sample	0.00	27.60	5.74	929 (30)
Submissiveness Affect				
0	0.02	0.02	1.00	742
1	−0.05	−0.05	0.92	71
2	−0.37	−0.36	0.94	18
3	0.14	0.15	1.10	38
4	−0.08	0.08	0.99	82
Entire sample	0.00	0.01	1.00	951 (8)

TABLE C1 (continued)

Group	Standard score	Mean	Standard deviation	Group size
Self-esteem Affect				
0	0.01	0.01	0.97	744
1	−0.01	−0.01	1.01	71
2	0.51	0.51	0.84	18
3	−0.21	−0.21	1.19	38
4	−0.05	−0.05	1.16	81
Entire sample	0.00	0.00	1.00	952 (7)
Well-Acquainted with Classmates (Single Item)				
0	0.00	2.59	0.69	749
1	0.06	2.55	0.71	71
2	0.17	2.47	0.80	17
3	−0.40	2.87	0.74	38
4	0.11	2.51	0.69	82
Entire sample	0.00	2.59	0.70	957 (2)
Stimulated by Other Students (Single Item)				
0	−0.01	1.81	0.73	748
1	−0.07	1.86	0.66	71
2	0.34	1.56	0.71	18
3	−0.41	2.11	0.76	38
4	0.25	1.62	0.71	82
Entire sample	0.00	1.81	0.73	957 (2)
Stimulated by Professors (Single Item)				
0	0.00	2.40	0.72	742
1	0.20	2.25	0.75	71
2	0.62	1.94	0.80	18
3	−0.59	2.84	0.79	38
4	−0.03	2.43	0.79	82
Entire sample	0.00	2.40	0.74	951 (8)
Happy with Current Studies (Single Item)				
0	0.00	2.24	0.79	749
1	0.18	2.10	0.74	71
2	0.73	1.67	0.69	18
3	−0.36	2.53	0.73	38
4	−0.15	2.37	0.84	82
Entire sample	0.00	2.24	0.79	958 (1)

261 Standard scores for political types

TABLE C1 (continued)

Group	Standard score	Mean	Standard deviation	Group size
Health Poor Past Year (Single Item)				
0	−0.02	1.45	0.66	748
1	0.04	1.49	0.77	71
2	−0.27	1.28	0.58	18
3	0.09	1.53	0.78	38
4	0.15	1.57	0.77	81
Entire sample	0.00	1.46	0.68	956 (3)
Number of Serious Childhood Illnesses				
0	−0.02	0.41	0.95	750
1	−0.09	0.34	0.86	70
2	0.16	0.59	0.94	17
3	−0.15	0.29	0.84	38
4	0.31	0.73	1.07	81
Entire sample	0.00	0.43	0.96	956 (3)
Number of Serious Adult (after age 15) Illnesses				
0	−0.01	0.10	0.37	747
1	−0.04	0.87	0.28	70
2	0.17	0.17	0.71	18
3	−0.20	0.03	0.16	38
4	0.13	0.15	0.43	79
Entire sample	0.00	0.10	0.37	952 (7)
Number of Minor but Enduring Ailments				
0	−0.03	0.67	0.91	748
1	0.16	0.85	0.86	71
2	−0.40	0.33	0.46	18
3	0.07	0.76	0.75	38
4	0.16	0.84	1.05	81
Entire sample	0.00	0.70	0.91	956 (3)
Number of Times Hospitalized Past Five Years				
0	−0.01	0.51	0.90	748
1	0.07	0.58	1.01	71
2	−0.20	0.33	0.49	18
3	0.01	0.53	1.11	38
4	0.06	0.57	0.94	81
Entire sample	0.00	0.51	0.91	956 (3)

D

Reference tables

TABLE D1
Distribution characteristics of opinion scales (factor score scales) for whole sample ($N = 959$)

Variable	Lower limit	Upper limit	Mean	SD	Skewness*	Kurtosis†	Missing cases
RRR	−2.30	2.60	0.01	0.99	0.72	−1.81	9
System Cynicism	−2.39	2.64	−0.02	0.99	1.30	−2.20	14
Student Power	−3.60	2.10	0.00	0.99	−3.46	0.72	17
Aimlessness	−1.30	2.50	0.01	0.99	6.48	−4.27	11
Contentment	−3.10	1.40	0.00	0.99	−8.41	−0.55	8
University Alienation	−2.00	2.50	0.00	1.00	3.75	−2.65	8
University Elitism	−1.60	3.60	0.01	1.00	7.89	0.51	10
University Militancy	−2.53	4.92	0.00	1.49	11.33	10.37	122
General Militancy	−7.77	2.84	0.00	1.58	−5.68	5.09	27
Survey F	−2.10	2.70	0.00	0.99	1.42	−3.79	18
Closed-Mindedness	−1.50	3.50	0.00	1.00	8.14	1.68	12
Submissiveness	−2.20	3.10	0.01	1.00	2.36	−1.82	8
Pessimism	−3.76	4.23	0.00	1.57	−0.09	−2.58	10
War	−1.40	3.80	0.00	0.99	7.00	−0.44	5
Religion	−2.43	2.11	0.01	1.01	3.28	−5.77	0
Alienation from People	−1.70	2.50	0.00	1.00	7.73	−2.30	13
Nurturance	−6.46	3.46	0.00	1.57	−4.88	1.63	15
Political Alienation	−3.04	2.92	0.00	1.17	−1.06	−2.42	8
Self-esteem	−4.60	1.50	0.00	1.00	−10.09	5.89	7
Mental Health	15.00	55.00	27.60	5.74	10.37	8.84	30
IPAT	−7.17	8.29	0.00	2.86	1.66	−2.17	27
Sensitive to Criticism	−2.97	2.40	0.02	0.99	0.35	−2.25	27
Depression	−2.33	3.84	0.00	1.01	6.94	3.67	27
Paranoia	−2.50	2.67	0.00	1.00	1.61	−3.90	27
Irritability	−2.28	2.52	−0.01	0.87	1.58	−1.37	27
Tension	−2.59	3.16	−0.01	0.99	4.00	−1.71	27

TABLE D1 (continued)

Variable	Lower limit	Upper limit	Mean	SD	Skewness*	Kurtosis†	Missing cases
Nurturance, Economic	−2.90	2.50	0.00	1.00	0.23	−1.81	15
Nurturance, General	−4.90	1.60	0.00	1.00	−14.35	13.40	15
Pessimism, Present	−1.90	3.00	0.00	1.00	5.90	−2.79	10
Pessimism, Future	−2.90	2.00	0.00	1.00	−4.40	−1.61	10
University Militancy, Moderate	−3.74	5.25	0.07	1.15	0.28	16.09	98
University Militancy, Extreme	−2.50	5.11	0.00	1.04	37.70	66.30	115
General Militancy Moderate	−5.03	1.02	0.00	1.03	−22.24	25.16	23
General Militancy Extreme	−3.85	2.97	−0.03	1.03	4.64	1.20	16

* Positive number indicates distribution is skewed to the right, negative number to the left.
† Positive values indicate leptokurtosis, negative values platykurtosis.

TABLE D2
Proportion of variance explained in opinions by activities using multiple regression

1. Analysis within Whole Sample ($N = 795$)

Independent variables	Cum. R^2	Simple R	B	Std. error B
Dependent variable Student Power				
Attend student debates	0.119	0.344	0.300	0.043
Discuss university politics	0.152	0.289	0.242	0.044
Participate in social change group	0.165	0.204	0.298	0.087
Tried to see administrator	0.166	0.014	0.103	0.080
Ran for university office	0.168	0.028	0.083	0.070
Campaigned for student council candidate	0.168	0.112	0.038	0.108
Addressed student council	0.168	0.116	0.004	0.110

Constant = 1.82   df = 7; 787   F = 22.68

Dependent variable Rejection of Radicals and Radicalism				
Attend student debates	0.093	0.304	0.284	0.043
Participate in social change group	0.129	0.262	0.517	0.088
Discuss university politics	0.139	0.206	0.143	0.045
Ran for university office	0.143	0.002	0.104	0.071
Tried to see administrator	0.144	0.011	0.089	0.081
Campaigned for student council candidate	0.146	0.053	0.102	0.110
Addressed student council	0.146	0.082	0.068	0.112

Constant = 1.59   df = 7; 787   F = 19.28

Dependent variable University Militancy				
Attend student debates	0.082	0.286	0.410	0.065
Participate in social change group	0.102	0.210	0.557	0.133
Discuss university politics	0.106	0.167	0.135	0.067
Ran for university office	0.109	0.005	0.154	0.107
Addressed student council	0.110	0.074	0.161	0.168
Campaigned for student council candidate	0.110	0.093	0.112	0.165
Tried to see administrator	0.111	0.020	0.075	0.122

Constant = 2.25   df = 7; 787   F = 14.02

TABLE D2 (continued)

2. Analysis within Opinion-Consistent Sample ($n = 338$)

Independent variables	Cum. R^2	Simple R	B	Std. error B
Dependent variable Student Power				
Attend student debates	0.195	0.442	0.381	0.079
Discuss university politics	0.235	0.378	0.343	0.082
Participate in social change group	0.265	0.338	0.534	0.145
Tried to see administrator	0.270	0.010	0.201	0.140
Ran for university office	0.271	0.046	0.104	0.115
Campaigned for student council candidate	0.273	0.167	0.182	0.178
Addressed student council	0.273	0.179	0.093	0.189

Constant = 2.59   df = 7; 330 F = 17.75

Dependent variable Rejection of Radicals and Radicalism				
Attend student debates	0.206	0.453	0.422	0.078
Participate in social change group	0.254	0.376	0.678	0.145
Discuss university politics	0.272	0.336	0.256	0.083
Tried to see administrator	0.279	0.023	0.245	0.141
Ran for university office	0.280	0.048	0.076	0.116
Campaigned for student council candidate	0.280	0.127	0.021	0.172

Constant = 2.52   df = 6; 331 F = 21.50

Dependent variable University Militancy				
Attend student debates	0.171	0.414	0.571	0.111
Participate in social change group	0.190	0.285	0.552	0.202
Discuss university politics	0.205	0.303	0.305	0.115
Ran for university office	0.211	0.001	0.257	0.160
Tried to see administrator	0.216	0.022	0.261	0.196
Campaigned for student council candidate	0.218	0.147	0.276	0.248
Addressed student council	0.219	0.147	0.186	0.264

Constant = 3.12   df = 7; 330 F = 13.21

Dependent variable New Consistency Student Power Score				
Attend student debates	0.175	0.419	0.286	0.058
Participate in social change group	0.207	0.324	0.400	0.107
Discuss university politics	0.231	0.336	0.208	0.061
Tried to see administrator	0.239	0.034	0.177	0.104
Ran for university office	0.243	0.015	0.101	0.085
Addressed student council	0.244	0.141	0.114	0.140
Campaigned for student council	0.245	0.117	0.042	0.131

Constant = 3.56   df = 7; 330 F = 15.26

E

Socialization variables: bivariate tables and intercorrelations

TABLE E1
Family 'warmth' by type: 'How close did you feel
to your mother and father when you were a child?'

			Very close	Fairly close	Not close at all
Passive	(71)	Mother	57.7[r]	39.4	2.8
conservatives	(71)	Father	39.4	46.5	14.1
Acting	(18)	Mother	55.6	38.9	5.6
conservatives	(18)	Father	27.8	55.6	16.7
Passive	(38)	Mother	57.9	36.8	5.3
radicals	(38)	Father	44.7	34.2	21.1
Acting	(80)	Mother	47.5	41.3	11.2
radicals	(80)	Father	28.0	50.0	22.0
Whole	(948)	Mother	55.9	39.3	4.6
sample	(948)	Father	38.2	47.4	14.1

r = row percentage.

TABLE E2
Family strictness by type: 'How strict were
your mother and father with you when you were a child?'

			Very strict	Moderately strict	Not strict at all
Passive	(68)	Mother	17.6[r]	70.6	11.8
conservatives	(71)	Father	29.6	64.8	5.6
Acting	(18)	Mother	33.3	55.6	11.8
conservatives	(18)	Father	11.1	77.8	11.1
Passive	(38)	Mother	5.3	73.7	21.1
radicals	(38)	Father	15.8	60.5	28.7
Acting	(81)	Mother	12.3	76.5	11.1
radicals	(82)	Father	28.0	56.1	15.9
Whole	(937)	Mother	11.8	76.9	11.2
sample	(944)	Father	23.3	65.0	11.7

r = row percentage.

TABLE E3
Punishment alternatives by type: 'When you were a child,
would you say your parents usually punished you by ...'

		Withdrawal of affection	Physical means	Withdrawal of privilege/perks	Never punished
Passive conservatives	(71)	5.6[r]	71.8	50.7	2.8
Acting conservatives	(18)	11.1	50.0	55.6	5.6
Passive radicals	(38)	18.4	65.8	39.5	5.3
Acting radicals	(82)	25.6	58.5	53.7	7.3
Whole sample	(953)	15.1	67.3	52.5	5.2

r = row percentage.

TABLE E4
Decision-allocation by type: 'Who would you say
made most of the decisions in your childhood family?'

		Mother	Father	Mother and father together
Passive conservatives	(70)	11.4^r	44.3	44.3
Acting conservatives	(18)	16.7	16.7	66.7
Passive radicals	(37)	21.6	27.0	51.4
Acting radicals	(80)	16.2	28.8	55.0
Whole sample	(950)	14.7	34.1	51.2

r = row percentage.

TABLE E5
Conflict by type: 'Would you say that your parents
argued a great deal when you were a child, or didn't argue?'

		Argued a great deal	Argued a fair amount	Argued only a little	Argued not at all
Passive conservatives	(71)	9.9^r	21.1	40.8	28.2
Acting conservatives	(18)	5.6	27.8	50.0	16.7
Passive radicals	(38)	2.6	31.6	52.6	13.2
Acting radicals	(82)	18.3	29.3	45.1	7.3
Whole sample	(951)	9.0	22.0	50.2	18.8

r = row percentage.

269 Socialization variables

TABLE E6
Frequency of parental argument by childhood complaint rate

Childhood complaint	Argued a great deal	Argued a fair amount	Argued only a little	Argued not at all	Total
Very often	53.8^r	15.4	15.4	15.4	
	16.3^c	1.9	0.8	2.2	2.7 (26)
Fairly often	9.7	26.1	50.7	13.5	
	38.4	43.0	36.4	25.7	36.0 (341)
Hardly ever	6.9	20.0	51.9	21.2	
	43.0	52.2	58.9	63.7	56.9 (539)
Never	4.9	14.6	43.9	36.6	
	2.3	2.9	3.8	8.4	4.3 (41)
Total	9.1	21.9	50.2	18.9	
	(86)	(207)	(475)	(179)	(947)

r = row percentage; c = column percentage.

TABLE E7
Childhood influence by type: 'How much influence
did you usually have on your parents' decisions?'

		A great deal	A fair amount	Only a little	None
Passive conservatives	(71)	5.6^r	36.6	38.0	19.7
Acting conservatives	(17)	5.9	52.9	29.4	11.8
Passive radicals	(38)	7.9	39.5	42.1	10.5
Acting radicals	(82)	–	42.7	46.3	11.0
Whole sample	(949)	4.3	34.0	51.0	10.6

r = row percentage.

TABLE E8
Childhood complaining by type: 'How often did you complain
about the decisions that your parents made?'

		Very often	Fairly often	Hardly ever	Never
Passive conservatives	(71)	2.8^r	25.4	69.0	2.8
Acting conservatives	(17)	–	23.5	70.6	5.9
Passive radicals	(38)	–	47.4	52.6	–
Acting radicals	(82)	6.1	45.1	46.3	2.4
Whole sample	(954)	2.7	36.3	56.7	4.3

r = row percentage.

TABLE E9
Complaint consideration by type: 'If you did complain,
how much difference did it usually make in your parents' decisions?'

		A great deal	Some difference	No difference	Never complained
Passive conservatives	(65)	4.6^r	55.4	36.9	3.1
Acting conservatives	(17)	–	64.7	35.3	–
Passive radicals	(35)	–	80.0	20.0	–
Acting radicals	(81)	1.2	74.1	22.2	2.5
Whole sample	(903)	2.0	65.7	28.9	3.4

r = row percentage.

TABLE E10
Overt political socialization by type: 'How often would you say
your parents discussed politics and community affairs when you were a child?'

		Very often	Fairly often	Hardly ever	Never
Passive conservatives	(70)	5.7^r	50.0	41.4	2.9
Acting conservatives	(18)	16.7	50.0	27.8	5.6
Passive radicals	(38)	5.3	60.5	28.9	5.3
Acting radicals	(82)	20.7	37.8	34.1	7.3
Whole sample	(953)	12.2	43.7	39.3	4.8

r = row percentage.

271 Socialization variables

TABLE E11
Childhood church-going by type: 'How often would you say that you ...
went to church or religious services, say until the time you were 15?'

		More than weekly	Weekly	2–3 times per month	Once a month	Few times a year	Never
Passive conservatives	(69)	15.9[r]	37.7	24.6	5.8	8.6	7.2
Acting conservatives	(18)	22.2	55.6	5.6	–	16.7	–
Passive radicals	(37)	5.4	48.6	16.2	5.4	18.9	5.4
Acting radicals	(79)	6.3	34.2	32.9	7.6	13.9	5.1
Whole sample	(924)	9.4	40.4	25.0	7.7	14.5	3.0

r = row percentage.

TABLE E12
Birth order by type: 'When your brothers and sisters are ranked
from eldest to youngest, are you the ...?'

		First-born or only	Sequential child
Passive conservatives	(71)	40.8[r]	59.2
Acting conservatives	(18)	33.3	66.7
Passive radicals	(38)	50.0	50.0
Acting radicals	(82)	58.5	41.5
Whole sample	(956)	42.1	57.9

r = row percentage.

TABLE E13

Childhood happiness by type: 'How happy would you say your childhood was?'

		Very happy	Fairly happy	Only a little happy	Not happy at all
Passive conservatives	(71)	35.2[r]	54.9	9.9	0.0
Acting conservatives	(18)	61.1	33.3	5.6	0.0
Passive radicals	(38)	36.8	57.9	2.6	2.6
Acting radicals	(82)	25.6	54.9	14.6	4.9
Whole sample	(955)	42.9	48.4	6.9	1.8

r = row percentage.

TABLE E14
Intercorrelations of socialization variables within whole and types' samples

	1	2	3	4	5	6	7	8	9	10	11	12	13	14	15	16
1 Male sex	1.00* / 1.00†	0.176 / 0.184	0.064 / 0.030	0.054 / -0.028	-0.066 / -0.073	-0.042 / -0.010	0.149 / 0.120	-0.016 / -0.113	0.007 / 0.180	0.061 / 0.101	0.014 / 0.020	-0.011 / 0.036	0.077 / -0.034	-0.063 / -0.009	0.021 / -0.054	0.050 / -0.039
2 Church-going as child^c (infrequent high)		1.00 / 1.00	0.088 / 0.077	0.124 / 0.044	-0.091 / -0.129	-0.084 / 0.027	0.073 / 0.111	0.073 / 0.080	0.054 / 0.098	0.073 / 0.085	0.003 / -0.176	-0.023 / -0.014	0.088 / 0.059	0.062 / 0.086	-0.048 / -0.121	0.078 / 0.032
3 First-born in family			1.00 / 1.00	0.015 / -0.086	0.050 / 0.042	-0.019 / -0.019	-0.001 / -0.018	-0.008 / -0.063	-0.003 / 0.011	-0.015 / -0.009	-0.001 / -0.147	-0.020 / 0.042	0.011 / -0.036	-0.043 / -0.019	0.071 / -0.003	0.009 / -0.004
4 Childhood happiness^c (negative high)				1.00 / 1.00	-0.333 / -0.224	-0.389 / -0.313	0.018 / -0.052	0.368 / 0.350	-0.106 / -0.029	-0.031 / 0.042	-0.098 / 0.009	-0.108 / -0.162	0.233 / 0.319	0.117 / 0.153	0.104 / 0.055	0.180 / 0.222
5 Felt close to mother					1.00 / 1.00	0.505 / 0.448	-0.040 / -0.021	-0.183 / -0.192	0.006 / -0.168	0.039 / -0.088	0.035 / -0.036	0.043 / -0.027	-0.127 / -0.060	0.003 / -0.050	-0.039 / -0.008	-0.103 / -0.032
6 Felt close to father						1.00 / 1.00	0.035 / 0.036	-0.232 / -0.208	0.067 / 0.062	0.001 / -0.005	0.048 / 0.061	0.036 / 0.076	-0.163 / -0.220	-0.028 / -0.033	-0.057 / -0.101	-0.150 / -0.148
7 Father dominated family							1.00 / 1.00	0.046 / 0.030	-0.204 / -0.219	0.068 / 0.099	-0.013 / -0.068	-0.102 / -0.117	0.206 / 0.253	-0.008 / 0.058	0.082 / 0.082	0.014 / -0.106
8 Parents fought frequently								1.00 / 1.00	-0.128 / -0.069	-0.028 / 0.019	-0.141 / -0.162	0.004 / 0.028	0.077 / 0.125	0.097 / 0.107	0.050 / -0.018	0.040 / 0.022
9 Father strict^c (negative high)									1.00 / 1.00	0.368 / 0.273	0.084 / 0.049	0.133 / 0.273	-0.187 / -0.273	0.035 / 0.050	-0.215 / -0.217	-0.014 / -0.016
10 Mother strict^c (negative high)										1.00 / 1.00	0.030 / -0.038	0.100 / 0.099	-0.131 / -0.223	-0.010 / 0.102	-0.147 / -0.142	0.004 / -0.003
11 Childhood complaining rate^c (negative high)											1.00 / 1.00	-0.233 / -0.194	0.108 / 0.067	-0.045 / -0.112	0.002 / 0.027	0.071 / 0.029
12 Felt views considered												1.00 / 1.00	-0.364 / -0.434	0.022 / 0.043	0.204 / 0.114	-0.125 / -0.105
13 Influence in childhood family^c (negative high)													1.00 / 1.00	0.022 / 0.043	0.204 / 0.114	0.126 / 0.123
14 Psychologically punished														1.00 / 1.00	-0.139 / -0.246	-0.002 / -0.030
15 Physically punished															1.00 / 1.00	0.081 / 0.149
16 Family discussed politics^c (infrequent high)																1.00 / 1.00

* Whole sample (n = 834) top row figure.
† Types (n = 186) second row figure.
c = continuous variable; all the rest are dichotomous.

TABLE E15
Intercorrelations of socialization variables within Radical and Conservative samples

	1	2	3	4	5	6	7	8	9	10	11	12	13	14	15	16
1 Male sex	1.00* 1.00†	0.170 0.254	0.071 -0.009	-0.050 0.025	-0.128 0.001	-0.029 0.017	0.091 0.150	-0.145 -0.049	0.171 0.027	0.274* 0.027	0.033 0.077	0.168 -0.115	-0.215* 0.194	0.044 -0.010	-0.051 -0.067	-0.085 0.031
2 Church-going as child^c (infrequent high)		1.00 1.00	0.012 0.073	-0.011 0.057	-0.134 -0.099	-0.068 0.178	0.133 0.151	0.055 0.047	0.042 0.117	-0.038 0.168	-0.268 0.096	0.071 -0.229*	-0.018 0.169	0.007 0.089	0.018 -0.300*	0.026 0.098
3 First-born in family			1.00 1.00	-0.146 -0.042	0.055 0.046	-0.068 0.055	-0.071 0.087	-0.182 0.069	0.045 -0.110	-0.120 0.079	-0.033* -0.241	0.038 -0.009	-0.112 0.059	-0.038 -0.112	-0.014 0.045	0.046 -0.061
4 Childhood happiness^c (negative high)				1.00 1.00	-0.237 -0.198	-0.295 -0.348	-0.174 0.173	0.362 0.304	-0.108 0.084	0.057 -0.022	0.068 -0.103	-0.358* 0.067	0.386 0.236	0.162 0.036	0.031 0.133	0.206 0.286
5 Felt close to mother					1.00 1.00	0.458 0.446	0.060 -0.135	-0.275* -0.071	-0.056* -0.400	0.000 -0.189	0.061 -0.039	0.000 -0.053	0.012 -0.159	-0.042 -0.081	-0.055 0.071	0.097* -0.265
6 Felt close to father						1.00 1.00	0.097 -0.053	-0.241 -0.149	0.171 -0.107	0.061 -0.088	0.068 0.040	0.089 0.073	-0.298* 0.073	0.000 -0.086	-0.044 -0.205	-0.123 -0.194
7 Father dominated family							1.00 1.00	-0.010 0.126	-0.212 -0.202	0.035 0.209	-0.028 -0.190	-0.032 -0.186	0.172 0.352	0.127 0.017	0.087 0.049	-0.176 -0.016
8 Parents fought frequently								1.00 1.00	-0.216* 0.133	0.010 -0.007	-0.124 -0.154	0.004 0.009	0.138 0.108	0.081 0.048	0.089 -0.147	0.019 0.048
9 Father strict^c (negative high)									1.00 1.00	0.317 0.185	0.038 0.191	0.303 0.189	-0.378 -0.142	-0.036 0.118	-0.235 -0.113	-0.060 0.108
10 Mother strict^c (negative high)										1.00 1.00	0.068 -0.109	0.040 0.123	-0.238 -0.210	0.087 0.056	-0.164 -0.092	-0.047 0.088
11 Childhood complaining rate^c (negative high)											1.00 1.00	-0.199 -0.116	0.069 0.074	-0.058 -0.052	0.069 -0.098	0.061 -0.067
12 Felt views considered												1.00 1.00	-0.453 -0.428	0.007 0.099	-0.255 -0.067	-0.209* 0.069
13 Influence in childhood family^c (negative high)													1.00 1.00	0.124 0.099	0.239* -0.067	0.241* 0.069
14 Psychologically punished														1.00 1.00	-0.255 -0.162	-0.020 -0.002
15 Physically punished															1.00 1.00	0.109 0.190
16 Family discussed politics^c (infrequent high)																1.00 1.00

* Radicals (n = 110).
† Conservatives (n = 76).
c = continuous variable; all the rest are dichotomous.

Notes

1 From an interview with the head of the Corporate and Commercial section of the Ontario bar admission course, quoted in 'Cracks Widen in Outdated Bar Admission Course,' *Globe and Mail*, 26 March 1977, pages 1 and 4. The official was explaining his reluctance to see the law students gather into large groups. The Ontario episode is an excellent example of the movement's effects. Students now routinely claim the right to air their grievances. Instructors and administrators are still routinely surprised and insulted.

2 E.J. Tanenbaum, in reporting on a sample of the Edmonton urban electorate, has found that of approximately 1,000 individuals surveyed, only seven had ever sought public office. The reader interested in the incidence of developed ideology in the mass public could begin with Angus Campbell et al. (1960), Lester Milbrath and M.L. Goel (1977), and Philip Converse (1964a, b).

3 I am grateful to an anonymous reader for clearly stating my theme in just these terms. The idea is, of course, similar to the notion that beliefs are qualified by their linkages with other beliefs as stated in *The Authoritarian Personality* (Adorno et al., 1950). It is discussed fully in chapters 2 and 3.

4 An exchange between R.D. Mathews and Tom Pocklington in *The Canadian Forum* in 1965, for example, put American faculty in the Department of Political Science at two out of a total of nine. My own count for the academic year 1968–69 puts the figure at eight Americans in a full-time faculty of twenty. This is something of an underestimate of American cultural influence, however, because at least two of the Canadian nationals had just returned from American graduate schools, as had two of the European nationals. The graduate student body was composed of perhaps one-quarter American citizens.

5 Harold Cardinal has changed less than most of the 'celebrated' radicals. He has not become outdated nor has he repudiated the sixties' stance. In the spring of 1977, for example, he was appointed regional director for Alberta for Indian Affairs, and shook up the system by moving some high-ranking Indian Affairs bureaucrats, replacing them with American Indian Movement activists. He was shortly thereafter fired.

6 Tallman's book, *Passion, Action and Politics*, provides a fairly complete introduction to the literature on social movements. His work integrates theories on social structural conditions with discussion of particular movements. A similar task is performed by a wide range of articles in McLaughlin (1969) and in Clark, Grayson, and Grayson (1975). The latter book deals with a range of Canadian social movements. Other representative books of the field, which emphasize personal motivations, are Hampden-Turner's *Radical Man*, Hoffer's *The True Believer*, and Toch's *The Social Psychology of Social Movements*. Kornhauser's *The Politics of Mass Society* and Eitzen's *Social Structure and Social Problems in America* are more attentive to social structural conditions. Viorst's *America in the 1960's* looks back at the student movement in the context of the general upheaval of the time. Altback's *Student Politics in America* provides useful background, as do virtually any of the articles and books by S.M. Lipset. A wealth of other references to the student movement per se is found in the bibliography.

7 This argument is explored in Todd Gitlin's book, *Mass Media in the Making and the Unmaking of the New Left*, which appeared just as I was completing this study.

CHAPTER 1

1 Physiological measures, disguised or indirect measures such as the ink-blot test and the story-completion tests, and behavioural observation are seldom used. When used, these measures are typically related to self-reports, or used in conjunction with self-reports. See Wahlke and Lodge (1972) for a useful discussion. They note that the literature reports correlations in the 0.25–0.30 range between physiological reactions and self-reported affect. This is the common range for correlations between self-reported affect and behaviour, also. See also Calder and Ross (1976).

2 The physiological expression of 'attitude' had previously been the link to 'science' or measurability, even in the absence of precise instruments for measurement. Without this component, attitude was in danger of being inaccessible. Thurstone's contribution was to circumvent the problem of establishing a standard or base: he offered pairs of attitudinal stimuli to subjects.

After all possible pairs had been ordered, a continuous scale of preferences was worked out. The result was an ordinal scale, as responses were relative to one another. Practical limitations on the feasibility of interpreting each subject's ranking encouraged search for a method which would establish a 'norm.' Thurstone solved the problem with the method of equal-appearing intervals. This involved prior submission of the set of attitude statements to a panel of judges, who would locate the statements on a graded continuum from least through neutral to most favourable. Subjects could be described in relation to the judges' approximation of the 'real' social attitude (Thurstone, 1927, 1931). The use of judges was cumbersome, and their views stood between the subject and the expression of his attitudes. Rensis Likert, in effect, made the attitude a Protestant proposition in 1932 by the now-obvious breakthrough of framing the questions so that the subject himself specified the strength and direction of affect. In this method, the statement-stimuli are presented, and the subject chooses a response category (generally presented as five options from 'strongly agree' through 'strongly disagree' or some such). Categories are adjusted for direction, given a numerical value, and summed for each subject over each item of the attitude 'scale.' This remains the basic tactic.

3 To take a well-known disvalued social attitude-cum-personality trait, 'authoritarianism' is consistently related to variables indicating lower socio-economic status. For reviews of empirical studies, see Christie and Cook (1958), Stewart and Hoult (1959), and Hopple (1976). Taking the supposed reverse of the F-concept, studies showing that support for democratic norms is socially located in higher strata include, notably, Berelson (1952), Stouffer (1963), McClosky (1964), Budge (1970), Budge et al. (1972), Prothro and Grigg (1960). Milbrath (1965) and Milbrath and Goel (1977) summarize findings as they relate to political participation. McClosky states the view succinctly: 'Democratic viability is ... saved by the fact that those who are most confused about democratic ideas are also likely to be politically apathetic and without significant influence. Their role in the nation's decision process is so small that their 'misguided' opinions or non-opinions have little practical consequence for stability' (1964: 376).

4 The measurement of a behavioural component of social attitudes (conceptualized as a latent or mediating stage between stimulus and response) follows from psychological theory of long standing (see Hilgard, 1979). Katz and Stotland (1959) recommended that attitude assessment should involve assessment of an evaluative (belief) component as well as the affective component. While the conceptualization usefully recognized that the expression of affect (liking or disliking) did not exhaust the evocative capacities of most social stimuli, it did not generate notable research. Bem (1968a: 198) notes that the additional

'components' were assessed by the same old method: statements were formed which specified belief in some view, or intent or liking for some activity, and the individual responded via the standard Likert items. Greenwald et al. (1968) note that the distinction between cognitive, affective, and conative components of attitude emerged from learning theory. The processes were theoretically separable, they said, but it did not necessarily make sense to extend the distinction. The existing tests of the relative ability of 'components' to predict to various criteria are unrevealing; see Insko and Schopler (1967), Mann (1959), Ostrom (1969), Woodmansee and Cook (1967). Kothandapani (1971) provides a replication of Ostrom's work using factor analysis to separate statements (previously generated to express the tripartite distinction) into their evaluative, cognitive, and conative 'scales.' The usefulness of factor analysis to sort item-statements into clusters homogeneous on content and semantic factors is demonstrated, if nothing else. Intention to act was the best, but still not statistically significant, predictor of behaviour. Fishbein's work on the role of beliefs in prediction of behavioural intentions (see his reader, 1967, for a sampling) is, of course, a conceptual cousin.

5 *Attribution: Perceiving the Causes of Behaviour*, edited by Edward Jones et al., is a comprehensive and convenient introduction to the literature. See also Jones (1979) and Kelley and Michela (1980). Ross (1977) is also of interest.

6 Rotter (1972) suggests that the felt need for consistency between what one may believe and what one may say or do should be treated as a characteristic which might vary from individual to individual; that is, as a learned rather than as a universal motivating cognitive process. The dissonance theorists, Rotter suggests, were investigating cultural factors in their investigation of individual tendencies to adjust cognitions favourably after the fact of a difficult choice. The opposite process – where post-choice cognitions would exaggerate the desirability of the not-chosen alternative – was the norm in his upbringing in Jewish Brooklyn, Rotter says.

7 In his paper Converse reminds the reader that Hartley in 1946 was able to collect 'a full set of ethnic attitudes towards groups that did not exist.' Converse estimates that only 10 to 15 per cent of the public has any 'belief system' about political matters. Angus Campbell and his associates deal with the ideological development of the mass public in chapters 8 to 10 of *The American Voter*. They find that they can classify 3 or 4 per cent of the public as ideologues (possessing a coherent grasp of some criterion ideology) and about 12 per cent as 'near ideologues,' possessing a couple of political beliefs that 'go together' in any customary sense. A 1975 review by Peterson and Dutton of 28 recent research reports includes a regret that consideration of the *existence* of the social attitude being investigated (as well as its centrality, extremity,

and intensity) was still being neglected. They recommend that those individuals who are ignorant of or indifferent toward the attitude object should be
located 'off the continuum' rather than at mid-point, which should be
reserved for conflicted or ambivalent feelings. Perry, Gillespie, and Parker
(1976) also insist on the importance of establishing that a genuine attitude is
held. They do this by developing an index of the importance of the topic to
the individual. Their elementary elaboration of 'attitude' adds to variance
explained in criterion action.

In contradiction, Achen (1975) performs a reanalysis of the data that Converse had used to demonstrate that most people did not have attitudes toward
many social objects which were of concern to scholars. My feeling is that
Achen turns what is a conceptual problem into a technical problem. He con-
tends that the sample was inconsistent across time and viewpoints because of
technical unreliability of the measures. The upper limit of correlation is
depressed by low reliability of measurement; hence correction for attenuation
of correlations due to unreliability would show that attitudes were much more
structured than Converse had contended. It seems to me that this viewpoint
ignores the fact that where the question is one of public knowledge and attentiveness to certain stipulated issues, 'good questions' have to be those to
which one wants answers rather than ones to which the public may know
some answers.

8 Personality theorists suggest a variety of modes of acquisition of 'attitudes'
and other individual differences. Sarnoff and Katz (1954:117) state that there
are three modes of acquisition: reality testing, in which the individual formu-
lates and tests summary frameworks for processing of information; social
reward and punishment in which something like habit is acquired in an
unexamined way; and dynamic ego-defensive motivations in which the individual's subconscious operates to defend the ego against an unpleasant truth
by transforming that reality into some non-threatening content. The work of
M. Brewster Smith (1958, 1968) and of Smith, Bruner, and White (1956)
postulates that attitudes and personality traits can be variously based in
different individuals. In the case of 'authoritarianism' as conceptualized by the
California group, the empirical (correlational) coherence of the logically contradictory elements of the syndrome signal presence of the 'disease process.'
In other words, for the data to make any sense, there *had* to be a disease. But
the researchers had postulated the syndrome, and also saw subjects in a clinical setting.

9 An analysis of cross-sectional survey data by Sniderman and Citrin (1971) is
typical in this regard. First, they specify that personality characteristics are general, attitudes are organized around specific objects, and opinions are even

more specific; next, they state that an operational version of self-esteem they work with is a personality characteristic, and that a measure of 'isolationism' is a political attitude; third, they establish covariation; fourth, they say that personality characteristics mediate some individuals' formation of political viewpoints.

10 The current fashion for 'causal modelling' has much to do with the dazzling promise of the name of the technique. For a corrective, see Blau and Duncan (1967: 177): 'The technique of path analysis is not a method for discovering causal laws but a procedure for giving a quantitative interpretation to the manifestations of a known or assumed causal system as it operates in a particular population.' The salient assumption on which one *proceeds* to attach magnitudes to the arrows between variables is that the causal relationship between the variables has already been correctly specified. In K.I. Macdonald's phrase, as quantitative social scientists we suffer from having the second-order account before owning much first-order activity. Hence we are in the business of continually recycling a few tired old causes through our bright new techniques. See Macdonald (1977a and b) and Macdonald and Doreian (1977) for expositions.

11 In their view of the attitude-behaviour controversy, Schuman and Johnson (1976) note that the three major collections of reprinted papers of the 1970s (K. Thomas, 1971; Deutscher, 1973; and Liska, 1974d) have only minor overlap in content, and that no single piece is reprinted in all three.

CHAPTER 2

1 The Determinants of Citizenship Orientation Project was fielded under the name 'Modern Life and Health Survey,' at the University of Alberta, 1968–70. The research was funded by the Canada Council, and directed by Drs Christian Bay, Susan Hunter-Harvey, and Ted Harvey. The project was broader than the study reported here: data were also collected from a random sample of the Edmonton city electorate. Student questionnaires were self-completed in the project accommodations, students attending at scheduled times following an invitation by mail. A student directory was used to ensure that there were no substitutions. Respondent identity was also controlled by issuing a small honorarium (three dollars) by cheque for each subject. Three waves of reminder letters were followed by telephone contacts. Project workers delivered and picked up questionnaires to respondents in hospital or otherwise incapacitated. Non-response was primarily due to dropping-out or to the staff's inability to locate and contact respondents. Data collection proceeded from February to May, and coding was complete by mid-June. Pre-

testing of measures had been conducted during 1968–69, S. Hunter-Harvey being primarily responsible for the work on Dogmatism, Humanitarianism (original to the project), Militancy, and Authoritarianism.

There is a good fit between basic parameters (i.e. sex, age, place of residence, and grade point average where available) derived from registrar's records and sample estimates within strata.

Full detail on all these topics has been provided by Dr S. Hunter-Harvey in a collection of research reports submitted to the Canada Council, 1968–71.

2 Guilford has established that 'the item-test correlations for well-constructed items range between .30 and .80 which means item intercorrelations approximately between .10 and .60. Items within these ranges of correlation should provide tests of both satisfactory reliability and validity' (1956: 481).

3 All work to the stage of data analysis was done in co-operation with a colleague, Jeremiah Ezekiel. For the independent Ezekiel analysis, see Ezekiel (1971b).

4 Dr N. Chi (now at Carleton University in Ottawa) suggested the sentence-completion technique. For a useful discussion of other researchers' uses of this technique, see Lemon (1973: 123–7).

5 All factor analyses reported from this point were performed with the University of Essex Saly Project 'Fact' Program. 'Fact' is adapted from the University of Michigan OSIRIS package, the extent of the adaptation being to accommodate the OSIRIS program to University of Essex hardware. In this program, 'factor extraction proper is accomplished by the principal axis method of Hotelling, using a Jacobi diagonalization of the correlation matrix to find the eigenvalues and their corresponding vectors' (*Saly User's Manual, 1971*: Fact −1). Where reference is made to orthogonal rotation (which assumes that the factors to be extracted will be unrelated to one another, or located orthogonally in factor space), it is the Saly varimax solution that has been applied. Varimax maximizes the differences between factors. Where reference is to oblique rotation, it is to the Saly Oblimin rotation. Oblique rotation allows factors to be related to one another. Throughout, communalities were used in the matrix diagonals, factors had to have eigenvalues greater than one to be retained, and no iterations were performed. Factor analysis of the large item pools was accomplished through a 75 per cent item overlap procedure.

Items were retained as useful indicators of the factor they loaded upon if the item loaded at 0.4 or higher on one factor and at no more than 0.15 on other factors patterned from the same universe of items.

6 For a discussion of coefficient alpha with cluster or factor analysis, see McKennell (1970) and Cronbach (1951). Alpha is related to the split-half method of estimating reliability in which test items are divided into two halves

and scores between these two halves are correlated and then corrected for the effects of halving. 'Several split-half coefficients can be obtained from the same testing, and these will vary somewhat, depending on which items are allocated to one or the other half-tests. It can be shown (Cronbach, 1951) that alpha is the mean of all possible split-half coefficients' (McKennell, 1970: 229). McKennell provides a short-cut formula for calculation of alpha, and a table from which one can locate the alpha coefficient for a test from the average inter-item correlation and the number of items in the test. This formula 'brings out very well how the reliability of a test depends on its internal consistency or homogeneity and its length' (McKennell, 1970: 230).

7 Recollect the history of the concept of authoritarianism: (1) a series of projects under one rubric resulted in a description of who the authoritarian was and speculated upon the significance for society of the findings (Adorno et al., 1950); (2) other research found that virtually all correlates of authoritarianism became insignificant if education was controlled (for example, Campbell et al., 1960) and that the measure was contaminated with an ideology component (Rokeach, 1960); (3) a burst of research utilized the concept, the operationalization being non-standard as various researchers became sensitive to particular flaws and 'redressed' these in their individual manners; (4) early consensus was dissipated and no new and true consensus could emerge because indicators were not comparable from study to study; (5) other concepts were substituted in ongoing research, for example, Dogmatism, Tolerance-Intolerance of Ambiguity, and Tough-Mindedness, which themselves followed much the same pattern. Result: no one knows what to believe about the authoritarian personality, or whether there is one. The fact that virtually every study must be remembered in terms of its own idiosyncracies and shortcomings means that any attempt at a powerful summary must result in an explosion of small facts, the wheat not obviously distinguishable from the chaff.

CHAPTER 3

1 Gross and Niman (1975), in their review of attitude-behaviour consistency, make the point that the distinction between attitude and behaviour is misleading. An attitude response, they say, is actually behaviour, whether a verbal or written response. Given this fact, the term attitude-and-behaviour should really be written as indicated – some kinds of behaviour and other kinds of behaviour. More scholarly references would be written in the style suggested by Kiesler, Collins, and Miller (1969): 'The Relationship between Certain Kinds of Behavior, Arbitrarily Designated by Most Social Scientists as

Measures of Attitude, and Other Kinds of Behavior, which, According to Theory, Should be Influenced by the Attitude in Question.'

2 Hase and Goldberg (1967) is a partial counter-example. They suggest that technical improvements will be inadequate to the task of improving attitude-behaviour relations. The principal finding of their study is that sets of scales constructed by each of four primary strategies of scale construction – factor analytic, empirical, theoretical, and rational – were equivalent in their validity across thirteen diverse criteria. Only randomly composed scales performed notably differently (worse). This is called a partial application because it is not truly multi-method, but really only a test of approaches within the confines of one method (verbal scales). Schuman and Johnson (1976) provide an excellent review of approaches to improving measured consistency between attitudes and behaviour.

3 This tactic seems greatly underexplored in survey research, with scholars generally as jealous of their 'n's' as a hen of her chicks. Resistance to the very idea seems often to be generated by the confusion between statistical significance and phenomenal importance. Statistical significance tells how likely it is that the observed results will represent true population differences: phenomenal importance tells how much of one phenomenon can be 'accounted for' by the variability of another phenomenon. Neither bears any privileged relation to theoretical importance, which is a question of where the result might fit in some established and closely reasoned body of knowledge about the events in question. Random sampling techniques ensure the representativeness of survey findings within a margin of error depending on the sample size. Most surveys are set at the size which will justify generalization of correlations of minuscule magnitude in terms of variance of one phenomenon accounted for by another. One can therefore 'afford' (in terms of degrees of freedom and statistical significance) to partition one's sample in non-obvious ways, just as one can 'afford' the degrees of freedom used up in techniques which relate two variables while controlling for a third, and more.

4 Gamma is a coefficient of correlation suitable for use with variables that are measured in ranks. It assesses the predictability of order on one variable from the rank or order on another. It can vary from -1.0 to $+1.0$. It is legitimate to interpret gamma as a proportional reduction of error measure: a gamma of 0.673, for example, means that we have reduced almost 70 per cent of the error we would incur by guessing without knowledge of the rank of the independent variable.

5 Factor analysis can serve as a heuristic device to show the loading of the activities index on a postulated underlying dimension of affect for student participation. The following loadings, indicating the correlation of the variable

with the dimension (factor), are obtained by a varimax rotation of the opinion scales RRR, SP, UMIL, with the summed university activities index. The loadings can be squared to indicate the amount of variance of the scale or index which is shared with the dimension.

Variable	Factor loading
Rejection of Radicals	0.828
Student Power	−0.828
University Militancy	−0.757
University Activities	−0.570

6 There is no interaction effect whatever between activities predicting to any of the attitude measures as the dependent variable.

7 The Consistency Student Power score was derived by the following procedure: those 77 persons who scored low on Student Power, low on University Militancy, and high on RRR were given a score of 1, for 'low'; those 77 persons who scored moderate on all three scales were given a score of 2, for 'moderate'; and those 65 persons who scored high on Student Power, high on University Militancy, and low on RRR were given a score of 3, for 'high.' Hence the sample 'n is 219, as none of the individuals who did not meet the consistency test could be given a rank on the new consistency affect score.

8 This is done by readjusting cutting points on the badly skewed distribution of University Militancy (see appendix D, table D1, for the distribution characteristics of this scale and other opinion scales). Until this point, scores on University Militancy had been trichotomized by the best attempt to divide the frequency distribution into even thirds, as had been done for Student Power and RRR. In the loosened conditions, the frequency distribution of University Militancy is divided into approximate fourths, the upper half being accepted as 'high' and the lower half as 'low.' A new Consistency Student Power score can be calculated for the loosened conditions by the following procedure: those 120 individuals who scored low on Student Power, low on University Militancy, and high on RRR score 1 for 'low'; those 77 persons who score moderate on Student Power, moderate on University Militancy (in either the second or third quarters of the distribution, and *not* in the lowest or highest quarter), and moderate on RRR score 2 for 'moderate'; and those 148 persons who score in the top third of Student Power, the top half of University Militancy, and the bottom third of RRR score 3 for 'high.' This new opinion-consistent subsample comprises 345 individuals, all those who do not meet the new loosened conditions being given the code of zero.

No great violence has been done to the consistency criteria by loosening the conditions for qualification in the way described above. This can be shown by using the *new* Consistency Student Power score as the dependent variable in a multiple regression with the same selection of university activities as the independent variables. When this is done, the fraction of variance in the new score which is explained by all the activities is 0.24, a drop of 0.04 from the figure of 0.28 for the old score.

It might be cautioned that the amount of variance that the independent activities can predict will be affected adversely for either consistency score because there are only three categories on each, in contrast with the many categories of either of the three continuous variables Student Power, Rejection of Radicals, and University Militancy. Hence claims about improvement in predictability of consistent individuals are conservative. This supposition can be tested by using the activities as dependent variables, and each of the three continuous distribution scales as independent variables, *within* the subsample of 345 individuals who have qualified for entry by the loosened conditions. When this is done, the amount of variance the activities explain in Student Power is 0.27 in RRR 0.28, and in University Militancy 0.21. Thus the continuous opinion scale scores of *consistent* individuals are more predictable than those for the whole sample – Table 3.4 gives the complementary figures for the whole sample as 0.16, 0.10, and 0.14. We see that the smaller number of categories in the consistency score variable does just slightly attenuate prediction. Appendix D, table D2 reports the regression analyses.

CHAPTER 4

1 A work which adopts a somewhat similar strategy of analysis is Verba and Nie's *Participation in America* (1972). They defined types through cluster analysis of a number of typical political activities. They then investigated the backgrounds and opinions of types which were 'specialist' in different kinds of activity. Meredith Watts in 'Efficacy, Trust, and Orientation toward Socio-political Authority: Students' Support for the University' (1973) also argues that individuals adopt characteristic stances. Watts found that general political trust and traditional values are related to university radicalism. Unfortunately, Watts reports no activities or behaviour dispositions.

2 The prediction that conservative types will have less accepting *views* of underprivileged groups is suggested by McClosky's finding that 'conservative' personality traits include contempt for weakness and intolerance of human frailty (1958: 38). This article, 'Conservatism and Personality,' has been very influential in shaping assumptions about the traits of the *party* Conservative (see Bay, 1967) although the correlation between McClosky's Conservatism scale and identification with a conservative political party is low (1958: 44). The Conservatism scale was derived from the writings of Edmund Burke.

McClosky notes that status and education factors account for a large share of the total variance in his data – uneducated and low-status individuals tending, of course, to conservatism.

3 Milbrath (1965: 17) suggests that 'political participation can be thought of as a special case of general participation in social and community activities.'

4 Under 'trivial, ad hoc reason' were coded responses such as 'it would be alright to speed if you were rushing a pregnant woman to the hospital.' Responses coded under the second summary heading suggested that laws could be ignored to protect the respondent's physical safety, most often in cataclysmic events in which the civil authority would lose the ability to maintain order and protect life. Responses under the third heading said that civil disobedience was justified if it could be seen that laws were unfairly discriminating against any group of people, it being stipulated that the group be one in which members would think of themselves *as* a group (i.e., Jews or native peoples). In the fourth and fifth categories, an appeal was made to a general and abstract right. Thus, in the fourth category were placed responses which said that disobedience was justified if and when a law promulgated by the civil authority was one that went against the religious views or the morality of *a group* of people. In the last category went responses which gave the individual *alone* the right to decide when to comply.

5 The New Democratic party is the most ideological of all Canadian political parties. The Conservative and Liberal parties are 'catch-all peoples' parties.'

6 Devall (1970) found that students who support the New Democratic party are much more likely to be libertarian than those who support the Progressive Conservative party. H. Astin (1969) found a correlation of 0.28 between protest activity and a left-wing self-label, and Gurin (1971) found that activism in a protest against the House UnAmerican Activities Committee predicted left political identification. Lyonns (1965), writing on the California police-car demonstration, found that demonstrators had a liberal political self-identification. Somers (1965), taking militants, moderates, and conservatives, found that militants had comparatively liberal-left political preferences. Tygart and Holt (1972: 965) reported that 'demonstrators in the early phase of the UCLA campus antiwar movement were much more likely to have worked in Democratic party precinct activities than respondents generally.' Tygart and Holt's article refutes Weinberg and Walker's (1969) view that student activism constitutes isolated and non-instrumental behaviour.

7 The finding is supported by the literature. Clarke and Egan (1971) found a relationship between left political ideology and involvement in demonstrations. Using 'New Left' scales, Fenton and Gleason (1969) found that those who scored high were likely to support student decision-making on course content,

and were against the war in Vietnam. Devall (1970) found that active students were more likely than inactive students to give libertarian responses regardless of their party adherence.

8 For a sympathetic finding, but outside the student activism literature, see Budge et al. (1972). Having selected a political stratum on amount of political involvement, Budge and his colleagues found that 'the greater political involvement associated with higher activity produces in common not only stronger attachments to procedures and a heightened political realism but also keener partisan feeling, *carried over more consistently to certain types of political attitude*' (p. 11; emphasis added). Budge et al. also find that 'activists express greater agreement in their assessment of the content of political problems' (p. 11), amount of activity being the strongest predictor of attitudes which were unaffected by party competition. See also Budge, *Agreement and the Stability of Democracy* (1970), chapter 5. A similar mechanism may be operating here to bring the actors' groups closer together than passive groups on some ideologically non-contentious issues.

9 Milbrath (1962: 63), using a short version of the F-Scale, finds a tendency for 'high scorers to shun political activity.' He thinks this is 'the first clear-cut finding that a high score on F reflects a barrier to political participation.' 'Our data suggest that they will shun the rough and tumble of partisan politics. Persons scoring high on F have repeatedly been shown to be prejudiced and to have antidemocratic attitudes: if these beliefs are seldom implemented through ordinary channels, as our data suggest, such persons may be less dangerous to a democratic political system than might be supposed' (1962: 63). Sutherland and Tanenbaum (1980) are in basic agreement.

With regard to comparable student activism studies, Donovan and Shaevitz (1973), taking subjects from left, right, and fraternity groups, found that radicals are hostile to authority and right-wing groups are strongly for authority figures. Schiff (1964) found that conservatives are distinguished from liberal subjects by higher scores in authoritarian conformity, ego control, and repression. Katz et al. (1968) note that the Berkeley Free Speech Movement arrestees were lower on authoritarianism and ethnocentrism than other groups. Working with dogmatism, Doress (1968) found that left activists were lowest on the trait, when compared with right and moderate activists. Baird (1970), however, found no relationship between dogmatism and activism.

Feldman and Newcomb (1970: 60) find that students learn liberalism from professors and books in the same way they learn history and French. As active radicals are in the most liberal faculties – arts and humanities – of all types, they will have differentially been exposed to this 'learning.' Korn (1968) notes that the major impact on reducing authoritarianism scores is that of 'sophistication.' Students learn which verbal nuances are disvalued, and learning opportunities will again be best in liberal faculties. The one finding that would not be vulnerable to the charge of ideological bias is that of Mussen and Warren (1952) that active individuals of both Republican and Democratic youth groups are less conventional, more idealistic and altruistic, and less likely to glorify parents than non-activists.

10 Cowdry et al. (1970) also found that the level of socio-political activities (especially protest) was related to levels of community service and political activity. Gastwirth (1965) studied leaders, followers, and non-participants in a demonstration, finding that leaders were also active in civil rights and peace movements.

11 Clarke and Egan (1971) found that higher levels of political cynicism were associated with left activism. Lyonns (1965) reports that experienced demonstrators express greater dissatisfaction with courses, examinations, professors, and are more willing to risk arrest and expulsion. Spreitzer and Synder (1971) report similar findings: left activists (defined by Christie's New Left scale and an activism index) are most dissatisfied with course offerings, degree requirements, and instruction in university.

12 Milbrath (1965: chap. 3) amply documents the case that all of political alienation, anomy, cynicism are related to political activity in much the same manner as personal effectiveness, political efficacy, etc., but in the opposite direction. Budge (1970: 126) finds that his group of politicians 'are overwhelmingly confident that political activity brings results and overwhelmingly reject the idea that politicians ignore the needs of ordinary people.' Schwartz (1973: 141) finds that student activists are significantly more 'alienated, reformist and cynical' than non-activists; but his 'alienation' measures tap belief that student protest is macro-political in meaning. On a one-item measure of 'effectiveness' (whether the student felt he could personally be effective in changing university structures) Schwartz found no differences between activists and non-activists. Clarke and Egan (1971) found, in an activism study, that political alienation was highest among illegal demonstrators, next highest in legal demonstrators. Silvern and Nakamura (1971) studied an activist population using a measure of internal versus external 'locus of control.' An internal locus of control, to explain, is the view that people are responsible for their life situations, which reflect effort and ability. Left-wing activists were high on the opposite view, 'externality.' Silvern and Nakamura found, not surprisingly, that the measure is strongly correlated with ideology – as would be true with many such measures. Thomas (1970) also found that internality-externality has a serious conservative bias.

13 Advances in cognitive psychology suggest that there is no reason to suspect that judgment is sometimes 'flawed' by interference from emotional aspects of

the personality. Robyn M. Dawes, in a provocative article called 'Shallow Psychology' (1976), argues that cognitive results are often less than optimally rational simply because human powers of cognition are intrinsically limited and, further, geared toward closure on recognition of any pattern. As an information processor, 'man' has a number of speedy routines which he applies whether they are appropriate or not.

14 An analysis of variance F-test on means and standard deviations of scores for groups of all types plus the residual group shows that all differences reported are 'significant' (not due to sampling error). Differences between groups are significant at the 0.0001 level on General Militancy, Nurturance, Left-Liberalism, Survey F, Outside Political Activity, and Informal Contacts; and at the 0.001 level for Club Contacts and Social Helping Activity (figure 4.2). Differences are significant at the 0.0001 level on Political Alienation, Closed-Mindedness, Pessimism, Religion, System Cynicism, and University Elitism; at the 0.001 level on War, University Alienation, and Aimlessness; and at the 0.05 level on Contentment (figure 4.3).

The pattern is much weaker for psychological variables. Differences between the five groups as above, again using F, are significant at the 0.01 level on Depression and Mental Health, and at 0.05 on Anxiety and Tension. No other differences reach significance (figure 4.4). Differences on 'stimulated by professors' are significant at 0.0001; on 'happy with current studies' at 0.001; and on 'stimulated by other students' at 0.01. No other differences reach significance (figure 4.5).

The T-test is used to test significance of differences between acting radicals and the residuals (not a type) group on the 'psychological' variables of figures 4.4 and 4.5. Separate variance estimates were used, with a two-tailed 'T' (null hypothesis). This tests the likelihood that one could have obtained a difference between group averages of the reported size by chance. *No* differences whatever are found on the variables of figure 4.4, indicating that the psychological of active radicals functioning is no better and no worse than that of the average student.

Considering the hedonic tone variables of figure 4.5, the only differences between active radicals and the residual that reach significance are 'stimulated by other students' and 'number of serious childhood ailments' (0.01 level). The hypothesis that 'radical man' acts from a basis of superior emotional robustness receives no support.

CHAPTER 5

1 According to the theory of institutional quality, there were 'protest-prompting' institutions. The highly selective multiversities were thought to gather so

much talent to their bosoms that a critical mass of critics was reached. Protest events occurred less because there were real issues at stake than because there were so many in one place who were clever, morally vigilant, and fearless through economic and social privilege. In his 1966 and 1968 studies Peterson linked incidence and type of protest to institutional quality in deservedly praised projects. Scott and El-Assal (1969) somewhat simplified the argument from institutional quality by showing that size *alone* was the most important predictor of incidence of protest. In any event, large institutions and quality institutions are overlapping categories in the North American context. Kahn and Bowers (1970) took a stratified random sample of 100 institutions to represent all types, and found that there is no consistent association between socio-economic background and activism *within* quality (institutional) contexts. This debate remains confused.

2 For example, L.E. Thomas (1971) found that when family psychological variables – permissiveness, warmth, conflict, interaction – were entered into a multiple regression with political preference controlled, these family variables were able to add only 2 per cent more to the amount of variance explained. Univariate relationships were, of course, higher, but vary in complex fashion across ideology and sex groupings. Similarly, Aron (1974) found that all his background factors (sociological and psychological) were able to explain only 6 per cent of the variance in activism, here defined on an index of non-university political activity and social-helping activities, the index as a whole being biased to protest options. Braungart (1971b) did somewhat better, but through selecting only the most active. Working with a subsample of activists alone, he was able to explain 28 per cent of the variance in student political *identification* with background factors. Despite this qualified success, he warns against taking background factors very seriously.

3 I regret that even this very loose sampling criterion forced me to omit several otherwise interesting studies. Those that fell victim were mainly questionnaire studies which drew some kind of random sample, then depended upon the students to return the questionnaire to the researcher. Where response rates fell below one-third, I reasoned that the sample could no longer claim to be representative of the student body. Hence claims about background characteristics of 'activists' drawn from these groups would not bear consideration.

4 There is, however, a fair amount of data on what is called the 'generational continuity' hypothesis. Keniston et al. (1973) make the point that much of the same data is used to support both the views that activists are rebelling against parents *and* that they are acting out values which the parents instilled in them. Sometimes those arguing the generational continuity view take group-group correlations between an aggregate of students and a cohort of adults and find

them high, as the distribution of opinion over a temporally appropriate left-right dimension will remain much the same from generation to generation. But if pair comparisons are made between each child and his own parents, the match is much less good. In pair comparisons, the discrepancy between parent and child is found to be greater at the liberal end of the political spectrum than at the conservative end.

While it would be difficult to argue that a broad ideology will always be logically entailing to a particular set of issues across generations (so that a reincarnated Burke, Mill, or Marx could, on any day in any country, instantly locate himself in detail on a check-list of issues), the stance-issue problem is perhaps more difficult for the left. The Friedman et al. study (1972) supports this view: the authors think that much of what is said in the name of the New Left was not recognizable by an Old Left parent as germane to his position. Conservatism by its nature is more likely to retain some detail across generations. (See also Edelstein, 1962.) Connell (1972) should also be cited here. He took 20 studies of opinions of parents and children in which the response rate was above 50 per cent (including Flacks's study but no other explicitly student protest research), and found that the *only* moderately high pair correlation was on party preference. He thinks this is because party is a clear-cut institutional loyalty, whereas issues are difficult and fleeting.

5 Spock (1946) also thought that a spanking was sometimes preferable to a long, drawn-out psychological battle because it cleared the air. Spock must only have seemed permissive in contrast to pre-war practices. Compared to current observed parental practice, he reads like a hard-liner. He suggests that discipline be begun early so that the parents run the child and not the reverse, that punishment and discipline be consistent and persistent because the child has to be civilized to live in accord with others, that psychological squabbling should be avoided, and that the balking and tantrum-throwing child be simply, cheerfully, but *physically* moved to a new, non-central and non-disturbing location.

CHAPTER 6

1 The average income of the university sample in 1970 was approximately 12,700 dollars per annum, whereas the average family income in Edmonton was approximately 7,250 dollars. The figure is from Eric Tanenbaum's analysis of the data set for the Edmonton urban area – a random sample of 1,200 electors conducted at the same time as the student study. Of the sample of Edmonton electors, 31 per cent had a professional or owner-manager occupation, 17 per cent had a college education, and 6 per cent had an income of

15,000 plus. In student data, in comparison, 52 per cent of fathers had such an occupation, 23 per cent had a college education (13 per cent of mothers), and 25 per cent of families had incomes of 15,000 plus. Tanenbaum further notes that 43 per cent of electors are of 'Anglo' origin: here students' parents are more than half 'Anglo' in background.

2 It appears most sensible to concentrate upon the control for ideology which Kerpelman (1969) and Keniston et al. (1973) urge. In addition, chapter 4, which delineates the enlarged ideology of the four types, has established validity credentials for the ideological definition.

3 Other central studies which stress a view of social viewpoints as learned within appropriate settings include Litt (1963), who argues that origins of political cynicism may be traced to community roots as well as to personality roots; Eitzen (1970), who finds that status inconsistents were more moderate in opinion on social welfare, civil rights, and internationalism than were persons whose status was consistently high or low; Harned (1961), who found that in his sample of party workers there was a relationship between the number of years of party activity and the degree of ideological partisanship; Rose (1962), who provides a similar interpretation of the lesser alienation and superior social integration in his sample of group leaders; Schoenberger (1968), who found that his sample of journalists, intellectuals, business and professional men who had formed a conservative party in New York in 1961 had a 'distinct and coherent ideology which, while limited in breadth is appropriate to their socio-economic position'; and Anderson et al. (1965), who found that high economic status is associated with economic conservatism.

4 Verba and Nie (1972: 148), find that political activity increases with length of exposure to politics, and with involvement and acquaintance with a place. Milbrath, under the heading 'community identification,' also notes findings which show that 'the longer a person resides in a given community, the greater the likelihood of his participation in politics' (1965: 133). Length of residence in a community, he says, is particularly strongly related to gladiatorial activities – the more difficult activities. Supportive studies cited by Milbrath include Agger et al. (1964), Birch (1950), Birch and Campbell (1950), Buchanan (1956), Lane (1959), and Lipset (1960).

5 See Patrick Doreian for a useful discussion of multivariate analysis and categorized data. Doreian says that 'in a bivariate situation when both variables are categorised it is clear that a cross-tabulation should be inspected before any attempt at regression is made' (1972: 271). He notes: 'Blau and Duncan (1967) suggest that we should analyse data in a variety of ways and then examine the different outcomes. We could be very conservative and use only a limited set of tools or we could make outrageous assumptions and see what

results. If little difference emerges between the two approaches then we can claim that little distortion has been introduced by the more sophisticated procedures' (1972: 254). In his article, Doreian inspects correlations between different categorizations of two variables. He finds that interrelations between the dichotomized and trichotomized variables are lower than those for categorizations with higher numbers of categories. He notes that categorization introduces measurement error, and therefore correlations are attenuated between dichotomized versions of variables. Hence, the overall effect will be to attenuate relationships, and results will be conservative – rather than suggesting relationships which do not 'really' exist.

Ideally, because of level of measurement considerations, cross-tabulations with controls would be the more suitable analysis technique. It is, of course, impossible to pursue because of small subsample numbers. But it is true that the regression analyses show that in most cases the impact of individual variables under controls is of roughly the same magnitude, and in the same direction, as the impact indicated in bivariate cross-tabulation analysis. This fact suggests that, in predictive terms, these independent variables are behaving autonomously. Thus the results of regression analyses allow a retrospective confidence in the direction and magnitude of cross-tabulation findings. That is, were n-level controls applied in cross-tabulation, the bivariate relationships in most cases would not diminish radically.

6 In the chapter, regression analysis is aimed at discovering factors that modulate the quantity of action output within ideological groups. But another interesting question is whether or not it is useful to regard activity as pursued by a distinctive type of individual. That is, can people be divided into categories of actors and non-actors according to background factors which describe them? The question was pursued by forming a dummy variable for membership or non-membership in the actor class, and performing multiple regression analysis with the same background factors. In a word, it was found that factors that predict membership in the actor class were the same as those that predicted *increased* activity (vis-à-vis university political activities).

7 Dummy variables were formed according to the following procedure. Let us begin with socio-economic status variables. Father's occupation is described with two dummy variables only: a 'professional father' category was formed, with the zero category containing all non-professional codes, and a 'farm father' category was formed, the zero category containing all non-farmer fathers. Two dichotomous variables were also formed to describe the mother's work history: 'working mother' describes women who worked for most or all of the first fifteen years of the respondent's childhood, the zero category taking in those who worked infrequently or not at all; 'professional mother'

describes those mothers with high-status occupations of the recoded mothers' occupation variable, the zero category including all others. Father's and mother's educational attainment are each described by a dichotomous variable, the split for both being made after high school, the highly educated group including from 'normal school' or teacher training college on through graduate degrees. This group is described as 'highly educated father' and 'highly educated mother' respectively, with all lower educational codes being subsumed in the zero category.

'Place' variables and religion were also used to form dummy variables. The variable 'Canadian parents' describes the student *both* of whose parents were born in Canada. All other contingencies are subsumed in the zero category. A second ethnic dummy variable, 'one foreign parent,' describes the case in which one parent was born in a nation *other* than Canada, the United States, or a 'founding' nation – i.e. the family in which there is an element of what might be called cultural disjointedness. All other cases fall in the zero category. Following on the earlier discussion dealing with rootedness in Alberta – long acquaintance with the provincial political environment – the attribute 'Alberta born and raised' describes the student who was both born in Alberta and spent the first fifteen years of his life in the province. All others fall in the zero category. Originally dummy variables for father's religion were formed, but as father's and mother's religions correlated very strongly, and as the correlation of students' religion was just marginally higher with the mother's religion than with the father's, it was decided to allow the mother's affiliation to stand alone for religious background, with one exception of a 'secular father' variable. For father's religion, therefore, only one dummy variable will be used: this describes the attribute secular father, i.e., having a father who has no religious affiliation. No secular category is formed for mothers, as the incidence of non-affiliated women is too low. 'Anglo-Protestant mother' describes women in Anglo/liberal Protestant denominations, zero including all others; 'Catholic mother' describes women of both Roman and Greek rites, zero including all others.

8 The stepwise multiple regression program of the Statistical Package for the Social Sciences was used for all regression analysis. To quote page 180 of the SPSS manual: 'The method recursively constructs a prediction equation one variable at a time. The first step is to choose the single variable which is the best predictor. The second independent variable to be added to the regression equation is that which provides the best prediction in conjunction with the first variable.' Variables are added step by step until no other variable will make a significant contribution, each being the optimum variable given the other variables in the equation.

The advantages and disadvantages of this program strategy have been discussed extensively in the literature (e.g. Draper and Smith, 1968, chapter 6). Missing data were handled by pairwise deletion in these analyses.

CHAPTER 7

1 This important article, 'The Structuring Principle: Political Socialization and Belief Systems,' attacks the socialization inferences. Searing and his colleagues test the potential of the socialization link by arguing that if childhood orientations are important to adult issue preferences, then adult orientations must be important to adult issue preferences. The entire model can only be as strong as its weakest link. Working with two samples of the American electorate, each about 1,500, they find that what they call 'personality factors' are not strongly related to issue preferences. In their work, the best linear combination of orientations (using multiple regression analysis) yields an R^2 of 0.15, predicting to issue preferences. Sutherland and Tanenbaum (1977), using three samples (two adult and one university student), were able to account for, at most, 6 per cent of variance in political preferences with contemporaneous personality factors.

2 For the now-traditional view of women in politics and how they get that way, see Greenstein (1961), Easton and Dennis (1969), and Lane (1959). Morgan (1974) reviews and attacks the work. The process of training into general-appropriate roles during childhood is also portrayed in Lambert (1969). Consequences of this socialization for adult women are summarized over a great array of literature in O'Leary (1974). See also Sutherland (1978) for a data-based discussion of the consequences for women of acceptance of the 'feminine psychology.'

3 Tables are not reported here because no one table is of great theoretical interest in the simple bivariate cross-tabulation. Tables that were statistically significant (including the category of 'not a type'), using chi-square and moving through the questions in the order described in the text, were strictness of mother and father (both at $p = 0.05$), psychological punishment ($p = 0.01$), childhood complaining ($p = 0.05$), childhood church-going ($p = 0.05$), first or only child ($p = 0.02$), childhood happiness ($p = 0.01$). On all other variables, the statement that there is a trend for differences between types refers to over- or under-representation of between 5 and 10 per cent in a category. See appendix E for detailed tables.

An examination of correlation matrices of these variables within the radicals and conservatives types and the whole sample shows that memories are not differently structured within groups, and relationships are no stronger within subsamples. In the whole sample, gender is not systematically related to any pattern of memories. In general, childhood happiness and sense of overall importance in the childhood family are related to memories of the family as having been warm but not particularly permissive.

4 Once more a dummy variable was formed in which '1' represented membership in the actors' group within the appropriate ideology classification and '0' represented all others. Factors that predicted membership in actors' groups were once more the same as had predicted increased intensity of university activity when the interval-level index was the dependent variable.

CHAPTER 8

1 Characteristics are called 'semi-voluntary' when they are factors over which the individual is at least potentially capable of exercising choice. The range of choices on a factor such as area of study will be constrained by parental attributes (for example, doctors' sons will not often choose to study agriculture) and perhaps by childhood experiences. But the individual does tend to take responsibility for the identity built up from these 'choices.'

2 But planless does not mean feckless. Both types of actors are more likely to be employed part-time than are other students (only 3 per cent of the sample was employed full time). Forty-five per cent of active conservatives were employed, as well as 43 per cent of active radicals. Figures are 34 per cent for passive radicals, and 27 per cent for passive conservatives. The result is significant (chi-squared) at 0.05.

3 A negative sign in a correlation thus signifies that the factor is associated with decreasing year of birth, hence *increasing* age.

4 Again a dummy variable was formed for membership in an actors' group and run as a dependent variable. Again factors that predicted membership were the same as those that predicted increased activity when the interval-level university political activities index was the dependent variable. And again factors accounted for roughly the same amount of variance in the dependent variable.

5 The dummy variable of having taken time out is associated with higher grades ($r = 0.238$), with the dummy variable for being married ($r = 0.393$), and with year of birth ($r = -0.518$). For radicals, the relationships for the same variables are -0.008, -0.290, and -0.396, respectively.

CHAPTER 9

1 See Lipset on 'Working-Class Authoritarianism' (1960: chapter 4) for an early and influential statement. For example: 'Isolation, a punishing childhood, eco-

nomic and occupational insecurities, and a lack of sophistication are conducive to withdrawal, or even apathy, and to strong mobilization of hostility. The same underlying factors which predispose individuals toward support of extremist movements under certain conditions may result in total withdrawal from political activity and concern under other conditions. In "normal" periods, apathy is most frequent among such individuals, but they can be activated by a crisis, especially if it is accompanied by strong millennial appeals' (1960: 116). Lipset cites survey evidence from the United States and Britain to show that where extremist movements are weak, individuals respond to extreme economic hardship with apathy, and mixed survey and impressionistic evidence from Europe to show that where extremist movements exist, individuals respond to extreme hardship by supporting these movements. He assumes that each individual or client group is potentially capable of either riot or withdrawal.

For a counter-argument that many disvalued personality traits of non-elite groups re *not* personality traits or sovereign attitudes but, rather, are beliefs grounded in subcultural teachings and in objective appraisals of reality, see Richard F. Hamilton's *Class and Politics in the United States* (1972). Hamilton's chapter 11 is a detailed critique of the Lipset formulation of working-class authoritarianism, which is rich with quantitative evidence. Hamilton challenges both the validity of measures like authoritarianism *and* the claims which could be made were the evidence acceptable. He argues that it is the upper middle class that is the repository of 'conservatism' as defined by disvalued personality traits and issue preferences.

2 I provide the significance figures simply because I have been asked for them on several occasions, and they are easily provided. I had been reluctant to include figures for significance of findings of differences between the types' groups (and the residual group) for several reasons. First, the strategy of analysis used here has been frankly investigative, descriptive, and iterative. Second, differences between types on independent variables are often minor in magnitude. Even where they are significant statistically, they would not be properly significant theoretically where prior directional hypotheses have not been stated (but are mildly interesting when several findings point together at some phenomenon). Third, it is difficult to know how to interpret 'significance' for the types' groups which are analytical aggregates. What is the population to which one would wish to make inferences? Further, there is no real context of comparison from other research. Where significance levels are presented elsewhere in the research for known groups, it is difficult to know how to interpret summary statistics which were developed to support inference to whole 'populations' from random samples. As well, most significance

figures are heavily dependent upon sample size. Proportional-reduction of error statistics would be much more useful, but are usually not obtainable for other work, and have already been provided for this research.

3 Campbell and his associates deal with the ideological development of the mass public in chapters 8 and 10 of *The American Voter*. They find that they can classify only between 3 and 4 per cent of voters as 'ideologues' and 12 per cent as 'near-ideologues.' Milbrath, summarizing findings across studies, speculates that somewhat less than 1 per cent of the American adult population can be called 'gladiators' when that term is applied only to those who hold office, contend for office, or solicit funds. About 4 or 5 per cent, he says, are active in a party, campaign, and attend meetings (1965: 19). Peterson (1968, 1970) says that only about 2 per cent of the student body of a given university, during years in which the movement was of great concern, ever figured as principled radicals. Hence, my figure of a 20 per cent incidence of 'ideologues' in a university setting seems about right, while the acceptance of roughly 10 per cent of the sample as *activists* of left and right is probably somewhat too optimistic. Criteria which are too loose will have a conservative effect on findings, in that activists, loosely defined, will resemble ordinary students more closely than if more difficult criteria were set.

4 Merelman and McCabe (1974) discuss education for politics. They studied the development of what they call 'formal and substantive' orientations toward policy debates in adolescence. A 'formal' orientation underlies a decision taken with regard to formal rules of decision-making. A 'substantive' orientation underlies a decision taken with regard to which *outcome* the student would himself prefer, regardless of whether any set of rules would favour that outcome. Indeed, in the substantive orientation, rules are not invoked. The authors find that formal orientations 'appear to be a function of age, mature cognitive capacities, political interest and the specific issue area' (1974: 65). Their findings lend qualified support to a subsidiary or derived hypothesis that rule-oriented cognition can be 'taught to older adolescents under proper learning conditions in the classroom – or through the rhetoric of political debate' (1974: 678). Interestingly, the authors do not recommend a program of teaching rule-orientation as a panacea: 'A society which slavishly applies decision rules in the face of strongly held substantive preferences may well reap a harvest of political trouble for its efforts' (1974: 680). They recommend Christian Bay (1971) for a different viewpoint.

5 When the same most important variables from each of the categories of parental attributes, socialization factors, and own attributes are used to explain activity levels in the various samples, but using stepwise regression without the stipulation that categories of variables enter in stages, results support the

contention that each category represents a fairly autonomous sphere. For each sample and for each of the activity indices, variables which enter as most important (given the other variables already entered) are the top two from each of the categories. In turn, these are ordered roughly according to the absolute magnitude of the correlation coefficient, with degree goals, of course, leading. A simple way to check the autonomy of variables is to study the correlation matrix for these last two analyses. Correlations are in fact low.

6 Sperlich (1971) has reviewed the evidence, concluding that cross-pressures theory to that date had not been a powerful explanatory device for empiricists. The formulation is muddy with regard to distinguishing between those who are genuinely cross-pressured, that is, holding equally salient but conflicting opinions, and those who have not yet formed any opinion. See also Eitzen (1970), Hunt and Cushing (1972), and Travis (1976).

7 This is not to say that all learning will be systematic. See Skinner (1976) on accidental conditioning, to which he attributes the origins of social superstitions. A good contemporary example is the behaviour of people in elevators. Many elevators are programmed to close their doors at specific intervals. Some people become irritated, and push the 'door close' button repeatedly. Eventually doors close, the elevator moves, and the impatient are satisfied. Those who know that the timing is preset and not to be affected by the buttons are amused.

8 There is evidence of increasing interest in what is called 'adult political socialization.' See Di Renzo (1977) for a useful discussion. Orum (1976) is also of great interest. He is one of the few writers to discuss processes as well as content outcomes from a social indoctrination perspective, still using many routine 'socialization' concepts. See also Schooler (1972).

9 There is already some exciting research in this area. One empirical stream is of 'reality testing' or learning formulations which suggest that political stances are learned as appropriate cognitive responses to particular environments. See McDill and Ridley (1962), Litt (1963), St. Angelo and Dyson (1968), Sallach et al. (1972), and, perhaps most outstanding, Form and Huber (1971). Fairly concise theoretical statements are to be found in Smelser (1968), Bengtson and Lovejoy (1973), Elder (1973), and Rothman and Lichter (1978).

Bibliography

Abelson, R.P., E. Aronson, W.J. McGuire, T.M. Newcomb, M.J. Rosenberg, and P.H. Tannenbaum (eds.). 1968. *Theories of Cognitive Consistency: A Sourcebook.* Chicago: Rand McNally

Aberbach, Joel D. 1969. 'Alienation and political behaviour,' *American Political Science Review* 63, 1: 86–99

Achen, Christopher H. 1975. 'Mass political attitudes and the survey response,' *American Political Science Review* 69, 4: 1218–31

Acock, Alan C., and Melvin L. Defleur. 1972. 'A configurational approach to contingent consistency in the attitude behaviour relationship,' *American Sociological Review* 37: 714–26

Adanek, R.J., and J.M. Lewis. 1973. 'Social control violence and radicalization: the Kent State case,' *Social Forces* 51: 342–7

Adelson, Joseph, and Robert P. O'Neil. 1970. 'Growth of political ideas,' pp. 50–64 in Roberta A. Sigel (ed.), *Learning about Politics: A Reader in Political Socialization.* New York: Random House

Adorno, Theodore, Else Frenkel-Brunswik, Daniel J. Levinson, and R. Nevitt Sanford. 1950. *The Authoritarian Personality: Studies in Prejudice.* New York: Harper and Row

Agger, Robert E., Daniel Goldrich, and Bert E. Swanson. 1964. *The Rulers and the Ruled: Political Power and Impotence in American Communities.* New York: John Wiley

Ajzen, I., R.K. Darroch, M. Fishbein, and J.A. Hornick. 1970. 'Looking backward revisited: a reply to Deutscher,' *American Sociologist* 5: 267–75

Ajzen, I., and M. Fishbein. 1970. 'The prediction of behaviour from attitudinal and normative variables,' *Journal of Experimental Social Psychology* 6: 466–87

– 1974. 'Factors influencing intentions and the intention-behaviour relation,' *Human Relations* 27, 1: 1–15

Albrecht, Stan L., and Kerry Carpenter. 1976. 'Attitudes as predictors of behaviour versus behaviour intentions: a convergence of research intentions,' *Sociometry* 39: 1–10

Albrecht, Stan L., M.L. Defleur, and L.G. Warner. 1972. 'Attitude-behaviour relationships – a re-examination of the postulate of contingent consistency,' *Pacific Sociological Review* 15, 2: 149–68

Alker, Henry A. 1972. 'Is personality situationally specific or intra-psychically consistent?' *Journal of Personality* 40, 1: 1–16

Allerbeck, K.R. 1972. 'Some structural conditions for youth and student movements,' *International Social Science Journal* 24, 2: 257–70

Allport, Gordon W. 1954. 'The historical background of modern social psychology,' pp. 3–56 in G. Lindzey (ed.), *Handbook of Social Psychology*. Cambridge, Mass.: Addison-Wesley

– 1960. 'The psychology of participation,' pp. 181–99 in *Personality and Social Encounter*. Boston: Beacon Press

Almond, G.A., and Sidney Verba. 1963. *The Civic Culture*. Princeton: Princeton University Press

Altbach, Philip G. 1974. *Student Politics in America: A Historical Analysis*. New York: McGraw-Hill

Altbach, Philip G., and D.H. Kelly. 1973. *American Students*. Toronto: Lexington Books

Altbach, Philip G., and R.S. Laufer (eds.). 1972. *The New Pilgrims: Youth Protest in Transition*. New York: David McKay

Altus, William D. 1966. 'Birth order and its sequelae,' pp. 210–44 in Liam Hudson (ed.), *The Ecology of Human Intelligence*. New York: Penguin

Alwin, D.F. 1973. 'Making inferences from attitude-behaviour correlations,' *Sociometry* 36: 253–78

– 1976. 'Attitude scales as congeneric tests: a re-examination of an attitude-behaviour model,' *Social Psychology* 39: 377–83

Anderson. B.M. et al. 1965. 'On conservative attitudes,' *Acta Sociologica* 8: 189–204

Andrews, Kenneth, and D.B. Kandel. 1979. 'Attitude and behaviour,' *American Sociological Review* 44, 2: 298–310

Arblaster, Anthony. 1972. 'Participation: context and conflict,' pp. 4–59 in G. Parry (ed.), *Participation in Politics*. Manchester: Manchester University Press

Archibald, W. Peter. 1976. 'Psychology, sociology and social psychology: bad fences make bad neighbours,' *British Journal of Sociology* 27, 2: 115–29

Aron, R. 1969. 'Student rebellion: vision of the future or echo from the past?' *Political Science Quarterly* 84: 289–331

Aron, William S. 1974. 'Student activism of the 1960's revisited: a multivariate research note,' *Social Forces* 52, 3: 408–14

Aronson, E., J. Turner, and M. Carlsmith. 1963. 'Communicator credibility and communicator discrepancy as determinants of opinion change,' *Journal of Abnormal Social Psychology* 59: 31–6

Astin, Alexander W. 1968. 'Personal and environmental determinants of student activism,' *Measurement and Evaluation in Guidance* 1: 149–62

– 1970. 'Determinants of student activism,' pp. 95–105 in J. Foster and D. Long (eds.), *Protest!! Student Activism in America*. New York: William Morrow

Astin, Helen S. 1969. 'Themes and events of campus unrest in twenty-two campuses and universities,' Bureau of Social Science Research, Washington, DC, unpublished

– 1970. 'Profiles of students during the 1968–1969 campus protest activities,' Bureau of Social Science Research, Washington, DC, unpublished

– 1971. 'Self-perceptions of student activists,' *Journal of College Student Personnel* 12, 4: 263–70

Auger, Cammilla, A. Burton, and R. Maurice. 1969. 'The nature of the student movement and radical proposals for changes at Columbia University,' *The Human Factor* (Journal of the Graduate Sociology Student Union, Columbia University) 9, 1: 18–40

Bachrach, Peter. 1967. *The Theory of Democratic Elitism*. Boston: Brown and Company

Backman, Earl L., and D.J. Findlay. 1973. 'Student protest: a cross-national study,' *Youth and Society* 5, 1: 3–45

Bagley, C., G.D. Wilson, and R. Bushier. 1970. 'The conservatism scale: a factor structure comparison of English, Dutch and New Zealand samples,' *Journal of Social Psychology* 81: 267–8

Bagozzi, Richard, and R.E. Burnkrant. 1979. 'Attitude organization and the attitude-behaviour relationship,' *Journal of Personality and Social Psychology* 37, 6: 913–29

Baird, Leonard L. 1970. 'Who protests: a study of student activists,' pp. 123–53 in Julian Foster and Durward Long (eds.), *Protest!! Student Activism in America*. New York: William Morrow

Bandler, R.J., G.R. Madaras, and D.J. Bem. 1968. 'Self-observation as a source of pain perception,' *Journal of Personality and Social Psychology* 9: 205–9

Bandura, Albert. 1971. *Social Learning Theory*. Morristown, NJ: General Learning Press

Bandura, A., and R.H. Walters. 1959. *Adolescent Aggression: A Study of the Influences of Child-Training Practices and Family Interrelations*. New York: Ronald Press

- 1963. *Social Learning and Personality Development*. New York: Holt, Rinehart and Winston

Baron, R.A. 1968. 'Authoritarianism, locus of control and risk taking,' *Journal of Psychology* 68: 141–3

Barry, Brian. 1970. *Sociologists, Economists and Democracy*. London: Collier-Macmillan

Barton, A.H. 1968. 'The Columbia crisis: campus, Viet Nam and the ghetto,' *Public Opinion Quarterly* 32: 333–52

Barton, A.H., and R.W. Parsons. 1977. 'Measuring belief system structure,' *Public Opinion Quarterly* 41: 159–80

Bass, A.R., and H. Rosen. 1969. 'Some potential moderator variables in attitude research,' *Educational and Psychological Measurement* 29: 331–49

Bay, Christian. 1965. 'Politics and pseudo-politics,' *American Political Science Review* 59, 2: 39–51

- 1967. 'Political and apolitical students: facts in search of a theory,' *Journal of Social Issues* 23, 3: 76–91

- 1971. 'Human development and political orientations: notes toward a science of political education,' pp. 145–85 in Gilbert Abcarian and John Soule (eds.), *Social Psychology and Political Behaviour*. Columbus: Charles E. Merrill

Beals, R., D.H. Krantz, and A. Tuersky. 1968. 'Foundations of multidimensional scaling,' *Psychological Review* 75: 125–42

Becker, S.W. (ed.). 1970. *Campus Power Struggle*. New York: Transaction Books

Becker, S.W., and J. Carroll. 1962. 'Ordinal position and conformity,' *Journal of Abnormal Psychology* 65: 129–31

Becker, W.C. 1964. 'Consequences of different kinds of parental discipline,' pp. 169–208 in M.L. Hoffman and Lois W. Hoffman (eds.), *Review of Child Development Research*. New York: Russel Sage Foundation

Bell, D., and I. Kristol (eds.). 1968. *Confrontation: The Student Rebellion and the Universities*. New York: Basic Books

Beloff, M. 1969. 'The L.S.E. story,' *Encounter* 32: 66–77

Bem, Daryl J. 1965. 'An experimental analysis of self-perception,' *Journal of Experimental Social Psychology* 1: 199–218

- 1967. 'Self perception: an alternative interpretation of cognitive dissonance phenomena,' *Psychological Review* 74: 183–200

- 1968a. 'Attitudes as self descriptions: another look at the attitude behavior link,' pp. 197–214 in A.G. Greenwald et al. (eds.), *Psychological Foundations of Attitudes*. New York: Academic Press

- 1968b. 'Dissonance reduction in the behaviorist,' pp. 246–56 in Robert Abelson et al. (eds.), *Theories of Cognitive Consistency: A Sourcebook*. Chicago: Rand McNally

- 1970. *Beliefs, Attitudes and Human Affairs*. Belmont, Calif.: Brooks Cole
- 1972. 'Constructing cross-situational consistencies in behavior: some thoughts on Alker's critique of Mischel,' *Journal of Personality* 40, 1: 16–26
Bem, Daryl, and Andrea Allen. 1974. 'On predicting some of the people some of the time: the search for cross-situational consistencies in behaviour,' *Psychological Review* 81, 6: 506–20
Bem, Daryl, and David C. Funder. 1978. 'Predicting more of the people more of the time: assessing the personality of situations,' *Psychological Review* 85, 6: 485–501
Bengston, V.L., and M.C. Lovejoy. 1973. 'Values, personality and social structure,' *American Behavioral Scientist* 16, 6: 880–912
Bentler, P.M., and G. Speckart. 1979. 'Models of attitude-behaviour relations,' *Psychological Review* 86: 75–81
Bereiter, C., and M.B. Freeman. 1962. 'Fields of study and the people in them,' pp. 563–96 in N. Sanford (ed.), *The American College*. New York: John Wiley
Berelson, B.R. 1952. 'Democratic theory and public opinion,' *Public Opinion Quarterly* 16, 3: 313–30
Berelson, B.R., P.F. Lazarsfeld, and W.N. McPhee. 1954. *Voting*. Chicago: University of Chicago Press
Berg, Nancy E., and Paul Mussen. 1976. 'Social class differences in adolescents' sociopolitical opinions,' *Youth and Society* 7, 3: 259–70
Berger, E.M. 1952. 'The relation between expressed acceptance of self and expressed acceptance of others,' *Journal of Abnormal and Social Psychology* 47, 4: 778–82
Bergmann, Gustav. 1951. 'The logic of psychological concepts,' *Philosophy of Science* 18, 2: 93–110
- 1968. 'Ideology,' pp. 123–38 in May Brodbeck (ed.), *Readings in the Philosophy of the Social Sciences*. New York: Macmillan
Berkman, Paul L. 1971. 'Life stress and psychological well-being: a replication of Langner's analysis in the Midtown Manhattan Study,' *Journal of Health and Social Behaviour* 12, 1: 35–46
Berkowitz, Leonard, and K.G. Lutterman. 1968. 'The traditional socially responsible personality,' *Public Opinion Quarterly* 32, 2: 169–86
Berlyne, Daniel E. 1968. 'Behavior theory as personality theory,' pp. 629–91 in Edgar F. Borgatta and William W. Lambert (eds.), *Handbook of Personality Theory and Research*. Chicago: Rand McNally
Berry, J.W. 1979. 'A cultural ecology of social behaviour,' *Advances in Experimental Social Psychology* 12: 177–206
Bickford, Hugh L., and A.G. Neal. 1969. 'Alienation and social learning: a study of students in a vocational training centre,' *Sociology of Education* 42, 2: 141–53

Birch, A.H. 1950. 'The habit of voting,' *Journal of the Manchester School of Economic and Social Studies* 23: 75–82

Birch, A.H., and P. Campbell. 1950. 'Voting behavior in a Lancashire constituency,' *British Journal of Sociology* 1: 197–208

Bishop, G.D., D.L. Hamilton, and J.B. McConahay. 1980. 'Attitudes and non-attitudes in the belief systems of mass publics,' *Journal of Social Psychology* 110: 53–64

Bissell, Claude. 1969. 'Academic freedom: the student version,' *Queen's Quarterly* 76, 2: 171–84

– 1974, *Half-way up Parnassus*. Toronto: University of Toronto Press

Blackstone, Tessa, K. Gales, H. Roger, and W. Lewis. 1970. *Students in Conflict*. London: Weidenfeld and Nicolson

Blackstone, Tessa, and H. Roger. 1971. 'Student protest in a British university: some comparisons with American research,' *Comparative Education Review* Feb.: 1–19

Blalock, H. Jr. 1960. *Social Statistics*. New York: McGraw-Hill

Blau, P.M., and O.D. Duncan. 1967. *The American Occupational Structure*. New York: John Wiley

– 1968. 'Review symposium,' *American Sociological Review* 33: 294–300

– 1976. *The American Occupational Structure*. New York: John Wiley

Blauner, R. 1960. 'Work satisfaction and industrial trends in modern society,' pp. 339–61 in W. Galenson and S.M. Lipset (eds.), *Labour and Trade Unionism*. New York: John Wiley

Blishen, Bernard R. 1958. 'The construction and use of an occupational class scale,' *Canadian Journal of Economics and Political Science* 14, 4: 521–31

– 1967. 'A socio-economic index for occupations in Canada,' *Canadian Review of Sociology and Anthropology* 4, 1: 41–53

Block, Jeanne H., N. Haan, and M. Brewster Smith. 1968. 'Activism and apathy in contemporary adolescents,' pp. 198–231 in James F. Adams (ed.), *Understanding Adolescence*. Boston: Allyn and Bacon

– 1969. 'Socialization correlates of student activism,' *Journal of Social Issues* 15, 4: 143–77

Blum, Richard. 1969. 'Epilogue: students and drugs,' pp. 361–83 in Richard Blum and Associates, *Students and Drugs: Drugs II*. San Francisco: Jossey-Bass

Blumberg, P. 1968. *Industrial Democracy: The Sociology of Participation*. London: Constable

Blume, Norman. 1972. 'Family and the socialization of YR and YD presidents in the Midwest,' *Youth and Society* 2, 2: 177–84

Booth, Alan, and Susan Welch. 1978. 'Stress, health and political participation,' *Social Biology* 25, 2: 102–14

Bossard, James H.S., and E.S. Boll. 1956a. 'Adjustment of siblings in large families,' *American Journal of Psychiatry* May: 889–92
- 1956b. *The Large Family System.* Philadelphia: University of Pennsylvania
Bottomore, T.B. 1975. *Sociology as Social Criticism.* London: George Allen
Bowers, K.S. 1973. 'Situationism in psychology: an analysis and a critique,' *Psychological Review* 80, 5: 307–36
Bradburn, N.M. 1969. *The Structure of Psychological Well-being.* Chicago: Aldine
Brannon, R. et al. 1973. 'Attitude and action: a field experiment joined to a general population experience,' *American Sociological Review* 38: 625–36
Brauen, M., and K.N. Harmon. 1977. 'Political socialization: a topical bibliography,' *Youth and Society* 8, 3: 299–320
Braungart, R.G. 1971a. 'SDS and YAF: a comparison of two student radical groups in the mid-1960's,' *Youth and Society* 2: 441–57
- 1971b. 'Family status, socialization and student politics: a multivariate analysis,' *American Journal of Sociology* 77, 1: 108–30
- 1974. 'The sociology of generations and student politics: a comparison of the functionalist and generational unit models,' *Journal of Social Issues* 30, 2: 31–54
Braungart, R.G., and M. Braungart. 1974. 'Protest attitudes and behaviour among college youth: a U.S. case study,' *Youth and Society* 6, 2: 219–48
Bray, D.W. 1950. 'The prediction of behavior from two attitude scales,' *Journal of Abnormal Psychology* 65: 64–85
Braybrooke, David. 1975. 'The meaning of participation and of demands for it: a preliminary survey of the conceptual issues,' pp. 130–49 in J. Roland Pennock and J.W. Chapman (eds.), *Participation, Nomos XV.* New York: Lieber
Brehm, J.W. 1956. 'Post-decision changes in the desirability of alternatives,' *Journal of Abnormal and Social Psychology* 52: 384–9
- 1960. 'A dissonance analysis of attitude-discrepant behavior,' pp. 169–97 in C.I. Hovland and M.J. Rosenberg (eds.), *Attitude Organization and Change.* New Haven: Yale University Press
Brim, O.G. 1955. 'Attitude content, intensity and probability expectations,' *American Sociological Review* 20: 68–76
- 1960. 'Personality development as role learning,' pp. 127–59 in I. Iscoe and H. Stevenson (eds.), *Personality Development in Children.* Austin, Texas: University of Texas Press
Brim, O.G. Jr. 1966. 'Socialization through the life cycle,' pp. 1–49 in O.G. Brim and S. Wheeler (eds.), *Socialization after Childhood: Two Essays.* New York: John Wiley
Brodbeck, May. 1959. 'Models, meaning and theory,' pp. 373–407 in C. Gross (ed.), *Symposium in Sociological Theory.* Evanston: Row Peterson
- (ed.). 1968. *Readings in the Philosophy of the Social Sciences.* New York: Macmillan

Brody, S. 1957. *Patterns of Mothering*. New York: International Universities Press

Bronfenbrenner, U. 1961. 'Some familial antecedents of responsibility and leadership in adolescents,' pp. 239–71 in L. Petrullo and B. Bass (eds.), *Leadership and Interpersonal Behavior*. New York: Holt, Rinehart, and Winston

Bronson, Wanda C. 1966. 'Central orientations: a study of behavior organization from childhood to adolescence,' *Child Development* 37: 125–55

Brown, Michael K. 1969. *The Politics and Anti-politics of the Young*. Toronto: Collier-Macmillan

– 1973. 'Student protest and political attitudes,' *Youth and Society* 4, 4: 413–42

Brown, Roger. 1965. *Social Psychology*. New York: The Free Press

Browning, R.P. 1968. 'The interaction of personality and political system in decisions to run for office: some data and a simulation technique,' *Journal of Social Issues* 24, 3: 93–109

Browning, R.P., and H. Jacob. 1964. 'Power motivation and the political personality,' *Public Opinion Quarterly* 28: 75–90

Buchanan, William. 1956. 'An inquiry into purposive voting,' *The Journal of Politics* 18: 281–96

Budge, Ian. 1970. *Agreement and the Stability of Democracy*. Chicago: Markham

Budge, Ian, J.A. Brand, M. Margolis, and A.L.M. Smith. 1972. *Political Stratification and Democracy*. Toronto: University of Toronto Press

Budner, S. 1962. 'Intolerance of ambiguity as a personality variable,' *Journal of Personality* 30: 29–50

Burgess, P.M., and R. Hofstetter. 1971. 'The "student movement": ideology and reality,' *Midwest Journal of Political Science* 15: 687–702

Burnstein, Paul. 1972. 'Social structure and individual political participation in five countries,' *American Journal of Sociology* 77, 6: 1087–1111

Burwen, L.S., D.T. Campbell, and J. Kidd. 1956. 'The use of a sentence completion test in measuring attitudes toward superiors and subordinates,' *Journal of Applied Psychology* 40: 248–50

Byrne, Gary C. 1970. 'Cognitive inconsistency and student protest behaviour,' *Summation* 2, 1: 17–35

Calder, B.J., and M. Ross. 1973. *Attitudes and Behaviour*. Morriston, NH: General Learning Press

– 1976. 'Attitudes, theories and issues,' pp. 3–35 in John W. Thibault and Janet T. Spence (eds.), *Contemporary Topics in Social Psychology*. Morristown, NJ: General Learning Press

Campbell, A. 1962. 'The passive citizen,' *Acta Sociologica* 6: 9–21

– 1964. 'Who are the non-voters?' *New Society* 68: 11–12

Campbell, A., and P. Converse (eds.). 1972. *The Human Meaning of Social Change*. New York: Gage

Campbell, A., P. Converse, W. Miller, and D. Stokes. 1960. *The American Voter.* New York: John Wiley

Campbell, D.T. 1963. 'Social attitudes, and other acquired behavioral dispositions,' pp. 94–172 in S. Koch (ed.), *Psychology: A Study of a Science*, Vol. 6. New York: McGraw-Hill

Campbell, D.T., and D. Fiske. 1967. 'Convergent and discriminant validation by the multitrait-multimethod matrix,' pp. 282–93 in Martin Fishbein (ed.), *Readings in Attitude Theory and Measurement.* New York: John Wiley

Campbell, E.Q. 1969. 'Adolescent socialization,' pp. 821–59 in David A. Goslin (ed.), *Handbook of Socialization Theory and Research.* Chicago: Rand McNally

Card, B. 1968. *Trends and Change in Canadian Society: Their Challenge to Canadian Youth.* Toronto: Macmillan

Cattell, R.B., and I.H. Scheier. 1963. *Handbook for the IPAT Anxiety Scale Questionnaire (Self Analysis Form)*, 2nd ed. Champaign, Ill.: Institute for Personality and Ability Testing

Chein, W.K.C. 1948. 'Behavior theory and the behavior of attitudes,' *Psychological Review* 55: 175–88

Christie, R., and P. Cook. 1958. 'A guide to published literature relating to the authoritarian personality through 1956,' *Journal of Psychology* 45: 171–99

Christie, R., and M. Jahoda (eds.). 1954. *Studies in the Scope and Method of 'The Authoritarian Personality.'* New York: The Free Press

Clark, S.D., P. Grayson, and L. Grayson (eds.). 1975. *Prophecy and Protest: Social Movements in Twentieth-Century Canada.* Toronto: Gage

Clarke, J.W., and J. Egan. 1971. 'Social and political dimensions of campus protest activity,' paper read at Florida Academy of Sciences, Melbourne, Florida (March), unpublished

Clausen, John A. 1966. 'Family structure, socialization, and personality,' pp. 1–53 in Lois W. Hoffman and M.C. Hoffman (eds.), *Review of Child Development Research*, Vol. 2. New York: Russell Sage Foundation

– (ed.). 1968a. *Socialization and Society.* Boston: Little, Brown

– 1968b. 'Recent developments in socialization theory and research,' *Annals of the American Association of Political Science* 377: 139–55

Cnudde, C.F., and D.E. Neubauer (eds.). 1969. *Empirical Democratic Theory.* Chicago: Markham

Cobb, Roger W. 1973. 'The belief systems perspective: an assessment of a framework,' *The Journal of Politics* 35, 1: 121–53

Cockburn, A., and R. Blackburn (eds.). 1969. *Student Power: Problems, Diagnoses and Action.* Harmondsworth, Middlesex: Penguin

Cohen, P.S. 1966. 'Social attitudes and sociological enquiry,' *British Journal of Sociology* 17: 341–52

Cohen, P.S., and A. Watson. 1971. 'The typical student?' *New Society* 4: 873–6
Collins, Barry E. 1968. 'Behavior theory,' pp. 240–245 in Robert Abelson et al.
(eds.), *Theories of Cognitive Consistency: A Sourcebook* Chicago: Rand McNally
Connell, R.W. 1972. 'Political socialization in the American family: the evidence
re-examined,' *Public Opinion Quarterly* 36: 323–33
Converse, Philip E. 1962. 'Information flow and the stability of partisan attitudes,'
Public Opinion Quarterly 16, 4: 578–99
– 1964a. 'New dimensions of meaning for cross-section sample surveys in
politics,' *International Social Science Journal* 16, 1: 19–35
– 1964b. 'The nature of belief systems in mass publics,' pp. 206–62 in David
Apter (ed.), *Ideology and Discontent*. Glencoe, Ill.: The Free Press
– 1970. 'Attitudes and non-attitudes: continuation of a dialogue,' pp. 168–89 in
Edward R. Tufte (ed.), *The Quantitative Analysis of Social Problems*. Reading,
Mass.: Addison Wesley
Cook, T.J., and F.P. Scioli Jr. 1972. 'Political socialization research in the United
States: a review,' pp. 154–74 in D.D. Nimmo and C. Bonjean (eds.), *Political
Attitudes and Public Opinion*. New York: David McKay
Cook, W.W., and C. Selltiz. 1964. 'A multiple-indicator approach to attitude
measurement,' *Psychological Bulletin* 62: 36–55
Corey, S.M. 1937. 'Professed attitudes and actual behavior,' *Journal of Educational
Psychology* 28: 271–80
Costner, Herbert L. 1963. 'Measures of association for cross-classification: III.
Approximate sampling theory,' *Journal of the American Statistical Association* 58:
310–64
– 1965. 'Criteria for measures of association,' *American Sociological Review* 30,
3: 341–53
Couch, A., and K. Keniston. 1960. 'Yeasayers and naysayers: agreeing response
set as a personality variable,' *Journal of Abnormal and Social Psychology* 97:
151–74
Cowdry, R.W., K. Keniston, and S. Cabin. 1970. 'The war and military obliga-
tions: private attitudes and public actions,' *Journal of Personality* 38, 4: 525–49
Crespi, Irving. 1971. 'What kinds of attitude measures are predictive of behaviour?' *Public Opinion Quarterly* 35, 3: 327–35
– 1977. 'Attitude measurement, theory and prediction,' *Public Opinion Quarterly*
41: 285–94
Crick, B., and W.A. Robson (eds.). 1970. *Protest and Discontent*. Middlesex:
Penguin
Cronbach, L.J. 1951. 'Coefficient alpha and the internal structure of tests,' *Psycho-
metrika* 16: 292–334
– 1975. 'Beyond the two disciplines of scientific psychology,' *American Psychologist* 30, 2: 116–27

Cronbach, L.J., and P. Meehl. 1955. 'Construct validity of psychological tests,' *Psychological Bulletin* 52: 281–302
Cutler, Neal E. 1976. 'Generational approaches to political socialization,' *Youth and Society* 8, 2: 175–207
Dahl, R.A. 1956a. 'Hierarchy, democracy, and bargaining in politics and economics,' pp. 83–90 in H. Eulan, S. Eldenveld, and M. Janowitz (eds.), *Political Behaviour*. Glencoe, Ill.: The Free Press
– 1956b. *Preface to Democratic Theory*. Chicago: University of Chicago Press
– 1961. *Who Governs?* New Haven: Yale University Press
– 1963. *Modern Political Analysis*. Englewood Cliffs, NJ: Prentice-Hall
Davidson, A.R., and J.J. Jaccard. 1979. 'Variables that moderate the attitude-behaviour relation – results of a longitudinal survey,' *Journal of Personality and Social Psychology* 37: 1364–76
Davidson, Carl. 1968. 'Blueprint for a student revolution,' *Vancouver Sun* (Thursday, 15 August): 6
Davidson, Donald. 1968. 'Actions, reasons and causes,' pp. 44–58 in May Brodbeck (ed.), *Readings in the Philosophy of the Social Sciences*. New York: Macmillan
Davidson, H.H., and L.P. Krugler. 1953. 'Some background correlates of personality and social attitudes,' *Journal of Social Psychology* 38: 233–40
Davies, James C. 1970. 'The family's role in political socialization,' pp. 108–16 in Roberta S. Sigel (ed.), *Learning about Politics: A Reader in Political Socialization*. New York: Random House
– 1973. 'Where from and where to?' pp. 1–27 in J.N. Knutson (ed.), *Handbook of Political Psychology*. San Francisco: Jossey-Bass
Davis, Keith E. 1968. 'Needs, wants and consistency,' pp. 327–30 in Robert Abelson et al. (eds.), *Theories of Cognitive Consistency: A Sourcebook*. Chicago: Rand McNally
Dawes, R.M. 1976. 'Shallow psychology,' pp. 5–20 in J.S. Carroll and J.W. Payne (eds.), *Cognition and Social Behaviour*. Hillsdale, N.J.: W.J. Lawrence
Dawson, R.E., and K.E. Prewitt. 1969. *Political Socialization*. Boston: Little, Brown
Day, R.C., and R.L. Hamblin. 1964. 'Some effects of close and punitive styles of supervision,' *American Journal of Sociology* 69, 5: 499–510
Dean, D.G. 1961. 'Alienation: its meaning and measurement,' *American Sociological Review* 26: 753–8
De Charms, Richard. 1968. *Personal Causation: The Internal Affective Determinants of Behavior*. New York: Academic Press
DeFleur, M.L., and F.R. Westie. 1958. 'Verbal attitudes and overt acts: an experiment on the salience of attitudes,' *American Sociological Review* 23: 667–730
– 1963. 'Attitude as a scientific concept,' *Social Forces* 42: 17–31

Demerath, N.J. III, G. Marwell, and M. Aiken. 1970. 'The dynamics of idealism: student activism and the Black Movement,' unpublished paper, Department of Sociology, University of Wisconsin

Dennett, D.C. 1978. *Brainstorms: Philosophical Essays on Mind and Psychology*. Ann Arbor, Mich.: Bradford Books

Dennis, Jack. 1968. 'Major problems of political socialization research,' *Midwest Journal of Political Science* 12: 85–114

De Quenetain, Tanneguy. 1970. 'The revolt of the student prince,' *Realities* March: 62–71

Deutscher, Irwin. 1966. 'Words and deeds: social science and social policy,' *Social Problems* 13: 235–54

– 1969. 'Looking backward: case studies on the progress of methodology in sociological research,' *American Sociologist* 4: 35–41

– 1973. *What We Say/What We Do*. Glenview, Ill.: Scott, Foresman

Devall, W.B. 1970. 'Support for civil liberties among English-speaking Canadian university students,' *Canadian Journal of Political Science* 3, 3: 433–50

DiPalma, G., and H. McClosky. 1970. 'Personality and conformity: the learning of political attitudes,' *American Political Science Review* 64, 4: 1054–73

DiRenzo, G.J. (ed.). 1974. *Personality and Politics*. New York: Doubleday

– 1977. 'Socialization, personality and social systems,' *American Review of Sociology* 3: 261–95

Dohrenwend, B.P., and B.S. Dohrenwend. 1969. *Social Status and Psychological Disorder: A Causal Inquiry*. New York: Wiley Associates

Donovan, J.M., and M.H. Shaevitz. 1970. 'A study of student political groups,' unpublished paper, Connecticut Mental Health Centre, New Haven

– 1973 'Student political activists: a typology,' *Youth and Society*, 4, 4: 379–411

Doob, Leonard. 1947. 'The behavior of attitudes,' *Psychological Review* 54: 135–56

Doreian, Patrick. 1972. 'Multivariate analysis and categorised data,' *Quality and Quantity* 6, 2: 253–73

Doress, Irvin. 1968. 'A study of a sampling of Boston University student activists,' unpublished EDD thesis, Boston University

Douglas, J.W.B. 1964. *The Home and School*. London: MacGibbon & Kee

Douvan, Elizabeth. 1963. 'Employment and the adolescent,' pp. 142–64 in F.I. Nye and Lois W. Hoffman (eds.), *The Employed Mother in America*. Chicago: Rand McNally

Draper, N.R., and H. Smith. 1968. *Applied Regression Analysis*. New York: John Wiley

Dunlap, R. 1970. 'Radical and conservative student activists: a comparison of family backgrounds,' *Pacific Sociological Review* 13, 1: 171–81

Eagly, A.H., and S. Himmelfarb. 1978. 'Attitudes and opinions,' pp. 517–54 in M.R. Rosenzweig and L.W. Porter (eds.), *Annual Review of Psychology* 29

Easton, D., and J. Dennis. 1967. 'The child's acquisition of regime norms: political efficacy,' *American Political Science Review* 61: 759–61
– 1969. *Children in the Political System*. New York: McGraw-Hill
– 1970. 'The child's image of government,' pp. 31–56 in Roberta S. Sigel (ed.), *Learning about Politics: A Reader in Political Socialization*. New York: Random House
Eckstein, Harry. 1966. *Division and Cohesion in Democracy*. Princeton: Princeton University Press
Edelstein, A.S. 1962. 'Since Bennington: evidence of change in student political behaviour,' *Public Opinion Quarterly* 26, 4: 564–77
Edwards, A.L. 1957a. *Techniques of Attitude Scale Construction*. New York: Appleton, Century Crofts
– 1957b. *The Social Desirability Variable in Personality Assessment Research*. New York: Dryden Press
Ehrlich, H. 1969. 'Attitudes, behavior and the intervening variables,' *American Sociologist* 4: 29–34
Eitzen, D.S. 1970. 'Social class, status inconsistency and political attributes,' *Social Science Quarterly* 51, 3: 602–9
– 1974. *Social Structure and Social Problems in America*. Boston: Allyn and Bacon
Elder, G.H. Jr. 1963. 'Parental power legitimation and its effect on the adolescent,' *Sociometry* 26: 50–65
– 1968. 'Adolescent socialization and development,' pp. 239–363 in Edgar F. Borgatta and William Lambert (eds.), *Handbook of Personality Theory and Research*. Chicago: Rand McNally
– 1973. 'On linking social structure and personality,' *American Behavioural Scientist* 16, 6: 785–800
Elder, G.H. Jr., and C.E. Bowerman. 1963. 'Family structure and child-rearing patterns: the effect of family size and sex composition,' *American Sociological Review* 28: 891–905
Elkin, F., and W.A. Westley. 1955. 'The myth of adolescent culture,' *American Sociological Review* 20: 680–4
Erbe, W. 1964. 'Social involvement and political activity: a replication and elaboration,' *American Sociological Review* 29: 198–215
Eriksen, C.W., and J. Pierce. 1968. 'Defense mechanisms,' pp. 1007–41 in E.F. Borgatta and W.W. Lambert (eds.), *Handbook of Personality Theory and Research*. Chicago: Rand McNally
Erikson, E.H. 1963. *Childhood and Society*, rev. ed. New York: Norton
Es, J.C. Van, and D.J. Koenig. 1976. 'Social participation, social status and extremist political attitudes,' *Sociological Quarterly* 17, 1: 16–26
Etzioni, A. 1968. 'Confessions of a professor caught in a revolution,' *New York Times Magazine* (15 Sept.): 89–102

Everson, David H. 1970. 'The background of student support for student protest activities in the university,' *Public Affairs Bulletin* 3, 2: 1–7

Ezekiel, Jeremiah. 1971a. 'The uses of naive psychology in survey research,' unpublished paper, University of Alberta

– 1971b. 'Correlates of student political attitudes,' unpublished MA thesis, University of Alberta

Farley, Jennie. 1968. 'Maternal employment and child behavior,' *Cornell Journal of Social Relations* 3, 2: 58–71

Fazio, R.H., and M.P. Zanna. 1978. 'Attitudinal qualities relating to the strength of the attitude-behaviour relationship,' *Journal of Experimental Social Psychology* 14: 398–408

Feldman, K., and T. Newcomb. 1970. *The Impact of College on Students*. San Francisco: Jossey Bass

Fendrich, J.M. 1967. 'A study of the association among verbal attitudes, commitment and overt behavior in different experimental situations,' *Social Forces* 45: 347–55

– 1974. 'Activists ten years later: a test of generational unit continuity,' *Journal of Social Issues* 30, 3: 95–118

Fendrich, J.M., and A.T. Tarleau. 1973. 'Marching to a different drummer: occupational and political correlates of former student activists,' *Social Forces* 52: 245–52

Fengler, A.P., and V. Wood. 1973. 'Continuity between the generations: differential influence of mothers and fathers,' *Youth and Society* 4, 3: 359–73

Fenton, J.H., and G. Gleason. 1969. 'Student power at the University of Massachusetts: a case study,' Bureau of Government Research, University of Massachusetts, unpublished

Festinger, L. 1957. *A Theory of Cognitive Dissonance*. Evanston, Ill.: Row-Peterson

Festinger, L., and J.M. Carlsmith. 1959. 'Cognitive consequences of forced compliance,' *Journal of Abnormal Social Psychology* 58: 203–10

Feuer, Lewis S. 1968. 'The new marxism of the intellectuals,' *The New Leader* (4 Nov.): 7–11

– 1969a. *The Challenge of Youth*. Garden City, NY: Basic Books

– 1969b. *The Conflict of Generations: The Character and Significance of Student Movements*. Garden City, NY: Basic Books

Finifter, Ada W. 1970. 'Dimensions of political alienation,' *American Political Science Review* 64: 369–410

Finney, Henry C. 1971. 'Political libertarianism at Berkeley: an application of perspectives from the new left,' *Journal of Social Issues* 27, 1: 35–61

Fischer, Edward H. 1971. 'Who volunteers for companionship with mental patients? A study of attitude-belief intention relationships,' *Journal of Personality* 39: 552–63

- 1973. 'Consistency among humanitarian and helping attitudes,' *Social Forces* 52, 2: 157–67

Fishbein, M. 1963. 'An investigation of the relationships between beliefs about an object and the attitude toward that object,' *Human Relations* 16: 233–9

- 1966. 'The relationship between beliefs, attitudes and behavior,' pp. 199–223 in S. Feldman (ed.), *Cognitive Consistency: Motivational Antecedents and Behavioral Consequences*. New York: Academic Press

- 1967. 'Attitude and the prediction of behavior,' pp. 477–93 in M. Fishbein (ed.), *Readings in Attitude Theory and Measurement*. New York: John Wiley

Fishbein, M., and I. Ajzen. 1974. 'Attitudes towards objects as predictors of single and multiple behavioural criteria,' *Psychological Review* 81: 59–74

Fishbein, M., and B.H. Raven. 1962. 'The AB scales: an operational definition of belief and attitude,' *Human Relations* 15: 35–43

Flacks, Richard. 1967. 'The liberated generation: an exploration of the roots of student protest,' *Journal of Social Issues* 23, 3: 52–75

- 1970a. 'The revolt of the advantaged: an exploration of the roots of student protest,' pp. 186–203 in Roberta Sigel (ed.), *Learning about Politics: A Reader in Political Socialization*. New York: Random House

- 1970b. 'Social and cultural meanings of student revolt: some informal comparative observations,' *Social Problems* 17: 340–57

- 1970c. 'Who protests: the social bases of the student movement,' pp. 134–57 in Julian Foster and Durward Long (eds.), *Protest!! Student Activism in America*. New York: William Morrow

- 1971a. 'The New Left and American politics after 10 years,' *Journal of Social Issues* 27, 1: 21–34

- 1971b. *Youth and Social Change*. Chicago: Rand McNally

- 1972. 'Young intelligentsia in revolt,' pp. 247–64 in R. Lejeune (ed.), *Class and Conflict in American Society*. Chicago: Markham

Fleming, Donald. 1967. 'Attitude: the history of a concept,' pp. 287–369 in D. Fleming and B. Bailyn (eds.), *Perspectives in American History*, volume 1. Harvard University: Charles Warren Centre for Students in American History

Form, W., and J. Huber. 1971. 'Income, race and the ideology of political efficacy,' *The Journal of Politics* 33, 3: 659–88

Foster, J., and D. Long (eds.). 1970. *Protest! Student Activism in America*. New York: William Morrow

Foulds, G.A., and T.M. Caine. 1965. *Personality and Personal Illness*. London: Tavistock

Frankfurt, H.G. 1971. 'Freedom of the will and the concept of a person,' *The Journal of Philosophy* 68, 1: 5–21

Fraser, John. 1970. 'The mistrustful-efficacious hypothesis and political participation,' *The Journal of Politics* 32, 2: 444–50

- 1971. 'Personal and political meaning correlates of political cynicism,' *Midwest Journal of Political Science* 15, 2: 347–65

Freeman, J.L. 1969. 'Parents; it's not all your fault, but ...,' *The Journal of Politics* 31: 812–17

Frideres, J.S., and L.G. Warner. 1980. 'Attitude-action relationships,' *Canadian Review of Sociology and Anthropology* 17, 2: 109–22

Frideres, J.S., L.G. Warner, and S.L. Albrecht. 1971. 'The impact of social constraints on the relationship between attitudes and behaviour,' *Social Forces* 50: 102–12

Friedman, Lucy N., A.R. Gold, and R. Christie. 1972. 'Dissecting the generation gap: intergenerational and intrafamilial similarities and differences,' *Public Opinion Quarterly* 36: 334–46

Friedman, S.R. 1973. 'Perspectives on the American student movement,' *Social Problems* 20: 283–99

Fruchter, B. 1954. *Introduction to Factor Analysis*. Princeton, NJ: Princeton University Press

Gabennesch, H. 1972. 'Authoritarianism as world view,' *American Journal of Sociology* 77, 5: 857–75

Gales, K.E. 1966. 'A campus revolution,' *British Journal of Sociology* 17: 1–19

Gamson, W.A. 1961. 'The fluoridation dialogue: is it an ideological conflict?' *Public Opinion Quarterly* 25: 526–37

- 1968. *Power and Discontent*. Homewood, Ill.: The Dorsey Press

Gamson, Z.F., J. Goodman, and G. Gurin. 1967. 'Radicals, moderates and bystanders during a university protest,' unpublished paper read at American Sociological Association, San Francisco, August

Garfinkel, H. 1967. *Studies in Ethnomethodology*. Englewood Cliffs, NJ: Prentice-Hall

Gastwirth, Donald. 1965. 'Why students protest,' unpublished student paper, Department of Psychology, Yale University

George, A.L. 1968. 'Power as a compensatory value for political leaders,' *Journal of Social Issues* 24, 3: 29–49

Gergen, M.K., and J. Kenneth. 1971. 'How the war affects the campuses,' *Change* 3: 10, 69–70

Geschwender, J.A. 1972. 'Continuities in theories of status consistency and cognitive dissonance,' pp. 292–308 in D. Nimmo and C. Bonjean (eds.), *Political Attitudes and Public Opinion*. New York: David Mckay

Geschwender, J.A., J.W. Rinehart, and P.M. George. 1974. 'Socialization, alienation and student activism,' *Youth and Society* 5, 3: 303–25

Gitlin, Todd. 1980. *Mass Media in the Making and the Unmaking of the New Left*. Los Angeles: University of California Press

Glazer, N. 1969. 'Jewish students and student activism,' *Fortune* 79: 112–13

Goertzel, T. 1972. 'Changes in the values of college students,' *Pacific Sociological Review* 15, 2: 236–44

Goffman, E. 1959. *The Presentation of Self in Everyday Life*. Garden City, NY: Doubleday

Gold, A.R., R. Christie, and L. Friedman. 1976. *Fists and Flowers: A Social Psychological Interpretation of Student Dissent*. New York: Academic Press

Gold, A.R., L.N. Friedman, and R. Christie. 1971. 'The anatomy of revolutionists,' *Journal of Applied Social Psychology* 1: 26–43

Goldhamer, H. 1950. 'Public opinion and personality,' *American Journal of Sociology* 55, 4: 346–54

Goodman, J. 1968. 'Alienation and commitment in contemporary American: speculations from a study of student activists at the University of Michigan,' unpublished paper, Department of Sociology, University of Chicago

Goodman, L. 1972. 'A general model for the analysis of surveys,' *American Journal of Sociology* 77: 1035–86

Goodman, P. 1968. 'The black flag of anarchism,' *New York Times Magazine* (14 July): 11–18

Gore, P.M., and J.B. Rotter. 1963. 'A personality correlate of social action,' *Journal of Personality* 31: 58–64

Gottfried, A. 1955. 'The use of psychosomatic categories in a study of political personality,' *The Western Political Quarterly* 8, 2: 234–47

Greene, L.R. 1979. 'Psychological differentiation and social structures,' *Journal of Social Psychology* 109: 79–86

Greenstein, F.I. 1961. 'Sex-related political differences in childhood,' *The Journal of Politics* 23: 353–71

– 1965. *Children and Politics*. New Haven, Conn.: Yale University Press

– 1968. 'Political socialization,' *International Encyclopedia of the Social Sciences* 14: 551–5. New York: Macmillan and The Free Press

– 1969. *Personality and Politics*. Chicago: Markham

– 1970a. 'Personality and political socialization: the theories of authoritarian and democratic character,' pp. 260–76 in Roberta A. Sigel (ed.), *Learning about Politics: A Reader in Political Socialization*. New York: Random House

– 1970b. 'A note on the ambiguity of political socialization: definitions, criticisms and strategies of inquiry,' *The Journal of Politics* 32, 4: 969–79

Greenstein, F.I., and N.W. Polsby. 1975. 'Political socialization,' pp. 93–153 in F. Greenstein (ed.), *Handbook of Political Science*. Reading, Mass.: Addison-Wesley

Greenwald, A.G., T. Brock, and T.M. Ostrom. 1968. *Psychological Foundations of Attitudes*. New York: Academic Press

Greer, S., and P. Orleans. 1962. 'The mass society and the parapolitical structure,' *American Sociological Review* 27: 634–46

Gross, S.J., and C.M. Niman. 1975. 'Attitude-behaviour consistency: a review,' *Public Opinion Quarterly* 29, 3: 358–68

Guilford, J.P. 1956. *Fundamental Statistics in Psychology and Education.* New York: McGraw-Hill

Gump, J.P. 1972. 'Sex-role attitudes and psychological well-being,' *Journal of Social Issues* 28, 2: 79–92

Gunderson, E.K., and J.L. Mahan. 1966. 'Cultural and psychological differences among occupational groups,' *Journal of Psychology* 62: 287–304

Gurin, G. 1971. 'A study of students in a multiversity,' Office of Education, Project S-0901, University of Michigan, unpublished

Gurin, G., J. Veroff, and S. Feld. 1960. *Americans View Their Mental Health.* New York: Basic Books

Haan, N., M.B. Smith, and J. Block. 1968. 'Moral reasoning of young adults: political-social behaviour, family background and personality correlates,' *Journal of Personality and Social Psychology* 10: 183–201

Hagan, J. 1975. 'Law, order and sentencing: a study of attitude in action,' *Sociometry* 38: 374–84

Hall, Calvin S. 1968. 'The relevance of Freudian psychology and related view-points for the social sciences,' pp. 245–319 in Gardner Lindzey and Elliot Aronson (eds.), *The Handbook of Social Psychology,* 2nd ed., vol. 1. Reading, Mass.: Addison-Wesley

Hall, Calvin S., and G. Lindzey. 1970. *Theories of Personality,* 2nd ed. New York: John Wiley

Halleck, Seymour L. 1967. 'Psychiatric treatment of the alienated college student,' *American Journal of Psychiatry* 124, 5: 96–104

Hamilton, Richard F. 1972. *Class and Politics in the United States.* New York: John Wiley

Hampden-Turner, Charles. 1970. *Radical Man.* Cambridge, Mass.: Schenkman

Handlin, Oscar. 1970. 'The vulnerability of the American university,' *Encounter* 35, 1: 22–30

Harding, James. 1968. 'From the midst of a crisis: student power in English-speaking Canada,' pp. 90–105 in G.F. McGuigan (ed.), *Student Protest.* Toronto: Methuen

– 1970. 'The New Left in British Columbia,' *Our Generation* 7, 2: 21–44

Harned, L. 1961. 'Authoritarian attitudes and party activity,' *Public Opinion Quarterly* 25, 3: 393–9

Harris, Janet (ed.). 1970. *Students in Revolt.* New York: McGraw-Hill

Hase, H.D., and L.R. Goldberg. 1967. 'Comparative validity of different strategies of constructing personality inventory scales,' *Psychological Bulletin* 67: 231–48

Hassenger, Robert. 1970. 'Protest and the Catholic colleges,' pp. 483–96 in Julian Foster and Durward Long (eds.), *Protest!! Student Activism in America*. New York: William Morrow

Hastings, P.K., and D.R. Hoge. 1970. 'Religious change among college students over two decades,' *Social Forces* 49, 1: 16–27

Hedlund, Ronald D. 1973. 'Psychological predispositions: political representatives and the public,' *American Journal of Political Science* 17: 480–505

Heider, F. 1958. *The Psychology of Interpersonal Relations*. New York: John Wiley

Heise, David R. 1977. 'Group dynamics and attitude behaviour relations,' *Sociological Methods and Research* 5, 3: 259–88

Helson, R., and V. Mitchell. 1978. 'Personality,' pp. 555–85 in M.R. Rosenzwig and L.W. Porter (eds.), *Annual Review of Psychology*, vol. 29

Hennessy, Bernard. 1970. 'A headnote on the existence and study of political attitudes,' *Social Sciences Quarterly* 51, 3: 463–76

Henriot, Peter J. 1966. 'The coincidence of political and religious attitudes,' *Review of Religious Research* 8, 1: 50–7

Henry, Franklin J. 1971. 'University influence on student opinion,' *Canadian Review of Sociology and Anthropology* 8, 1: 18–31

Hess, E.H., A.L. Seltzer, and J.M. Shlien. 1965. 'Pupil response of hetero and homosexual males to pictures of men and women: a pilot study,' *Journal of Abnormal Psychology* 70: 165–8

Hess, R.D., and J.V. Torney. 1967. *The Development of Political Attitudes in Children*. Chicago, Ill.: Aldine

Hilgard, E.R. 1979. 'The trilogy of mind: cognition, affection and conation,' *Journal of Historical Behavioural Science* 1: 3–29

– 1980. 'Consciousness in contemporary psychology,' pp. 1–26 in M.R. Rosenzweig and L.W. Porter (eds.), *Annual Review of Psychology*, vol. 31

Hobbart, Charles. 1972. 'Implications of student power for high schools,' pp. 323–33 in H.A. Stevenson et al. (eds.), *The Best of Times: The Worst of Times: Contemporary Issues in Canadian Education*. Toronto: Holt, Rinehart & Winston

Hoffer, Eric. 1951. *The True Believer*. New York: New American Library

Hoffman, Lois W. 1972. 'Early childhood experiences and women's achievement motives,' *Journal of Social Issues* 28, 2: 129–55

– 1977. 'Changes in family roles, socialization and sex differences,' *American Psychologist* 32, 8: 644–57

Hoffman, Martin L. 1962. 'The role of the parent in the child's moral growth.' *Religious Education Research Supplement* 57

– 1977. 'Personality and social development,' pp. 295–321 in M.R. Rosenzweig and L.W. Porter (eds.), *Annual Review of Psychology*, vol. 28

Hogan, R., C. DeSoto, and C. Solano. 1977. 'Traits, tests and personality research,' *American Psychologist* 32, 4: 255–64

Hoge, D.R. 1976. 'Changes in college students' value patterns in the 1950's, 1960's and 1970's,' *Sociology of Education* 49: 155–63

Holian, J. Jr. 1972. 'Alienation and social awareness among college students,' *Sociological Quarterly* 13: 114–25

Holt, R.R. 1970. 'Yet another look at clinical and statistical prediction: or, is clinical psychology worthwhile?' *American Psychologist* 25: 337–49

Homant, Robert. 1969. 'Semantic differential ratings and the rank-ordering of values,' *Educational and Psychological Measurement* 29: 885–9

– 1970. 'Denotative meaning of values,' *Personality* 1, 3: 213–19

Hopple, Gerald W. 1976. 'Protest attitudes and social class: working class authoritarianism revisited,' *Sociology and Social Research* 60, 3: 229–45

Horner, Matina S. 1972. 'Toward an understanding of achievement-related conflicts in women,' *Journal of Social Issues* 27, 2: 157–75

Hovland, C.I. 1959. 'Reconciling conflicting results derived from experimental and survey studies of attitude change,' *American Psychologist* 14: 8–17

Hovland, C.I., and M.J. Rosenberg (eds.). 1960. *Attitude Organization and Change*. New Haven: Yale University Press

Howarth, E., and J.A. Browne. 1971. 'An item-factor-analysis of the 16 PF,' *Personality* 2, 2: 117–39

Hunt, J. 1965. 'Traditional personality theory in the light of recent evidence,' *American Scientist* 53: 80–96

Hunt, L.L., and R.G. Cushing. 1972. 'Status discrepancy, interpersonal attachment and right-wing extremism,' pp. 324–38 in D.D. Nimmo and C. Bonjean (eds.), *Political Attitudes and Public Opinion*. New York: David Mckay

Hyman, H.H. 1959. *Political Socialization*. Glencoe, Ill.: The Free Press

Iglitzin, Lynne B. 1972. 'Sex-typing and politicization in children's attitudes: reflections on studies done and undone,' prepared for delivery at the 1972 Annual Meeting of the American Political Science Association, Washington, 5–9 September

Inkeles, Alex. 1968. 'Society, social structure, and child socialization,' pp. 73–129 in John A. Clausen (ed.), *Socialization and Society*. Boston: Little Brown

Insko, C.A. 1967. *Theories of Attitude Change*. New York: Appleton-Century-Crofts

Insko, C.A., and J. Schopler. 1967. 'Triadic consistency: a statement of affective-cognitive-conative consistency,' *Psychological Review* 74: 361–76

Irving, J.A. 1969. *The Social Credit Movement in Alberta*. Toronto: University of Toronto Press

Issaak, Robert A. 1971. 'Student alienation and ideology: attitude consistency and future implications,' prepared for delivery at the Annual Meeting of the American Political Science Association, Washington, 7–11 September

Jaccard, J. et al. 1977. 'Attitudes and behaviour: an analysis of specificity of attitudinal predictors,' *Human Relations* 30: 817–24

Jackman, M.R. 1973. 'Education and prejudice or education and response-set?' *American Sociological Review* 38: 327–39

– 1976. 'The relation between verbal attitude and overt behaviour: a public opinion application,' *Social Forces* 54: 646–68

Jackman, Robert W. 1970. 'A note on intelligence, social class, and political efficacy in children,' *The Journal of Politics* 32: 984–9

– 1972. 'Political elites, mass publics and support for democratic principles,' *The Journal of Politics* 34, 3: 753–74

Jackson, D.W., and S.V. Paunonen. 1980. 'Personality structure and assessment,' pp. 503–51 in Mark R. Rosenzweig and L.W. Porter (eds.), *Annual Review of Psychology*, vol. 31

Jacobs, Paul, and S. Landau. 1966. *The New Radicals: A Report with Documents*. New York: Vintage Books

Jahoda, Marie. 1958. *Current Concepts of Positive Mental Health*. New York: Basic Books

Jameson, J., and R.M. Hessler. 1970. 'The natives are restless: the ethos and mythos of student power,' *Human Organization* 29: 81–94

Jansen, D.G., B.B. Winborn, and W.D. Martinson. 1968. 'Characteristics associated with campus social-political action leadership,' *Journal of Counseling Psychology* 15, 6: 552–62

Jennings, M.K., and R.G. Niemi. 1974. 'The transmission of political values from parent to child,' pp. 295–305 in A.R. Wilcox (ed.), *Public Opinion and Political Attitudes*. New York: John Wiley

Johnson, D.W., and D.C. Neale. 1968. 'The effects of models, reference groups and social responsibility norms upon participation in prosocial action activities,' *Journal of Social Psychology* 81: 3–8, 87–92

Johnson, H.M. 1936. 'Pseudo-mathematics in the mental and social sciences,' *American Journal of Psychology* 48: 342–51

Jones, Edward E. 1979. 'Rocky road from acts to dispositions,' *American Psychologist* 34: 107–17

Jones, E.E., and K.E. Davis. 1965. 'From acts to dispositions: the attribution process in person perception,' pp. 220–66 in Leonard Berkowitz (ed.), *Advances in Experimental Social Psychology*, vol. 11. New York: Academic Press

322 Bibliography

Jones, E.E., D.E. Kanouse, H.H. Kelley, R.E. Nisbett, S. Valins, and B. Weiner. 1971. *Attribution: Perceiving the Causes of Behaviour*. Morristown, NJ: General Learning Press
Jones, E.E., and R.E. Nisbett. 1971. *The Actor and Observer: Divergent Perceptions of the Causes of Behavior*. New York: General Learning Press
Jones, Ruth S. 1977. 'Institutional change and socialization research: the school and politicization,' *Youth and Society* 8, 3: 277–98
Jones, W.H. et al. 1977. 'Self-concept as a function of political ideology and activism,' *Psychological Reports* 40: 1295–6
Kahle, L.R., and J. Berman. 1979. 'Attitudes cause behaviours: a cross-lagged panel analysis,' *Journal of Personality and Social Psychology* 37: 315–21
Kahn, R.M., and W.J. Bowers. 1970. 'The social context of the rank-and-file student activist: a test of four hypotheses,' *Sociology of Education* 43: 38–56
Kariel, Henry A. 1967. 'The political relevance of behavioral and existential psychology,' *American Political Science Review* 61, 2: 334–42
Kasahara, Y. 1968. 'A profile of Canada's metropolitan centres,' pp. 67–76 in B. Blishen et al. (eds.), *Canadian Society: Sociological Perspectives*, 3rd ed. Toronto: Macmillan
Kasschau, P., H.E. Ransford, and V.L. Bengston. 1974. 'Generational consciousness and youth movement participation: contrasts in blue collar and white collar youth,' *Journal of Social Issues* 30, 3: 69–93
Katz, Daniel. 1974. 'Factors affecting social change: a social-psychological interpretation,' *Journal of Social Issues* 30, 3: 159–80
Katz, Daniel, and Ezra Stotland. 1959. 'A preliminary statement to a theory of attitude structure and change,' pp. 423–76 in S. Koch (ed.), *Psychology: A Study of a Science*, vol. 3. New York: McGraw-Hill
Katz, Joseph et al. (eds.). 1968. *No Time for Youth*. San Francisco: Jossey-Bass
Kavanagh, Dennis. 1972a. 'Political behaviour and political participation,' pp. 102–25 in G. Parry (ed.), *Participation in Politics*. Manchester: Manchester University Press
– 1972b. *Political Culture*. London: Macmillan
Kelley, H.J. 1967. 'Attribution theory in social psychology,' pp. 192–238 in D. Levine (ed.), *Nebraska Symposium on Motivation*. Lincoln: University of Nebraska Press
Kelley, H.J., and J.L. Michela. 1980. 'Attribution theory and research,' pp. 457–502 in M.R. Rosenzweig and L.W. Porter (eds.), *Annual Review of Psychology*, vol. 31
Kelly, George A. 1973. 'Man's construction of his alternatives,' pp. 200–11 in Hariet N. Mischel and Walter Mischel (eds.), *Readings in Personality*. New York: Holt, Rinehart and Winston

Kelman, H.C. 1953. 'Attitude change as a function of response restriction,' *Human Relations* 6: 185–214
– 1958. 'Compliance, identification and internalization: three processes of opinion change,' *Journal of Conflict Resolution* 2: 51–60
– 1974. 'Attitudes are alive and well and gainfully employed in the sphere of action,' *American Psychologist* 29: 310–24
Kelvin, R.P., C.J. Lucas, and A.B. Ojha. 1965. 'The relation between personality, mental health and academic performance in university students,' *British Journal of Social and Clinical Psychology* 4: 244–53
Keniston, Kenneth. 1960. *The Uncommitted: Alienated Youth in American Society.* New York: Delta
– 1967. 'The sources of student dissent,' *Journal of Social Issues* 23, 3: 108–37
– 1968. *Young Radicals: Notes on Committed Youth.* New York: Harcourt, Brace and World
– 1971. *Youth and Dissent: The Rise of a New Opposition.* New York: Harcourt, Brace, Jovanovich
Keniston, Kenneth, and M. Lerner. 1971. 'Campus characteristics and campus unrest,' *Annals of the American Academy of Political and Social Science* 395: 39–53
Keniston, Kenneth et al. 1973. *Radicals and Militants: An Annotated Bibliography of Empirical Research on Campus Unrest.* Lexington, Mass.: D.C. Heath
Kenrick, D.T., and D.O. Stringfield. 1980. 'Personality traits and the eye of the beholder: crossing some traditional philosophical boundaries in the search for consistency in all of the people,' *Psychological Review* 87, 1: 88–104
Kerlinger, Fred N. 1966. *Foundations of Behavioral Research.* New York: Holt, Rinehart and Winston
Kerlinger, Fred N., and Elazar J. Pedhazur. 1973. *Multiple Regression in Behavioral Research.* New York: Holt, Rinehart and Winston
Kerlinger, F.N., and M. Rokeach. 1966. 'The factorial nature of the F and D scales,' *Journal of Personality and Social Psychology* 4: 391–9
Kerpelman, Larry C. 1969. 'Student political activism and ideology,' *Journal of Counseling Psychology* 16, 1: 8–13
– 1970. 'Student activism and ideology in higher education institutions,' Office of Education, Project no. 8–A–028, University of Massachusetts, unpublished.
Key, V.O. Jr. 1966. *The Responsible Electorate.* Cambridge: Harvard University Press
Kiesler, C.A., B.E. Collins, and N. Miller. 1969. *Attitude Change.* New York: John Wiley
Kiesler, C.A., and P.A. Munson. 1975. 'Attitudes and opinions,' pp. 415–56 in M.R. Rosenzweig and L.W. Porter (eds.), *Annual Review of Psychology*, vol. 26

324 Bibliography

Kim, Jae-On, N. Nie, and S. Verba. 1974. 'The amount and concentration of political participation,' *Political Methodology* 1, 2: 104–32

King, A.J.C. 1968. 'Ethnicity and school adjustment,' *Canadian Review of Sociology and Anthropology* 5, 2: 84–91

Kirby, D. 1971. 'Counter-culture explanation of student activism,' *Social Problems* 19: 203–16

Kirk, B.A., and L. Sereda. 1969. 'Accuracy of self-reported college grade averages and characteristics of non and discrepant reporters,' *Educational and Psychological Measurement* 29: 147–55

Kirkpatrick, Samuel A. 1970. 'Political attitudes and behaviour: some consequences of attitudinal ordering,' *Midwest Journal of Political Science* 14: 1–24

Kirsht, J.P., and R.C. Dillehay. 1967. *Dimensions of Authoritarianism: A Review of Research and Theory*. Frankfort: University of Kentucky Press

Kline, Paul. 1972. *Fact and Fantasy in Freudian Theory*. London: Methuen

Knutson, Jeanne N. 1972. *The Human Basis of the Polity: A Psychological Study of Political Man*. Chicago: Aldine Atherton

– (ed.). 1973. *Handbook of Political Psychology*. San Francisco: Jossey-Bass

– 1974. 'The political relevance of self-actualization,' pp. 367–99 in A.R. Wilcox (ed.), *Public Opinions and Political Attitudes*. New York: John Wiley

Koch, H.L. 1954. 'The relation of "primary mental abilities" in five- and six-year-olds to sex and characteristics of his sibling,' *Child Development* 25: 209–23

Koch, Sigmund. 1964. 'Psychology and emerging conception of knowledge as unitary,' pp. 1–42 in T.W. Wann (ed.), *Behaviourism and Phenomenology*. Chicago: University of Chicago Press

Kohn, Melvin L. 1959. 'Social age and parental values,' *American Journal of Sociology* 64: 337–51

– 1972. 'Class, family and schizophrenia: a reformulation,' *Social Forces* 50: 295–304

Kohn, M.L., and J.A. Clausen. 1956. 'Parental authority behavior and schizophrenia,' *American Journal of Orthopsychiatry* 26: 297–313

Korn, Harold A. 1968. 'Personality scale changes from the freshman year to the senior year,' pp. 162–84 in Joseph Katz and Associates (eds.), *No Time for Youth*. San Francisco: Jossey-Bass

Kornberg, Allan, and Mary Brehm. 1970. 'Ideology, institutional identification, and campus activism,' *Social Forces* 49, 2: 445–59

Kornhauser, William. 1959. *The Politics of Mass Society*. New York: Free Press

Kothandapani, Virupaksha. 1971. 'Validation of feeling, belief and intention to act as three components of attitude and their contribution to prediction of contraceptive behavior,' *Journal of Personality and Social Psychology* 19, 3: 321–34

Kraut, Robert. 1971. 'Parental conflict and political ideology,' unpublished paper, Department of Psychology, Yale University

Krout, M.H., and R. Stagner. 1939. 'Personality development in radicals,' *Sociometry* 2: 31–46

Kuhn, T.S. 1962. *The Structure of Scientific Revolutions*. Chicago: University of Chicago Press

Kutner, B., C. Wilkins, and P.R. Yarrow. 1952. 'Verbal attitudes and overt behavior involving radical prejudice,' *Journal of Abnormal and Social Psychology* 47: 649–52

Labovitz, Sangford. 1970. 'The nonutility of significance tests: the significance of tests of significance reconsidered,' *Pacific Sociological Review* 13: 141–8

Lader, M., and I. Marks. 1971. *Clinical Anxiety*. London: Heineman

Laird, James D. 1974. 'Self-attribution of emotion: the effects of expressive behavior on the quality of emotional experience,' *Journal of Personality and Social Psychology* 79, 4: 475–86

Lambert, R.D. 1969. *Sex Role Imagery in Children: Social Origins of Mind*. Studies of the Royal Commission on Status of Women in Canada, no. 67. Ottawa: Information Canada

Lane, Robert E. 1959. *Political Life*. Glencoe, Ill.: The Free Press

– 1970. 'Fathers and sons: foundations of political belief,' pp. 116–29 in Roberta A. Sigel (ed.), *Learning about Politics: A Reader in Political Socialization*. New York: Random House

Langner, T.S. 1962. 'A twenty-two item screening score of psychiatric symptoms indicating impairment,' *Journal of Health and Human Relations* 111, 3: 269–76

Langton, Kenneth. 1969. *Political Socialization*. New York: Oxford University Press

– 1974. 'Peer group and school and the political socialization process,' pp. 310–20 in A.R. Wilcox (ed.), *Public Opinion and Political Attitudes*. New York: John Wiley

LaPiere, R.T. 1934. 'Attitudes vs actions,' *Social Forces* 13: 230–7

Lasswell, Harold D. 1930. *Psychopathology and Politics*. Chicago: University of Chicago Press

– 1960. *Psychopathology and Politics*, rev. ed. New York: Viking Press

– 1962. *Power and Personality*. New York: Viking Press

– 1968. 'A note on types of political personality: nuclear, co-relational, developmental,' *Journal of Social Issues* 24, 3: 81–91

LaTouche, Daniel. 1968. 'The Quebec student movement,' pp. 113–32 in G.F. McGuigan (ed.), *Student Protest*. Toronto: Methuen

Laumann, E.O., and D.R. Segal. 1971. 'Status inconsistency and ethno-religious group membership as determinants of social participation and political attitudes,' *American Journal of Sociology* 77, 1: 36–61

Lauzon, Adele. 1970. 'The New Left in Québec,' *Our Generation* 7, 1: 14–31

Laxer, James. 1969. 'Student movement and Canadian independence,' *Canadian Dimension* 6: 27–34, 69–70

Lazarsfeld, Paul F. 1972. 'Problems in methodology,' pp. 17–24 in P.F. Lazarsfeld, A.K. Pasanella, and M. Rosenberg (eds.), *Continuities in the Language of Social Research*. New York: The Free Press

Lehtiniemi, L. 1972. 'A tested theory of student unrest,' *Alberta Journal of Educational Research* 43: 51–8

Leiserson, Avery. 1968. 'Empirical approaches to democratic theory,' pp. 13–39 in Oliver Garceau (ed.), *Political Research and Political Theory*. Cambridge: Harvard University Press

Lejeune, Robert (ed.). 1972. *Class and Conflict in American Society*. Chicago: Markham

Lemon, Nigel. 1973. *Attitudes and Their Measurement*. London: B.T. Batsford

Levenson, H., and J. Miller. 1976. 'Multidimensional locus of control in sociopolitical activists of Conservative and Liberal ideologies,' *Journal of Personality and Social Psychology* 33: 199–208

Levin, H., and B. Fleischmann. 1968. 'Childhood socialization,' pp. 215–38 in E.F. Borgatta and W.W. Lambert (eds.), *Handbook of Personality Theory and Research*. Chicago: Rand McNally

Levinson, D.J. 1958. 'The relevance of personality for political participation,' *Public Opinion Quarterly* 22, 1: 3–10

– 1968. 'Political personality: conservatism and radicalism,' pp. 21–29 in D. Sills (ed.), *International Encyclopedia of the Social Sciences*. New York: Macmillan

Levitin, T., and W.E. Miller. 1972. 'The new politics and partisan realignment,' paper prepared for delivery at meeting of the American Political Science Association, Washington, DC

Levitt, Eugene E. 1968. *The Psychology of Anxiety*. London: Staples Press

Levy, S.G. 1970. 'The psychology of political activity,' *Annals of the American Academy of Political and Social Science* 391: 83–96

Lewis, S.H., and R.E. Kraut. 1972. 'Correlates of student political activism and ideology,' *Journal of Social Issues* 28, 4: 131–49

Lieberman, S. 1956. 'The effects of changes in roles on the attitudes of role occupants,' *Human Relations* 9: 385–402

Light, D. Sr., and J. Spiegel (eds.). 1977. *The Dynamics of University Protest*. Chicago: Nelson-Hall

Likert, R. 1961. *New Patterns of Management*. New York: McGraw-Hill

Linn, L.S. 1965. 'Verbal attitudes and overt behavior: a study of racial discrimination,' *Social Forces* 43: 353–64

Lipset, Seymour M. 1960. *Political Man*. London: Heinemann

- 1965. 'University student politics,' pp. 137–49 in S.M. Lipset and S. Wolin (eds.), *The Berkeley Student Revolt: Facts and Interpretations.* Garden City, NJ: Anchor/Doubleday
- 1968a. 'The activists: a profile,' *The Public Interest* 13: 39–51
- 1968b. 'Students and politics in comparative perspective,' *Daedalus* 97, 1: 1–19
- 1969. 'The possible political effects of student activism,' *Social Science Information* 8, 2: 7–29
- 1972. *Rebellion in the University: A History of Student Activism in America.* London: Routledge and Kegan Paul
- 1973. 'American student activism in comparative perspective,' pp. 78–9 in P.K. Manning (ed.), *Youth: Divergent Perspectives.* New York: John Wiley
Lipset, Seymour M., and P. Altbach. 1967. 'Student politics and higher education in the United States,' pp. 222–44 in S.M. Lipset (ed.), *Student Politics.* New York: Basic Books
Lipset, Seymour M., and E.C. Ladd Jr. 1971a. 'College generations and their politics,' *New Society* 1: 654–7
- 1971b 'College generations – from the 1930's to the 1960's,' *The Public Interest* 25: 99–113
Lipset, Seymour M., and S.S. Wolin (eds.). 1965. *The Berkeley Student Revolt: Facts and Interpretations.* Garden City, NJ: Anchor/Doubleday
Lipsitz, D. 1964. 'Work life and political attitudes,' *American Political Science Review* 58, 4: 951–62
Lipsitz, Lewis. 1965. 'Working-class authoritarianism: a reevaluation,' *American Sociological Review* 30, 1: 103–9
- 1974. 'On political belief: the grievances of the poor,' pp. 273–87 in A.R. Wilcox (ed.), *Public Opinion and Political Attitude.* New York: John Wiley
Liska, Allen E. 1974a. 'Attitude-behavior consistency as a function of generality equivalence between attitude and behaviour objects,' *Journal of Psychology* 86: 217–28
- 1974b. 'Emergent issues in the attitude-behavior consistency controversy,' *American Sociological Review* 39: 261–72
- 1974c. 'The impact of attitude on behaviour: attitude social support interaction,' *Pacific Sociological Review* 17, 1: 83–97
- (ed.). 1974d. *The Impact of Attitude on Behaviour: The Consistency Controversy.* Cambridge, Mass.: Schenkman
Litt, Edgar. 1963. 'Political cynicism and political futility,' *The Journal of Politics* 2, 25: 312–23
- 1970. 'Civic education, community norms and political indoctrination,' pp. 328–36 in Roberta S. Sigel (ed.), *Learning about Politics: A Reader in Political Socialization.* New York: Random House

Lubell, Samuel. 1968. 'That generation gap,' *The Public Interest* 13: 52–60
Ludz, Peter C. 1973. 'Alienation as a concept in the social sciences: a trend report and bibliography,' *Current Sociology* (Special Issue) 21, 1: 1–115
Lykken, David. 1968. 'Neuropsychology and Psychophysiology in personality research,' pp. 413–510 in Edgar F. Borgatta and W.W. Lambert (eds), *Handbook of Personality Theory and Research*. Chicago: Rand McNally
Lyonns, Glen. 1965. 'The police car demonstration: a survey of participants,' pp. 519–30 in S.M. Lipset and S.S. Wolin (eds.), *The Berkeley Student Revolt: Facts and Interpretations*. New York: Anchor Books
Lyons, Schley R. 1970. 'The political socialization of ghetto children: efficacy and cynicism,' *The Journal of Politics* 32, 2: 288–305
McArthur, C. 1956. 'Personalities of first and second children,' *Psychiatry* 19: 47–54
McCandless, Boyd R. 1969. 'Childhood socialization,' pp. 791–819 in David A. Goslin (ed.), *Handbook of Socialization Theory and Research*. Chicago: Rand McNally
McClelland, David C. 1956. 'Personality: an integrative view,' pp. 322–65 in J.L. McCary (ed.), *Psychology of Personality: Six Modern Approaches*. New York: Logos Press
McClintock, C.G. 1958. 'Personality syndromes and attitude change,' *Journal of Personality* 26: 479–93
McClosky, Herbert. 1958. 'Conservatism and personality,' *American Political Science Review* 52, 1: 27–46
– 1964. 'Consensus and ideology in American politics,' *American Political Science Review* 58, 2: 361–83
McClosky, Herbert, and J.H. Schaar. 1965. 'Psychological dimensions of anomy,' *American Sociological Review* 30, 1: 14–40
Maccoby, Eleanor E. 1965. 'The choice of variables in the study of socialization,' pp. 56–68 in Ivan D. Steiner and Martin Fishbein (eds.), *Current Studies in Social Psychology*. New York: Holt, Rinehart and Winston
McCoy, C., and J. Playford (eds.). 1967. *Apolitical Politics*. New York: Cromwell
McCrone, D., and C. Cnudde. 1967. 'Toward a communications theory of democratic political development,' *American Political Science Review* 61: 72–9
McDill, E.L., and J.C. Ridley. 1962. 'Status, anomia, political alienation and political participation,' *American Journal of Sociology* 68, 2: 205–13
Macdonald, K.I. 1977a. 'Causal modelling in politics and sociology,' *Quality and Quantity* 10: 189–208
– 1977b. 'Path analysis,' pp. 81–104 in C. O'Muircheartaigh and C. Payne (eds.), *The Analysis of Survey Data*: vol. II: *Model Fitting*. London: John Wiley

Macdonald, K.I., and P. Doreian. 1977. *Regression and Path Analysis*. London: Methuen

McFalls, J.A., and B.J. Gallagher. 1979. 'Political orientation and occupational values of college youth,' *Adolescence* 14: 641–55

Macfarlane, J.W., L. Allen, and M.P. Honzik. 1954. *A Developmental Study of the Behavior Problems of Normal Children between 21 Months and 14 Years*. University of California Publications in Child Development, vol. 2. Berkeley: University of California Press

McGregor, D. 1960. *The Human Side of Enterprise*. New York: McGraw-Hill

McGuigan, Gerald F. 1968. *Student Protest*. Toronto: Methuen

McGuire, William J. 1966. 'Attitudes and opinions,' *Annual Review of Psychology* 17: 475–514

– 1969. 'The nature of attitudes and attitude change,' pp. 136–314 in G. Lindzey and E. Aronson (eds.), *The Handbook of Social Psychology*, vol. III, rev. ed. Reading, Mass.: Addison-Wesley

MacIntyre, Alasdair. 1967. 'A mistake about causality in social science,' pp. 48–71 in Peter Laslett and W.G. Runciman (eds.), *Philosophy, Politics and Society*. Oxford: Basil Blackwell

McKennell, Aubrey C. 1970. 'Attitude measurement: use of coefficient alpha with cluster or factor analysis,' *Sociology* 4, 2: 227–45

– 1974. 'Surveying attitude structures,' *Quality and Quantity*, Special Issue, 7, 2: 203–94

McKinney, David W. Jr. 1973. *The Authoritarian Personality Studies: An Inquiry into the Failure of Social Science Research to Produce Demonstrable Knowledge*. The Hague, Paris: Mouton

McLaughlin, Barry. 1969. *Studies in Social Movements: A Social Psychological Perspective*. New York: The Free Press

Macpherson, C.B. 1968. *Democracy in Alberta: Social Credit and the Party System*. Toronto: University of Toronto Press

Malcolm, N. 1964. 'Behaviorism as a philosophy of psychology,' pp. 141–55 in T.W. Wann (ed.), *Behaviorism and Phenomenology*. Chicago: University of Chicago Press

Manis, Jerome G. 1974. 'The concept of social problems, vox populi, and sociological analysis,' *Social Problems* 21: 305–15

Manis, Melvin. 1978. 'Cognitive psychology and attitude change,' *American Behavioral Scientist* 21, 5: 675–90

Mankoff, Milton. 1970. 'The political socialization of student radicals and militants in the Wisconsin student movement during the 1960's,' unpublished PHD dissertation, University of Wisconsin

Mankoff, M., and R. Flacks. 1971. 'The changing social base of the American student movement: its meaning and implications,' *Annals of the American Academy of Political and Social Science* 395: 54–62

Mann, J.H. 1959. 'The relationship between cognitive, behavioral and affective aspects of racial prejudice,' *Journal of Social Psychology* 49: 223–8

Manning, Peter K. (ed.). 1973. *Youth: Divergent Perspectives*. New York: John Wiley

Manzer, Ronald. 1974. *Canada: A Socio-political Report*. Toronto: McGraw-Hill

Marsh, Allan. 1977. *Protest and Political Consciousness*. Beverly Hills: Sage

Marston, Wilfred G. 1969. 'Social class segregation within ethnic groups in Toronto,' *Canadian Review of Sociology and Anthropology* 6, 2: 65–79

Mathews, R.D. 1965. 'University crisis and the commonweal: with a reply by T.C. Pockington,' *The Canadian Forum* May: 32–4; July: 76–8

Mathews, R.D., and J. Steele (eds.). 1969. *The Struggle for Canadian Universities*. Toronto: New Press

Mayo, Elton. 1945. 'Hawthorne and the Western Electric Company,' pp. 68–86 in E. Mayo, *The Social Problems of an Industrial Civilization*. Andover, Mass.: Andover Press

Megargee, E.I., and G.V.C. Parker. 1971. 'Relationship of familial and social factors to socialization in middle-class college students,' *Journal of Abnormal Psychology* 77, 1: 76–89

Meier, H.C., and W. Orzen. 1971. 'Student legitimation of campus activism: some survey findings,' *Social Problems* 19: 181–92

Meile, R.L., and P.N. Haese. 1969. 'Social status, status incongruence and symptoms of stress,' *Journal of Health and Social Behaviour* 10, 3: 237–44

Merelman, Richard M. 1966. 'Learning and legitimacy,' *American Political Science Review* 60: 548–61

– 1969. 'The development of political ideology: a framework for the analysis of political socialization,' *American Political Science Review* 68, 3: 750–68

– 1971. *Political Socialization and Educational Climates*. New York: Holt, Rinehart and Winston

Merelman, R.M., and A.E. McCabe. 1974. 'Evolving orientations toward policy choice in adolescence,' *American Journal of Political Science* 18, 4: 665–80

Merton, Robert K. 1940. 'Fact and factitiousness in ethnic opinionnaires,' *American Sociological Review* 5: 13–39

Meyer, Marshall W. 1971. 'Harvard students in the midst of crisis,' *Sociology of Education* 44, 3: 245–69

Middleton, R., and S. Putney. 1963. 'Political expression of adolescent rebellion,' *American Journal of Sociology* 48: 527–35

Milbrath, Lester W. 1960. 'Predispositions toward political contention,' *The Western Political Quarterly* 13: 5–18

- 1962. 'Latent origins of Liberalism-Conservatism and party identification: a research note,' *The Journal of Politics* 24: 679–88
- 1965. *Political Participation.* Chicago: Rand McNally
Milbrath, L.W., and M.L. Goel. 1977. *Political Participation* 2nd ed. Chicago: Rand McNally
Milbrath, L.W., and W.W. Klein. 1962. 'Personality correlates of political participation,' *Acta Sociologica* 6: 53–66
Miller, N.E., and J. Dollard. 1941. *Social Learning and Imitation.* New Haven: Yale University Press
Mills, C.W. 1940. 'Methodological consequences of the sociology of knowledge,' *American Journal of Sociology* 46: 316–30
Milne, R.A., and K.J. Meier. 1976. 'Graphic approach to Rosenberg's affective-cognitive consistency theory,' *Human Relations* 29: 273–85
Minard, R.D. 1952. 'Race relationships in the Pocahontas coal field,' *Journal of Social Issues* 8, 1: 29–44
Mischel, H.N., and W. Mischel (eds.). 1973. *Readings in Personality.* New York: Holt, Rinehart and Winston
Mischel, Theodore. 1969. 'Scientific and philosophical psychology: a historical introduction,' pp. 1–40 in T. Mischel (ed.), *Human Action.* New York: Academic Press
Mischel, Walter. 1968. *Personality and Assessment.* New York: John Wiley
- 1973. 'Toward a cognitive social learning reconstruction of personality,' *Psychological Review* 80: 252–83
- 1977. 'On the future of personality measurement,' *American Psychologist* 32, 4: 246–54
Moon, J. Donald. 1975. 'The logic of political inquiry: a synthesis of opposed perspectives,' pp. 131–228 in F.I. Greenstein and N.W. Polsby (eds.), *Handbook of Political Science*, vol. 2. Reading, Mass.: Addison-Wesley
Moore, W.E. 1969. 'Social structure and behavior,' pp. 283–323 in G. Lindzey and E. Aronson (eds.), *The Handbook of Social Psychology*, vol. 4, 2nd ed. Reading, Mass.: Addison-Wesley
Morgan, Jan. 1974. 'Women and political socialization: fact and fantasy in Easton, Dennis and in Lane,' *Politics* 9, 1: 50–5
Morgan, S.W., and B. Mausner. 1973. 'Behavioural and fantasied indicators of avoidance of success in men and women,' *Journal of Personality* 41: 457–69
Morrow, Conrad. 1971. 'Biased interpretation of a communications effort within an academic hierarchy: a study of hierarchy, people and politics,' unpublished paper, University of Alberta
Morse, S.J., and S. Peele. 1971. 'A study of participants in an anti-Vietnam War demonstration,' *Journal of Social Issues* 27, 4: 113–36

Mowrer, O.H. 1963. 'Cognitive dissonance or counterconditioning? A reappraisal of certain behavioral "paradoxes,"' *Psychological Record* 13: 197–211

Mueller, Conrad G. 1979. 'Some origins of psychology as science,' pp. 9–29 in M.R. Rosenzweig and L.W. Porter (eds.), *Annual Review of Psychology*, 30: 9–29

Mussen, Paul H. 1961. 'Some antecedents and consequents of masculine sex-typing in adolescent boys,' *Psychological Monographs* 75, 2

– 1969. 'Early sex-role development,' pp. 707–31 in A. Goslin (ed.), *Handbook of Socialization Theory and Research*. Chicago: Rand McNally

Mussen, P.H., and A.B. Warren. 1952. 'Personality and political participation,' *Human Relations* 5, 1: 65–83

Mussen, P.H., and A. Wyszynski. 1952. 'Personality and political participation,' *Human Relations* 5: 65–82

Nachmias, David. 1974. 'Modes and types of political alienation,' *British Journal of Sociology* 25, 4: 478–93

Nagel, Ernest. 1968. 'The subjective nature of social subject matter,' pp. 34–44 in May Brodbeck (ed.), *Readings in the Philosophy of the Social Sciences*. New York: Macmillan

Nagel, Julian (ed.). 1969. *Student Power*. London: Merlin Press

Newcomb, Theodore M. 1958. 'Attitude development as a function of reference groups: the Bennington study,' pp. 265–75 in T.M. Newcomb, E.E. Maccoby, and E. Hartley (eds.), *Readings in Social Psychology*, 3rd ed. New York: Holt, Rinehart and Winston

Nie, Norman et al. 1969. 'Social structure and political participation: developmental relationships,' *American Political Science Review* 63: 361–78, 808–32

– 1975. *Statistical Package for the Social Sciences*. New York: McGraw-Hill

Niemi, R.G. et al. 1978. 'Similarity of political values of parents and college age youths,' *Public Opinion Quarterly* 42: 303–20

Niemi, R.G., and B.I. Sobieszek. 1977. 'Political socialization,' *American Review of Sociology* 3: 209–33

Nisbett, R.E. 1970. 'Who killed the student revolution?' *Encounter* 34: 10–18

Nisbett, R.E., and T. DeCamp Wilson. 1977. 'Telling more than we can know: verbal reports on mental processes,' *Psychological Review* 84, 3: 231–59

Nisbett, R.E., and S. Valins. 1972. 'Perceiving the causes of one's own behavior,' pp. 63–79 in E. Jones, E.D. Kanouse, and B. Weiner (eds.), *Attribution: Perceiving the Causes of Behavior*. Morristown, NJ: General Learning Press

Norman, R. 1975. 'Affective-cognitive consistency, attitudes, conformity and behaviour,' *Journal of Personality and Social Psychology* 32: 83–91

O'Leary, V.E. 1974. 'Some attitudinal barriers to occupational aspirations in women,' *Psychological Bulletin* 81: 809–26

Olsen, M.E. 1962. 'Liberal-Conservative attitude crystallization,' *Sociological Quarterly* 3: 17–26
- 1965. 'Alienation and political opinion,' *Public Opinion Quarterly* 29, 2: 200–12
- 1969. 'Two categories of political alienation,' *Social Forces* 47: 288–99
Oppenheim, Felix E. 1975. 'The language of political inquiry: problems of clarification,' pp. 283–335 in F. Greenstein and N.W. Polsby (eds.), *Handbook of Political Science*. Reading, Mass.: Addison-Wesley
Orum, Anthony M. 1976. 'On the explanation of political and social change,' *Youth and Society* 8, 2: 147–74
Orum, A.M., R.S. Cohen, and A.W. Orum. 1974. 'Sex, socialization and politics,' *American Sociological Review* 39: 197–209
Osgood, C.E., G.J. Suci, and P.H. Tannenbaum. 1957. *The Measurement of Meaning*. Urbana, Ill.: University of Illinois Press
Osgood, C.E., and P.H. Tannenbaum. 1955. 'The principle of congruity in the prediction of attitude change,' *Psychological Review* 62: 42–55
Ostrom, Thomas M. 1968. 'The emergence of attitude theory: 1930–1950,' pp. 1–32 in A.G. Greenwald et al. (eds.), *Psychological Foundations of Attitude*. New York: Academic Press
- 1969. 'The relationship between the affective behavioral and cognitive components of an attitude,' *Journal of Experimental Social Psychology* 5: 12–30
Paige, Jeffrey M. 1971. 'Political orientation and prior participation,' *American Sociological Review* 36, 5: 810–19
Palmore, E., and C. Luikart. 1972. 'Health and social factors related to life satisfaction,' *Journal of Health and Social Behaviour* 13, 1: 68–80
Palumbo, Dennis J. 1969. *Statistics in Political and Behavioral Science*. New York: Appleton-Century-Crofts
Parenti, Michael. 1970. 'Power and pluralism: a view from the bottom,' *The Journal of Politics* 32, 3: 501–31
Parry, Geraint. 1972. 'The idea of political participation,' pp. 3–39 in G. Parry (ed.), *Participation in Politics*. Manchester University Press: Rowman and Littlefield
- 1976. 'Trust, distrust and consensus,' *British Journal of Political Science* 6, 2: 129–42
Parsons, Talcot. 1962. 'Youth in the context of American society,' *Daedalus* 91: 97–123
Pateman, C. 1970. *Participation and Democratic Theory*. Cambridge: Cambridge University Press
Paulus, George S. 1967. 'A multivariate analysis study of student activist leaders, student government leaders, and non-activists,' EDD dissertation, Michigan State University

Pavalko, Ronald M. 1967. 'Socio-economic background, ability and the allocation of students,' *Canadian Review of Sociology and Anthropology* 4, 4: 26–39

Perry, Ronald W. 1976. 'Attitude scales as behaviour estimation devices: scale specificity and prediction accuracy,' *Journal of Social Psychology* 100: 137–42

Perry, R.W., and D. Gillespie. 1976. 'An analysis of intervening variables in the attitude behaviour relationship,' *Journal of Social Psychology* 98: 281–9

Perry, R.W., D. Gillespie, and R. Lotz. 1976. 'Attitudinal variables as estimates of behaviour; a theoretical examination of the attitude-action controversy,' *European Journal of Social Psychology* 6, 2: 227–43

Perry, R.W., D. Gillespie, and H.A. Parker. 1976. 'Configurations in the analysis of attitudes, importance and social behaviour,' *Sociology and Social Research* 60, 2: 135–46

Pervin, L.A., L.E. Reik, and W. Dalrymple (eds.). 1966. *The College Drop-out and the Utilization of Talent.* Princeton: Princeton University Press

Peterson, K.K., and J.E. Dutton. 1975. 'Centrality, extremity, intensity: neglected variables in research on attitude-behavior consistency,' *Social Forces* 52, 2: 393–414

Peterson, Richard E. 1968. 'The student left in American higher education,' *Daedalus* 97: 293–317

– 1970. 'The scope of organized student protest,' pp. 72–85 in J. Foster and D. Long (eds.), *Protest!! Student Activism in America.* New York: William Morrow

Philipps, Derek L. 1967. 'Mental health status, social participation and happiness,' *Journal of Health and Social Behaviour* 8, 14: 285–91

Pike, Robert M. 1970. *Who Doesn't Get to University ... and Why?* Ottawa: Association of Universities and Colleges of Canada

Pinard, M., J. Kirk, and D. von Eschen. 1969. 'Processes of recruitment in the sit-in-movement,' *Public Opinion Quarterly* 3: 355–69

Pinner, Frank A. 1965. 'Parental overprotection and political distrust,' *Annals of the American Academy of Political and Social Science* 361: 58–70

– 1971. 'Students – a marginal elite in politics,' *Annals of the American Academy of Political and Social Science* 395: 127–38

Pinner, F.G., C. Bay, and J.E. Fletcher. 1980. 'Dreams of power,' paper presented at the Third Annual Scientific Meeting of the International Society of Political Psychology, Boston, Mass. 4–7 June

Prewitt, Kenneth. 1974. 'Political ambitions, volunteerism and electoral accountability,' pp. 619–35 in A.R. Wilcox (ed.), *Public Opinion and Political Attitudes.* New York: John Wiley

Prewitt, K., H. Eulau, and B.H. Zisk. 1966. 'Political socialization and political roles,' *Public Opinion Quarterly* 30, 4: 569–83

Price, Richard. 1970. 'The new left in Alberta,' pp. 41–59 in D.J. Roussopoulos (ed.), *The New Left in Canada*. Montreal: Our Generation Press

Prothro, J.W., and C.M. Grigg. 1960. 'Fundamental principles of democracy: bases of agreement and disagreement,' *The Journal of Politics* 22, 2: 276–94

Pruitt, D.G., and J.P. Gahagan. 1974. 'Campus crisis: the search for power,' pp. 349–94 in J.T. Tedeschi (ed.), *Perspectives on Social Power*. Chicago: Aldine

Pugh, M.D. et al. 1971. 'Participation in anti-war demonstrations: a test of the parental continuity hypothesis,' *Sociology and Social Research* 56: 19–28

Pugh, M.D., B. Perry Jr., E.E. Snyder, and E. Spreitzer. 1972. 'Faculty support of student dissent,' *Sociological Quarterly* 13, 4: 525–32

Putnam, Robert D. 1974. 'Studying elite political culture: the case of ideology,' pp. 239–69 in A.R. Wilcox ed.), *Public Opinion and Political Attitudes*. New York; John Wiley

Quarter, Jack. 1972. *The Student Movement of the Sixties: A Social-Psychological Analysis*. Toronto: Ontario Institute for Studies in Education Occasional Papers

– 1974. 'Shifting ideologies among youth in Canada,' *Youth and Society* 5, 4: 448–74

Raden, David. 1977. 'Situational thresholds and attitude-behaviour consistency,' *Sociometry* 40: 123–30

Ransford, H.E. 1968. 'Isolation, powerlessness and violence: a study of attitudes and participation in the Watts riot,' *American Journal of Sociology* 73: 581–91

Regan, D., and R. Fazio. 1977. 'On the consistency between attitude and behaviour: look to the method of attitude formation,' *Journal of Experimental Psychology* 13: 28–45

Reid, T., and J. Reid (eds.). 1969. *Student Power and the Canadian Campus*. Toronto: Peter Martin

Renshon, Stanley A. 1975a. 'Personality and family dynamics in the political socialization process,' *American Journal of Political Science* 19, 1: 63–80

– 1975b. 'Psychological needs, personal control, and political participation,' *Canadian Journal of Political Science* 8, 1: 107–16

– 1977. 'Models of man and temporal frameworks in political socialization theory: an examination of some assumptions,' *Youth and Society* 8, 3: 235–73

Resnick, Philip. 1970. 'The New Left in Ontario,' *Our Generation* 7, 1: 35–51

Rim, Y. 1970. 'Values and attitudes,' *Personality* 1, 3: 243–50

Robins, Lee N. 1969. 'Social correlates of psychiatric disorders: can we tell causes from consequences?' *Journal of Health and Social Behavior* 10, 2: 95–103

Robinson, J.P., J.G. Rusk, and K.B. Head. 1968. *Measures of Political Attitudes*. Ann Arbor: Institute for Social Research, University of Michigan

– 1972. 'Criteria for the construction and evaluation of attitude scales,' pp. 101–11 in D.D. Nimmo and C. Bonjean (eds.), *Political Attitudes and Public Opinion*. New York: David McKay

Robinson, J.P., and P.R. Shaver. 1969. *Measures of Social Psychological Attitudes* (rev. ed. 1973). Ann Arbor: Institute for Social Research, University of Michigan

Rodgers, Harrell R. 1974. 'Toward explanation of the political efficacy and political cynicism of black adolescents: an exploratory study,' *American Journal of Political Science* 18, 2: 257–83

Rogers, Evan D. 1972. 'Intelligence and student political activism,' *Social Science Quarterly* 53, 2: 557–62

Rokeach, Milton. 1960. *The Open and Closed Mind*. New York: Basic Books

- 1967a. 'Attitude change and behavior change,' *Public Opinion Quarterly* 30: 529–50

- 1967b. 'Value systems in religion,' *Review of Religious Research* 2, 1: 3–39

- 1968. *Beliefs, Attitudes and Values*. San Francisco: Jossey-Bass

- 1971. 'The measurement of values and value systems,' pp. 21–39 in G. Abcarian and J. Soule (eds.), *Social Psychology and Political Behavior*. Columbus, Ohio: Charles E. Merrit

- 1973. *The Nature of Human Values*. New York: The Free Press

Rokeach, M., and B. Fruchter. 1956. 'A factorial study of dogmatism and related concepts,' *Journal of Abnormal and Social Psychology* 53: 356–60

Rokeach, M., and D.D. McLellan. 1972. 'Feedback of information about the values and attitudes of self and others as determinants of long-term cognitive and behavioral change,' *Journal of Applied Social Psychology* 2, 3: 236–51

Rose, Arnold M. 1961. 'Inconsistencies in attitudes toward Negro housing,' *Social Problems* 8: 286–92

- 1962. 'Alienation and participation: a comparison of group leaders and the "mass,"' *American Sociological Review* 27, 6: 834–8

Rosenberg, Morris J. 1954. 'Determinants of political apathy,' *Public Opinion Quarterly* 18, 4: 349–66

- 1956. 'Misanthropy and political ideology,' *American Sociological Review* 21, 6: 690–5

- 1962. 'Self-esteem and concern with public affairs,' *Public Opinion Quarterly* 26, 2: 201–12

- 1965. *Society and the Adolescent Self-image*. Princeton, NJ: Princeton University Press

- 1968. 'Hedonism, inauthenticity and other goals: toward expansion of a consistency theory,' pp. 73–112 in R.P. Abelson et al. (eds.), *Theories of Cognitive Consistency: A Sourcebook*. Chicago: Rand McNally

Ross, J. 1970. 'Multi-dimensional scaling,' pp. 279–94 in G. Summers (ed.), *Attitude Measurement*. Chicago: Rand McNally

Ross, L. 1977. 'The intuitive psychologist and his shortcomings: distortions in the attribution process,' *Advances in Experimental Social Psychology* 10: 173–220

Ross, M., C.A. Insko, and H.A. Ross. 1971. 'Self-attribution of attitude,' *Journal of Personality and Social Psychology* 17: 292–7

Rothman, S., and S.R. Lichter. 1978. 'Power, politics and personality in post-industrial society,' *The Journal of Politics* 40: 675–707

Rotter, Julian B. 1972. 'Beliefs, social attitudes and behavior: a social learning analysis,' pp. 335–50 in J.B. Rotter, J.E. Chance, and J. Phales (eds.), *Applications of a Social Learning Theory of Personality*. New York: Holt, Rinehart and Winston

Roussopoulos, Dimitrios J. 1970a. 'Towards a revolutionary movement,' *Our Generation* 7, 2: 45–59

– (ed.). 1970b. *The New Left in Canada*. Montreal: Black Rose Books

Rubenstein, R., and H.D. Lasswell. 1966. *The Sharing of Power in a Psychiatric Hospital*. New Haven: Yale University Press

Rummell, R.J. 1967. 'Understanding factor analysis,' *Journal of Conflict Resolution* 11: 444–80

– 1970. *Applied Factor Analysis*. Evanston, Ill.: Northwestern University Press

Ryle, Gilbert. 1969. *The Concept of Mind*. New York: Barnes and Noble

St. Angelo, D., and J.W. Dyson. 1968. 'Personality and political orientation,' *The Midwest Journal of Political Science* 12, 2: 202–23

Salisbury, Robert H. 1975. 'Research on political participation,' *American Journal of Political Science* 19, 2: 323–41

Sallach, D.L., N. Babchuck, and A. Booth. 1972. 'Social involvement and political activity: another view,' *Social Science Quarterly* 52, 4: 879–93

Salter, B. 1973. 'Explanations of student unrest: an exercise in devaluation,' *British Journal of Sociology* 24: 329–40

Sample, J., and R. Warland. 1973. 'Attitude and prediction of behaviour,' *Social Forces* 51: 292–319

Sampson, Edward E. 1965. 'The study of ordinal position: antecedents and outcomes,' pp. 125–228 in B. Maher (ed.), *Progress in Experimental Personality Research* vol. 2. New York: Academic Press

– 1967. 'Student activism and the decade of protest,' *The Journal of Social Issues* 23, 3: 1–33

Sanders, William B. (ed.). 1976. *The Sociologist as Detective*, 2nd ed. New York: Praeger

Sanford, Nevitt. 1956. 'The approach of the authoritarian personality,' pp. 254–319 in J.L. McCary (ed.), *Psychology of Personality: Six Modern Approaches*. New York: Logos Press

– 1966. *Self and Society: Social Change and Individual Development*. New York: Atherton Press

Sarnoff, I. 1960. 'Psychoanalytic theory and social attitudes,' *Public Opinion Quarterly* 24: 251–79

Sarnoff, I., and D. Katz. 1954. 'The motivational bases of attitude change,' *The Journal of Abnormal and Social Psychology* 49, 1: 115–24

Sartori, Giovanni. 1972. 'Politics, ideology and belief systems,' pp. 58–80 in D.D. Nimmo and C. Bonjean (eds.), *Political Attitudes and Public Opinion*. New York: David McKay

Schachter, S. 1963. 'Birth order, eminence and higher education,' *American Sociological Review* 28: 757–68

Schachter, S., and J. Singer. 1962. 'Cognitive, social and physiological determinants of emotional state,' *Psychological Review* 69: 379–99

Schachter, S., and L. Wheeler. 1962. 'Epinephrine, chlorpromazine and amusement,' *Journal of Abnormal Psychology* 65: 121–8

Schedler, P. 1966. 'Parental attitudes and political activism of college students,' unpublished Masters' thesis, Committee on Human Development, University of Chicago

Schiff, Lawrence. 1964. 'The obedient rebels: a study of college conversions to conservatism,' *Journal of Social Issues* 20, 4: 74–95

– 1966. 'Dynamic young fogies: rebels on the right,' *Transaction* Nov.: 31–6

Schoenberger, R.A. 1968. 'Conservatism, personality and political extremism,' *American Political Science Review* 62, 3: 868–77

Schonfeld, William R. 1975. 'The meaning of democratic participation,' *World Politics* 28, 1: 134–58

Schooler, Carmi. 1972. 'Social antecedents of adult psychological functioning,' *American Journal of Sociology* 78, 2: 299–322

Schroder, H.M., M.J. Driver, and S. Streufert. 1967. *Human Information Processing: Individuals and Groups Functioning in Complex Social Situations*. New York: Holt, Rinehart and Winston

Schuman, Howard. 1972. 'Attitudes vs actions versus attitudes vs attitudes,' *Public Opinion Quarterly* 36: 347–53

Schuman, H., and M.P. Johnson. 1976. 'Attitudes and behaviour,' *Annual Review of Sociology* 2: 161–207

Schwartz, Carol C., J.K. Myers, and B.M. Astrachan. 1975. 'Comparing three measures of mental status: a note on the validity of estimates of psychological disorder in the community,' *Journal of Health and Social Behaviour* 14, 3: 265–73

Schwartz, David C. 1973. *Political Alienation and Political Behavior*. Chicago: Aldine

Schwartz, S.H. 1968. 'Words, deeds and the perception of consequences and responsibility in action situations,' *Journal of Personality and Social Psychology* 10: 232–42

Schwartz, S.H., and R.C. Tessler. 1972. 'A test of a model for reducing attitude-behaviour discrepancies,' *Journal of Personality and Social Psychology* 24: 225–36

Schwartz, Sandra K. 1977. 'The validity of adolescents' political responses,' *Youth and Society* 8, 3: 212–14

Scott, J.W., and M. El-Assal. 1969. 'Multiversity, university size, university quality and student protest: an empirical study,' *American Sociological Review* 34: 702–9

Scott, William A. 1957. 'Attitude change through reward of verbal behaviour,' *Journal of Abnormal and Social Psychology* 55: 72–5

– 1959. 'Attitude change by response reinforcement: replication and extension,' *Sociometry* 22: 328–35

– 1968a. 'Attitude measurement,' pp. 204–74 in G. Lindzey and E. Aronson (eds.), *The Handbook of Social Psychology*, vol. 2. Reading, Mass.: Addison-Wesley

– 1968b. 'Conceptions of normality,' pp. 974–1006 in E.F. Borgatta and W.W. Lambert (eds.), *Handbook of Personality Theory and Research*. Chicago: Rand McNally

Scriven, Michael. 1964. 'Views of human nature,' pp. 163–90 in T.W. Wann (ed.), *Behaviorism and Phenomenology*. Chicago: University of Chicago Press

Searing, D.D., J.J. Schwartz, and A.E. Lind. 1973. 'The structuring principle: political socialization and belief systems,' *American Political Science Review* 67, 2: 415–32

Sears, David O. 1975. 'Political socialization,' pp. 93–153 in F.I. Greenstein and N.W. Polsby (eds.), *Handbook of Political Science*. Reading, Mass.: Addison-Wesley

Sears, Robert R. 1951. 'A theoretical framework for personality and social behaviour,' *American Psychologist* 6: 476–83

Sears, Robert R., E. Maccoby, and H. Levin. 1957. *Patterns of Child Rearing*. New York: Row, Peterson

Seeman, Melvin. 1966. 'Alienation, membership and political knowledge: a comparative study,' *Public Opinion Quarterly* 30, 3: 353–68

Seiler, Lauren H. 1973. 'The 22-item scale used in field studies of mental illness: a question of method, a question of substance and a question of theory,' *Journal of Health and Social Behaviour* 14, 3: 252–64

Selltiz, C., M. Jahoda, M. Deutsch, and S.W. Cook. 1959. *Research Methods in Social Relations*. New York: Holt, Rinehart and Winston

Selvin, Hanan C., and W.O. Hagstrom. 1968. 'Determinants of support for civil liberties,' pp. 155–78 in Ronald M. Pavalko (ed.), *Sociology of Education*. Ithaca, Ill.: F.E. Peacock

Shaver, P. 1970. 'Authoritarianism, dogmatism and related measures,' pp. 211–368 in J. Robinson and P. Shaver (eds.), *Measures of Social Psychological Attitudes*. Ann Arbor, Mich.: Institute for Social Research

Shaw, M.E., and J.M. Wright. 1967. *Scales for the Measurement of Attitudes*. New York: McGraw-Hill

Sheffe, Norman (ed.). 1970. *Issues for the Seventies: Student Unrest*. Toronto: McGraw-Hill

Shils, Edward. 1954. 'Authoritarianism: right and left,' pp. 24–49 in R. Christie and M. Jahoda (eds.), *Studies in Scope and Method of the Authoritarian Personality*. Glencoe, Ill.: The Free Press

– 1969. 'Plenitude and scarcity,' *Encounter* 32, 5: 37–57

Shoben, E. Joseph Jr. 1970. 'The climate of protest,' pp. 554–81 in J. Foster and D. Long (eds.), *Protest!! Student Activism in America*. New York: William Morrow

Shoben, E.J. Jr., P. Werdell, and D. Long. 1970. 'Radical student organizations,' pp. 210–29 in J. Foster and D. Long (eds.), *Protest!! Student Activism in America*. New York: William Morrow

Sigel, Roberta S. (ed.). 1970. *Learning about Politics: A Reader in Political Socialization*. New York: Random House

Silvern, L.E., and C.Y. Nakamura. 1971. 'Powerlessness, social-political action, social-political views: their interrelation among college students,' *Journal of Social Issues* 27, 4: 137–57

Simpson, J.H., and W. Phillips. 1976. 'Understanding student protest in Canada: the University of Toronto strike vote,' *The Canadian Journal of Higher Education* 6, 1: 59–67

Simpson, R.L., and M. Milles. 1963. 'Social status and anomia,' *Social Problems* 10: 256–64

Skinner, B.F. 1964. 'Behaviorism at fifty,' pp. 79–108 in T.W. Wann (ed.), *Behaviorism and Phenomenology*. Chicago: University of Chicago Press

– 1976. *About Behaviorism*. New York: Vintage Books

Smelser, Neil J. 1968. 'Personality and the explanation of political phenomena at the social system level: a methodological statement,' *Journal of Social Issues* 24: 111–26

Smith, D. 1967. 'Prairie revolt, federalism and the party system,' pp. 204–16 in H. Thoburn (ed.), *Party Politics in Canada*. Toronto: Prentice-Hall

Smith, E.R., and F.D. Miller. 1978. 'Limitations on perception of cognitive processes: a reply to Nisbett and Wilson,' *Psychological Review* 85, 4: 355–62

Smith, M. Brewster. 1958. 'Opinions, personality and political behavior,' *American Political Science Review* 52, 1: 1–17

– 1968. 'Personality in politics: a conceptual map, with application to the problem of political rationality,' pp. 77–102 in D. Garceau (ed.), *Political Research and Political Theory*. Cambridge: Harvard University Press

– 1974. 'Morality and student protest,' pp. 582–96 in A.R. Wilcox (ed.), *Public Opinion and Political Attitudes*. New York: John Wiley

Smith, M.B., J.S. Bruner, and R.S. White. 1956. *Opinions and Personality*. New York: John Wiley

Smith, M.B., N. Haan, and J. Block. 1970. 'Social psychological aspects of student activism,' *Youth and Society* 1: 261–88

Sniderman, Paul. 1975. *Personality and Democratic Politics*. Berkeley: University of California Press

Sniderman, P., and J. Citrin. 1971. 'Psychological sources of political belief: self-esteem and isolationist attitudes,' *American Political Science Review* 65, 2: 401–17

Social Science Research Council Work Group on Family Size and Birth Order. 1965. 'Family size and birth order as influences upon socialization and personality: bibliography and abstracts,' prepared by J.A. Clausen (July)

Solomon, F., and J.R. Fishman. 1964. 'Youth and peace: a psycho-social study of student peace demonstrators in Washington, D.C.', *Journal of Social Issues* 20: 54–73

Somers, Robert H. 1965. 'The mainsprings of the rebellion: a survey of Berkeley students in November 1964,' pp. 530–9 in S.M. Lipset and S. Wolin (eds.), *The Berkeley Student Revolt: Facts and Interpretations*. New York: Anchor Books

Somit, Albert. 1972. 'Review Article: biopolitics,' *British Journal of Political Science* 2: 209–38

Spaeth, Joe L. 1969. 'Public reactions to college student protests,' *Sociology of Education* 42, 2: 199–206

Spence, J.T., and R. Helmreich. 1972. 'Who likes competent women? Competence, sex-role congruence of interests, and subjects. Attitudes toward women as determinants of interpersonal attraction,' *Journal of Applied Social Psychology* 2, 3: 197–213

Sperlich, Peter W. 1971. *Conflict and Harmony in Human Affairs: A Study of Cross-pressures and Political Behavior*. Chicago: Rand McNally

Spiegel, John. 1977. 'The group psychology of campus disorders: a transactional approach,' pp. 139–70 in D. Light Jr. and J. Spiegel, (eds.) *The Dynamics of University Protest*. Chicago: Nelson-Hall

Spock, B. 1946. *The Commonsense Book of Baby and Child-Care*. New York: Duell, Sloan and Pearce

Spreitzer, E., and E. Snyder. 1971. 'Rank and file student activism at a non-elite university,' unpublished paper, Department of Sociology, Bowling Green State University

Srole, Leo. 1956. 'Social integration and certain corollaries,' *American Sociological Review* 21: 709–16

Srole, Leo et al. 1962. *Mental Health in the Metropolis*. New York: McGraw-Hill

Star, Shirley A. 1966. 'The screening of psychoneurotics in the army: technical development of tests,' pp. 486–548 in S.A. Stouffer et al. (eds.), *Measurement and Prediction*, vol. IV. New York: John Wiley

Stefensmeier, R., and D. Stefensmeier. 1975. 'Attitudes and behaviour toward hippies: a field experiment accompanied by home interviews,' *Sociological Quarterly* 16: 393–400

Stewart D., and T. Hoult. 1959. 'A social-psychological theory of the authoritarian personality,' *American Journal of Sociology* 65, 3: 274–9

Stinchcombe, E. 1973. 'Theoretical domains and measurement' (two parts), *Acta Sociologica* 16, 1: 3–12; 16, 2: 79–97

Stock, D.L. 1949. 'An investigation into the interrelations between the self-concepts and feelings directed toward other persons and groups,' *Journal of Consulting Psychology* 13: 176–80

Stone, William F. 1974. *The Psychology of Politics*. New York: Macmillan

Stouffer, Samuel A. 1963. *Communism, Conformity and Civil Liberties*. Gloucester, Mass.: Peter Smith

Straus, M.A. 1962. 'Conjugal power structure and adolescent personality,' *Marriage and Family Living* 24: 17–25

Strickland, B. 1965. 'The prediction of social action from a dimension of internal-external control,' *Journal of Social Psychology* 66: 353–8

Strodtbeck, F. 1958. 'Family interaction, values and achievement,' pp. 135–94 in D.C. McClelland, A.L. Baldwin, U. Bronfenbrenner, and F.L. Strodtbeck (eds.), *Talent and Society*. Princeton, NJ: Van Nostrand

Suchman, Edward A. 1962. 'An analysis of "bias" in survey research,' *Public Opinion Quarterly* 26, 1: 102–11

Sullivan, J.L., G.E. Marcus, and D.R. Minns. 1975. 'The development of political ideology: some empirical findings,' *Youth and Society* 7, 2: 148–70

Summers, G. 1970. *Attitude Measurement*. Chicago: Rand McNally

Surgeon, George P. 1969. 'Political attitudes at Wesleyan,' unpublished paper, Wesleyan University, Connecticut

Susmilch, C.E., G.C. Elliott, and S.H. Schwartz. 1975. 'Contingent consistency and the attitude-behavior relationship – a comment,' *American Sociological Review* 40: 682–6

Sutherland, S.L. 1969. 'Dimensions of attitudes toward student power and toward the university experience,' unpublished MA thesis, University of Alberta

– 1975. 'An empirical study of political ideologies,' unpublished doctoral dissertation, University of Essex

– 1978. 'The unambitious female: women's low professional aspirations,' *Signs* 3, 4: 774–94

Sutherland, S.L., and E. Tanenbaum. 1975. 'Rokeach's value survey in use: an evaluation with criterion attitude scales and party identification,' *Canadian Review of Anthropology and Sociology* 12, 4: 551–64

- 1977. 'Political preferences and psychological functioning,' paper presented at June 1977 Annual Meeting of the Canadian Political Science Association, Quebec City
- 1980. 'Submissive authoritarians: need we fear the fearful toadie?' *Canadian Review of Anthropology and Sociology* 17, 1: 1–23
Sutton-Smith, B., and B.G. Rosenberg. 1966. 'Sibling consensus on power tactics,' paper presented at Fall Meetings, American Psychological Association
Symons, Thomas. 1975. *To Know Ourselves: The Report of the Commission on Canadian Studies*, vols. 1 and 2. Ottawa: Association of Universities and Colleges of Canada
Tallman, Irving. 1976. *Passion, Action and Politics: A Perspective on Social Problems and Social Problem Solving*. San Francisco: W.H. Freeman
Tanenbaum, Eric. 1981. 'Patterns of political preferences,' unpublished doctoral dissertation, University of Essex
Tannenbaum, A.S. 1957. 'Personality change as a result of an experimental change of environmental conditions,' *Journal of Abnormal and Social Psychology* 55: 404–6
Tarter, D.E. 1969. 'Toward prediction of attitude-action discrepancy,' *Social Forces* 47: 398–405
- 1970. 'Attitude: the mental myth,' *American Sociologist* 5, 3: 276–8
Teevan, R.C. 1954. 'Personality correlates of undergraduate field of specialization,' *Journal of Consulting Psychology* 18: 212–18
Templeton, F. 1966. 'Alienation and political participation: some research findings,' *Public Opinion Quarterly* 30, 2: 249–61
Tessler, M.A. 1970. 'Student-faculty attitudes toward the November Vietnam moratorium,' paper read at Midwest Political Science Association, Chicago
Thomas, K. 1971. *Attitudes and Behaviour*. London: Penguin
Thomas, L. Eugene. 1970. 'The I-E scale ideological bias and political participation,' *Journal of Personality* 38: 273–86
- 1971. 'Family correlates of student political activism,' *Developmental Psychology* 4: 206–14
- 1974. 'Generational discontinuity in beliefs: an exploration of the generation gap,' *Journal of Social Issues* 30, 3: 1–22
Thomas, W.I., and F. Znaniecki. 1918. *The Polish Peasant in Europe and America*. Boston: Bader
Thompson, Richard. 1970. 'The New Left in Saskatchewan,' *Our Generation* 7: 52–66
Thurstone, L.L. 1927. 'The method of paired comparisons for social values,' *Journal of Abnormal and Social Psychology* 21, 3: 384–400
- 1928. 'Attitudes can be measured,' *American Journal of Sociology* 33: 529–54

- 1931. 'The measurement of social attitudes,' *Journal of Abnormal and Social Psychology* 26: 249-69

Tittle, C.R., and R.J. Hill. 1967. 'Attitude measurement and prediction of behavior: an evaluation of conditions and measurement techniques,' *Sociometry* 30: 199-213

Toch, Hans. 1966. *The Social Psychology of Social Movements*. London: Methuen

Tousignant, M., G. Denis, and R. Lachapelle. 1974. 'Some considerations concerning the validity and use of the health opinion survey,' *Journal of Health and Social Behaviour* 15, 3: 241-52

Travis, Russell. 1976. 'Status consistency and political orientation: a test of alternative perspectives,' *Sociology and Social Research* 60, 3: 247-62

Trent, James W. 1970. 'Revolution, reformation and reevaluation,' pp. 23-54 in E.R. Sampson and H.A. Korn (eds.), *Student Activism and Protest*. San Francisco: Jossey-Bass

Trent, J.W., and J.L. Craise. 1967. 'Commitment and conformity in the American college,' *Journal of Social Issues* 12, 3: 34-51

Turner, R.H. 1972. 'Campus peace: harmony or uneasy truce?' *Sociology and Social Research* 57: 5-21

Tygart, C.E. 1975. 'Political liberalism-conservatism among university students: the question of dimensionality,' *Youth and Society* 6, 3: 298-308

Tygart, C.E., and N. Holt. 1971. 'A research note on student leftist political activism and family sociological status,' *Pacific Sociological Review* 14, 1: 121-8

- 1972. 'Examining the Weinberg and Walker typology of student activists,' *American Journal of Sociology* 77, 5: 957-66

Valins, S. 1966. 'Cognitive effects of false heart rate feedback,' *Journal of Personality and Social Psychology* 4: 400-8

Verba, Sidney. 1961. *Small Groups and Political Behaviour*. Princeton: Princeton University Press

Verba, S., and N. Nie. 1972. *Participation in America: Political Democracy and Social Equality*. New York: Harper and Row

Veroff, Joseph. 1978. 'Social motivation,' *American Behavioral Scientist* 21, 5: 709-30

Viorst, Milton. 1980. *America in the 1960's*. New York: Musson

Wachtel, P.L. 1969. 'Psychology, metapsychology and psychoanalysis,' *Journal of Abnormal Psychology* 74: 651-60

- 1973. 'Psychodynamics, behavior therapy, and the implacable experimenter: an inquiry into the consistency of personality,' *Journal of Abnormal Psychology* 82, 2: 324-34

Wada, G., and J.C. Davies. 1957. 'Riots and rioters,' *The Western Political Quarterly* 10, 4: 864-74

Wahlke, John C., and M.G. Lodge. 1972. 'Psychophysiological measures of political attitudes and behavior,' *Midwest Journal of Political Science* 16, 4: 505–37

Wallace, Walter. 1966. *Student Culture*. Chicago: Aldine

Waly, P., and S.W. Cook. 1966. 'Attitude as a determinant of learning and memory: a failure to confirm,' *Journal of Personality and Social Psychology* 4: 280–8

Warner, L.G., and M.L. Defleur. 1969. 'Attitude as an interactional concept: social constraint and social distance as intervening variables between attitudes and action,' *American Sociological Review* 34: 153–69

Warr, P.B., and T.L. Coffman. 1970. 'Personality, involvement and extremity of judgement,' *British Journal of Social and Clinical Psychology* 9: 108–21

Watts, Meredith W. 1973. 'Efficacy, trust, and orientation toward socio-political authority: students' support for the university,' *American Journal of Political Science* 17, 2: 282–301

– 1974. 'Alienation and support for the political system among college students,' pp. 105–27 in A.R. Wilcox (ed.), *Public Opinion and Political Attitudes*. New York: John Wiley

Watts, W.A., S. Lynch, and D. Whittaker. 1969. 'Alienation and activism in today's college-age youth: socialization patterns and current family relationships,' *Journal of Counseling Psychology* 16: 1–7

Watts, W.A., and D. Whittaker. 1966. 'Free speech advocates at Berkeley,' *Journal of Applied Behavioral Science* 2, 1: 41–62

Weigel, K.H. et al. 1974. 'Specificity of the attitude as a determinant of attitude-behaviour congruence,' *Journal of Personality and Social Psychology* 30, 6: 724–8

Weinberg, I., and K. Walker. 1969. 'Student politics and political systems: toward typology,' *American Journal of Sociology* 75: 76–97

Weinstein, Alan G. 1972. 'Predicting behavior from attitudes,' *Public Opinion Quarterly* 36: 355–60

Weissberg, C. 1968. 'Students against the rank,' unpublished master's thesis, Department of Sociology, University of Chicago

Weissberg, Robert. 1972. 'Adolescents' perceptions of political authorities: another look at political virtue and power,' *Midwest Journal of Political Science* 16, 1: 147–69

– 1976. 'The politics of political socialization,' *Youth and Society* 8, 2: 117–46

Welch, Susan. 1975. 'Dimensions of political participation in a Canadian sample,' *Canadian Journal of Political Science* 8, 4: 553–60

Westby, D.L., and R.G. Braungart. 1966. 'Class and politics in the family backgrounds of student political activists,' *American Sociological Review* 31: 690–2

– 1970. 'The alienation of generations and status politics: alternative explanation of student political acts,' pp. 476–89 in R.S. Sigel (ed.), *Learning about Politics: A Reader in Political Socialization*. New York: Random House

Westhues, Kenneth. 1972. *Society's Shadow*. Toronto: McGraw-Hill
– 1975. 'Inter-generational conflict in the sixties,' pp. 387–408 in S.D. Clark et al., *Prophecy and Protest: Movements in Twentieth-Century Canada*. Toronto: Gage
White, Eliott S. 1968. 'Intelligence and sense of political efficacy in children,' *The Journal of Politics* 30, 3: 710–31
White, Peter. 1980. 'Limitations on verbal reports of internal events: a refutation of Nisbett and Wilson and of Bem,' *Psychological Review* 87, 1: 105–12
White, R., and R. Lippitt. 1960. 'Leader behaviour and member reaction in three social climates,' pp. 527–54 in D. Cartwright and A. Zander (eds.), *Group Dynamics*, 2nd ed. London: Tavistock
Whitehorn, John C. 1956. 'Stress and emotional health,' *American Journal of Psychiatry* 16: 774–6
Wicker, A.W. 1969. 'Attitudes versus actions: the relationship of verbal and overt behavioral responses to attitude objects,' *Journal of Social Issues* 25: 41–78
– 1971. 'An examination of the other-variables explanation of attitude-behaviour inconsistency,' *Journal of Personality and Social Psychology* 19: 18–30
Wiebe, G.D. 1953. 'Some implications of separating opinions from attitudes,' *Public Opinion Quarterly* 17, 3: 328–52
Wilker, H.R., and L.W. Milbraith. 1970. 'Political belief systems and political behaviour,' *Social Science Quarterly* 51, 2: 477–93
Williams, Roger J. 1956. *Biochemical Individuality*. New York: John Wiley
Winch, Peter. 1958. *The Idea of a Social Science*. London: Routledge
Wood, James L. 1971. 'The role of radical political consciousness in student political activism: a preliminary analysis,' paper read at the American Sociological Association, Denver, September
Woodmansee, J.J., and S.W. Cook. 1967. 'Dimensions of verbal racial attitudes: their identification and measurement,' *Journal of Personality and Social Psychology* 7: 240–50
Worcester, Robert. 1972. 'The hidden activists,' *New Society* June 8: 512–13
Wright, James D. 1975. 'The socio-political attitudes of white college-educated youth,' *Youth and Society* 6, 3: 251–97
Wylie, Ruth. 1979. *The Self Concept*, rev. ed. Lincoln: University of Nebraska Press
Yamamoto, Kaoru (ed.). 1968. *The College Student and His Culture* Boston: Houghton Mifflin
Yankelovich, Daniel. 1972. *The Changing Values on Campus*. New York: Washington Square Press
Yarrow, M.R., P. Scott, L. Deleeuw, and C. Heinig. 1962. 'Child-rearing in families of working and non-working mothers,' *Sociometry* 25: 122–40

Yinger, J.M. 1963. 'Research implications of a field view of personality,' *American Journal of Sociology* 68, 5: 580–92

Young, W. 1969. *Democracy and Discontent: Progressivism, Socialism and Social Credit in the Canadian West.* Toronto: Ryerson

Zanich, Michael. 1962. 'Relationship between maternal behaviour and attitudes towards children,' *Journal of Genetic Psychology* 100: 155–65

Zellman, G.L., and D.O. Sears. 1971. 'Childhood origins of tolerance for dissent,' *Journal of Social Issues* 27, 2: 109–36

Zigler, E., and V. Seitz. 1978. 'Changing trends in socialization theory and research,' *American Behavioral Scientist* 21, 5: 731–56

Name index

Subject index

academic discipline: *see* Faculty of enrolment

academic success: of first-born children 151; *see also* Scholarship

action: as willed behaviour 28; as ground for attitudes 32; personal style 108; systemic opportunities for 207, 218–20

activists, mass public: proportion in population 5, 298

activists, student: characteristics 6, 7, 10, 18, chapters 5, 9 passim; as proportion of student body 10, 13, 19, 91, 298; specifying analytic types 100; general criteria for 139–41; *see also* Radical activists, Conservative activism, Ideologues

activity, student: options for university political activity 5, 47, 85–7, 89–94, 107, 108, 113, 117, 212; activities predicting attitudes 92, 264–5; characteristic activities of types 104–6; informal and social-organizational 107, 108, 111, 113, 119–22, 212, 214; outside the university 106–9, 113, 117, 118, 212; 'social-helping'

or community 107, 108, 111, 113, 118, 119, 212; as qualifying commitment 133; direction of ideology controlled 141; and elite characteristics 207; summary of factors facilitating 216–17; indexes, standard scores 255–6

affect: as congenital characteristic 39; *see also* Attitudes, as affect

age: relation to activism 153, 191, 193, 198, 204, 296

Aimlessness (scale) 49, 58, 122, 124, 212; items, factor loadings 237; standard scores 257

Alberta: local student protest 12, 13; provincial politics 11; University of 10, 11; *see also* Edmonton

Alienation from People (scale) 64, 65; items, factor loadings 241

Alienation, Political (scale) 64, 122, 123, 124, 212, 288; items, factor loadings 241; standard scores 256

Alienation, University (scale) 49, 58, 122, 124, 212; items, factor loadings 238; standard scores 257

alpha, reliability coefficient 54, 281